IN THE ARENA

IN THE ARENA

A Memoir of Love, War, and Politics

Chuck Robb

Virginia Governor, Senator, and U.S. Marine

University of Virginia Press • *Charlottesville and London*

University of Virginia Press
© 2021 by Charles S. Robb
All rights reserved
Printed in the United States of America on acid-free paper

First published 2021

9 8 7 6 5 4 3 2 1

Library of Congress Cataloging-in-Publication Data
Names: Robb, Charles S., author.
Title: In the arena : a memoir of love, war, and politics / Charles S. Robb.
Description: Charlottesville : University of Virginia Press, [2021] | Includes bibliographical
    references.
Identifiers: LCCN 2020037876 (print) | LCCN 2020037877 (ebook) | ISBN 9780813946108
    (hardcover) | ISBN 9780813946115 (ebook)
Subjects: LCSH: Robb, Charles S. | United States. Congress. Senate—Biography. | United
    States. Marine Corps—Officers—Biography. | Legislators—United States—Biography. |
    Governors—Virginia—Biography. | United States—Politics and government—1989– |
    Virginia—Politics and government—1951–
Classification: LCC E840.8.R585 A3 2021 (print) | LCC E840.8. R585 (ebook) | DDC 328.73/092
    [B]—dc23
LC record available at https://lccn.loc.gov/2020037876
LC ebook record available at https://lccn.loc.gov/2020037877

Cover photo by Ron Chapiesky. (Courtesy of Linda Zember and the estate of Ron Chapiesky)

To Lynda, from whom I learned about unconditional love

CONTENTS

Illustrations gallery follows page 176

FOREWORD

ON THE EVENING of July 17, 1984, Governor Chuck Robb of Virginia stood at a podium in the Moscone Center in San Francisco and delivered a brave speech.

The occasion was the 1984 Democratic National Convention. "We cannot afford to cling to the ghost of a time now vanished," Robb told us. To succeed in a new era, he said, Democrats must prove themselves "not only compassionate enough to care, but tough enough to govern."

Convention speeches are supposed to get people cheering, but Robb's speech did more than that: it got people thinking, about the future of our party and of our country. Although we were about to lose the fourth of the last five presidential elections, not everyone was ready to take up the challenge he posed. But those of us who shared his vision of a party that was more about the future than the past were more than ready.

That Chuck Robb—a man of courage and conviction—is present on every page of this remarkable book. I am not an unbiased reader. I like and admire Chuck Robb very much and treasure the times Hillary and I have shared with him and Lynda.

I knew about Chuck long before we met. As an undergraduate at Georgetown in the 1960s I supported President Johnson's civil rights, voting rights, and antipoverty agenda and opposed his Vietnam policy. I was intrigued by the young Marine Corps officer who, on assignment to the White House, fell in love with and married the president's older daughter, Lynda, and was sent into combat in Vietnam.

Until I read his book, I didn't know much about Chuck's family and his early years before joining the military, or how he had to push for combat duty in Vietnam. The book offers a clear explanation about why he did it and how his experience shaped the rest of his life in public service.

We got to know each other in the early 1980s, while Chuck was governor of Virginia and I was governor of Arkansas. By then, I had come to admire him as a dedicated public servant and an eloquent voice for new ideas. When Chuck ran for governor in 1981, the Democratic Party was losing its hold on the South. The New Deal coalition that had for so long served as the party's foundation was crumbling, just as President Johnson predicted when he signed the bills that became the Civil Rights and Voting Rights Acts. Some worried that states like Virginia, which had elected three Republican governors in a row, had become impossible to win.

With his election, Chuck helped prove that a new breed of Democrat—progressive but pragmatic, guided by the past but not held hostage to it—could win statewide office in the South, even during the Reagan years. His election also helped bring Democrats into the offices of lieutenant governor and attorney general.

After his inauguration, he brought a diverse, dynamic new group of leaders into Virginia's government, including a historic number of women and Black Americans. His example and support prompted many others to run for and win offices themselves. At the end of his term he helped Democrats hold on to the top three offices and keep Virginia on a progressive course.

What Chuck did for Virginia, he worked to do for America as well. As a cofounder of the Democratic Leadership Council, Chuck brought together a group of like-minded Democrats—of which I was one—committed to making the national party a force again.

During his years in the U.S. Senate, Chuck worked steadily to strengthen our economy and our national security. Sometimes that meant breaking ranks to reach across the aisle. Other times, it meant putting political self-interest aside to stand up for his beliefs, as when he stood strong in support of LGBTQ Americans.

I was fortunate in my eight years in the White House to have Chuck Robb as an ally in Congress. His support in the Senate helped us secure passage of landmark legislation such as the Federal Assault Weapons Ban and the 1993 economic plan that erased the deficit, sparked our longest peacetime expansion, and led to the most broad-based prosperity in fifty years. The bill passed by just one vote in both houses of Congress. Chuck risked his career because he believed in fiscal responsibility, opposed trickle-down economics, and wanted to lift the lives of all Americans.

I'm especially proud to have worked with Chuck in normalizing relations with Vietnam. As both a veteran and the proud son-in-law of President Johnson, Chuck saw this as not just a foreign-policy issue; it was personal. He knew that I had been opposed to the war, but he never saw that as an obstacle to our working together. And so, along with other veterans in the Senate and House, including John McCain, John Kerry, Bob Kerrey, and Pete Peterson, we were able to help heal the wounds of war and extend a hand of friendship to a former adversary, now a strong ally.

Through it all, as you'll read in this book, Chuck has been fortunate to have Lynda by his side, a true partner in every sense. Her political insight, compassion, and sense of humor are at the very center of this story, right where they belong. Together, Chuck and Lynda have carried forward the legacy of President Johnson: the belief that government can, and government must, do all it can to provide security and extend opportunity to Americans of every background in every part of our country.

Almost twenty years ago now, in January 2001, I stood at Andrews Air Force Base and bid farewell to many of the officials, friends, and supporters with whom I had the privilege of working as president. I remember looking out at the crowd and seeing Chuck, and I called to him. He had just lost a close Senate race, and I was so grateful he was there—because he had been there all along, all the way back to the 1980s, working toward peace, security, and shared prosperity in a welcoming, inclusive America.

In my lifetime, few have served our country as ably and honorably as Chuck Robb. His quiet dedication to doing what he believed was right will inspire readers of this book—including a younger generation of Americans who will take up that challenge he posed to us all: get into the arena.

Bill Clinton

PREFACE

On November 11, 1985, I was invited to speak at a Veterans Day event at the Vietnam Veterans Memorial in Washington, D.C. As I took the walk along the length of the wall, I saw all the notes and mementos left by friends and families of the men and women who never returned. I heard the quiet sobs of those who stood close to that smooth black granite wall, tracing their loved ones' names. Looking at name after name, I remembered aloud: "We put them in body bags and zipped the bags up. That's a pretty tough way to say goodbye."

I hadn't been back to the memorial since I spoke at the groundbreaking ceremony three years earlier. I hadn't been avoiding going to see it, but I had been waiting for the right time for what I knew would be a powerful, emotional moment. I held no bitterness from my experience in Vietnam— I had wanted to serve there and had requested the assignment. My proclivity for keeping my feelings tightly under control may also have protected me when I returned from the war. But on this Veterans Day, sixteen years after I had returned safely, I found my carefully guarded emotions suddenly spilling out and my eyes growing moist.

Taking my place at the lectern, I saw the crowd of more than 2,500, many wearing old combat uniforms, their shirts dotted with faded ribbons. There were also parents, widows, and children who had lost their loved ones in the Vietnam War. Looking out at those faces, I realized that my prepared speech didn't measure up to the emotions we all felt on that day. So, I put my notes aside.

"I can't use anything but my gut reaction today," I began. "I have a pretty good reputation for keeping it on a straight plane. . . . [But today] I started walking down there and it all came back. There are so many people who don't understand."

I was interrupted by the roar of airplanes from National Airport and Park Service helicopters flying overhead. The sound of the aircraft, I said, recalled when the military helicopters arrived "when we really needed them. . . . There were times when those noises sounded awfully good."[1]

Lynda stayed close by my side, tears periodically rolling down her cheeks from beneath her sunglasses. I tried to lighten the mood a little.

"Lynda has come along to see if I really do show emotion," I said, attempting a smile. "I've hidden it in so many ways."

I looked out at the faces and saw nods of recognition.

"Those who are listed here paid the price, whether or not they understood or agreed with their country's policies. To those whose names are inscribed on this memorial, we say that we remember. We understand what you did. Your country called, and you answered the call."

I was there that day, speaking to this crowd, because I'd served as an officer in the Marine Corps, and that service had led to a series of other high-profile events. I had married the daughter of a president in the White House, run for public office, and was currently the governor of Virginia, just across the Potomac River. My successor in that office (Virginia governors can't succeed themselves) had been elected just the week before, and three years later I would be elected to a seat in the U.S. Senate, in which I would serve two terms.

My life, which began simply enough with a middle-class upbringing, has taken me places that I never anticipated. This book is about the twists and turns that got me there, and the decisions that I made along the way.

Many of those decisions were based on core values that I learned as a young Marine officer. One of the most important was that respect is an essential element of leadership. The key to getting people to follow your orders—whether those orders were to march in a parade or to risk their lives taking a heavily enemy-fortified hill—is to first develop respect. As President Dwight D. Eisenhower once said, "You do not lead by hitting people over the head—that's assault, not leadership."[2]

When I entered politics, it became clear that this type of respect was just as important in political leadership. We develop that respect by listening—to the ideas of staff members, to the advice of experts, to the needs of constituents, and to the other side.

In politics, I never saw the other side as an enemy, and I never bought into the ugly tribalism that has been taking over much of our political system. Some called me a moderate, but I never considered myself wedded to a spot on the ideological spectrum. I tried to listen carefully to all sides and do what I thought was right, regardless of party or political positioning. I tried to be loyal to my party, and I didn't like to defy my own party leadership, even when I felt I had to, but I never minded taking politically unpopular positions that I saw as principled and right.

I've always seen duty as not simply a box that we check, but a responsibility, when we are presented with a need, to act, and when duty calls, to join the fray. President Theodore Roosevelt—as he so often did—said it best: "The credit belongs to the man who is actually in the arena, whose face is marred by dust and sweat and blood . . . who knows the great enthusiasms, the great devotions; who spends himself in a worthy cause; who at the best knows in the end the triumph of high achievement, and who at the worst, if he fails, at least fails while daring greatly, so that his place will never be with those cold and timid souls who know neither victory or defeat."[3]

I have lived a life of incredible events and interesting stories. I led a company of Marines on combat missions at night through the pitch-black Vietnamese bush. I accepted the responsibility of being the last member of the family to look upon the body of President Lyndon Johnson. I've sat down with warlords in their jungle hideouts and had tea in Israel with Golda Meir. I've stood proudly for politically unpopular causes and worked quietly to change the system from within. I've led a sweep of statewide offices and faced electoral loss. I've had ups and, as on any good roller-coaster ride, there've been some downs. Throughout it all, I'm grateful that I had the chance to spend so much of my life "in the arena."

PART I

SEMPER FIDELIS

I WASN'T BORN a Marine. But reporting to Marine Corps Base Quantico in the summer of 1960, I found an identity and an ethos that would remain at my core for the rest of my life. And so, in some sense, my story does start with becoming a Marine, even though my life had begun twenty-one years earlier.

I arrived at Quantico the summer between my junior and senior years of college and reported to Officer Candidate School (OCS), then called the Training and Test Regiment. I was one of hundreds of highly motivated young men of approximately the same age, all eager to earn the title of "Marine."

That summer was a series of trials meant to challenge our leadership ability, our physical stamina, and our ability to perform under extreme conditions. The course included elements of small-unit leadership and infantry tactics, but the most memorable were the physical trials. Among the physical trials, one that stood out was the Hill Trail.

The Hill Trail was a physical test shared by every Marine officer candidate in that era—a grueling march through a heavily wooded area on a rocky trail that tested our strength, endurance, and ability to gut it out while straggling up and down steep hills carrying full combat gear: a rifle, helmet, field pack, and two full canteens.

The endurance course started early, just after dawn. Steam rose from the single-file line of sweating Marine officer hopefuls that stretched as far as I could see up the hill in front of me. We couldn't look up for long, though, for fear of tripping on one of the many exposed, ankle-breaking tree roots.

The trail had six steep hills, some so steep that we had to use exposed roots and underbrush, anything that we could get our hands on, to make it up hill after hill. Footholds had been worn in the trail by the steps of the Marines who had been there before. Scrambling to close gaps and keep the forced-march pace set by the drill instructors, we had to keep our minds focused so that we didn't trip and fall flat on our faces.

The downhill could be even more of a challenge. The dirt trail often turned into slippery mud as we stepped through streams between the hills. The gear weighed us down and flopped against our bodies with each step, and the heat made the gear feel twice as heavy. Heat exhaustion would occasionally overwhelm someone, and their body would go limp right on the trail.

Not everyone would make it. But that was the challenge—to push this mass of young would-be Marine officers to our physical limits and sometimes beyond. In a letter I sent to my parents, I told them matter-of-factly about my own minor injuries and discomforts before reporting on the more serious injuries in the regiment, including one death, one critically injured, and two in comas. I ended the letter with a deadpanned, "The program is rigorous."

But the physical challenges only energized me even more. I was by no means an Olympian, but I was a fair athlete, and at six feet two inches tall, 185 pounds, and twenty-one years old, I considered myself a lean, green fighting machine. It was the competition with the other officer candidates that pushed all of us. The tougher the trials, the more I seemed to relish them, whether it was long marches, running the obstacle course, or drilling in the sweltering heat or pouring rain.

Throughout that long, hot summer of 1960 in Quantico, Virginia, I began to think of myself first and foremost as a Marine. I began to fully embrace all that it encompassed: the discipline, the commitment, and the honor. It was clear to me that the Marine Corps offered a chance to excel, and I was determined to meet the challenge.

1

The Path to Quantico

ALTHOUGH MY STORY begins in Quantico, I didn't arrive there by accident, or by a straight path. My life up to that point had been neither charmed nor particularly difficult. My parents were not wealthy, but they were fundamentally even-keeled, and my childhood showed little evidence of hardship. It was a very normal, if somewhat itinerant, middle-class upbringing of the 1940s and 1950s. We moved around the country more than average, due mostly to my father's career and, occasionally, his adventurous spirit.

James S. Robb was a trim, dark-haired, enterprising man who was ever diligent and organized—never one to shirk his duties. He kept meticulous records and ensured that our family was always able to live a middle-class life, if one without many frills. His playful side shone through whenever he was spinning stories for friends and family or penning funny poems to send out on holidays. He enjoyed adventure and pursued it when he could. He was, in many ways, the quintessential American dreamer: the entrepreneur willing to take big risks in the hope of reaping big rewards. But my father at times appeared frustrated that he somehow had failed to fulfill the unspoken expectations of his own father.

My paternal grandfather, Charles Spittal Robb (after whom I was named), came to this country at age five from Glasgow, Scotland, in 1873. My grandfather was industrious and bright. After graduating as high school valedictorian, he took a job with the West Virginia Central & Pittsburgh Railway Co. In fifteen years, he worked his way up from office boy to top executive.

He married Susan Gay Estill, who descended from one of the first settler families in West Virginia (then a part of Virginia) and Kentucky, and whose ancestors fought in the Revolutionary War.

After taking a job as general manager of the Davis Colliery Co., my grandfather got a taste of politics by working for the unsuccessful Democratic presidential ticket of Alton Parker and former U.S. senator Henry Gassaway Davis, heir to Davis Colliery. Grandfather Robb later moved his family to Washington, D.C., where he would serve as the "confidential secretary" (now known as chief of staff) to Senator Stephen B. Elkins of West

Virginia, and my grandparents would spend several decades working and socializing with the political and social leaders of the day.

Trim and smartly dressed, my grandfather was a pragmatic, ambitious businessman who expected his four children—of whom my father was the eldest—to display a similar level of ambition and achievement.

My father, however, showed an independent streak early on. Despite being sent to the Choate School, an illustrious preparatory boarding school in Connecticut, with the clear expectation that he would go on to college when he graduated, my father instead chose to enroll in the new Spartan School of Aeronautics, a pioneering aviation school in New Mexico. He earned his commercial pilot's license in 1930, a time when flying was still a hazardous profession and commercial flights weren't yet commonplace. He used to tell me how, when landing at Washington, D.C.'s Hoover Field (the site that is now the Pentagon) in the 1930s, the pilot had to radio ahead to the tower to activate a traffic light on Route 1, the main road leading south out of Washington, because it crossed over the airport landing strip.

My father loved flying, but he reluctantly gave it up for something less perilous. Family lore says that he was given strong encouragement in that direction from his father, who, in those early, uncertain days of aviation, considered flying a plane as akin to driving a bus and wanted his son to become a more conventional businessman. My father stayed in the airline business, however, switching over to the sales and management side with American Airlines.

That is how my father happened to be sitting behind a relatively unexciting desk at the American Airlines ticket office in downtown Washington when in walked a pretty young woman dressed in a neat summer suit. Stepping up to the counter with a smile, she asked my father if she could use the office telephone. This quiet introduction marked the beginning of my parents' long and devoted relationship.

Frances Woolley Robb was an attractive, loving, and attentive mother and wife. She proved to be the steadying keel that helped guide and focus my father's adventurous ambitions. She was the glue that held the family together, and though never particularly forceful or outgoing, my mother was a constant, reliable presence that kept us grounded throughout the occasional turbulence of financial difficulties and frequent moves.

Her family were prominent members of Washington, D.C., society when my parents met, and the Woolleys had a long history in American politics that went back to the 1600s. My mother's father, Robert W. Woolley, was a dapper and engaging man who had known many of the nation's key political leaders in the first half of the twentieth century. He started as a journalist and was working as a D.C. correspondent for the *New York World* when he got to know future president Woodrow Wilson. Grandfather Woolley became a member of Wilson's "Kitchen Cabinet" of trusted advisors and is credited with coining the famous campaign slogan that helped Wilson win reelection in 1916: "He kept us out of war." However, Grandfather Woolley would grumble that this shortened version changed the meaning of his original phrase: "*With honor,* he kept us out of war." He later served as the director of the U.S. Mint, as publicity director for the Democratic National Committee, as an Interstate Commerce commissioner, as the president of a finance company on Wall Street, and, in 1932, he helped to persuade Franklin Roosevelt to run for president.

Following her high school graduation from the private Holton-Arms School for Girls, then located in Washington, D.C., my mother attended art school and began a career working as a fashion illustrator. She drew the simple but chic pen-and-ink figures that adorned newspaper ads and catalogues. Though my mother stopped working full-time after having children, she went back part-time when the family finances needed it and continued working as a freelance artist for local newspapers and magazines well into her sixties.

James Robb and Frances Woolley were married in October 1936 at my maternal grandparents' Georgetown row house in Northwest Washington, D.C. A short time later, my father took a position in Phoenix as the regional sales manager for American Airlines. It was there, in the sweltering "Valley of the Sun," that I was born on June 26, 1939.

My Grandfather Woolley wrote me—his first grandchild—a letter on the occasion of my first birthday. In this letter, written a few days after France fell to Nazi Germany, my grandfather captures the atmosphere in which I was raised:

June 26, 1940

My precious Grandson:

On this day, the first anniversary of your birth, I salute you.

When you are old enough to read and understand this letter, either there will at last be peace on earth again, or civilization will have had its Gethsemane. Today Adolph Hitler . . . and his Huns are devastating

Europe with their mechanized warfare, destroying millions of God-fearing people whose only offending was that they dared to fight for what they believed to be right—in defense of their homes and the faith of their fathers.

Thank God, it will only be a memory while you are still a child, but it will carry a lesson which you and your generation must heed. May love of country, love of liberty in its finest sense (in defense of both of which you must ever be ready to offer your life if necessary) always find sanctuary in your heart. May you grow to manhood the splendid fruit of a fine ancestry, a comfort to and the pride of your parents—and be a gentleman ever.

Your devoted grandfather,

Robert W. Woolley

As a toddler, I was too young to understand my grandfather's words, but the sentiment that he captured was a common one in the generation in which I was raised, in the shadow of the Great Depression and World War II. Our parents, grandparents, teachers, heroes, and political leaders had lived through the trauma of these cataclysmic events, and it would color how they shaped our world. We were too young to fight in World War II alongside the "Greatest Generation," but our formative years, during Truman's presidency, were full of patriotic movies and the glory of serving one's country. These years during and immediately after the war lacked the carefree materialism of the 1950s. One of my earliest memories was of carefully rolling up toothpaste tubes from the bottom to squeeze out every last bit. We had to turn in the tube, which was made of rationed metal, to be able to buy a new one. Rationing continued until 1946, the year I turned seven, and I remember holding on to our little coupon book—with stamps for items considered precious, such as sugar, coffee, and meat—as I went into the grocery store with my mother.

When the war ended, there were new fears to contend with. Though Nazi Germany was beaten, the giant in the East—the Soviet Union—was now at its most threatening. The Red Menace, as we knew it then, now controlled well more than half of Europe through the Eastern Bloc countries, and its influence was stretching into Asia. The United States' use of the atomic bomb on the Japanese cities of Hiroshima and Nagasaki was a recent memory, and it felt very real that such a horrific weapon could be used again. Our elementary school teachers had us practice hiding (futilely) under our desks to prepare for a possible nuclear attack.

There was also the fear of a postwar recession, as had happened after the First World War, or that the country would return to the prewar decade of depression. My parents' own families, which had both been comfortably well off in the 1920s, had been severely affected by the Great Depression. The story has also been passed down that, although my Grandfather Robb's losses were minimal because of his status as a preferred stockholder, he felt obligated to pay off the debts to common stockholders who lost everything, increasing his own debt considerably. According to the *Sunday Star,* my Grandfather Robb "lost all his money in the crash but never declared bankruptcy. He got a job with the Home Owner's Loan Corp and paid up every penny of his indebtedness."[1]

My Grandfather Woolley was also "cleaned out" by the crash. Ever the self-made man, he joined a law firm to get a steady salary, despite, according to the *Sunday Star,* having passed the bar after having only completed one year at Fordham Law School.[2]

Though neither side of my parents' families would be left penniless, after the Great Depression they were no longer prosperous, and any inheritance that my parents could have expected to receive was no longer significant. Making ends meet would always be a concern for my parents, though they generally managed their more limited finances well.

That's not to say that I was particularly conscious of these factors during my childhood, but I was likely affected by the atmosphere of my upbringing, whether I was aware of it at the time or not. Around the same time the Soviets were testing their first atomic bomb, I was busy riding my bike to see the movie *The Sands of Iwo Jima* at a twenty-five-cent Saturday matinee. This was the typical fare of the time: John Wayne as Marine Corps sergeant John M. Stryker, whipping up a band of young recruits into an elite fighting corps. The Marines seemed like supermen to a boy growing up in the shadow of World War II, hearing stories of the heroes of the war.

WHEN I WAS eight years old, my family moved from Phoenix to rural Arizona, following one of my father's more adventurous ambitions: running a dude ranch. We moved first to a small town called Patagonia, then to the blink-and-you-missed-it town of Sonoita. The sole teacher in our one-room schoolhouse was the wife of the owner of the only gas station.

Then, when I was ten, after the dude ranching didn't pan out, my father went back into the airline business with Pan American World Airways. We moved to a big old house in the country an hour northeast of Cleveland, Ohio. Five years after that, another job opportunity, back with American Airlines, took us to Alexandria, Virginia, in the suburbs of Washington, D.C.

Despite the number of moves, I was a pretty typical boy for the era: keen on all kinds of sports, working as a newspaper delivery boy and mowing lawns, and going to the movie theaters on Saturday afternoons to see the war films and Westerns. I was an athletic child, very competitive, and spent most of my free time outside playing whatever sport was in season.

By the time we moved to Ohio, I had three younger siblings. Robert Wickliffe (Wick) Robb was two years younger than I was, and David MacGregor Robb came along three years later. Marguerite Trenholm (Trenny) Robb, my only sister, was also the baby of the family and a full eight years younger than I was.

I spent the most time with my brother Wick, who was closest to me in age and with whom I shared the most common interests, even if we did not share physical similarities. I was dark-haired, with an angular jaw and often tan skin, whereas Wick was a towheaded, fair-skinned blond. When we got older and I hit a late growth spurt, the disparity in our height made the differences even more striking.

If there was a distinguishing characteristic about me early on, it would have been that I was more serious than most kids my age. Some of this was simply my nature, and some perhaps due to my birth order. I was the classic oldest child: responsible, careful, and dutifully performing all the things expected of me. My mother later told the *Washington Post* that my very first word was "'away,'—as in 'store the toys away neatly.'"[3] My earnest nature was pronounced enough to earn me the nickname of "the little judge."

We weren't a fervently religious family, though we went to church every Sunday, said grace before meals, and recited prayers before bed. I always had a sense of some larger force behind the order of the universe that kept an eye out for right and wrong. When my brother Wick and I got into little arguments, the highest oath we would make to each other was, "I promise God," and that was one that was not to be broken.

Even my hobbies had an earnest bent. I had an extensive collection of baseball cards, which I managed to fund creatively by buying packs of five cards that also included two sticks of bubblegum and cost a nickel. I would then resell the sticks of gum to my siblings or other neighborhood children, netting me the baseball cards for free. Then I'd turn a profit by selling off my duplicate cards to the neighborhood kids. It was a profitable enterprise until my three-year-old sister, Trenny, discovered my stash of gum and the whole endeavor ended up as chewed-up wads on the floor.

My parents later described me as a "very composed, well organized person who always had money in the bank."[4] My father recalled that I earned enough money selling newspapers that I "went downtown in Cleveland and bought . . . a good English bicycle." And that I "was only 12 at the time."[5]

I got good grades throughout primary and secondary school, but I freely admit that I was almost never truly challenged; my good grades had more to do with a system that favored athletes than they did with my own study habits. I was a quarterback on the high school football team—until a broken arm on the field in my sophomore year cut short my season. My matronly Latin teacher gave almost anyone playing a school sport an A, and to this day I remember only a few words in that language. I did have an abiding interest in math, however, and my test scores were good enough that, in my senior year of high school, I was made a National Merit Scholarship Finalist and won an engineering scholarship to Cornell University.

The engineering scholarship was critical because my parents weren't in a position to pay for my college education. The result of the Depression on their families and their own modest means meant that, though they had both attended prominent private prep schools, they had very little money to help pay for my college tuition. So, while I was also accepted to the engineering programs at Yale and Dartmouth—the only other schools to which I had applied—the scholarship to Cornell made all the difference in my decision process.

In the fall of 1957, I set out on a train bound for Ithaca, New York, with a suitcase in my hand and a fedora on my head—in deference to my father, who believed a proper young man should wear a hat. I was eager to show I was ready for the Ivy League.

I was not prepared, however, for that wholly new environment. It probably didn't help that I didn't have the kind of guidance that one might get from parents who had attended college. And, after receiving nearly all As through high school, I reached college with a naive sense of confidence surrounding the difficulty of serious study. At Cornell, I pursued the social opportunities of college life—joining Chi Phi fraternity and going to football games, fraternity and sorority parties, and social mixers—with a good deal more enthusiasm than I showed for my academic courses. I fit studying into whatever time was left, and I wasn't particularly concerned about grades. I had picked engineering based on a fascination with the space race (I began college the same fall that the Soviets launched Sputnik) and my affinity for mathematics and science. Not surprisingly, the academic atmosphere at Cornell was competitive, and the grading was tough. Engineering turned out to be a more challenging and less exciting field than I had expected, and the newly found freedoms of college life proved enticing. All of this came to a head at the end of my freshman year when, although I had passed all of my courses, my grades were not quite good enough to place me in the top third of my class, as my scholarship required, and I lost it. While I could have continued on at Cornell, without a scholarship I simply couldn't afford it. It was a good lesson to learn early on in life.

This could easily have been devastating news, but around the same time I learned that I'd been awarded a competitive appointment to the U.S. Naval Academy. Accepting the appointment to the Naval Academy would mean I'd have to repeat my first year of college—all midshipmen are required to attend the academy for four years. At nearly the exact same time, I found out that I had also been offered a Navy ROTC (NROTC) scholarship. With the NROTC scholarship, I wouldn't have to repeat anything, but I'd spend my summers in military training, and after graduation I would be obligated to serve for a minimum of four years as a commissioned officer in either the Navy or the Marine Corps. I had enjoyed NROTC so far—I'd signed up at the beginning of my freshman year—and the training and service felt like a challenge worth taking on. So, I accepted the NROTC scholarship offer, and because it was the beginning of the summer, I was ordered to report to Norfolk for duty, to undergo midshipman third class training on a World War II destroyer, the USS *Harlan R. Dickson.*

The only downside to the NROTC scholarship was that Cornell didn't have a vacancy for an NROTC scholarship student, so I'd have to transfer to a school that did. My parents, who had recently moved to Milwaukee, urged me to consider the University of Wisconsin at Madison, which had an opening, and I decided to make the transfer. I also decided, during my sophomore year, that engineering didn't appear to be my calling after all, and I switched my major to business administration.

It was at the University of Wisconsin at Madison that my innate seriousness of purpose truly found an outlet and I began to find my place.

I became focused on my NROTC activities and the idea of becoming a Marine. The work was physical and mental, focused and structured, and perfectly tailored for my disciplined nature. I even joined the silent drill team, a group that performed complex, choreographed marching and rifle drills, including an intricate series of rifle spins and tosses, all without a single spoken order.

I was encouraged to choose the Marines by the NROTC's Marine Corps officer instructor and the sponsor of the drill team, Major Reverdy Morton Hall. Built like a fireplug with almost no neck and a broad, muscled chest, he looked and carried himself like the embodiment of the Marine Corps ethos. Despite his bulldog looks and sometimes ornery demeanor, Major Hall was also an extremely sophisticated conversationalist. He had the distinction of being, simultaneously, one of the most articulate and profane officers that I would ever meet.

At Wisconsin, Major Hall became a constant figure in my life and an early role model. He made a special effort to recruit me for the Marines, not that I needed much of a push. The Marines, which were a part of the naval service, were more selective and smaller than the other branches—they were permitted to take only up to one-sixth of each graduating class from both the NROTC and the Naval Academy. The recruitment process for the Marines had a toughness to it that attracted a certain type of individual. Instead of trying to entice recruits with sweeteners, the Marines said, in essence, "if you think that you are tough enough to join our ranks, then prove it."

That challenge sparked something in my competitive nature. There was a certain mystique to the Corps. Though I was drawn to the idea of being a trained fighting man in any branch—self-confident and physically fit— the Marines seemed tougher and more squared away. Becoming a Marine meant that I could count myself among those I saw as the military's crème de la crème, the service designed to be "the first to fight."

With Major Hall's guidance and a solid record in my NROTC program, I was accepted to undergo training in the Marine Corps' Officer Candidate School (OCS) at Quantico, Virginia, for that pivotal summer between my junior and senior years of college. One of the things that sets the Marines apart from the other four branches of the United States military is what happens at the Marine Corps Base Quantico. Whereas the other branches thrive on specialization, the Marine Corps makes every Marine a rifleman first. That means that to become a Marine, everyone—from a pilot to a gunnery sergeant to a member of the Drum & Bugle Corps—has to go through the intense physical and mental training of OCS or boot camp.

There was a distinct feeling, as soon as I set foot on the base at Quantico, that I was going through these trials to be a part of something larger, a member of an elite team with a common goal.

I knew that I had to personally push myself to earn the title of "Marine." That prize focused my competitive instincts and single-minded determination. The instructors would post scores for the various tests and rank the would-be Marine officers throughout the summer. Once I saw myself getting even close to the top of the rankings, I pushed harder. My primary goal was to simply complete the course, but the idea of being among the top finishers became a greater motivator, particularly after my less-than-stellar grade-point average at Cornell.

When the summer was over, I found out that I had done well enough in the OCS training program that I was selected as the brigade commander of all the ROTC units on campus for my senior year at Wisconsin, and I worked through the year with a renewed sense of purpose. Then, on June 5, 1961, I found myself standing in the uniform of a Marine Corps officer amid a sea of caps and gowns as I graduated from the University of Wisconsin with a bachelor of arts in business administration. That same day, I was commissioned as a second lieutenant in the United States Marine Corps.

Before I could get my first regular duty station assignment, however, I'd have to go back to Quantico for an even longer training course. I'd spend the next six months at Marine Corps Officers Basic School, known as The Basic School (TBS), a kind of postgraduate school for recently commissioned Marine officers. While OCS had tested our physical, mental, and emotional stamina, at TBS we were constantly being tested and evaluated in three areas: leadership skills, physical fitness, and academic work in military strategy and tactics, with points awarded on performance in each area.

Through a seemingly infinite number of exercises and simulations, we learned military history, tactics, and basic battlefield engineering, navigation, and marksmanship. In the field, we learned how to conduct operations, handle our equipment and weapons, and function as a unit. Instructors would set up exercises such as a navigational challenge, where a small group of officers would be dropped in a far-flung spot, given tactical map coordinates, and told to find their way back to base headquarters many miles away, through a heavily wooded training area.

Throughout, instructors would rotate the leadership of groups from within our numbers, allowing each person a chance to lead in various capacities. Our leadership score was based on a combination of the ratings by our instructors and the peer evaluations of the Marines we had led. To the great credit of the Marine Corps, our training emphasized the importance of leadership as an act of respect, not force or superior rank.

"You've got to lead by persuasion, by logic, by convincing your peers that your approach is right," retired General Carl Mundy Jr.—who had been an instructor of mine at TBS and later commandant of the Marine Corps—explained to a reporter in 2000. "You get graded on that. At two or three points along the way you sit down and do a peer evaluation—and put down, 'I would or would *not* follow this guy.'"[6]

The physical fitness portion of TBS was the brutal Physical Readiness Test (PRT). Surrounded by a highly motivated group of strong young Marine officers, I was determined to not just pass the PRT but to "max out" and prove myself worthy of the best of the best.

The toughest part of the PRT was a three-mile run in full battle gear—helmet and combat boots, a full field pack, two filled canteens, and a rifle. In order to pass, we had to traverse the course in the summer heat in twenty-eight minutes. But in order to "max out," this had to be done in eighteen minutes, averaging six minutes or less per mile. The additional gear weighed about forty pounds, and when you ran, the gear bounced, jostled, and dug in wherever it touched your body. Today, I'd be hard-pressed to run three miles in eighteen minutes even without all the weight of combat gear, but at TBS, fueled by adrenaline and the competition, I finished the run in just under the eighteen-minute mark.

This is, perhaps, the greatest strength of the Marine Corps: its unique ability to take ordinary young men (and now, I am proud to say, women), challenge them to do something extraordinary, and convince them that they are, in fact, capable of achieving their maximum potential. My fellow second lieutenants were the toughest of the tough, and I wanted to be able to stand tall and proudly look even the strongest of them in the eye as an equal. I considered it the best kind of peer pressure.

Periodically, our rankings among the class were posted, an event that naturally drew considerable attention in such a competitive environment. In the last few weeks, I knew I was doing well, ranking right at the top of my platoon and company, but with about a week to go before graduation, one of my company officers let me know that as long as I didn't screw up in the last few days, I'd end up at the top of the whole class, a position called the class "honor graduate." I was proud and mildly surprised. That hadn't been my conscious goal, though I had constantly been pushing to excel. General Mundy said it pretty well in the interview in 2000: "To be measured by your peers, to be measured by your instructors, who are paid to be critical of you, to meet all the standards of physical fitness, tactical ingenuity, knowledge, leadership skills, and to come out No. 1 of (a class of) extraordinarily competitive individuals is a pretty doggone-good achievement."[7]

My company officer told me in advance so I'd be able to make sure my parents came to the upcoming graduation ceremony. They were already planning to make the trip from Wisconsin to Quantico, so I decided to let them be surprised. After filing into the darkened, cavernous auditorium of Little Hall and settling into their seats, however, my parents leafed through the list of graduates printed in the program and began to worry when they didn't see my name. Having overlooked the page listing me as the honor graduate, my mother was apprehensive throughout the opening ceremonies, wondering whether I'd somehow failed the training at the last minute. When my name was announced and I walked onto the stage to receive the honor graduate's engraved, pearl-handled Marine Officer's Mameluke sword, my mother burst into tears, but it's fair to surmise that they were tears of relief as much as pride.

Receiving that sword and completing my training, I felt like the archetypal military man. I had internalized the Corps' lessons as I went through training, developing the strength and command presence that had initially drawn me to the Corps. The control and order of the Marines was now a part of what I identified as who I was. The macho, all-male culture of TBS reinforced my belief that real men didn't cry and that keeping emotions in check was the way a man ought to conduct himself. I learned how to handle a leadership role during a crisis and project an aura of calm, focus, and control, a skill that would prove fundamental—both professionally and as a part of my personality—for the remainder of my life.

I didn't fully realize just how much I was learning at the time. Or how much I had yet to learn. Looking at pictures of myself then, I'm surprised at not just how young I looked, but how earnest. The Marines had instilled a sense of purpose, and youth added a feeling of invincibility. I had conquered TBS, and now, I thought, I could take on anything. The Marine ethos had become a part of my DNA.

For my first regular active duty assignment, I was eager to see combat. Not because I relished the idea of war itself, but because I wanted to prove myself worthy of the honor that the Marines had given me in naming me the honor graduate. An essential part of being a Marine is *earning* your honors, not being *given* anything. And a Marine earns his honors on the battlefield, with the "muddy boots Marines."

When I graduated from TBS, the war in Vietnam was just starting to heat up. Many of the officers I'd trained with at Quantico would soon be fighting in Vietnam, and I wanted to join them. I requested a combat duty assignment at every opportunity.

But what I didn't realize when I was competing for top of my class was that winning the honor would mean that I wouldn't get to see combat anytime soon. The Marine Corps would instead be sending me on a series of what were considered "plum posts." While they were great duty assignments, I had not requested them, and I admit that I was disappointed each time my request to be assigned to Vietnam was not approved.

These early, highly sought-after assignments did have their memorable moments. When I shipped out as the executive officer of the Marine detachment aboard the USS *Northampton*—affectionately referred to as the "Snort'n Nort'n"—soon after my graduation from Quantico, there was every possibility that the ship would end up hosting some of the country's top leaders. Though this was highly classified at the time, the ship was configured to serve as the National Emergency Command Post Afloat (NECPA), a floating command center for the president of the United States in the event of nuclear war. And on April 13, 1962, we did get a visit from President John F. Kennedy, though under much grander and less apocalyptic circumstances.

I had met Kennedy one time before, during his campaign stop in Madison, Wisconsin. I had a part-time job during college as a bellhop, and I was going in to start my shift as the then presidential candidate was coming out of the hotel where I worked. I didn't see any Secret Service with him, and hardly any entourage at all. Still, he had a kind of presence about him that made me remember the meeting.

Just a few years later, President Kennedy and his guests—including Secretary of State Dean Rusk, Secretary of Defense Robert McNamara, and the members of the Joint Chiefs of Staff, including the commandant of the Marine Corps—were on board the *Northampton* to oversee a number of high-level command and control exercises. The second day of the president's visit was the highlight, and one that was to happen only once in the twentieth century: nearly the entire Atlantic fleet executed a "pass in review" for their commander in chief.

The ship's newsletter later described the scene:

> The Presidential party gathered on the Admiral's Veranda. . . . Suddenly, steaming toward them over the horizon were the world's largest aircraft carriers, the Enterprise and the Forrestal. As they came closer it could be seen that they each led a column of ships as far as the eye could see.
>
> The NORTHAMPTON, with every few feet of her rail on all eight levels manned by the crew, sailed majestically down the center. As the leaders passed they saluted the President with a simultaneous twenty-one gun salute. . . . Besides three aircraft carriers there were six amphibious ships, three cruisers, two guided missile frigates, and thirty destroyers. From horizon to horizon the might of the Atlantic Fleet was displayed for the President, and he was noticeably impressed.[8]

For a young Marine officer, it was an unforgettable experience.

A few months later, in October 1962, many of those same ships were ordered to participate in the blockade off of the island of Cuba during the Cuban Missile Crisis, the closest that America had ever gotten to a full nuclear war. Onboard the *Northampton,* the adrenaline was pumping as we all prepared to join in the blockade. "This is it!" we thought.

But it was not to be. The *Northampton*'s unique function as a command center meant that we were soon ordered north to the Chesapeake Bay, where President Kennedy could easily reach us by helicopter in the event of nuclear war. Ours was an important role, but, for a gung-ho young Marine officer like myself, it was frustrating and disappointing to be tucked away reasonably safely in the bay.

My next assignment, to the 2nd Marine Division at Camp Lejeune, North Carolina, was no nearer to actual combat. I was selected as the aide for the incoming commanding general of the 2nd Marine Division, Major General William J. Van Ryzin. As a rule, I headed the general's personal staff and served as his gatekeeper, coordinator, and briefer. But I was also assigned to staff visiting dignitaries who were touring the base, including, on two separate occasions, Lieutenant General Chesty Puller, the most decorated Marine in American history, and Navy Admiral John McCain Jr., who would soon go on to command the Pacific fleet in the Vietnam War.

It was awe-inspiring, as a young first lieutenant, to have the opportunity to spend an entire day with these two living legends, sitting next to them in the back of the commanding general's staff car and listening to war stories. Puller in particular, legendary as a "Marine's Marine," lived up to my ideal of a quintessential fighting man, famous for quotes like "We've been looking for the enemy for some time now. We've finally found him. We're surrounded. That simplifies things." As I watched him interact with the enlisted Marines, I could see his devotion to his men. He embodied his personal motto, "Lead by example."

There were moments like these in my early years as a Marine officer that were unforgettable, and I learned valuable lessons from each post, but I still continued to hope, with each new assignment, that I would be posted to combat. From Camp Lejeune, I embarked with a battalion landing team headed for operations in the Mediterranean as the executive officer of H Company, 2nd Battalion, 2nd Regiment, 2nd Marine Division. From there, I requested specifically to be assigned next to Fleet Marine Force Pacific, the command furnishing Marines for the increasing combat buildup in Vietnam. I was again disappointed to find that my request was not granted. This time, however, my disappointment would have been tempered if I had known how much my next assignment would change the course of my life.

In the winter of 1965–66, I was ordered to report to the Marine Corps Barracks at Eighth and I Streets in Southeast Washington, D.C—often shortened to "Eighth and Eye"—the post that provides, among other duties, military social aides to the White House. And it was at this post that I would meet a remarkable young woman: the president's eldest daughter, Lynda.

2

The President's Daughter

"A DATE WITH Lynda Bird Johnson for lunch . . . is a unique experience," began one article in the *Washington Post* on January 21, 1966.

> Lynda is a challenging combination of attractive qualities. She has the innocence of childhood, the wisdom and maturity of middle age, and the intellectual flair of the honor student that she is. . . .
>
> The girl is understandably fed up with what she calls "the match-making of you reporters." She assures you absolutely that she is not serious about any boy and has no marriage or engagement plans. She has many dates, she says, and in the last couple of months she has gone out more than once with at least four men, including a young movie actor named George Hamilton, who has made the papers as Lynda's date in recent weeks.
>
> "Really, there's something more in life than men," Lynda says at one point.
>
> As luncheon progresses, the most remarkable quality this girl reveals is her modesty and her awareness of the fleeting nature of fame.
>
> "You're not ever as important as you think you are," Lynda said, in talking about the job of being the daughter of the President and the First Lady.[1]

A few months after this article was published, Lynda graduated from the University of Texas (UT) and returned to Washington, D.C., in the summer of 1966 in the midst of a media blitz: the fairy-tale wedding of her nineteen-year-old sister, Luci, to Patrick Nugent in an elaborate ceremony at Washington's Shrine of the Immaculate Conception. It was at Luci's wedding reception that Lynda and I first appeared in the same photograph, an event that will have to serve as the beginning of our de facto story together, because our recollections differ about when we first met. I remember meeting Lynda at a party at Eighth and Eye, a short time before Luci's wedding. Lynda believes our first encounter was at the White House around the same time. Perhaps not surprisingly, we each claimed our own turf as the venue for that first meeting.

At the time of Luci's wedding, I was twenty-seven, and Lynda was twenty-two, a tall, striking brunette with a very slight, but charming, Texas accent. She was a recent graduate with honors in history. She had finished near the top of her class, and her record would have qualified her for the Phi Beta Kappa Society if she had stayed at UT for all four years, but she had spent two of her four years at George Washington University at the request of her father, who had just become president, to be closer to her family. (The technicality of her initial exclusion from Phi Beta Kappa was overcome in 1992, when Lynda was formally inducted into the prestigious honor society in Washington, D.C., making her the only Phi Beta Kappa in the Robb household.)

Lynda was an obvious magnet for attention at the many social gatherings that summer. She had been conscious of the spotlight from a young age, though not always eager to be in it. Lynda had been only four years old when her father became a U.S. senator and sixteen when he was sworn in as vice president. When she was nineteen, Lynda was thrust unexpectedly into a new level of national attention when her father became president of the United States after the assassination of President John F. Kennedy on November 22, 1963.

A few weeks later, the *Washington Post* noted that something as common as attending school had become complicated for Lynda and her sister: "They are learning what it's like to lead a parade. The parade consists of the inevitable Secret Service man and a long string of photographers."[2]

The life of the daughter of the president was exciting, and sometimes thrilling, but these were mixed with an equal part of absurdity. One night, Lynda rose from her bedroom at the White House and walked down the corridor in her bathrobe, only to run into Frank Sinatra, who was getting a tour of the residence by Vice President Hubert Humphrey. Though she was giddy on the inside, Lynda, then only a teenager, kept her composure and warmly greeted the famous guest.

By the time I met her in 1966, I had become a fairly regular face at the White House for the staff and First Family. My official assignment was as the barracks adjutant at Eighth and Eye, the oldest ceremonial post in the Marine Corps. Eighth and Eye is home to the commandant of the Corps and his family, and it provides the Marines detailed to ceremonies at the White House, Camp David, the Pentagon, and Arlington National Cemetery. Marines posted at the barracks provide the honor guard for the president, the funeral escort for Marines and high-level government dignitaries, and the silent drill team that performs at parades like the Sunset Parade on the barracks' parade field and the Sunset Parade at the Iwo Jima Memorial. In addition to my duties as adjutant, I was selected to serve as one of the two Marine Corps military social aides to the White House and then as the officer in charge of the White House Color Guard.

At the White House, many of my duties were ceremonial. At the beginning of each state dinner, I would lead the president and the visiting king, prime minister, or president down the grand staircase, where we would pause for photos before continuing into the East Room to greet the assembled guests. Whenever you see a president and a visiting dignitary in pictures or on the news, flanked by Marines in their formal dress uniforms, you're seeing my old post in action.

My additional duties as a military social aide were fairly straightforward: do whatever was needed to make social or ceremonial functions at the White House move as smoothly as possible. This would usually include a variety of more formal events in the East Room or the State Dining Room as well as the occasional less formal events, parties, and barbecues on the South Lawn. Frequently, I was assigned to stand beside the president in the receiving line and introduce, by name and title (if appropriate), each official guest to the president—from the secretary of state to the ambassador of France—to avoid unintentional slights.

When social events included dancing, the social aides were expected to ensure that no ladies were left without dance partners. In this particular administration, President Johnson gave us one additional duty: whenever he gave a certain signal—usually a slight nod in our direction—while he was dancing, we were to cut in on him so he could change partners. There were times when the president liked to dance with several ladies during a single number, and, as might be expected, each lady wanted her special turn with the president to last as long as possible. I'm sure there were many glamorous White House visitors who were left grumbling at the brash young military aide who dared cut in on their dances with the president.

It was undeniably exhilarating to take part in official White House dinners, to mingle with kings, queens, prime ministers, presidents, and ambassadors along with movie stars, writers, artists, sports stars, political leaders, business leaders, and anyone else important enough to garner an invitation

to the White House. I wasn't at every function, since there were several social aides from each of the services who rotated through events, but I was
one of the regulars. And it was an empowering feeling to drive up to the illustrious residence in my spanking-new sports car—a 1966 Austin-Healey
convertible in British racing green that I had bought overseas while embarked with the battalion landing team in the Mediterranean. In an era
before today's much heavier security, the White House police would see my
Austin-Healey approaching and simply open the gates. I'd drive through
with a nod and park in the driveway of the White House.

But while I spent much of my time at the White House standing next to
the president, introducing dignitaries, my relationship with him was purely
professional. During this period, I don't think that we once shook hands or
had a real conversation. I was, to be honest, like all the military social aides,
an extension of the White House support system—a part of the furniture.

With the president's daughters, who were closer in age to the social
aides, the relationship was more personal. We would sometimes see them at
both social and official events. Occasionally, following official White House
functions, Lynda would invite one or two friends or military social aides
up to the Solarium to play bridge. The Solarium, a room on the top floor of
the White House with an impressive panoramic view of the National Mall,
was a place where the First Family could relax and entertain close friends.
Lynda later liked to tease, when asked how we ended up together, that she
picked me out of the class of military social aides by pointing a finger in my
direction and saying, "I'll take *that* one."

I was certainly drawn to Lynda from the beginning—she was a vivacious
young woman with sparkling dark eyes who exuded an irresistible air of
vitality, intelligence, and wit.

But our relationship didn't get off to a quick start. It wasn't until the
spring of 1967 that it started to become clear that Lynda and I were enjoying
each other's company even more than the game of bridge. We found that
we had a lot in common—we were both the firstborns in our families and
the more serious of our siblings, and we shared a love of the theater and
bridge. But perhaps the most compelling thing about Lynda was simply
how much I enjoyed her company. No matter what the day had been like, I
could always find comfort and contentment being with her.

I didn't see it as "dating" in the formal sense, because I didn't ring her
up and ask her out on a date or ask her to be my steady girlfriend. It was

much more casual than that, and Lynda took a leading role. She would ask me to accompany her to events to which she had been invited—sometimes formal ones where it was expected that she would have an escort and other times more casual social events—or ask me to partner with her in bridge. We did see more and more of each other socially, but I didn't make any grand romantic gestures. I didn't think of it this way at the time, but I can see now that, subconsciously, I was self-conscious of looking too eager to date the president's daughter. Wooing her with flowers and chocolates, or asking her out on formal dates, felt inherently presumptuous. She was, to use a modern term, out of my league. I was an officer of the United States Marine Corps, of which her father was commander in chief, and it didn't feel entirely proper for me to be pursuing her. At the same time, I was wary, again subconsciously, of being seen as a publicity hound or as trying to get close to her because of who her father was.

There are many peculiarities about going out with the daughter of the president. One of the more noticeable ones was the fact that Lynda (whose code name was "Velvet") had round-the-clock Secret Service protection. Most of the agents were very easy to get along with, and many became lifelong friends. They did their best to stay out of the way during dates, but their first responsibility was always to keep the president's daughter safe. We had to give them a schedule ahead of every date so that the agents could advance the locations. There were no spontaneous or surprise outings. Driving Lynda in my Austin-Healey gave the agents serious heartburn, so we were usually driven in one of their cars. We got used to arriving for dinner at a restaurant in the back of a large black sedan with two agents in the front seat.

We didn't try to "ditch" her agents—there didn't seem to be much point to it because they did their job both well and inconspicuously. The one time that Lynda did blend into a tour group, just to see what people talked about on the tours, she turned around before they reached the gates. She knew that the agents would get in trouble if she left with the tourists, and she would have felt terrible.

Unsurprisingly, most of our "dates" ended up taking place in the White House itself, usually up in the Solarium, where the agents generally stayed well out of the way.

We tried our best to keep our burgeoning relationship a private affair, but the *Washington Star*'s gossip page did take note when Lynda invited me to escort her to an event at the Peruvian embassy in June 1967. Soon thereafter, short items about us began appearing in more newspapers, as we continued to see each other outside of official White House functions.

Predictably, the press was keenly interested in the First Daughter's dating life. Over the Fourth of July weekend in 1967, Lynda and I—and, of course, her Secret Service detail—took a trip to Rehoboth Beach, Delaware. We'd kept the trip as quiet as we could, but as we lay sunning on a strip of sand called Whiskey Beach, an enterprising photographer with a telephoto lens snapped a picture of us together. That picture, which appeared in newspapers all over the country the next day, was even more popular because as far as the press knew, Lynda was still involved in a glamorous romance with actor George Hamilton. By then, not only were George and Lynda no longer an item, but she and I were fast reaching a turning point.

Later that month, Lynda prepared for a trip to England. As we lingered over our farewells at the White House doors, she leaned close and said, "We've got to talk when I get back." A light went on in my head, and, for the first time, I started to think about the possibility that Lynda and I might be interested in each other in a more serious way. It was new territory for me—though I'd dated several delightful young ladies in high school and college, I had never been in a committed, exclusive relationship. I'd also never been in love, in the "swept off your feet" sort of way. I wasn't particularly swift at picking up on signals from the fairer sex and probably missed several hints along the way. Even though Lynda and I had been spending a lot of time together, I hadn't realized how close we had grown. But for those two weeks while Lynda was in Europe, I, for the first time, took a critical look at how I felt about her and realized that I was starting to think of her as a more permanent and indispensable part of my life. The idea of being with Lynda exclusively began to appeal to me more and more.

On August 9, a few days after Lynda's return from England, we were invited to the home of White House curator Jim Ketchum and his wife, Barbara, for dinner along with two other couples—the first time Lynda and I had been formally invited to an event as a "couple." Afterward, we returned to the White House and went up to the Solarium.

Over the next several hours, we talked of many things—about Lynda's trip, about the latest D.C. gossip, and finally about us. We came to realize how much our feelings had sneaked up on us, how deeply we valued each other's company, and how much we really wanted to be together. It was one of the deepest and most meaningful conversations I have ever had, and we connected on a much more profound level than I ever had with anyone before. I had never realized what falling in love really meant, but I knew then that what I had with Lynda was the real thing.

We also talked about Vietnam. After several requests for duty there, Lynda and I both knew that I would almost certainly be sent to a combat zone for my next assignment. That meant that I would only remain in Washington for another six or seven months before shipping out.

I don't know who mentioned it first, but somehow the conversation turned in a longer-term direction. We knew that Vietnam put a kind of time pressure on us that we might not have otherwise had. We were also aware that as soon as we were seen in public together more frequently, our relationship would be a source of interest for the media.

We talked for hours, and very late that night, or more accurately early the next morning, with the romantic vista of the moonlit Mall sparkling outside the Solarium window, and the rest of the White House very quiet, we decided to marry.

Shortly thereafter, I departed to get back to Eighth and Eye, but Lynda wanted to tell her mother right away. As she later recounted in *McCall's* magazine:

> I was very nervous and still too excited to sleep—and since my mother was leaving for Texas early in the morning, I wanted to tell her before she left. Now, when we were children, if my sister, Luci, was sick, I would go into my parents' room and get Mother by crawling across the room and tapping her on the hand, to keep from waking my father, who is a very light sleeper. I hadn't done that for years, of course, but I decided to try it.
>
> Her side of the bed is very close to the wall, so I just kind of inched in. Just about the time I got next to her, she suddenly sat up and asked, "Who is it?" Only then did it occur to me that she might have been so startled to find a stranger in her room that she might have set off an alarm and wakened the whole White House! In any event, she saw me and asked, "Do you want me to come with you?" Just then my father woke up and asked, "What's going on?" I blurted out something about wanting to talk to Mother, and then he said, sounding a little hurt, "Don't you want to talk to me, too?"
>
> Well, they pulled me into their bed—it's a large, large bed—and although I didn't think I could sit still for a minute, I sat there and told them that Chuck and I were going to get married.[3]

The next morning, I sent Lynda a dozen red roses with a romantic note, but the moment was nearly lost when they were mistakenly delivered to her mother instead. When Lynda saw them, she blurted out, "Those are for me!" And with a smile, her mother handed them over lovingly.

I'm sure many newly engaged couples spend the first few days in a happy fog, reveling in excitement and anticipation before they tackle the wedding details. I'm probably not the type to do that anyway, but under our unusual circumstances, I'd never have the chance to find out. As soon as we'd made our decision, we had to move fast. We had a very conspicuous wedding to plan within a few short months, and we needed to get organized before our happy news was prematurely leaked to the media.

Though Lynda and I, both independent adults, had made our own decision to marry, I still wanted to ask for her hand in the old-fashioned way. So, I called the president's secretary and requested a few minutes of his time for "a personal matter," and she squeezed me into his appointment book for a fifteen-minute slot.

For me, my bride-to-be's father was every inch the larger-than-life figure he's remembered as today. A consummate, gregarious politician, President Lyndon B. Johnson was a man whose mere presence in a room commanded attention. His manner was pure down-home Texas, and he knew how to put anyone at ease, or, conversely, to make anyone feel his wrath. Although I had been dating his eldest daughter for more than six months, and we'd had countless interactions in my official capacity—I had, by then, been working as a White House military social aide for more than a year—this would be my first real meeting with President Johnson alone.

As the president entered the Queen's Sitting Room, we exchanged a warm handshake, sat down, and I got straight to the point.

"Mr. President," I began, "I assume you know why I asked for this meeting." In response, he smiled broadly.

"Yes," he answered. "I think I do." Knowing how busy he was, I quickly expressed my intentions and formally asked his permission for his daughter's hand in marriage.

"You have it," he responded quietly, "and my love." We spoke briefly of the plans Lynda and I had started working on, and with that, our meeting ended.

Our speedy courtship seemed to have taken both the Johnsons by surprise. The same day I met with the president, Mrs. Johnson wrote in her diary: "A sweetly sad thought came to me when I went into Lynda's room. I noticed something different and for several moments I couldn't decide what it was. And then I knew—gone, gone were all the pictures of George Hamilton—the romantic-devilish one on the chest of drawers, the patrician-handsome one, and lots of other little mementos—a faded telegram pasted on the mirror. She hadn't said a word about it. They had simply been removed."[4]

Mrs. Johnson noted that, though she knew little about me, I played "a good game of bridge" and looked as if I "ought to be on a poster for the Marines."[5] She pointed out that my "all-American boy" manner differentiated me from the crowd Lynda usually socialized with: "people on the stage and screen, café society people, people who are very rich or very talented or very social."[6] Though it seemed I was initially marked in her mind more by what I wasn't than by what I was, I apparently passed muster, at least enough to marry her daughter and become a part of the family.

The same day that I asked her father for her hand, Lynda and I discussed our tentative plans with her mother. Though I'd had a few more substantive conversations with Mrs. Johnson than with the president, this was also the most personal interaction I had had with her up to this point, and she was just as warm, steady, and poised in person as she was by her husband's side. Lady Bird Johnson was an incredible asset for her husband, hosting events, making amends for people LBJ may have inadvertently offended, and, most important of all, having a calming influence on the president. Years later, Lynda would do the same thing for me, smoothing ruffled feathers and winning people over on my behalf.

We talked through our plans with Mrs. Johnson, going over our tight timeline and the kind of event we envisioned. Lynda, a history major in college, wanted a historic wedding in the White House, something that hadn't happened since the 1914 wedding of Woodrow Wilson's daughter Eleanor in the Blue Room. Two of Wilson's daughters were married in the White House, but those weddings had been relatively small affairs. We knew that our wedding would be most compared to Alice Roosevelt's, who married Nicholas Longworth in a large East Room affair in 1906.

We quickly realized that a White House wedding would take a lot of extra planning, and time was running short. I was expecting to ship out for Vietnam as early as March 1968, and it was already mid-August. We tentatively set the date for December 9, giving us nearly four months to prepare, and time enough after the wedding for a short honeymoon.

It was an extraordinarily hectic and surreal four months, and I had little time to reflect on how much my life was changing. In the span of a few months I'd found the person with whom I wanted to share the rest of my life, was planning to marry her in the White House, and soon thereafter I would finally get a chance to test myself on the battlefield. Even if I had been prone to introspection, I wouldn't have had time for it. All I knew was that I'd never felt happier.

So far, only a select few knew of our plans, and we hoped to keep it that way for at least another couple of weeks.

Since I had always kept personal matters mostly to myself, my parents were a bit surprised when I called them in Wisconsin to deliver the happy news. They had known about my relationship with Lynda but didn't know—partially because I hadn't known myself—how serious it had become. They gave their congratulations and expressed their excitement, of course. But most of the excitement, especially for my mother, was over the mystery of the wedding details: when and where the wedding would be, how many people would be invited, who to invite, and when they could say something about it.

In a way, even though they had never met, my parents already knew my fiancée and her parents far better than most future in-laws. They could read full profiles on Lynda and her parents in *Life* magazine and see pictures of Lynda at events in the "Style" section of their hometown paper. Just a month before, they would even have seen my picture in the papers with Lynda as we sunned on Rehoboth Beach.

I was pleasantly surprised at how smoothly my parents took in the fact that not only would I be marrying the president's daughter but the wedding would be in the national spotlight of the White House itself. I easily forgot that my parents had both spent much of their childhood in Washington and that their fathers had both moved in high-level political circles.

I was, however, a little worried about how the rest of my family would react to the news. Unlike the Johnsons, the Robbs weren't accustomed to press scrutiny. How would they deal with the whirlwind of attention that would descend on them as soon as word of our engagement got out? Ready or not, their lives were about to change, too, and I wanted to help make the transition as smooth as possible. So, in late August, I wrote my parents a six-page letter telling them what to expect and suggesting what to do and what to avoid. I realize in hindsight that I wasn't always as tactful as I should have been:

When things do break, please do all you can to help me keep the far-flung members of the family quiet. I'm thinking particularly of [Aunt] Marguerite, but other members should also be cautioned in a nice way about making any comments or answering any questions which could get into print. . . . I'd like family and friends to refer all questions and requests to the White House Press Office. . . .

Please forgive me for sounding like I'm lecturing, which I certainly don't mean to do. It's just that we could all spend many years trying to live down a slip of the tongue.

I even suggested, to avoid the barrage of phone calls, that my parents get an unlisted telephone number for this period. To their credit, they did just that, and mailed out little slips of paper with the new number to family and friends.

A few weeks later, we set the date to announce the engagement, but my siblings—Wick, David, and Trenny—still didn't know. Trenny, who was then nineteen, remembers my parents arranging a phone call with her on a Sunday under partially false pretenses: what to do about Grandmother Robb, whose health had been failing. At the appointed time, Trenny called, and my parents also told her that Lynda and I were scheduled to publicly announce our engagement within a few hours.

The weekend had begun in secrecy, when, unbeknownst to the White House press corps, I'd flown down to Texas with the Johnsons. Lynda's father enjoyed the clandestine exploits and had arranged for me to be spirited onto Air Force One before any of the traveling press corps arrived. The press corps then stayed behind in Austin while we flew on to the LBJ Ranch. Thus, for most of the weekend, no one in the press corps knew I was in Texas.

This was my first time at the famed LBJ Ranch, and we spent a leisurely Saturday there, with the president driving us around on the dusty roads in his white Lincoln convertible to check on his cattle and to see the exotic deer he loved to show to visitors to the ranch. There were large areas fenced off for the special deer, antelope, and other wildlife that President Johnson had gradually been collecting from friends and foreign lands.

Then on Sunday, September 10, 1967, Lynda and I flew with her parents from the ranch to Randolph Air Force Base in San Antonio. And while the president and Mrs. Johnson thoughtfully stayed out of sight, Lynda and

I descended the plane's steps, faced the White House press corps on the tarmac, and announced our engagement.

With that one simple announcement—no more than fifteen minutes long—I stepped into the public eye.

At the time, of course, this was not on my mind. I was twenty-eight years old and had just won the prize of a lifetime: Lynda. I was thinking mostly about the next three months and the White House wedding at the end of it. Luckily, the instant transition from private citizen to public figure was made somewhat easier by my position as a White House military social aide. For over a year, I had been around the White House press corps, the national media, and the herd of reporters and photographers who followed the First Family with their klieg lights, cameras, and notepads. I had existing relationships with several members of the press corps and felt comfortable with them personally. But until now I'd never been the subject of their stories. I'd now have the press scrutinizing every aspect of my life. I didn't think that I had any reason to be concerned about the scrutiny and was confident that I could handle it.

For the most part, I was right. Much of the press coverage of our engagement was focused on the lighter side of wedding excitement. One "news conference" held at the Eighth and Eye was covered mostly by society page writers, and the questions—such as "Will you cut the wedding cake with your sword?"—were not exactly hard-hitting.

I was certainly self-conscious about "screwing up" something with the press. One of my larger interviews was over breakfast at a Washington hotel with the White House correspondents for the three major broadcast news networks: John Chancellor of NBC, Dan Rather of CBS, and Frank Reynolds of ABC. I parted with the reporters on the sidewalk outside of the hotel, and, in a hurry to get back to Marine Barracks, I started to take a shortcut across the middle of the street to get to my car. Suddenly realizing that I was jaywalking and that the three White House correspondents were still watching, I caught myself and went down to an intersection to cross with the light. My self-consciousness prompted smiles from all three men and a cute newspaper story about the "added public scrutiny" I'd have to get used to.

Unfortunately, not every story was as lighthearted—or even based on fact. One weekend while I was playing in a regular touch football game with friends, I got word that the White House press secretary, Liz Carpenter, was trying to reach me. I jogged off the field and called Liz from a pay phone. She read me an item by the *Washington Post* gossip columnist Maxine Cheshire, titled "Vietnam on Waiting List for Capt. Robb?," that had appeared in that morning's paper. Cheshire claimed to have witnessed part of a conversation I'd had with Sir Angus Ogilvy, the husband of British Princess Alexandra, at the White House the evening before. According to Cheshire, I'd told Ogilvy that I was trying to have my tour of duty in Vietnam postponed because Lynda and I were "hoping to have some time together first."[7]

I was stunned. Nothing even resembling such a conversation had taken place, and I was incredulous that a writer for a respected national newspaper would simply make up something like that out of whole cloth. I'd been pushing for an assignment to Vietnam since long before Lynda and I ever met. I had never made a secret of my desire to be assigned to a unit in combat—it was something about which I'd told Lynda from the outset of our relationship. I deeply resented the implication that I was trying to weasel my way out of it. For a young Marine officer, it was nearly as insulting as saying I'd committed an act of cowardice on the battlefield.

Following our conversation, Liz called everyone from the British embassy to the publisher of the *Washington Post,* Katharine Graham, attempting to correct the record. But, although Ogilvy and I both stated flatly, for the record, that no such conversation had taken place, the *Post* refused to run a correction. For her part, Maxine Cheshire insisted her report was true, though she admitted she hadn't actually heard me say the words that she had quoted in her story. She said she'd read my lips from across the room.

Even then, the rules of the press were starting to shift, and that was enough to keep the piece in the newspaper with no retraction. This was my new reality, and I'd have to learn to live with it.

3

A White House Wedding

FROM THE MOMENT Lynda and I announced our engagement, cameras and reporters were at every event, documenting every congratulatory celebration, bridal shower, and bachelor party, and even some of the behind-the-scenes White House wedding planning.

"Private moments are few and far between," said NBC White House correspondent Nancy Dickerson over footage of Lynda and me being prepped for one of our many interviews under the glare of television lights.[1] Nearly every event of our three-month engagement was filmed, usually by the White House Communications Agency (WHCA), and turned into an hour-long television program, called *Once in a Lifetime* and narrated by Dickerson and her cohost, CBS White House correspondent Dan Rather. Dickerson's narration continued: "A courtship that had begun quietly, confided in only family and intimate friends, was now spotlighted in the national news. It would be a long time before Chuck and Lynda would again know the quiet moments they had shared during the summer of 1967."

The interest in our wedding wasn't all that surprising. Shortly before our engagement, one of the president's top advisors, Tom Johnson (no relation to the president), had joked: "The only thing that can save us now, in terms of public opinion, is to have another wedding." Clearly this quip had nothing to do with our decision to get married, but it spoke to the feeling, in the White House and across the country, that people wanted something to feel good about. Our wedding, and the social swirl around it, was an ideal diversion for the White House during the difficult days of 1967. That fall, President Johnson's approval ratings had plummeted to an all-time low, largely due to a drumbeat of bad news from Vietnam that cast a pall over the country. At the same time, the First Family had an air of glamor and celebrity, especially the president's two beautiful daughters. As the designer of Lynda's wedding dress, Geoffrey Beene, said, "The First Family represents the idea of royalty."[2] So it was only natural that so many were excited for details about the closest thing that America could get to a "royal wedding."

As Nancy Dickerson said in *Once in a Lifetime*: "The marriage of a president's daughter is so rare, the event so intriguing, that the public seizes upon every facet of the bride and groom's activities, their hopes for the future, their outlook on life."

The pre-wedding festivities kicked off with a black-tie dinner dance at the City Tavern Club in Washington celebrating our engagement, hosted by longtime Johnson family friends Nell and Jack Hight. Lynda looked every bit the movie star in a yellow gown that glittered as we danced to the song "Thoroughly Modern Lynda," a play on the title track from *Thoroughly Modern Millie,* with lyrics rewritten to fit the occasion:

> Everything tonight is thoroughly Lynda (may we say specifically);
> No two lovers look as happy as this (I mean as terrifically);
> It's just, like a fairytale, that came through and how;
> Beat the drums 'cause here comes Lynda Bird and her
>   captain now.

The cameras were also at Lynda's first bridal shower, held at the Washington Club.

"Bridal showers are a uniquely feminine innovation," said Dickerson, "and this one especially so because the theme was lingerie." America got to watch Lynda open her gifts and make poised, witty comments as each lacy item came out of its box.

Dan Rather cut in to deliver the comic contrast: "With Lynda caught up in the spirit and fun of her first showers, Chuck whiled away the hours quietly pursuing his favorite pastimes." *Once in a Lifetime* cut to clips of my regular Sunday-afternoon touch football game—my friends and I looking very serious as we huddled and ran each play. The show made a running joke out of this dichotomy, striking a gendered tone that was more appropriate for the 1960s than it would be today. The contrast, though exaggerated, was also not too terribly far from the truth.

More than a dozen parties followed, thrown by good friends, family, and Washington officials. Congressman Hale Boggs and his wife, Lindy, hosted a party with lots of longtime personal friends of both the Johnson and Robb families. The entire diplomatic corps organized a party with the ambassadors from around the world and their spouses at the home of Ambassador-at-large Averell Harriman. And the White House social aides threw a costume party for us with the theme of "Great Lovers of the World." Couples showed up in elaborate and creative costumes, and milling about the party, cocktails in hand, were Bonnie and Clyde, Anna and the King of Siam, and even two friends dressed as Lynda and me. For our part, Lynda and I went Shakespearean, dressing as Petruchio and Kate from *Taming of the Shrew*. The lively evening included plenty of gag gifts, including a large picture of the then commandant of the Marine Corps, General Wallace Green, with my face superimposed over his. This was accompanied, of course, by a lot of good-natured ribbing about how rapid my promotions would be after the wedding. One good friend, Brian Lamb, created a hilarious audiotape by splicing together unrelated public comments made separately by President Johnson and by me to make ludicrous combinations of questions and answers. Then a Navy lieutenant (junior grade) and fellow White House social aide, the media-savvy Lamb would later go on to found C-SPAN.

Interspersed with shots of the glittering events, *Once in a Lifetime* showed a room at the White House filling with presents arriving from friends, family, and the occasional surprise. We were overwhelmed by the generosity and intrigued by the sometimes exotic gifts. Among the fondue sets, electric skillets, and ornate candy dishes was an antique silver egg coddler from John Wayne and a set of small teak tables from General Chiang Kai-shek of Taiwan.

The streams of gifts highlighted a problem that the television cameras did not capture: the guest list. When we started planning, we knew the wedding would be big. But even so, we imagined something like a large family affair. We did not envision that the complex diplomatic and political issues of the day would turn the wedding of LBJ's eldest daughter into the equivalent of a state dinner. While the wedding ceremony itself would take place in the East Room, guests would be spread through the East Room, the Great Hall, and the Entrance Foyer, with the overflow relegated to the other official rooms on the first floor. Even with guests spread throughout the many rooms of the state floor of the White House, it looked like we could only invite about five hundred people. For the family of a sitting president with many political and social obligations, five hundred was not going to be enough invites to include everyone we'd like. The list included the members of the Supreme Court, numerous members of Congress, cabinet members, and ambassadors, which left an ever-dwindling number of invites for our extended family and friends. After many hours of painful deliberation, we pared down the list, knowing that most of those we couldn't invite would be hurt at missing this storybook "once in a lifetime" event.

The preparations needed to host the wedding in the White House were immense. The staff and a team of workers took care of every detail. False walls, columns, and an altar transformed the East Room into a beautiful ceremony location. Risers and lighting rigs ensured access for a press corps desperate for every detail about the gown, the food, and the attendees. There was even a press release devoted entirely to the details of the wedding cake—a 250-pound, five-tier traditional pound cake covered in white fondant icing. Reporters started a pool to guess the number of raisins. The winner, Malvina Stephenson of the *Tulsa World,* guessed 1,511 raisins and won $3.85. Sadly, the accomplished pastry chef who was tapped to create the six-foot-tall confection, Clement Maggia, died of a heart attack three days before the wedding. He had finished the main work on the cake but never got to see his finished creation.

Everything had to be thoroughly considered, as every detail would be scrutinized by the five hundred reporters and photographers who had been assigned to cover the wedding. Thankfully, we were in the capable hands of the president's social secretary, Bess Abell; press secretary, Liz Carpenter; and the rest of the White House staff.

As November turned into a snowy December, the preparations intensified. About a week before the wedding, my family came to Washington. "The James Robbs will return to the White House in December as considerably more than shy members of the bridegroom's family," wrote Betty Beale, the society reporter for the *Washington Evening Star.* Beale listed the connections to Washington, D.C., on both sides of my family: "They have dozens of upper-crust friends in the permanent Washington and Virginia society, and they both visited the White House several times when they were young and living in Georgetown."

My parents had met Mrs. Johnson the month before, when she had flown to Milwaukee, where they were then living, to talk about wedding details. Graciously, she and the president invited my parents and my sister, Trenny, who would be part of the official wedding party, to stay at the White House, while my brothers, Wick and David, stayed with friends in the D.C. area. Even though Wick and his family weren't staying at the White House, they spent time there during that week, and Wick still fondly remembers how warmly the president treated his young daughters, giving them free rein in the first floor of the White House residence.

My siblings, of course, were under a great deal of media scrutiny as well. To the press, they were three potential sources for stories about the newest member of the First Family. I didn't have to worry too much about Wick, who was still my closest sibling in both age and occupation. He had joined the military, going on active duty in the Navy even before I joined the Marine Corps, and eventually rising to the rank of senior master chief, the highest rank for a noncommissioned officer. Though we shared military service, we had turned out as different from each other in looks and temperament as night and day—Wick was still a towheaded blond, stood a couple of inches shorter, and had inherited my father's love of jokes and puns. He was—and is—a more expressive and colorful personality.

Wick's skills at press relations were tested early in the engagement when he agreed to talk to a reporter at the *San Diego Tribune* who was friends with the press officer for his Naval base. The reporter asked, "What will you ask the president for when your brother gets married?" Wick's smart-aleck response ended up in the story. I was especially sensitive to the impression that anyone associated with me could get special favors from the president, and, as Wick tells it, I made that "very clear" in a phone call the day after the story appeared. Even after this minor slipup, I knew that I could count on Wick's discipline around the press.

Wick and I both paled in the "colorful" category compared to our two younger siblings, David and Trenny. Though only five and eight years younger than I was, respectively, they seemed not only to be from a different generation but quite possibly from a different planet.

At the time of the wedding, David was a senior at the University of Wisconsin in Madison, where he would remain a student for far more than the traditional four years. When he finally got his undergraduate degree in 1988—366 credits after enrolling in college—the *Wisconsin State Journal* ran an article headlined "Diploma Caps 25-Year Effort." David told the *Journal:* "I haven't missed a home football game since 1962."[3]

Trenny, the baby of the family and my parents' only daughter, was a self-described "hippie chick." When she got married in 1970, Trenny and her ponytailed groom stood barefoot in a mountain stream to take their vows. A wedding photo shows the happy pair and their many long-haired, bell-bottomed friends standing in the water next to my stiffly posed father in a dark suit, his shoes dampening in the stream.

For Trenny, who was an aspiring model and a bridesmaid, the White House wedding and surrounding events proved to be a promising national stage. As *Time* magazine reported, Trenny "set the White House a-sparkle during the wedding week with her five rings, her silver miniskirts, her flowing brown tresses and her Twiggy eyelashes." The attention that she received during the wedding sparked her budding modeling career, and she ended up landing a contract with the Eileen Ford Agency in New York.

And it wasn't just her looks that got Trenny attention—she also proved to be the most quotable member of the wedding party. "You know," read one quote in *Time,* "I ought to start a romance with George [Hamilton]—wouldn't that be the end?"

In another interview, the completely apolitical Trenny was asked, "Are you a dove or a hawk?" Her response was, "I'm not the bird, Lynda is!"

The week of the wedding, my brothers joined a large gathering at the Army Navy Country Club to celebrate my bachelor party. For a bachelor party, mine was a somewhat formal affair. The seated dinner had a head table where I sat with my groomsmen and the commander in chief, the podium in the center bearing the seal of the president. Despite the buttoned-up setting, the whiskey flowed for a series of toasts, and the content was lighthearted.

"I'm glad that you gave me a legitimate excuse for a night out," said the president when he stood at the podium.

I even got my own song, performed by the White House chief of protocol, Jim Symington. Donning an Eisenhower-style jacket from his World War II Marine uniform, he had rewritten the words to the Marines' hymn, "From the Halls of Montezuma," in a "tribute" to my courtship that concluded with:

> Although the goal was far away
> he determined to pursue it,
> A true Marine, he'd never say
> "Why not let George do it?"
> So like Caesar this young captain came
> and conquered what he saw,
> Now he's proud to claim the title
> of United Son-in-Law!

The following night, December 8, was the rehearsal dinner. In keeping with tradition, my parents hosted the gathering, which was held at the City Tavern in Georgetown. President Johnson captured the tone of the dinner beautifully during his toast. With an impeccably dry sense of comic timing and a Texas drawl, the president turned to me.

"Chuck," he said, "I want to give you a very special wedding present tonight, and I want to do it here in the presence of your family and your friends." The president took out a large sheaf of paper which he held up for the room to see. "I'm now going to proceed to tear up, in your presence, all the Secret Service reports"—he paused as ripples of laughter began to spread around the room—"for the courting period. That is the period when you lost interest in leading us down the stairway and just being a bridge partner. And you started spending your weekends at Whiskey Beach."

With a sly smile, he peered down at the top paper and announced: "This first report starts out on Saturday at 2 p.m., completed Sunday at 3 a.m. Top Secret, stamped Whiskey Beach . . ." As the room erupted in laughter, he tore the report in two and tossed it aside with a flourish. He looked at me and concluded, "Chuck, here's all your bachelor past, reduced to a bunch of wedding confetti." It was pure theater that only Lyndon Johnson—Texas politician and unabashed ham—could carry off.

When the laughter died down, the president grew serious and continued quietly: "It seems like it was just yesterday when a lady in white attending the door at Garfield Hospital showed us a very small object in a very pink blanket, and she was pinker than the blanket. And I can still feel tonight the wonder that I felt on that very incredible night in March. I think it's a feeling that comes over every father with his firstborn. And this is what life is really all about."[4] The television camera caught Lynda gathering her napkin to wipe a tear from her eye.

After we all raised our glasses to the president's toast, Lynda stepped to the podium and pulled out a piece of creased, yellowed onionskin copy paper. She spoke about my service in the Marines and my upcoming deployment to Vietnam. Then, to my surprise, she began to read aloud the letter my maternal grandfather, Robert Wickliffe Woolley, had written to me on my first birthday in 1940 about the devastating war in Europe, including the line: "May love of country, love of liberty in its finest sense (in defense of both of which you must ever be ready to offer your life if necessary) always find sanctuary in your heart." As my fiancée read aloud my grandfather's words that evening, three months before I would be leaving the young woman I loved to fight in a war myself, I couldn't help but think how oddly prescient his words had been, and how thoughtful Lynda was to read them.

AT LAST, OUR wedding day—Saturday, December 9, 1967—arrived. The day began overcast and gray, though, as Mrs. Johnson noted in her diary, "with the promise of the sun breaking through."[5] The months of planning by Lynda, her mother, and the White House staff had paid off: the beautiful and complex dance of setup, ceremony, costume changes, set changes, and party for hundreds of our friends and relatives went off without a single noticeable hitch. It is a true testament to the staff at the White House and our many helpful friends and family that such an event, which can often go wrong on a much smaller and less public scale, went so smoothly.

The media surely had a hard time deciding who to feature in their pictures of the event as guests started to arrive in the midafternoon chill. Photos of Henry Ford, Governor Nelson Rockefeller, and future defense secretary Clark Clifford appeared alongside those of George Hamilton, Hollywood-handsome and sporting his famous tan, and actress Carol Channing.

The White House had been transformed by the small army of staff with poinsettias, red and white carnations, and evergreens, and dotted with hundreds of lights, all sparkling in the ten-foot chandeliers. Despite our best efforts to keep the numbers manageable, more than seven hundred people had been invited. Family, friends, fellow Marine officers, political leaders, and diplomats stood elbow-to-elbow in the East Room and then overflowed through the other rooms on the state floor. Guests were held back by red-ribboned stanchions through the Entrance Hall and hallway on either side of the makeshift red-carpeted aisle that ran from the grand staircase into the East Room.

Promptly at 4:00 p.m., the thirty-two-person chamber orchestra of the U.S. Marine Band struck up Jeremiah Clarke's "Trumpet Voluntary" and my parents came down the staircase. My father looked serious in a morning coat and horn-rimmed glasses, with my elegant mother smiling radiantly next to him.

Mrs. Johnson came down next, looking beautiful as always and perfectly at ease with the crowd, on the arm of my friend and fellow social aide Brian Lamb, followed by the groomsmen, and then the bridesmaids. The dramatic red-velvet, high-necked gowns worn by Lynda's bridesmaids had been designed by the same leading fashion designer, Geoffrey Beene, who had designed Lynda's dress specifically for her. Beene agreed to keep the fashion details secret until the wedding day, refusing to leak details even to the fashion editor of *Women's Wear Daily,* who held a grudge for years, never writing about Beene's work again.

Once the parade of beautiful bridesmaids ended, all eyes turned to the staircase, waiting for the first glimpse of the bride. A few moments later, Lynda appeared on the arm of her father. They paused on the last step as the trumpets blasted the final notes of "Trumpet Voluntary." Standing there next to the president, Lynda looked beatific and regal in a long-sleeved, high-collared silk-satin white dress. With her hair swept back under a hairpiece embroidered with glistening pearls and her veil cascading around her face and down to the floor, Lynda looked like Renaissance royalty.

Many a groom has had an attack of the jitters, and, considering the press attention and the buildup to the event, it would have been completely natural for me to feel a bit nervous on the big day. But as I stood in my dress blue uniform watching my beautiful bride walk down the aisle, I felt nothing but comfort and certainty. Perhaps it was because we'd had a chance to get to know each other out of the spotlight by keeping our early courtship relatively quiet. Perhaps it was because there was so much pomp and ceremony involved that it simply proved a distraction. It may just be my nature not to ruffle in such circumstances. Whatever the reason, as I watched Lynda walk down the aisle that day, I felt serenely happy.

The ceremony itself was fairly simple, conducted efficiently by Reverend Canon Gerald McAllister, a priest at the Episcopalian church in Texas that the Johnsons sometimes attended. Lynda and I had agreed to allow television coverage of the ceremony itself only if it could be done unobtrusively. The faux columns constructed in the East Room hid television cameras, and a single pool reporter would be allowed into the ceremony to report on our vows directly, but that reporter would have to remain hidden. Reporter Bonnie Angelo of *Time* magazine was chosen because, at five feet tall and ninety-seven pounds, she was the only member of the press corps who could crouch inside the stately, waist-high white altar built for the occasion that stood behind the celebrant. How she managed to remain concealed in the altar, unobserved throughout the ceremony, I still don't know.

Bonnie didn't have a lot to report on, for all of her effort. The ceremony had no gaffes or surprises, and everyone in the intricately choreographed ceremony hit their marks and delivered their lines. A mere eighteen minutes after I saw Lynda enter the East Room, we were married.

After the ceremony, we walked together through the arch of crossed swords held aloft by my fellow Marines from Eighth and Eye, out of the East Room and back upstairs to the Yellow Oval Room for formal pictures. This part of the festivities had the only gaffe, when President Johnson came into the room holding his favorite dog, a mutt named Yuki, who had been dressed by one of the staff in a red outfit with "Congratulations" sewn in sequins on the side. Lynda's mother briskly intercepted her husband and made clear that the dog was not to be in the photos.

The reception was a happy blur of perfectly appointed buffet tables, cutting our five-tiered wedding cake (with my sword), and a long formal reception line. I don't remember all of it, which, I've been told, is fairly normal for one's wedding day.

When the wedding and reception were finished, Lynda and I bid good-bye to our guests and then did a disappearing act. With our bags packed and plane tickets in hand, we left through an exit from the White House that isn't publicly visible, while friends and family deflected media inquiries. We spent the first night of our honeymoon in Washington, D.C., confusing the gossip columnists and photographers who were staking out various airports in the region. A couple of television reports actually "confirmed" our destinations, but all were pure guesswork and dead wrong.

The next morning, the Secret Service spirited us away to the airport, where we were escorted to a plane with a tiny first-class section in the front that had been curtained off from view of the other passengers. When we arrived at our destination, Secret Service agents were waiting to discreetly whisk us away. It was quite a cloak-and-dagger affair. Happily, we were able to enjoy our first days of marriage, relishing the sun and the surf in complete privacy—except, of course, for the agents, who came with us everywhere.

For two people very much in the spotlight at the time, Lynda and I are both fundamentally private people, and after making ourselves available for all manner of press coverage up to and during the wedding, we were determined to keep every detail about our honeymoon a secret. To this day, the Secret Service, Lynda, and I are the only ones who know for sure where we spent our honeymoon.

Despite our determined secrecy around the honeymoon, the experience of a "national wedding" was, nevertheless, a very happy one. The press corps who greeted us at every event were pleasant—not the aggressive paparazzi-style that we sometimes see today—and we were on friendly terms with many of them. We never felt harried or harassed, and we were so busy and happy that most of the time we barely noticed them. The constant presence of media was just part of the reality of marrying the daughter of the president.

Lynda and I both understood that people were interested in every little detail of our wedding. But there was a silver lining to the constant press coverage of our engagement and wedding—we have a real-time record of some of the happiest moments of our lives. In the decades since, Lynda and I have made it an anniversary tradition to gather friends and family who were at our wedding every five years to watch it all over again in *Once in a Lifetime*.

4

The Weight of War

WHEN LYNDA LIVED in the White House, her bedroom in the second-floor residence faced Pennsylvania Avenue. Through her window, she could hear the near-constant protesters shouting across the street in Lafayette Park: "Hey, hey, LBJ! How many kids did you kill today?"

I had become part of the Johnson family during a particularly difficult time for the president. By the end of 1967, the war in Vietnam had progressed from an advisory and limited bombing campaign into a bloody ground war. In the almost two years since the first combat troops entered Vietnam, the American forces on the ground had grown rapidly and were now nearly half a million strong.

Protests against the war had also accelerated, growing loud and fierce. As Lynda and I were blissfully engrossed in wedding planning, an estimated seventy thousand protesters gathered around the Lincoln Memorial on October 21, 1967, and then marched to the Pentagon, surrounding the building in an act of civil disobedience that lasted two days. For the first time, coverage of the protests—images of young American men burning their draft cards on college campuses and the self-immolation of Buddhist monks—was playing out daily on the evening news.

It was hard to watch my father-in-law's anguish as the war overtook his presidency. He had felt deep reservations about the conflict from the very beginning. In a May 1964 telephone conversation with McGeorge Bundy, his special assistant for national security affairs, the president worried that "we're getting into another Korea. It just worries the hell out of me. I don't see what we can ever hope to get out of there with, once we're committed."[1]

In the same conversation, however, LBJ raised the real concern that he and his advisors shared about not engaging in Vietnam: "I believe that the Chinese communists are coming into it. . . . Of course, if you start running from the communists, they may just chase you right into your own kitchen."[2]

President Johnson and his advisors were all Cold War warriors, and he truly feared the "domino effect," the theory that losing Vietnam to Communist control could lead to similar losses throughout Southeast Asia, and then potentially in the Western Hemisphere. In a conversation with Defense Secretary Robert McNamara in February 1964, McNamara asked what he should say about Vietnam in a speech, to which the president responded: "All right, I'll tell you what I would say about it. I would say that we have a commitment to Vietnamese freedom. Now we could pull out of there. The dominoes would fall, and part of the world would go to the communists. We could send our Marines in there, and we could get tied down in a Third World War or another Korean action. The other alternative is to advise them and hope that they stand and fight."[3]

The loss of life, on both sides of the war, tortured him. There was a perception among some Americans who opposed the war that President Johnson and his advisors were callous about its human costs, but it was obvious to all who knew him that he was painfully aware that the troops—not only our own, but those of the enemy as well—were real, flesh-and-blood human beings, with families and lives. In several conversations he spoke of picturing the people around him when he sent more troops into the conflict, putting faces he knew to the inevitable loss of life.

"I've got a little old sergeant that works for me over at the house," he said in a May 1964 conversation with Senator Richard Russell of Georgia, "and he's got six children and I just put him up as the United States Army, Air Force, and Navy every time I think about making this decision and think about sending that father of those six kids in there. And what the hell are we going to get out of his doing it? And it just makes the chills run up my back."[4]

The president felt terribly conflicted. "I just haven't got the nerve to do it, and I don't see any other way out of it," he said. Russell replied, "It's one of these things where 'heads I win, tails you lose.'"[5]

He felt duty-bound as the leader of the world's democratic superpower to stop Communist aggression. Yet this was not the war that he had set out to fight. Johnson was eager to fight the battles on the home front that he saw as long overdue: hunger, poverty, civil rights, and poor-quality education. To take on these topics in the American South in the 1960s was to address the issues of empowerment and opportunity, something that could be politically unpopular, even toxic at the time. But LBJ's commitment to the overlooked in America went far beyond political calculation.

In the early 1990s, Lynda and I were discussing her father with then senator Joe Biden.

"You know," Joe remarked, "I've read almost every book written about President Johnson, and the one thing I still don't understand is where this man from Texas developed his passion for civil rights. What's the explanation?" Lynda smiled and gave a clear, one-word answer: "Cotulla."

Back in 1928, a twenty-year-old Lyndon Johnson had been a schoolteacher in a small, dry South Texas town called Cotulla. Nearly all of the school's students were Mexican Americans, and while bright, caring, and eager to learn, most came to school without proper clothes, often hungry, and sometimes barefoot. Johnson couldn't stand to see their suffering, and he promised himself then that if he ever had the opportunity to do something about it, he would.

He never forgot that promise, and in a speech before a joint session of Congress in March 1964, he announced his intention of fulfilling it: "I never thought then, in 1928, that I would be standing here in 1964. It never even occurred to me in my fondest dreams that I might have the chance to help the sons and daughters of those students and to help people like them all over this country. But now I do have that chance—and I'll let you in on a secret: I mean to use it."[6]

And use it he did, leading the nation to greater strides in civil rights and poverty reduction than any other president in the twentieth century. In my view, his lasting legacy will always be the crusade to pass the Civil Rights Act of 1964, the landmark law that outlawed major forms of discrimination against African Americans and women. And he signed the law knowing full well that his signature was politically poisonous for the Democratic Party in the South. Then, instead of backing off after his victory, President Johnson pushed further, fighting for and signing into law the Voting Rights Act of 1965. But in the late 1960s, the country was turning its focus from civil rights to the war in Vietnam, where thousands of Americans in uniform were losing their lives.

The protests against the war were also becoming increasingly personal. In November 1967, while Lynda and I were traveling with her parents to historic Williamsburg, Virginia, for a Gridiron Club event the month before our wedding, we planned to attend Sunday-morning services at the historic Bruton Parish Church. The president often turned toward religion to wrestle with the difficult life-and-death decisions of the war. He had always been interested in religious teachings, and after early exposure to the preaching of his mother's Baptist congregation, he decided to join the Protestant Christian Church (also called the Disciples of Christ), of which he remained a member for the rest of his life. He frequently attended churches of different denominations, and the renowned evangelist Billy Graham had become a close friend and spiritual advisor. After Luci converted to Catholicism when she married Pat Nugent, she would talk to her father about matters of faith. Later in his presidency, he would increasingly seek solace from Catholic priests, whom he sometimes referred to as "my little monks."

Like Lynda and me, Mrs. Johnson was an Episcopalian, and the president often joined his wife to worship at Episcopal churches on Sundays, which was why the trip to the Episcopal Bruton Parish Church was added to the schedule. Hoping to enjoy a restorative service, the president asked his advance team to make certain that the preacher didn't plan to lecture him from the pulpit. Ahead of the service, a presidential advance man and a Secret Service agent each independently spoke with the rector, Reverend Cotesworth Pinckney Lewis, who assured them both that he was not planning to use his homily to criticize the president.

But with national media attention focused on his church, and the president captive in the front row, the temptation proved too great.

"We are mystified," Reverend Lewis intoned as the president sat before him in the first row, "by news accounts suggesting that our brave fighting units are inhibited by directives and inadequate equipment from using their capacities to terminate the conflict successfully. While pledging our loyalty, we ask humbly: 'Why?'"

I sat in the pew, embarrassed and angry. It wasn't so much that the preacher had used the pulpit to launch a political harangue—it was certainly his right—but that he had blindsided the president at a church where he'd gone to seek solace. It was an agonizing experience.

Characteristically, when my mother-in-law recounted the incident in her memoir, she expressed the greatest concern for me, though she and her husband were the real victims of the vicar's decision.

"Somehow," she wrote, "I felt even sorrier for Chuck than I did for Lyndon. He looked so peculiarly vulnerable, hurt, questioning, uncertain what a young man who is about to go out and fight this war should think or do about that sort of performance by a minister at home."[7]

As we exited the church in a daze, my mother-in-law made a heroic attempt to remain polite, and as she passed the rector, the only thing she said to him was: "The choir was beautiful."

Following the service, I joined the president and Congressman Jake Pickle from Texas for a round of golf. This was the first time I'd been invited to play with the president, and I had hoped the more informal setting would allow me to get to know my future father-in-law a little better personally. Unfortunately, Reverend Lewis had struck a chord, and we played the course as President Johnson vented his frustration. When we'd all sunk our putts on the seventeenth green, the president announced that we were finished. The spectators and the press would be waiting at the end of the eighteenth hole, and he was still too hurt and angry to face them.

LBJ took that kind of condemnation very personally, and it showed. The immense pressure and relentless criticism were taking a serious toll on his health and spirit, and Mrs. Johnson, Lynda, and Luci were all worried about it. It's important to know that as a practical matter—and Lyndon Johnson was very much a pragmatist—the president didn't think he would live very many years more. His parents had both died relatively young, a fact that he was somewhat obsessed by, and that drove his thinking. The war, pressure, protests, and his health were all pushing him to a difficult decision. By the winter of 1967–68, he had come to the painful conclusion that the bitterly divisive war, and his role in guiding America's involvement there, had become so traumatic to the national psyche that it was not possible for him to unify the country. It was time, he had reluctantly concluded, to step aside for the good of the country. He would not be running for reelection in 1968.

He had privately shared his decision with the family, including his sons-in-law. But by the time of the State of the Union address on January 17, 1968, he had not yet told the nation. He had hinted to us that he might make the announcement during his speech that night, and as Lynda and I sat with her family above the chamber floor, we were the only ones in the room who knew that this would be LBJ's last State of the Union address. At the president's request, I wore my green service uniform to the event. I imagine that he made the request to remind Americans that he too had a personal connection to the war, though I'm not sure that I was ever shown on camera.

We sat in anticipation through the whole speech, expecting the president to announce his decision at any moment. But when it ended, the president hadn't said a word about the presidential race. More than a little puzzled, we left the chamber. When we climbed into the presidential limousine with him for the short ride back to the White House, we couldn't bring ourselves to ask why he hadn't made his announcement, and he didn't offer any explanation. He later talked about the night in his own memoir:

> When I went to the Capitol that night, I thought I had the statement with me but I discovered that I had failed to bring it. Frankly, I cannot say what I would have done that night if the paper had been in my pocket. But my best guess is that I would not have read it. Although the State of the Union occasion would have provided an excellent forum for my announcement, I sensed that the timing was not the best. I was asking the Congress that night for a heavy and demanding program. To couple such a request with a statement that I was not going to run for President might suggest to various people that I was not willing to fight for what I was asking.[8]

Following the State of the Union address, the news from Vietnam got worse. At the end of January, the North Vietnamese and Viet Cong launched the Tet Offensive, a bloody series of attacks on cities and towns in South Vietnam, planned to coincide with Tet, the Vietnamese lunar New Year. The American public was not prepared for that kind of coordinated assault by an enemy often described as not all that sophisticated.

In early February, a stark photograph brought home the war's brutality. It showed South Vietnamese general Nguyen Ngoc Loan executing a Viet Cong prisoner by shooting him in the head at point blank range. Television clips of the shooting were even more graphic, showing the prisoner slumping to the ground, blood spurting from his head. During this first war to be televised in almost real time, footage from Vietnam reached the public with little censorship or editing. The clip was even more shocking because this gruesome execution was perpetrated by our ally—a representative of the government for whom American troops were risking their lives to restore to power. Such graphic spectacles of war being beamed into American living rooms—a far cry from the antiseptic newsreels of World War II and Korea—helped fuel growing resentment about the war.

And then, in March 1968, the *New York Times* revealed that President Johnson's administration was considering the Pentagon's request to send 206,000 more troops to Vietnam. Americans feared that the war was escalating beyond their expectations and spinning out of control.

It was during this time of uncertainty that I was finally heading to my long-requested combat assignment. My decision was met with some skepticism, as there were those who thought it might be a political stunt: the president's son-in-law rushing to the front. The truth was that I both felt a very strong obligation to serve, and I wanted to go.

Some suggested that it would have been easier on the president if I stayed home. It wouldn't help him, they argued, to make the momentous decisions about the war while worrying about his daughter's brand-new husband. In hindsight, it may have been selfish on my part not to consider how I might add to his burden, but I think he was proud of the fact that I wanted to go.

My father-in-law was also careful not to share his doubts about the war with me, though we now know that he regularly discussed them with members of his staff and military leaders. He knew that I had been determined to go long before I met Lynda, and he respected my decision. I think that he just didn't want to dispirit me about a posting that he knew I was determined to take.

There were a few people on the staff, however, who thought they could do me a favor by getting me out of going to Vietnam altogether. One morning shortly after Lynda and I announced our engagement, a senior White House staffer pulled me aside in the Lincoln Sitting Room: "If you'd like to resign your commission right now," he said, "you can still get married on the date you've picked, because you've more than completed your obligated service. You don't have to go to Vietnam." I thanked him politely and then told him respectfully, but emphatically, that I *wanted* to go to Vietnam.

I don't think many people really understood my decision to go to Vietnam. The only answer that I could give is that I saw it clearly and without hesitation as my duty, and my father-in-law's position did not change that. For a Marine, particularly an infantry officer, combat is the ultimate test. Performing well in Basic School, and becoming the honor graduate, assured me that I had the skills I needed. But I knew I still had something to prove to myself. Most of the Marines I'd trained and served with had, by then, already been to Vietnam, and a few were on their second tour of duty. Several friends had lost their lives. Yes, I was grateful for each of the plum assignments I'd been given in my then six-plus years of active duty in the Marine Corps. But I had repeatedly requested a combat assignment, and I felt like I'd be shirking my responsibility if I let this opportunity pass me by.

I didn't realize that my decision would also affect the other Johnson son-in-law: Luci's husband, Pat Nugent. Pat could have remained safely at home in the Air National Guard Reserve, which he had joined in 1965, but the media attention put on my decision to go to Vietnam created an unintended contrast between presidential sons-in-law. Though it was an unfair comparison, the pressure on Pat was unrelenting, and within weeks he too was on a fast track to Vietnam.

IN THOSE FINAL days before departure, without telling Lynda or anyone else, I quietly stopped by the office of her father's press secretary, Liz Carpenter. I left with her a signed statement to be released only in the event that I was killed or captured. Intended to deflect any criticism from the president, it said that I had volunteered to go to Vietnam and that I believed in the cause for which we were fighting.

I was grateful that Lynda supported my decision. Though she worried about what might happen to me overseas, she admired my sense of duty and never tried to convince me not to go. She knew that I was doing something I believed was honorable. We were both taking risks, but we both agreed that they were risks that had to be taken.

Just before I left, Lynda gave me a framed poem titled "To Lucasta, on Going to the Wars," by the seventeenth-century poet Richard Lovelace. Though it was written more than three hundred years before—and with the spelling of the time—I thought it accurately summed up our feelings, especially the last two lines: "I could not love thee, deare, so much, Lov'd I not honour more."[9]

MY ORDERS WERE to leave for Vietnam on March 30, 1968. The week prior, I would report to Camp Pendleton, the Marine Corps' training base near San Diego, California, for an intensive orientation on what to expect in Vietnam, including an update on booby traps and Viet Cong ambush techniques. Like many military wives whose husbands were about to deploy, Lynda planned to come with me to Camp Pendleton and see me off on my departure day. But first, we had time for a few days to ourselves.

We flew to Acapulco, Mexico, where the owner of the Las Brisas resort generously put us up in the secluded honeymoon cabin—a special suite atop a rocky hill, with its own private pool that extended all the way into the bedroom, so you could dive off the bed right into the water. Although we were in a beautiful setting, the trip was hardly the relaxing break we'd hoped for. I wasn't always the most attentive new husband, as my mind was often on my upcoming assignment. Though we spent many hours relaxing by the pool, I was preoccupied through most of them with listening intently to my

Vietnamese-language instructional tapes. Lynda was sick much of the time, the side effect of a suspected and welcome new development that wouldn't be confirmed until I'd been in Vietnam for six weeks: she was pregnant.

If I hadn't been scheduled to depart for Vietnam so soon after our wedding, we'd have waited longer before having children. We took measures to prevent Lynda from getting pregnant in the first month of our marriage in order to prevent the appearance that our short engagement had been intended to mask an out-of-wedlock pregnancy in the White House. It sounds old-fashioned now, but this was back when people still counted the months between a wedding and the appearance of a firstborn.

We knew that the timing meant I would be away for almost the entire pregnancy, the birth of our first child, and the first few months of his or her life—not an ideal situation for anyone. But in her typical energetic and optimistic way, Lynda thought of this as a "project" that she could work on in my absence, something that would give her a focus besides worrying about my safety and the progress of the war.

Though we'd lived in a small rented house in Arlington, Virginia, for our three months of married life together, she decided to move back into the White House while I was in Vietnam, where we knew she'd have the constant support of family and friends, as well as the best medical care available. Lynda said that the idea of having our child would be a comfort if anything were to happen to me in Vietnam.

On our way from Acapulco to Camp Pendleton, we made a quick stop in Los Angeles, where the always generous and gentlemanly George Hamilton threw a dinner party for us at his home. Seated at his elegant dinner table next to the stunning actress Candice Bergen, eating a beautifully prepared meal in his gorgeous home, I thought about the stark contrast with the C-rations I'd soon be eating in Vietnam.

I arrived at Camp Pendleton for a final week of orientation. The week seemed to fly by. When the day of my departure arrived, Lynda and I quickly found ourselves back on public display. Dozens of reporters flocked to the crowded airport terminal area where Lynda and I—and hundreds of other Marines and their wives and families—stood together and said tearful goodbyes. It was a chaotic scene: the departure area was crowded with apprehensive young Marines and anxious relatives, some of whom were being jostled by journalists maneuvering to photograph Lynda and me as I departed. I had accepted the fact that the press was going to cover my departure, but both Lynda and I were upset that the ruckus was interfering with other families' final moments together.

"We're not the only ones here, let's give everyone here some room!" I shouted over the din to the photographers and reporters, who acknowledged—a bit sheepishly—and backed off.

Surrounded by clicking cameras, with Lynda near tears and nauseous with morning sickness, we said our farewell. I had never felt such a sharp rush of sadness, excitement, and anticipation all at once. I'd wanted this assignment for almost as long as I'd been a Marine, and now I was about to get my chance, but it was coming at a cost. In some ways, I knew our impending separation would be more painful for Lynda. She'd be facing her first pregnancy alone, surrounded by the places and memories of the past year together, while I'd be half a world away, in a completely different and very hostile environment. When the time came to go, I found it even more difficult than I'd expected to pull myself away from her arms and walk to the plane.

I was already on the first leg of my journey to Vietnam when Lynda arrived back at the White House in the predawn of the next morning. The president and the First Lady were waiting—in pajamas and bathrobes—to greet her out on the South Lawn. As her father later wrote in his memoir:

> Lynda was tired, and she seemed lonely and bewildered. War and separation were cruel intrusions into her young life. . . . Lynda had been reading about those demonstrators and critics who looked on such sacrifices as hers and Chuck's as meaningless, or worse. The hurt that had been building up inside her was now released in a flood of tears. Why, she asked, was her husband going away to fight, and maybe die, for people who did not even want to be protected? It was a question that might have been asked by any young woman who had just seen her husband off to Vietnam. I wanted to comfort her, and I could not.[10]

Later that same morning, Lynda's mother told her and Luci that their father would publicly announce his planned retirement that very evening. In a televised address devoted primarily to developments in the war, President Johnson, in conclusion, told a stunned nation: "I do not believe that I should devote an hour or a day of my time to any personal partisan causes or to any duties other than the awesome duties of this office—the presidency of your country. Accordingly, I shall not seek, and I will not accept, the nomination of my party for another term as your president."[11]

The brave mask that Lynda had worn to see me off had disintegrated. Her mother described the day in her memoir: "Both [Lynda and Luci] were emotional, crying and distraught. What does this do to the servicemen? They will think—What have I been sent out here for? Was it all wrong? Can I believe in what I've been fighting for? Lynda and Luci seemed to feel that Lyndon has been the champion of the soldiers, and that his getting out would be a blow to them. Lynda said, with an edge of bitterness, 'Chuck will hear this on his way to Vietnam.'"[12]

I did, in fact, hear that the president had finally made his announcement while I was at the American military base on the Japanese island of Okinawa, doing my final processing. A couple of reporters stationed there sought me out for comment, but I was not surprised—as I had known for months of my father-in-law's decision—and had nothing to add. At that moment, I had other things on my mind.

Between the comforts of home and the fighting in Vietnam was the U.S. military base on Okinawa. There, I—and every other Marine headed to Vietnam—completed a simple task: I was given a cardboard storage box and told to place my personal possessions into it. Most of us didn't have much—maybe a watch that we didn't want to lose, a wallet, or the clothes we had worn when we first reported to Camp Pendleton. If I was wounded in Vietnam and evacuated, my box with my belongings would be shipped to me in the States, and if I was killed, the Marine Corps would send it to Lynda. I decided to keep my wedding ring—my only meaningful or valuable possession—on my finger, and cover over its glinting reflection with tape while on missions in the jungle. I don't remember precisely what items I put in that box. All I remember is the act itself: a point of no return when I left my life in the States behind and embarked on a new chapter in war. It was an equalizing, unifying act—no matter who I was or who the man next to me had been back home, our personal items both fit into the same kind of small cardboard box.

I finished these administrative details and boarded a hulking four-engine C-130 along with dozens of my fellow Marines. A short time later, we stepped onto a busy tarmac under overcast skies outside of Da Nang. My first impression of Vietnam was this air base—a blast of humid air, the acrid smell of jet fuel, and a vast series of runways. My overriding concern now that I was finally on the ground in Vietnam was whether I would get the assignment that I most wanted: the command of an infantry company in combat.

GIVEN MY RELATION to the commander in chief, I knew that some in the chain of command might have reservations about sending me out into the bush. I was concerned that, after years of service and requests for combat assignments, I would finally reach Vietnam only to find myself "in the rear with the gear." Behind-the-front-lines support is a critical responsibility in any war, but not one I wanted at this point in my career.

My orders directed me to report to the commanding general of the 1st Marine Division, who at the time happened to be Major General Donn Robertson, whom I knew well from my days at Camp Lejeune, where I had been General Van Ryzin's aide. After renewing acquaintances, General Robertson sent me on to the 7th Marine Regiment. I was pleasantly surprised to find that the 7th Marines were commanded by none other than Colonel Reverdy Morton Hall, the same profane, eloquent fireplug of an officer who, as a major, had recruited me into the Marine Corps in my NROTC unit in college. We caught up briefly, then Colonel Hall sent me to the 3rd Battalion, under the command of then lieutenant colonel Roger Barnard. I didn't know Barnard at that point, but he would have gotten my service record, and I'm sure that Colonel Hall would have communicated informally with him about me as well. My first impression of Colonel Barnard was that he was a truly squared away Marine—a leader that I looked forward to working with.

It was from Colonel Barnard that I finally got the type of assignment that I'd been hoping for—on April 8, 1968, I was given command of India Company, 3rd Battalion, 7th Marines.

5

Boots on the Ground

THE JUNGLE AT night isn't like it is seen in the movies, where it always appears to be half-lit in a gauzy blue from some mysterious source. In Vietnam in 1968, there were many nights when there was no moon and the jungle was pitch-black. It was the kind of dark that drew over your face like a blindfold and left you practically unable to tell the difference between closing and opening your eyes. The use of night-vision devices was still in its early stages, and the types of goggles that let troops see an unlit battlefield in greenish hues wouldn't be widely used until the Gulf War in 1991. So, on moonless nights in Vietnam, the only way to advance through the thick, inky vegetation was by moving forward single file, each Marine with a hand on the man in front of him.

One night, as a part of a battalion operation called Mameluke Thrust, my company headed out from our combat base and along the Song Vu Gia, a river in Quang Nam Province. When we got to a spot where the river was low enough to wade across, we held our weapons and ammunition over our heads and crossed into an area U.S. forces had nicknamed the Arizona Territory. Leading the advancing column, I would have one Marine "walking point," a highly vulnerable position that had to be rotated frequently during the night. As we walked single file through the dense vegetation, the Marine walking point quite literally stepped on a sleeping North Vietnamese soldier. There was one stunned moment before M16 and AK-47 shots rang out in short bursts. And then, almost as suddenly as it began, the firing stopped. It was so dark that neither side could see where it was shooting. I asked my artillery forward observer to get us some "willy peter." He radioed to the artillery battalion some five miles behind us, requesting that they fire burning white phosphorous into the air over our heads. In a few minutes we heard the pop of the artillery shell opening and saw the bright-white flare of the burning willy peter, held aloft by a tiny parachute, floating toward the earth, drifting with the wind. Each flare illuminated the area between us and the enemy, giving us eerie bursts of half light—snapshots of the battlefield. These thirty seconds of twilight were enough to give us a picture of the situation as we held our position and waited the hour or so until dawn.

The new visibility in the first light brought intense fighting. Now the bullets were really flying, and I saw one of my men get hit and fall in a spot where any attempt to rescue him would almost certainly result in more casualties. An enemy soldier was firing in the area where my man had fallen, either to make sure he'd hit his mark or to knock out rescuers, and the only way we could hope to pull him to safety would be to create a diversion.

Suddenly, a Marine I had disciplined only days earlier—one of the very few times I'd had to discipline a Marine in my company—stood up to fire, exposing himself, and drawing the attention of the enemy gunner. It was a perfect diversion, allowing two other Marines to crawl over and drag the wounded Marine to safety. But no sooner had the first Marine stood up than he was cut down, ripped apart by bullets from an enemy AK-47. I'll never know for certain whether he intentionally created a diversion or whether he'd simply stood up to get a better firing position, but it didn't matter. He had displayed great courage in the line of duty, and I subsequently recommended him for a posthumous decoration.

We engaged the enemy, but, having lost their advantage of darkness and faced with superior firepower, they didn't stick around for long. We regrouped and made sure that our casualties—including the courageous Marine killed creating a diversion and the man he helped to save—were medevacked to battalion headquarters. Then we moved to a new location to lie low during the day. We waited for the cover of nightfall to move out once again.

COMBAT CONTINUED EVERY day, whether that day was your first or your ninety-first, and there was no additional training period for new commanders. The day that I had gotten command of India Company I got in the company's Jeep and rode out to our combat base, a four-acre fortified zone about twenty miles southwest of Da Nang, called Hill 65. The numeric name was consistent with the American military system of naming hills for their height in meters. India Company, 3rd Battalion, 7th Marines (I/3/7) consisted of three infantry platoons of, on average, forty-one men each and several attached units assigned for specific missions. This meant that an average of between 130 and 150 men were under my operational control at any given time from that point forward.

The Marines were all likely sizing me up on that first day. They understood that whoever was giving the orders was going to put them in a situation where they could be injured or killed, and it was up to me to do my job effectively and earn their respect.

I can't say how many of them knew about my connection to the commander in chief on that first day, but I'm sure they all found out through word of mouth eventually. Aside from a few innocuous questions along the lines of "What is it like to visit the White House?" I don't believe that I ever spoke about it with the troops while I was in country, because it simply wasn't relevant.

One Marine who served in my company told a reporter after returning from Vietnam that "Of course everybody had heard about Robb coming over to Vietnam . . . but he's just a regular Marine captain." I thought he put it best when he said, "If you're wearing Marine green they shoot at you . . . and it doesn't matter who you are."[1]

The men in my company came from every walk of life and every part of the country. Military service is one of the rare equalizers in our society, and the strength of our training and experiences in battle developed a solid bond between brothers-in-arms. I spent the first few days getting to know the men in my company, the missions they'd conducted, the operations of my command post (CP), and the conditions in our tactical area of responsibility (TAOR). I got to know the strengths and weaknesses of the very capable officers under my command—the platoon leaders and the other staff in my immediate circle, like the company gunnery sergeant and tactical radio operators. We would all need to work together effectively, because we were all dependent on each other for our mission's success and our survival.

Like all companies in Vietnam, India Company was made up of a mixture of experienced fighters and young men fresh from boot camp. At the time, troops were rotated individually, instead of by unit, so Marines started and finished their thirteen-month tours at different times. This policy contrasted with the unit rotation that America had used in previous conflicts, like the Second World War and Korea. Some of the men in the company were nearing the end of their tour, while others had almost their whole combat tour ahead of them. Some amount of unit cohesion was lost when a unit didn't arrive in country as a team, carry out combat missions as a team, and return home together, as a team. Thankfully, the Marines returned to rotations by intact units after Vietnam.

The strong feeling of comradeship that I shared with the Marines I served with has never diminished over the decades since I hung up my utilities. Like most who serve in combat, I developed stronger personal connections with the Marines who served directly around me, such as my gunnery sergeant and my platoon commanders. In May 1968, a young second lieutenant named Terry Hale was assigned as one of my replacement platoon commanders, leading about forty men. A recent graduate from the University of Texas (UT), Hale was likeable and gung-ho.

Lieutenant Hale sticks in my memory because in the first few days after he reported in, I got to know and like him. Lieutenant Hale and I traded stories about UT—he shared the alma mater with my wife—and the UT football team, where he had been team manager. We talked about the platoon he was taking over and what we'd seen outside the wire. Fair-haired and lean in his new gray-green combat utility uniform, he had that clean, healthy look of a recent college graduate, ready to take on the world.

And on his very first operation in the bush, Lieutenant Hale was killed by a booby trap. Sadly, and without warning, he was gone.

When one of my Marines was killed, the company first sergeant, who normally remained at the combat base, would see to the proper preparation of the Marine's body. But if an officer was killed, I—if I was not on an extended operation away from my combat base—traveled to division headquarters and personally identified the officer's remains.

The first thing that hit me when I entered the mortuary tent at division headquarters was the smell. It wasn't the smell of decomposition but that of the chemicals that preserve bodies. The chemicals were used in large quantities to counter the effects of the heat, and the result, when several of those bodies were together in one tent, was overwhelming to the senses. The bodies themselves quickly lost their color of life. Pale and still in an unzipped black rubber bag, Terry Hale was laid out for identification. It is not something one forgets. The astringent smell stayed in my nostrils long after I left the tent.

There was no time for the fitting ceremonies and remembrances that I'm sure Lieutenant Hale received when his body was returned to the States. As company commander, I didn't even get to write to Hale's parents—that was always done back at battalion headquarters, where all the personnel records were kept. I did receive a letter from his parents a short time later, however, as they were hoping to find out more about how their son had died. They also asked if we might be able to find the new Bowie knife that they had given him before he shipped out. Though we made a quick search for it in the area where Hale had been killed, the Bowie knife—a prized possession if happened upon by the local Vietnamese—was, sadly, never found.

I would have liked to have had time to grieve for Lieutenant Hale, but war doesn't allow for that kind of luxury. I simply headed back to my combat base and got back to the daily life of combat operations. Within a few days, a replacement for Lieutenant Hale arrived at Hill 65.

THE COMPANY COMBAT base was always in motion, with patrols cycling in and out of operations, Marines ending their combat tours or arriving at their new post, men preparing for the next mission and cleaning their weapons from the last. The smallest type of U.S. military base in Vietnam, there was nothing especially fancy or permanent about it, and the Marines sheltered in canvas structures that had been improved and added on to over the months with available materials: poncho liners, cardboard salvaged from C-rations and ammo boxes, and the odd packing crate. The best shelter was made by using the crater of a previous ordnance blast as a dugout—or creating one yourself using entrenching tools—which protected you from shrapnel, though certainly not from a direct hit. When they could, the men slept in these makeshift shelters on inflatable mats we called "rubber ladies." They clustered by platoon, with my small command hut near the center.

We were by no means constantly under siege by the enemy, but there was always a heightened awareness, even when we were on our combat base. To one side of Hill 65 was the Song Vu Gia and to the other a valley that was full of Viet Cong and North Vietnamese Army (NVA) soldiers. There were always Marines on watch, stationed in a guard post made of sandbags with slits for their weapons to fire out and clear overlapping fields of fire. The perimeter at the base of the hill was mined with Claymore antipersonnel mines, ready to be blown if the enemy breached our rings of concertina wire that encircled the hill.

Even with these defenses, we were still vulnerable to mortar and rocket attacks on the combat base, which were not overwhelmingly accurate, though they were deadly if they reached their target. Even if you avoided a direct hit, mortars and rockets sent shrapnel flying in every direction, which could easily kill or seriously wound. Small trenches, technically called "defensive positions," dotted the bases. When they were available, the Navy Seabees dug these small trenches with a backhoe, with the unfortunate side effect that they were the size and shape of an open grave.

We faced similar dangers at the larger bases as well. One morning when I was back at battalion headquarters for intelligence updates, I was walking toward the command bunker, inside the defensive perimeter, when I heard the unmistakable whine of incoming rockets. I wrote to Lynda about the incident later in the day:

> Even before the first round hit I yelled "incoming" and dived for the nearest hole just as the first round landed about 20 meters away.
>
> Within 10 seconds, other Marines had dived into the very same hole on top of me which was only big enough for two people to begin with. Rounds continued to land all around us for the next minute or so, then there was a pause of about 30 seconds and one last round landed right on the opposite edge of the foxhole. Fortunately all the shrapnel went forward in the same direction the round was headed and none of it came back into the foxhole.[2]

The only injuries in the foxhole were mild concussions suffered by two of the Marines who had piled in on top of me. Had that round landed just five inches shorter, all of us would have been killed. "Today I was a very lucky man," I wrote Lynda.[3] Not as lucky was a small dog that I had seen trotting by just as the attack began, a mutt that probably belonged to one of the Vietnamese who worked on the base. The dog didn't jump in a foxhole at the sound of the incoming rockets and had been literally blown away.

There were also times on Hill 65 when we were under sustained attack from the enemy. I wrote to Lynda in the midst of one enemy offensive in May 1968:

> It's been 49 hours since I had a wink of sleep so please understand if I don't seem to make much sense. We have been in almost constant contact since I wrote you at midnight or so yesterday. . . .
>
> We've taken a whole lot more incoming mortars on my CP than most other areas because we've got two batteries of heavy artillery on the hill with us and this is a top priority target for the enemy because he has to try to suppress our fires while he's attacking. So far we've heard or seen the enemy mortars and rockets fired and had a couple

of seconds to dive into fox holes. Sunday morning very early and again early Sunday evening the enemy mortars were right on target, landing just a few feet from many of the fox holes but none actually landed in them and all we suffered were a few shrapnel casualties but no KIA's on this hill so far.[4]

From our base, my company patrolled our TAOR, an area of rice paddies and dense vegetation that stretched from southwest of Da Nang, across the narrow middle of the country, to the Laotian border in the west. The *Virginian-Pilot* newspaper later described the area around our base: "[Hill 65] rose from sun-baked bottomland in the north-east Quang Nam Province, 25 miles out of Da Nang. West of it loomed a 3,400-foot mountain chain, known to the grunts as 'Charlie Ridge.' To the south, beyond the Vu Gia and Thu Bon rivers, lay the Arizona Territory, a quiltwork of rice paddies, forests and low hills that the Marines crisscrossed but never fully controlled. To the southeast was Dodge City."[5]

The nicknames "Dodge City" and "Arizona Territory" were apt, as these areas were like the Wild West. We could expect a fight when we moved into either area, and we usually didn't have to wait long to get it. On my first day of command, I described it to Lynda: "I made it through what is called 'Ambush Alley' to check with some of my troops in the 'Dodge City' area. This is a real dangerous area which we are hoping to clear up in the next few months. Right now it's pure V[iet] C[ong] country and no one even ventures near it with less than a full company. More action now so I'll have to close."[6]

India Company's tasks were as straightforward as they were hazardous: patrol our TAOR, engage enemy troops, and protect crucial bridges necessary for resupplying troops with ammunition, food, and water. Executing these tasks, however, required very different tactics than those I'd seen in World War II newsreels as a kid at the Saturday matinee. We didn't move on recognizable fronts, against enemies identified by a different uniform, in the orderly progression of troops from one side of a country to the other. In Vietnam, at any given time, in any area, the enemy could come at you from any direction. Our TAOR was sliced out of the Marine 1st Division's TAOR, which backed up against the euphemistically named "demilitarized zone" (DMZ) dividing North and South Vietnam. The truth was that no area in Vietnam was truly demilitarized because the NVA was supplying and aiding the Viet Cong (VC), an organization of indigenous guerilla fighters in South Vietnam and Cambodia.

The Viet Cong were a formidable force. Lacking in conventional firepower, they were easily underestimated. But they more than made up for their lack of firepower with expert use of the elements of stealth, deception, and surprise. And unlike the young conscripts of the NVA, who wore more conventional uniforms and fought with traditional weapons and tactics, the Viet Cong were older, wiser, and blended in easily with the civilian population.

The Viet Cong were not, however, always allied with the local civilian population, and there were many instances of the VC committing robbery and terrorism against civilians. I wrote to Lynda in May 1968 about an offensive by the enemy:

> The civilian population has not fared so well as they have born[e] the brunt of the VC attack. The VC have slaughtered peasants in every hamlet in the area and set fire to several entire villages with satchel charges. Two entire villages were over 90% destroyed by fire shortly after the attack started yesterday morning.
>
> The VC have not gone scot-free in my area of responsibility however. The ambush which I set out last night turned out to be the most successful move in the entire regiment for the last 48 hours. We caught part of a VC company which was coming to attack our positions and burn two villages right next to us completely off guard. They thought we were spread too thin to put out any offensive force. I won't go into the details but among others we killed their company commander who had been terrorizing this area for a long time and found many usable documents on the bodies. One wounded VC was trying to eat a very important document but we managed to salvage it.[7]

During the daytime, the Viet Cong were indistinguishable from the many farmers and villagers you'd pass on patrol or see around base camp. These local Vietnamese were an essential part of life on the combat base because they set up small businesses just outside the perimeter of Hill 65. Women would charge a few pennies to take your clothes down to the nearby streams, beat them with rocks and sticks, and hang them in the sun to dry. Even straight from the "laundry," the clothes always had an earthy smell, but we still valued the service. Vietnamese men would sometimes set themselves up as company barbers. These entrepreneurs were essential around a makeshift combat base that had no such services for its Marines.

At night, the Viet Cong could melt into the dense vegetation and, using their knowledge of the terrain, could attack patrols and set up ambushes working with their NVA counterparts. The ambushes were sometimes highly coordinated operations. After one particularly successful ambush in which another company had lost several men, I wrote to Lynda: "One of the NVA bodies turned out to be an officer and he had all of his official and classified documents on him including very detailed plans and sketches of the ambush that actually took place. The infinite detail with which they plan each operation of this nature is amazing. If it weren't for our superiority of supporting arms we'd have a tough time beating them."[8]

No matter what we were up against, I was constantly impressed by the ability and discipline of the Marines under my command. On one moonless night, India Company was moving through a dry rice paddy when we were caught by an enemy ambush. The enemy had dug into the surrounding tree line, whereas we were completely exposed in the open field. We couldn't see the enemy in their entrenched position among the trees, so we were unable to effectively return fire. I ordered the men to hit the deck and we dropped on our bellies into the brush, where the enemy could no longer see us. I could hear the unmistakable "zip-zip-zip" of bullets flying just over our heads. I gave the order for the men to crawl through the field to the cover of the nearby trees and absolutely hold their fire. From the trees, we could get enough cover to return fire. More than one hundred men, spread in a single line, crawled noiselessly through the open field. The enemy kept up their barrage of firing, but they could no longer spot our exact positions, and their bullets whizzed past. If just one man had lost his nerve and returned fire, the flash from the tip of his weapon's muzzle would have given away the location of the whole company. But India Company held its nerve. We inched our way to cover, maintaining perfect fire discipline, and didn't lose a single man in that encounter. This incident was by no means isolated. It was one of the many times that I felt unmitigated pride in my company and the ethos of the Marine Corps.

Night movements were a constant part of our missions in Vietnam, and we conducted many in late June 1968, during our battalion's turn in the massive, long-term operation known as Operation Mameluke Thrust, in which companies rotated in and out of operations, spending several weeks at a time in the bush. We would engage with the enemy wherever we could find him throughout the Arizona Territory, sleeping in shifts during the day and moving under the cover of night.

It was while out on Operation Mameluke Thrust, one evening just before dark, that we received a supply of C-rations and ammunition from a helicopter drop. Resupply helicopters were both essential and very risky because they loudly proclaimed our position to the enemy. The key was to time a supply drop right as the sun was low in the sky, execute it as quickly as possible, and immediately move to a new position. On this occasion, we had already set a specific regroup location, but we didn't get the chance to make it there. Mortar fire started coming in as soon as the enemy spotted the helicopters.

With enemy fire coming from an unknown location, the best course of action was to hold our fire, hit the deck, and crawl to a new position to regroup. We hastily selected an alternative regroup location just as darkness descended. With mortar rounds exploding all around us, I ordered the men to dig in quickly at the new location. But with entrenching tools in hand, several men soon discovered an unsettling fact: we were in a Vietnamese graveyard. We'd seen enough such graveyards to know that the bodies would be buried just a foot or so below the surface, wrapped only in cloth or plastic.

Two diametrically opposed motivating forces were hard at work. Some men hesitated, recoiling at the idea of digging up, and then lying down with, recent Vietnamese remains. Training and survival kicked in, though, and soon every Marine was digging in the graveyard, deep enough to avoid the shrapnel from mortars exploding around us.

At the time, the event barely registered as strange. Life and death sat side by side in Vietnam. Death in the Vietnam War was not at all like death in civilian life, where we are accustomed to seeing people fade out over a long illness. In Vietnam, someone was alive one moment and dead the next. Injury and death didn't favor one type of person or another—no matter how careful or alert we were, incoming mortar or artillery fire, a booby trap, or a mine could get anyone.

I had one staff sergeant, then an acting platoon commander, who had, before I took command of India Company, a malfunctioning M16 rifle. Not content simply to swap it for a new one issued by the Marine Corps, he wrote a letter, on a lark, to the manufacturer. To his delight, they shipped him a personal replacement directly to Vietnam, and he carried it proudly.

No more than a week after he received the new weapon, we were on a night movement in the Dodge City area. There were no visible artificial lights, just a little moonlight through the trees, and we were spread out, moving through dense vegetation. The staff sergeant hit a trip wire, triggering a booby trap made from one of our own unexploded U.S. projectiles—a 105mm round—hidden in a hedgerow.

I happen to be closest to him when the shell exploded, but I was just far enough away to avoid being directly hit by the blast. I called in a medevac helicopter, and another Marine and I carried him toward a cleared road where the helicopter could land. I could hear the gurgle in his throat as he struggled to breathe. We hurried toward the helicopter, but the sounds he made grew fainter and fainter, and by the time we reached the thumping chopper, he was silent. The staff sergeant was the first of two Marines who would die in my arms during my thirteen months in Vietnam. There was no fanfare or extraordinary drama to it; the life simply slipped from his body.

AMBUSHES AND BOOBY traps were major tactics of the formidable guerilla force of the Viet Cong. They could launch attacks in the pitch black of night or set mines and booby traps along routes frequented by U.S. or allied forces. We suffered more casualties from those mines and booby traps than we did from conventional direct-fire weapons, so spotting and disarming them was a major part of any foray away from the company combat base. For the most part, our methods were reliable, but they were by no means foolproof.

When we saw a suspected mine in our path, the demolition engineer assigned to our company had a nerve-shredding and dangerous task. Once, as we walked on a narrow path through dense vegetation, a Marine directly ahead of me spotted some suspicious recently disturbed dirt. I gave the order to halt in place while a demolition specialist moved up to take a closer look. We watched as he walked ahead, knelt about twenty-five feet in front of us, bayonet in hand, and gently slid the flat tip under the dirt. Because detonators are usually located on the tops of mines, sliding a flat bayonet blade in to tap the side of an object was the least dangerous way to quickly learn whether a mine was present. Silently, carefully, he listened and felt for the telltale tap on the metal casing of an explosive device buried just beneath the surface. If he felt the tap, we could then detonate it in place with C4 plastic explosive and keep the convoy moving forward.

I put out the word for everyone to hit the deck, and we watched in complete silence as the demolition expert did his work. Suddenly, there was a violent explosion. I instinctively looked away as debris flew past my face, and when I turned back all I saw was a cloud of dust and smoke. None of the men around me were hurt—the explosion had been designed to direct its force upward to the underbelly of a passing heavy truck or tank. We ran forward to help the demolition expert, but he was simply gone.

With my ears still ringing from the explosion, I ordered a quick search of the area for any remains that we could send home to his family for burial. All we could find was one foot, still encased in his combat boot. The rest of the demolition expert had been vaporized instantaneously by the force of a blast meant to knock out a tank or a heavy truck. We would have liked to have searched longer but staying stationary in this difficult-to-defend area increased the risk of losing more men, so I quickly pushed the mission forward.

The threat of ambushes made one of our more dangerous tasks the forays by supply convoys, called "rough riders." These convoys helped move supplies to remote outposts deep in enemy territory, close to the Laotian border, and it was our job to provide security for them. The supply missions were critical to the overall battle effort, but they were always tricky and frequently resulted in casualties. The enemy would invariably see us coming with our large armored, amphibious, tracked vehicles (known as amtracs), tanks, and heavy-duty combat trucks, and they would lay mines, set booby traps, and organize ambushes as we tried to get the convoy through. This violent game was played over and over, with countless variations, as we learned the lessons of a new kind of warfare.

The return trip to our combat base was more dangerous because, by laboriously clearing a path through the dense vegetation on our way to the isolated outpost, we alerted the enemy to our route. We made every effort to quickly retrace our route back to our combat base before they could lay fresh mines. On one return trip, I split my company up among the three amtracs and several trucks for the bumpy, hurried ride. We were nearly two-thirds of the way back to the combat base when the amtrac immediately ahead of me, carrying most of the members of my second platoon, nearly thirty men, hit a mine.

The concussive explosion was deafening, but ordinarily it wouldn't have resulted in many serious casualties—the vehicle's heavy armor would have absorbed most of the shock. But the blast had ignited the amtrac's gas tank, sending up a blue ball of flame that instantly engulfed almost every man on board.

The explosion was large enough to be physically stunning and disorienting. My ears rang, and I caught the bitter, earthy smell of explosives and dirt in the air. Smoke blurred my vision, and a few burning tear gas grenades made my eyes water. I quickly took in the situation: the vegetation was thick on both sides of our column—thick enough to hide enemy troops waiting for our convoy to hit the mine. The amtrac in front of me was now unmovable, and there were many Marines injured. I immediately halted the rest of the convoy and set up a makeshift perimeter in case of an ambush. Around me, the whole company shook off the impact and leapt into action—some securing the convoy while others assisted the wounded. There was a danger to rescuing our comrades because the men on the burning amtrac were carrying ammunition and explosives, such as hand grenades, that could "cook off" in the heat of the flames. We rushed to get Marines off the burning amtrac as quickly as possible, away from the heat source before secondary explosions caused more injuries. The sounds coming from the wounded Marines were sickening—some Marines were still on fire and cried out in agony, their smoldering skin peeling off as they were lifted off the wreck. I was able, by radio, to divert two large helicopters from medevacs in a nearby area, and we got the seventeen most serious cases out in almost record time. A few minutes felt like hours as we stabilized the injured as best we could and left behind the smoldering hull of the destroyed amtrac.

The injured Marines were medevacked back to medical facilities to be patched up, and either sent home or reassigned. I would rarely get any sort of update on the status of our company's injured or even whether they survived. The helicopters simply swooped the injured Marines away forever, as much like angels as anything else I've ever encountered. The swift arrival of the helicopters that day likely saved several lives, I wrote to Lynda, "because they were all alive when we put them [on] board. The rest will be up to the doctors and the Almighty."[9]

In closing, I wrote: "I was very proud of the company again. When the chips are down they're tremendous."[10]

6

Bulletproof

IN A COMBAT situation, a letter from home is a treasured item. When we were out on a long mission in the bush, I couldn't send any letters to Lynda, but she continued to write to me every day. When I returned to the combat base, I received a whole stack of her letters and cards. It was like Christmas.

After only three short months of married life together, the long separation was hard on both of us. Nothing would increase my morale more than a letter from Lynda, and we wrote to each other as often as possible. If no writing paper was available while I was out on an operation, I could write on almost anything, even the flap of an empty C-ration carton or a little scrap of cardboard, addressing the back like a postcard. We wrote the word "FREE" in the space where a stamp would normally go, which was especially helpful because there was no way that a stamp would have stayed on in the Vietnamese humidity.

Experiences in war are varied and personal, but they share common themes. In that way, my letters to Lynda were similar to so many other service members' letters to loved ones. Usually I just told Lynda about my day, reassured her that I was unharmed, and expressed how much I loved and missed her. I tried to spare her the most gruesome details of war, but I now realize that I could have spared her even more:

May 13, 1968

Dear Lynda,

Boy, what a night so far. Not to mention the day and last night to boot. Things really started popping right after I finished my letter to you last night. By one a.m., there were huge fires in most of the hamlets and villages for as far as the eye could see. Some were almost completely destroyed. Not to mention mortars and rockets which also took a heavy toll. . . .

Tonight, just about thirty minutes before dark, as I was briefing an ambush patrol, the NVA opened up on us with some of the most accurate 82 millimeter mortar fire and rocket fire we've had yet. All of their rounds were on target. The first one hit 15 meters from where I was standing. I was lucky and didn't get even a scratch. But we had to emergency Medevac one of the men I was briefing. . . .

I'll try to write about happier things tomorrow. I miss you so much . . .[1]

May 22, 1968

Dearest Lynda,

Today has been a bad day all day through. We ran completely out of food and more important water and couldn't be resupplied until late evening. As you know hunger makes me cranky enough as is.

To add to my misery one of my patrols hit another booby trap and I had five more WIA (wounded in action) to worry about. The only bright spot was the actions of the corpsman who bandaged up the other 4 wounded for evacuation despite [being injured himself]. I've already written him up for a medal. I also signed 3 other medal recommendations for the other men from action 3 days ago.[2]

To that grim news, Lynda responded: "I received your letter in which you told me that you didn't have food or water and then you had 5 WIA. I cried when I read your letter because I felt such compassion for that medic. I also cried because I knew how selfish I am in not appreciating all the luxuries I have."[3]

For a young bride so far from the action and able only to imagine what war was like, the casual comments about rockets, mortars, and ambushes probably only added to her anxiety. But I wanted to give Lynda a sense of what I was experiencing, and I knew that if anything terrible did happen to me, she would find out well before receiving what would have been my last letter home.

Lynda and I were also able to send each other audiotapes, thanks to a small portable recorder that her father had given each of us before I left. The recorder made it easy to ramble on, and I tried to tell her a little bit about the mundane aspects of war—the food, the transportation, the waiting. At one point I mused about "all the little things that we so often take for granted, and I know that I'll begin taking them for granted again as soon as I get back home. But things that you tend to miss, things like plumbing, lights that go off and on, doors that shut, having a nice soft bed, and having a room that you can control the temperature to some degree in, a chest of drawers. There's just so many things that we all take for granted."[4]

It was a real treat to be able to hear Lynda's voice on her tapes. Lynda was much better at sending them than I was, and the ones that I sent were of much poorer quality. The batteries for the recorder—in 1968—needed to be kept cool and grew weak very quickly in the intense heat of Vietnam. As a result, my tapes were often recorded at an unintelligible speed. Lynda later told me her father kidded her more than once: "Why doesn't that smart young man you married know enough to be able to change the batteries?" Fortunately, helpful White House communications technicians were usually able to rerecord them at a normal speed.

Lynda sent me packages with cookies, including my favorite homemade oatmeal raisin cookies. And she would enlist any method necessary to see the cookies delivered, including the unlikely deliverymen of top Army and Marine Corps brass. One time she asked General William Westmoreland, who was visiting the White House to brief her father, to deliver a tin that she'd baked. He was kind enough to honor her request, but he had an aide slip it to me in private so I wouldn't be embarrassed that the commanding general of the entire Southeast Asian operation was delivering cookies to me.

I did my best to save Lynda's letters and—for reasons more sentimental than practical—kept the cookie tins in my supply tent back at my combat base. But at some point, while I was out on an operation, rockets hit the base and put shrapnel through all of the tins and some of her letters.

In many ways, my tour in Vietnam was much harder on Lynda than it was on me. I was in a new environment, constantly on the move, and had a complex job that required my undivided focus. Lynda, though, had plenty of time to ponder my dispatches from the front. From the moment we said goodbye, she was faced with time to fill: waiting for me to come home, waiting for the phone to ring and hoping it wasn't bad news, waiting for the birth of our first child, and waiting for her father's difficult last year in office to come to a close. It must have seemed almost endless for her. Because she was pregnant, we decided to delay my five-day R&R trip—standard for every service member during his Vietnam tour—until December 1968, when Lynda was well enough to travel to Bangkok to meet me. We spent most of our five days together in private, but when we did venture out as tourists, we were trailed everywhere by photographers, making this brief respite from war seem even more surreal.

In her letters, she described the discomfort of her pregnancy, her worry about her father's emotional state, and the loneliness of our separation. But she also shared the joy of feeling our baby's movements and reminded me of the normal pieces of everyday life back home. I loved reading her countless small, intimate details: news of her moods, weight, sleep patterns, thoughts, and feelings as the birth date drew near. She speculated on possible Secret Service code names for the baby. All the Johnsons had code names beginning with "V": "Velvet" for Lynda, "Volunteer" for her father, and "Victoria" for Lynda's mother, so Lynda offered her own suggestions for our child: "Velour" for a girl and "Varmint" for a boy.

In late October 1968, I got a letter from the president that read:

Dear Chuck:

This has been a week of waiting, of rumors, and of hopes for a turn toward peace, which have not been fulfilled.

It is a hard thing to turn from the attitudes and methods of war to serious negotiations and peace. It is particularly hard, apparently, in Hanoi. It is not easy in Saigon, although we are confident that the South Vietnamese are with us. While we ache to see this turn in the road, I must be absolutely sure that every step we take is consistent with the sacrifices made by our men in the field and with their security. Those will be my standards right down to January 20, 1969.

This has been a week of waiting also, and much hope, for the arrival of another Robb at the Mansion. Lynda has decreed Sunday as the big day and we hope she is right, but we are all willing to wait as long as necessary for something so precious as another child in this family. . . .

One of the newspaper people asked Lynda if you would be here with her when the baby came, and she replied "If the Marines wanted him to have a wife, they would issue him one."

News is scarce around here—as I said in the beginning we are just waiting.

We send all our love.
Sincerely,

Lyndon B. Johnson[5]

At the bottom of the letter, he added a handwritten postscript: "8 p.m. Lynda has just left with Luci and her mother for the hospital."[6]

On October 25, 1968, Lynda gave birth to our first child, whom we named Lucinda Desha Robb. Lynda and I had been discussing names for months, though most of the negotiations had revolved around names for boys. Lucinda was a name Lynda and I easily agreed to; it was a combination of Luci and Lynda. Desha was an old family name on Lynda's side. I thought that after bearing the child for nine months, Lynda should get a large say in the naming.

Although I couldn't be there for the birth, the ever-present Secret Service agents were, and one who'd also traveled with us on our honeymoon even caused a bit of a stir when he nearly accompanied Lynda into the delivery room. Lynda, jokingly exasperated, later remarked, "He was practically there for the conception; he might as well have been there for the delivery!"

For my part, I had prepared two letters for Lynda—one in case our child was a boy, one for a girl—and had asked Doug Davidson, the best man at our wedding, to deliver the appropriate one following the birth.

A special benefit of being the son-in-law of the president was that I got to see a picture of my newborn daughter sooner than any other new father in Vietnam, when the armed forces newspaper, *Stars and Stripes,* ran a photo of her on the front page. Regularly available at all military bases and installations around the world, bundles of *Stars and Stripes* were also included with the resupply of "bullets, beans, and band-aids" to combat bases. Within forty-eight hours of Lucinda's birth, I got to look her in the eye—in black-and-white newsprint, at least.

After Lucinda was born, Lynda would chronicle her development in the letters she sent, and sometimes I could even hear Lucinda cooing on the tapes.

Although I didn't entirely expect my tapes to Lynda to be shared, I was still careful in my comments, knowing there was no way to ensure they would be heard only by her. The president listened to some tapes, although they were not intended for him, causing Lynda some lighthearted consternation:

July 30, 1968

Tonight I let Daddy listen to the first side of your tape. He then told me, "I want you to give me all your letters from Chuck. After all, they are just letters to you, but they are important information for me!" Men do not understand! Your letters are only lifeblood for me! He asked me to ask you how many men in your company have been killed, and how many wounded since you took over?[7]

The president even played one of my tapes to Lynda for his cabinet. A dramatic photograph that was first published in *Life* magazine years after the war shows President Johnson sitting alone at the cabinet table, his head lowered on his hands in seeming despair, as he listened to a tape in which I spoke about a dramatic nighttime medevac rescue of one of my Marines who was severely injured during Operation Mameluke Thrust. I described the helicopter lowering a basket through the dense "triple canopy" of trees and vegetation as it hovered, rotators thumping, in the pitch black over our heads. Gunfire can be clearly heard in the background of the recording.[8]

It was clear that the president was genuinely interested in what our troops were experiencing on the ground in Vietnam. He also took care to write his own personal letters to me, letters that were immediately recognizable by their distinctive pale-green presidential stationery. Typewritten, but informal in tone, with the occasional enclosed photo or handwritten note at the bottom, his letters included news about Lynda, the rest of the Johnson family, military personnel, and sometimes his thoughts on Vietnam. I suspect some of the chattier sections on social events were the work of his secretary rather than the president himself. A typical example was his letter to me of May 3, 1968:

Dear Chuck,

I understand Lynda has been on Haywood [Colonel Haywood Smith, the senior Marine aide to the president] daily about the poor mail service. How Haywood plans to improve it, I haven't yet found out. . . .

The young ladies in the East and West Wings seem to be of the opinion that the new crop of Aides is not as attractive and mature as ones of your vintage and social grace who have been departing. . . .

The big news today is, of course, that at 1:00 am we received a cable that Hanoi would meet us in Paris on May 10th. We have immediately accepted and hope and pray that this first step toward negotiations for peace will have successful results.

Mrs. Johnson joins me in sending our love and affection.

Sincerely,

Lyndon B. Johnson[9]

These letters from the commander in chief were one of the very few ways in which my time in the service was different from others'. On the whole, I was treated like any other Marine officer, which was exactly how I wanted it to be. But that nearly changed one afternoon when international intelligence sources picked up information that I was a kidnap target.

Kidnapping had always been a threat because high-value hostages, such as a relative of the commander in chief, were greatly sought after by the enemy for bargaining leverage. At the time, the North Vietnamese were holding then naval aviator John McCain III, whose father became Commander in Chief, Pacific Command (CINCPAC) in July 1968, as a prisoner and were attempting to use him as a very public bargaining chip. McCain, with whom I would later serve in the U.S. Senate, withstood five and a half years of horrific conditions, repeatedly refusing the special treatment offered by the North Vietnamese, which they hoped to use as a propaganda measure.

I was aware of the danger, but I was also confident in myself and my training. There had been several false reports of my capture, but nothing had ever come of it. This time, though, the rumor seemed a little more credible than usual. According to a report, a Warsaw Pact country had passed message traffic that enemy agents were planning to kidnap me in order to exert leverage in the upcoming Paris peace negotiations. I learned about the threat when two Marines from division headquarters drove up to me one afternoon in a jeep while I was traveling between two combat bases. One stepped out and said: "Sir, we've been asked to provide additional security for you. A threat against you has been intercepted." I was incredulous. Not only did I not want to be treated differently than any other Marine, but it seemed obvious that having an extra security detail was exactly the wrong way to go about it. Walking around with two guards on my tail would just make me stand out to North Vietnamese snipers, when the greatest protection I had was my anonymity as a field commander. I immediately radioed my battalion commander, told him of my concerns, and said, "I'm sending these men back to headquarters." I volunteered to provide my rationale when I got back to the battalion command post, but I never heard anything more about any kidnapping threats.

In August 1968, after almost five months in command of India Company, I learned I was on the list of captains who had been selected for promotion to major. Shortly thereafter, I was also ordered to report to division headquarters outside of Da Nang for reassignment.

Disappointed at being sent to the "rear with the gear," I made a request that I remain with my battalion or at least my regiment. I was acutely conscious of the possible perception that I was getting special treatment by being sent out of harm's way. My protests were noted, but the orders remained, and I soon found myself at 1st Marine Division headquarters serving as the assistant G4, or logistics officer for plans and operations. Of course, logistics for a major combat operation is a critical part of the mission. Getting ammunition, food, and medical supplies out to the troops in a timely, organized manner could make all the difference in battle. But now, as a staff officer, I was no longer commanding an infantry unit, and the only time I had a direct role in the execution of specific combat operations thereafter was on helicopter trips to coordinate division support operations—which I did whenever possible.

I expressed my displeasure at the transfer in a letter to Lynda and reiterated that I didn't want it to look like I was getting special treatment. In a response dated August 25, 1968, she wrote: "I got your Aug. 16 letter explaining your transfer. Please know that neither I nor the President had anything to do with it. Your letter stated that you didn't want 'help.' My only 'help' has been cookies and letters, etc. I love you and I want you happy." A week later, to my surprise, I received a note from her father:

Dear Chuck,

You and I have a lot in common at this time, and I completely appreciate your sentiment at being reassigned, for I know how much your company has meant to you. I am proud of the skill with which you have commanded it, every action you have taken, and your reluctance to leave it.

But, having attained sixty years, and mellowed a little with each birthday, I am better able than you to accept the changes that come. At least, I like to think I am a new subscriber to the theory that things beyond control have to be accepted, philosophically, in anticipation of perhaps better things to come.

Something to remember, I think, is that you have had the company longer than any other current company commander [in the battalion], and the way in which you are able to perform your new duties will be greatly enhanced by the experience you have had in the field. . . .

Mrs. Johnson is busy with the household chores that keep this place running, but she has just stopped by to say that she sends a heart full of love, as do Lynda and I.

Sincerely,

Lyndon B. Johnson[10]

I relinquished my command of India Company on August 18, 1968, and proceeded to my new post at division headquarters. The division HQ was much bigger than my company combat base had been. I described it as "not particularly spartan" on a tape to Lynda:

> We have Southeast Asia huts as we call them, or hooches, and they are certainly adequate. . . . It's . . . nicer than living out in the field . . . they have little cots . . . to sleep on, and if you are lucky enough to get a mosquito net, you can keep some of the mosquitos out. . . . Of course, they have no plumbing, and you only have power or electric light when the generator is running. But basically, it's not too bad. We have a mess hall there, and [they] serve hot rations most of the time. And while they certainly aren't gourmet delicacies, they are . . . tasty enough.[11]

Division headquarters was heavily fortified, so there was little likelihood of being hit by enemy rifle fire or ambushes, but rockets were fired at the base with some regularity from areas outside the security wire. In February 1969, the enemy penetrated the defenses at the division headquarters for the first time. I wrote to Lynda while standing watch in the logistics operations bunker:

> It's now actually a little after 0200 on the 24th but it's the first moment I've had to write you since my last letter about 26 hours ago. . . .
>
>   As you might guess, all hell has broken loose since I wrote you last. . . .
>
>   The enemy struck with rocket, mortar and sapper attacks throughout the Danang [sic] area with the primary emphasis on the 1st Mar. Div. C.P. area. His objective doesn't appear to be any large scale military victory and he won't achieve this. But he should get all the headlines he's looking for at home and in Paris.
>
>   Among the most significant statistics so far during the first 24 hours are the following: 36 Marines killed and over 200 wounded just in the 1st Mar. Div. C.P. area. Over 100 enemy killed inside or just outside our innermost defensive positions. . . .
>
>   Our main generator was just knocked out and it took about an hour to get an emergency generator started so we could have power and I could see to continue writing this letter. It's now about 0330 and an eerie calm has settled temporarily. The flares continue to light the

78 SEMPER FIDELIS

sky and the artillery, air, and naval gunfire can still be heard but there has been no small ammo fire in the CP area for the past few minutes.

Since the attacks began a little over 24 hours ago the tempo has picked up and subsided several times. . . . The Division Band, which man the final defensive positions and about never gets in a real ground fight, has lost about 1/3 of its men as casualties but has really acquitted itself well in some pretty heavy fighting and retook a couple of positions right after they were overrun. . . .

I know my descriptions of some of the day's happenings may cause you some concern but by the time you receive this, things should have quieted down and there will be nothing to worry about.

It's thoughts of you that keep me going when the going gets rough.

All my love,

Chuck[12]

Aside from the occasional full-scale assault, rocket attacks could begin out of nowhere. On another night at division HQ, I was in my office, a small, wood-frame building with a corrugated metal roof and thin walls. These were good enough for shelter but offered no protection from rocket fire or shrapnel. I was talking with three other Marines inside when we all heard the distinctive sound of incoming rockets and immediately dove for cover. They all hit the deck, but I ran out of the shelter and dove into a ditch. When the rocket hit, all three of the others were hit by shrapnel, two critically, while I was unscathed, save for a few scratches. The other able Marine and I tried to aid the one who was bleeding most heavily. When we picked him up, he was injured but alive, and we started carrying him to a road where a medevac jeep could take him to the division hospital. But his injuries were too severe, and he breathed his last breath as we held him by the road.

When the rockets fell, men lived or died depending on whether they jumped right or left. It was truly random—just part of life in war. One day it was the dog out looking for scraps in the wrong place; the next, the Marine in your office who hit the deck instead of heading for the ditch. With the benefit of time, I realize now that I approached combat with a near-fatalistic sense of that randomness. I felt there was either a bullet out there with my name on it or there wasn't. Deciding to believe I had little control over what happened meant I could go about my duties in a straightforward way, detaching the very reasonable fear of death or injury from the job that had to get done. That helped me respond judiciously to the needs of whatever situation I found myself in. It also heightened my sense of self-confidence and certainly helped to define my personality—not just as a Marine, but also as a man.

THOUGH MY TIME in Vietnam had its share of dramatic events, I do not claim to have had any single heroic, life-altering combat experience. Still, Vietnam changed me. I had had the chance to command an infantry company in combat. I had seen hundreds of Marines and Vietnamese killed and wounded, and I'd been lucky enough to come back whole, both physically and mentally. It solidified my confidence into a sense of feeling almost bulletproof. The inner discipline that had served me so well in the heart-pumping moments under enemy fire became a permanent part of my psyche. The values of leadership that had been instilled in Basic School at Quantico and tested on the battlefield became second nature. My pride in the ethos of the Marine Corps fused with my own sense of self.

I did not, however, feel as though my service had been any sort of gallant, heroic gesture. And I didn't want it to be seen that way. I was proud that I had done a good job under challenging conditions, but I did not claim to be a hero. My service was simply that: *service,* which I, and every soldier, sailor, airman, and Marine with me had rendered to our country. The mundane truth is that my service in Vietnam was no more or less remarkable than that of the other Marines with whom I served.

7

Returning Home

On April 30, 1969, exactly thirteen months to the day after I'd left for Vietnam, I returned home. After landing in California, I continued on to Texas, where Lynda and our baby, Lucinda, had been living with the Johnsons since Lynda's father had left office in January. As I got off the plane in Dallas and walked down the jetway, a member of the Secret Service pulled me aside and escorted me to a holding room, where Lynda and her parents were waiting. Lynda held out six-month-old Lucinda to greet her father for the first time.

"You are just as cute as can be," I said to Lucinda, whose face could charitably be described as confused as she stared at the strange man suddenly looming before her. "I can see right now that we're going to have to get much better acquainted."[1]

Standing behind Lynda and our baby were the former president and First Lady, just three months out of the White House, as well as my own parents, who had flown in from Wisconsin. I had a very warm welcome home.

Unfortunately, the America that I returned to in April 1969 had changed significantly since I had left it in March 1968. While I was gone, the country had gone through a violent, tumultuous upheaval, enduring assassinations, riots, and protests. Ultimately, 1968 would come to be known as a year that forever changed America.

On April 4, 1968, less than a week after my arrival in Vietnam, Dr. Martin Luther King Jr. was assassinated, setting off widespread violence and looting in several major cities, including Washington, D.C. Lynda's letters to me were filled with anguish. She wrote on April 5: "Oh, I am glad you aren't here. It is a time that tries men's souls. The country is in such an upheaval. . . . I miss you so much. I hope we can get you out of one war before another breaks out here."[2]

Rioters looted and burned whole blocks of our nation's capital as fearful residents stayed indoors. Lynda wrote to me again on April 6: "It is horrible to see your Washington so bombed out. . . . By now you will have heard about a lot of the trouble. I pray that it will be over by the time you get this. There have been 8 killed. Fear runs rampant. . . . I haven't been allowed out. It is so strange."[3]

President Johnson insisted that many of the members of his staff sleep in the White House to avoid traveling through the riots and that anyone who needed to go home to their families be driven in White House cars. Knowing that Mrs. Johnson was out of town and Lynda had just seen her husband off to war, he asked one of his personal assistants—a young woman who was close to Lynda—to spend the night in Mrs. Johnson's room. Apparently, he told the assistant that the arrangement was for Lynda's sake, while he told Lynda that it was for the safety of the assistant, but the arrangement likely accomplished both. The violence in D.C. subsided the next week, but it left lasting scars on both the city and the national psyche.

Then, only two months later, news reached us in Vietnam of yet another shooting of a national leader. On June 5, Senator Bobby Kennedy was shot and gravely wounded while campaigning in California for the Democratic nomination for president. Hearing the news, I remembered, like so many others, where I had been when his brother, President John Kennedy, was shot. I was in a helicopter with General Van Ryzin traveling back to the 2nd Marine Division Headquarters at Camp Lejeune, North Carolina, from a visit to a remote training facility, and one of the pilots motioned for me to put on my headset.

"We've just gotten word," the pilot said, "that President Kennedy has been shot."

I stared at him for a moment in shock and then turned to inform the general. The general had no headset, so I was forced to shout the news over the deafening clatter of the helicopter blades. I saw the general's jaw stiffen, but the noise made it impossible to communicate, so his only reply was a nod.

Less than five years later, I heard the news of the shooting of President Kennedy's brother Robert while I was on a combat base in Vietnam, and the whole terrible event seemed very distant from the realities of combat.

I got a much fuller picture of what was happening at home from Lynda's letters. On June 5, she began:

I wish I could understand what is going on in our country. Today when I woke up I read the headlines and found out about the terrible shooting of Sen. Bobby Kennedy. . . .

You know how I felt about [Robert Kennedy's] treatment of my father. I did not agree with [Kennedy] on many questions, but I hate to have his career snuffed out this way. Violence will serve no end. It will only breed more violence. . . . I am scared for our nation. Everyone in public office is in danger. I fear for you. I fear for my father. So many of my feelings I cannot tell you in a letter.[4]

The next day, she wrote again:

Everyone has been glued to the TV for so long that we are all beginning to grow TV "rabbit ears." It is a morbid fascination. . . . Today I walked like a zombie around the house. Everyone has been up for so many night hours that daylight is a stranger.[5]

The same day, from half a world away, I wrote to Lynda about my fears for the country:

We just heard a couple of hours ago that Senator Kennedy died as a result of the shooting yesterday. I offered a little prayer for his soul and for the comfort of his family. I pray also that his death will not spark any new violence along either religious or racial lines and that the country will respond sensibly. . . .

But I hope that the grief many Americans will feel and the martyrdom which will follow will not cause the people to blindly follow a "cause" (particularly with respect to our commitment in Vietnam) which could destroy all that the President and most Americans have worked so hard to achieve. I guess only time will tell just what effect this event will have on our future, particularly on the leadership of the country.[6]

Lynda wrote again two days later:

Every time I hear the "Battle Hymn of the Republic" I will think of the scene by the Lincoln Memorial where the Kennedy group stopped tonight to hear this song on the way to Arlington [National Cemetery]. Tonight when I saw it on TV, I felt like crying. There is nothing I can say to Ethel Kennedy but I feel such compassion for her. It was after 10 p.m. when Bobby was buried by his brother's side but it was so sad with the candles flickering. My heart is heavy. I am scared. . . . I miss you so much. I worry about you all the time. Please be careful. I don't want a hero or a martyr but a husband and a father for my child.[7]

The assassination of Robert Kennedy left the country in mourning and was deeply jarring to the many who saw him as a bright hope for the nation's future. Kennedy had been a leading contender for the presidency when he was murdered, and the Democrats went into the Democratic National Convention in Chicago in August with uncertainty. Protests over the war had intensified all summer, and at the Chicago convention the tension over the war came to a head when approximately ten thousand protestors clashed with police in Grant Park and the situation quickly erupted into a riot.

Protests against the Vietnam War grew in strength while I was overseas and continued to escalate after I returned home from Vietnam at the end of April 1969. By November 1969—six months after I'd returned—a half million people marched on Washington, the largest antiwar protest in America's history.

A month after that, in December 1969, I got a small, very personal taste of the backlash of antiwar furor being reported in the media. One morning, I was contacted by CBS News and asked to respond to a column detailing allegations that I had led my company in small-scale, Mai Lai–type massacres. A syndicated column by Jack Anderson claimed that I instructed my men: "If it moves, kill it. If it doesn't, burn it." It was a shocking and hurtful accusation, and I was livid. I would never have condoned anything like that sort of murderous activity in my company.

The source of the allegations was a twenty-four-year-old real estate and investment broker named Anthony Martin-Trigona. A year earlier, as a student journalist for the University of Illinois school newspaper, he had spent a couple of days visiting my combat base and talking to some of my men. Martin-Trigona now claimed that one of my men had bragged about killing a pregnant woman and that others had claimed to have shot up several hamlets.

Despite a total lack of evidence, the claims drew attention because of the completely justified public outrage at the Mai Lai Massacre in March 1968. Once the story broke, CBS was the first to track me down with a television crew. I told them that the claims were categorically false, and they went to work running down the details. Being the first on the story, they had plenty of time to determine that the allegations were, in fact, completely bogus, so they killed the story. NBC and ABC arrived later in the day and had only a short time to put together a report before the evening news deadline. Under the additional time pressure, NBC and ABC didn't check the accuracy of the allegations but presented both the accusations and my categorical denials and let their viewers decide—the kind of presentation that invariably leaves viewers with doubts about who's telling the truth.

While I was disappointed that the story made it on the air at all, I will be forever grateful for the thorough and professional handling of the situation by the Marine Corps. The Corps' legal team conducted an immediate investigation, individually interviewing many former members of India Company and spending two days interviewing Martin-Trigona. Their conclusion was swift and unequivocal: the allegations were entirely baseless. In a memorandum, Secretary of the Navy John H. Chafee wrote:

> Throughout more than eight hours of discussion during two days, Mr. Martin-Trigona was unable to provide any evidence of wrongdoing by Marines, or to offer any reasonable point of departure for any investigation of wrongdoing by Marines. He saw no such incident. He gave the name of no witness to any avoidable civilian casualty, and said he was unable to identify any Marine who had reported such an incident. . . . In short, he provided no factual information upon which to base further investigation. . . . In view of the foregoing, it is considered that Mr. Martin-Trigona's allegations are unfounded and unsupported.[8]

Many years later, I would find out that the same former student journalist had made a kind of career out of this type of rumor-baiting. As a law student, Martin-Trigona had begun a pattern of making unsubstantiated claims against prominent figures, filing frivolous lawsuits, and unsuccessfully running for public office as many as nineteen times. At the time that he made the claims about the Marines under my command, Martin-Trigona was running for Illinois state representative. Eventually he filed so many frivolous lawsuits that his ability to file further legal actions was limited by the courts.[9] Among many others, he filed the unsuccessful lawsuit in Hawaii to have then presidential candidate Barack Obama's birth certificate released and is credited as the origin of the false rumor that Obama was secretly a practicing Muslim.[10]

The Marine Corps' legal team considered the case closed and gave me a complete file on the investigation. They advised me to hang on to it in case it ever became an issue in the future, but it never came up again.

The vehemence of my response to the accusations betrayed a personal sensitivity. As I said to an audience in Atlanta in October 1969: "The charge [against American forces in general] of reckless killing and destruction hurts the most. Our forces consistently bent over backwards to avoid even the possibility of harm to innocent civilians or their possessions, to a point that astonishes most Vietnamese, and encourages the enemy to take advantage of the value we place on human life."[11]

One tragedy of war is that civilians may be killed or injured. But as far as I was concerned, there was a huge difference, morally and legally, between unintentional civilian deaths—what we now call collateral damage—and the wanton murder of innocents. A mission is not helped by the murder of civilians, and no well-trained member of the military or self-respecting human being would engage in such unconscionable behavior. The intentional killing of civilians is a deeply dishonorable act and is anathema to our training and ethos. The soldiers who participated in the horrors of the Mai Lai Massacre ultimately stained the honor of everyone who served in Vietnam. Even the most fearless fighters are not sociopaths, nor are they indifferent to the suffering around them. The military goes to great lengths to teach ordinary men and women the extraordinary discipline and strength necessary to use violence appropriately and to cope with the stresses of war.

The accusations against me gained traction more quickly than they might have because I was the son-in-law of former president Johnson and my service in Vietnam was a matter of public interest. That relation also made me a particularly visible, symbolic target of antiwar protests, which were then common on college campuses. The year that I returned from Vietnam, protests at Columbia University led to the banning of the ROTC program altogether. It just so happened that a core part of my very next assignment, in April 1969, was speaking on college campuses in my dress blue uniform as head of the Platoon Leaders Class (PLC) program.

The PLC program was the Marine Corps' largest officer recruiting program, providing more Marine officer recruits than either the Navy Reserve Officers Training Corps (NROTC) program or the Naval Academy. Recruiting on college campuses, the PLC program enrolled college students in a program of training at Quantico, Virginia, during their summers. My new role meant that I was responsible for the administration of all the PLC officer recruitment in the United States. In addition to approving all applications to the program, the assignment required visiting with officer selection officers (OSOs) at campuses around the country, and occasionally giving speeches.

I tried to better understand the opposition, listening to them and reading about their views, all to get a sense of where many of the students and protesters were coming from. Speaking to a Kiwanis Club in Atlanta, Georgia, just a few days before the Vietnam Moratorium protest in October 1969, I said: "It would be a mistake to ignore [protestors], for this only widens the gaps of understanding which are already evident. Instead, I urge you to listen carefully, very carefully in fact, but listen to what they say and don't be unduly influenced by how they say it."[12]

The following year, when Yale professor Charles A. Reich published his best-selling book *The Greening of America,* an ode to the 1960s counterculture movement, I read the first copy I could get my hands on. And though the book hardly convinced me to resign my commission and pick up an antiwar sign, it did help me better understand the movement and some of its arguments.

In general, I respected conscientious objectors who declared that they were opposed to war on moral grounds yet were willing to accept the consequences of their decisions, which could include fines and jail time. But I felt less charitable toward those who tried to beat the system, either through deception or by fleeing the country.

I found, when I visited campuses, that keeping a clear head was the perfect antidote to the heated protestors. If I could remain steady under enemy fire, I was pretty sure I could handle angry college students. In fact, I enjoyed surprising protestors by applying a little bit of straightforward reason, and occasional humor, to the encounter.

In February 1970, I visited several colleges in the Philadelphia area, including the University of Pennsylvania and La Salle University, where I did a talk for students titled "Pacification in Vietnam." Not surprisingly, the antiwar protestors were out in force, with hundreds outside the Union Theatre wearing skull masks, shouting, and carrying signs. Inside, the theater was packed, with an overflow crowd of more than four hundred.

I walked onstage alone in my Marine Corps dress blue uniform with its ribbons, badges, and gold buttons, a walking poster for everything this crowd opposed. The auditorium was already noisy, and when I began to speak, the heckling intensified. But I had no intention of bullying them about who was "right" or "wrong" about American involvement in Vietnam. The *La Salle Magazine* recorded the event:

> Addressing an audience that included many highly-vocal anti-war protesters, Robb said that "I don't like being engaged in war. I find nothing satisfying about it."
>
> [Robb] obviously did not change opinions of the war dissenters with his answers to questions about U.S. policy in Vietnam. But he did succeed in winning over the audience with his calm, sincere personality. His replies frequently received warm applause.
>
> At one point, a student shouted, "You are teaching people to kill. What does this have to do with pacification?" Robb replied calmly, "Most people know how to kill already. We don't have to teach them that." The audience clapped.[13]

I surprised the crowd with my responses, and, in spite of their hostility, a few students laughed. It broke the tension—once they had laughed, it was impossible to sustain the level of animosity with which they'd come armed. My strategy was to respond directly to their arguments and questions, without seeming to be close-minded or dismissing the opposition out of hand, and engage the audience in a kind of dialogue. The result was that I was, as the *Philadelphia Inquirer* put it, "roundly applauded for some of [my] snappier comebacks to queries," and I "succeeded in establishing rapport with an audience that was initially hostile."[14]

The dialogue surprised some students, who must have expected me to simply spout promilitary rhetoric at them. At the very least, I hoped to give them a sense that I, like other returning veterans, was not an automaton or a warmonger but a human being, not so different from any of them and fully capable of developing personal opinions. I don't know if I changed anybody's stance on the war that day, but by the time I finished, the audience gave me a standing ovation.

Because the event was covered on the front page of the *Philadelphia Inquirer* the next day, I soon received a letter on the telltale pale-green stationary of the Oval Office from President Nixon, commending me on having won over the hostile crowd.

I certainly wasn't impartial on the complex topic of the Vietnam War. After all, I was a recently returned veteran who had joined willingly and requested combat duty, and my new bride's father had been president of the United States during the war. And my own views at the time were very much influenced by the military chain of command. I was generally supportive of the "domino theory," which held that if we let Vietnam fall to the Communists, the rest of Asia would go the same way. Like many other Cold Warriors, I saw America as a force for freedom and democracy, halting the spread of Communism.

As I said in a speech to the Kiwanis Club in Atlanta soon after I returned from Vietnam: "As a military officer and as a private citizen, I stand unashamedly behind our Vietnam commitment. Stated in the simplest terms, our government is fulfilling both a moral and legal obligation to assist the government and people of South Vietnam in thwarting aggression and determining their own future."[15] While I understood the need to serve our own national interests as well, I believed that "we can't abruptly turn our back on an ally just because we grow weary of helping. If a man is no better than his word, certainly the same can be said of a nation."[16]

In the decades since Vietnam, we've learned more about what was presented to those making the decisions about the war and their thinking at the time. These accounts have given us a fuller understanding of the decisions that were made along the way. The situation that the U.S. military entered in Vietnam in 1963 was far more complex than it appeared to be at the time.

As Edwin Reischauer, a Harvard professor of East Asian studies and former ambassador to Japan, said in testimony before Congress in 1967: "We have failed sometimes to understand the deeply rooted historic forces at work in Asia—anticolonialism, nationalism, the eagerness to wipe out past humiliations and the determination to advance rapidly without losing national identity."[17]

We have since reevaluated the strategy of General William Westmoreland, commander of U.S. forces in Vietnam from 1964 to 1968, who approached the conflict as a "war of attrition." Based on his experience, with America's superior firepower, he believed that the fastest way to win the war was to kill a large number of the enemy, who would see the futility of the fight and end hostilities. His strategy was built on the assumption that the conflict was being fought by two powers over the spread of Communism. Success was measured, under Westmoreland's command, by body count, while the efforts or ability of the South Vietnamese to defend themselves or maintain political and economic stability were underappreciated. But Westmoreland's strategy reflected a World War II mindset that didn't entirely take into account the motivations of the enemy or reflect the role of nationalism or patriotism in the fight for their country.

Over many decades, I have come to better understand the impact of the nationalist sentiment in Vietnam, which had a long history of fighting off foreign invaders. The Vietnamese had been clashing for centuries with the Chinese, the Khmers (of present-day Cambodia), and the Mongols. More recently, they had chafed under French colonialization starting in the nineteenth century. We now recognize how strongly the French occupation solidified Vietnamese nationalist feelings and allowed Ho Chi Minh, the cunning and talented leader of the Communist faction, to channel those feelings into an independence movement. While the Communists were the strongest component of the nationalist movement, nationalism was a much stronger motivation for the North Vietnamese and the Viet Cong than we realized at the time.

With the leaking of the Pentagon Papers in 1971 (after I had returned from Vietnam and retired from active duty), we saw fuller documentation of the history of U.S. involvement in Vietnam, including prior U.S. support to Ho Chi Minh's guerilla forces against the Japanese in World War II, our backing of France's efforts to recolonize Vietnam after the war, and, after France's defeat, the extent of our support for the South Vietnamese and our part in the military coup that overthrew and murdered their president, Ngo Dinh Diem, in 1963.

When the Pentagon Papers were initially released, much of my focus was on the harm that could be done by the release of these classified documents rather than on the information the papers contained. Over time, I've come to better appreciate the content of the Pentagon Papers themselves and the picture they gave of America's long-term involvement in Vietnam leading up to the war.

As historians have scrutinized the war in the last five decades, most have developed a more nuanced view about the circumstances and the history of Vietnam. Reischauer, Bernard Fall, and others who studied Vietnam were probably right that we ought to have been aiding the nationalist spirit of the Vietnamese and supporting their self-determination instead of fighting it.

However, I never doubted the good faith of our senior leadership in the Vietnam War. Though not privy to the policy discussions at the time, I was privileged to get to know on a more personal basis many of those involved in the policy and its execution. With the benefit of time and history, it is easy to critique decisions that might have been made differently, but I remain very much convinced that the decisions that were made were made by honorable people in what they believed to be the best interest of our country. There were certainly failures of information, but in hindsight it is harder to judge the decisions of those who had to make them in circumstances that were less than clear or calm.

The more I've learned about Vietnam, both the country and the war, the more complex and less clear the picture has become. But that complexity has broadened my understanding of why we were there, why we eventually pulled out, and the arguments of those opposed to the war. A true study of the Vietnam War reveals a picture that is not simply black-and-white, and sides that are not wholly right or wrong. After many years of reflection, we've found that the picture involves many shades of gray.

It was always important to me, both when I was giving speeches as head of the PLC program and in the many years since, that no one thought that their loved one had died in the Vietnam War in vain. When I took command of India Company, I was surrounded by Marines who were fighting, and sometimes dying, for the man on their right and their left. But in the broader sense, they believed that they were acting in the best interest of their country and the world. Many of them, like me, were volunteers, and these men did not go thousands of miles from home to fight out of bloodlust. We all raised a hand and took an oath to support and defend the Constitution of the United States from all enemies foreign and domestic. Our country called upon us to serve, and we answered that call.

8

A Growing Family

My assignment to head the Platoon Leaders Class (PLC) program at Headquarters Marine Corps wasn't the only new step for me in that first year after Vietnam. I had left for combat as a newlywed and returned home as a husband and a father of a six-month-old baby girl. Little Lucinda had been a bit wary of me at first, but a bond came with time. It was an added benefit that my new assignment allowed me to spend time with Lynda and our growing family.

Six months after my return from Vietnam, when Lucinda was just one year old, we found out that Lynda was pregnant again. Over the winter and spring of 1969–70, I got to participate in her pregnancy in a way that I'd only read about in Lynda's letters when she carried Lucinda. Like many other new fathers, I was impressed with how calmly Lynda coped with the physical and mental stresses of pregnancy while chasing around a toddling Lucinda.

After missing the birth of our first daughter, I was determined to be there for the birth of our second child. By the beginning of June, Lynda was three weeks overdue, and we were anxiously awaiting the new arrival. On Friday, June 5, I was ready to bow out of a morning golf tournament that I had long been scheduled to play in, but Lynda and her mother encouraged me to keep the engagement while they made arrangements at the hospital to start an induced delivery. Naturally, just as I was teeing off, Lynda went into labor, and—long before cell phones—no one was able to reach me for some time. When I found out that the baby was coming, I rushed to the Bethesda Naval Hospital, which was very close to the golf course. In my haste, I burst, momentarily, into the wrong birthing room just at that crucial moment. It took only a few seconds for me to realize that the moment isn't as special if it's not your child, and I beat a hasty retreat. But I did make it to the correct room, next door, and just in time. Our second daughter, Catherine, was born that afternoon. And it did, with my own child, feel like a miracle. Being there to support Lynda and share at least part of the experience of bringing a new child into the world was awe-inspiring to say the least.

Having also missed the first six months of our firstborn daughter's life, I didn't fully appreciate how challenging raising children can be. Lynda had it all well in hand and truly embraced the role of caretaker in the family. She was not only the heart of the family, but the multitasking engine whose energy never seemed to flag.

Lynda's style as a mother was not to be an authoritarian figure or a drill sergeant. She always seemed more like a big sister to our girls, especially as they got older. I've always been pleased with how much Lynda and our girls all simply enjoyed doing things together. She hardly ever seemed to need to discipline them—when there was a disagreement, Lynda worked with them to find a solution instead of scolding, and her patience was impressive. I benefited greatly from her talent for raising our three daughters, and her instincts are primarily responsible for what we've always called our "almost perfect daughters."

I, on the other hand, had to learn a lot about small children very quickly. By the summer of 1970, Lynda and I had been married for more than two and a half years, but we had lived together for only a total of about eighteen months, and in that time we had added two adorable little people to our family. Those early years of marriage, when couples learn how to live together and combine two personalities into one family, were somewhat condensed for us by my thirteen months in Vietnam and the early addition of our two daughters.

They say that opposites attract, and that was certainly true in our case. Lynda, like her father, is very emotional and warm, and expresses her feelings freely. I am more restrained and generally keep a fairly cool head.

My response to crisis tends to be calmly logical. Many years later, the *Washington Post* recounted that, while I was on a trip to Angola, a tarantula crawled up my leg. I don't remember the incident, but the response certainly sounds like me. According to the *Post,* all I said was, "Don't worry. It'll move."[1]

Lynda's mother once observed that I would be a good person to have around in an emergency, but Lynda didn't always appreciate my rational approach.

On Labor Day weekend in 1971, while I was working inside the house on law school assignments, Lynda was outside washing the family car. (She liked to note that "only first wives wash cars, you know!") We lived on a quiet cul-de-sac, and our house was perched atop an eight-foot embankment that dropped off steeply in the backyard. It was a pleasant, late-summer day until Lynda suddenly heard the squeal of car tires near the front of our house.

In an instant, Lynda realized she didn't know where our one-year-old Catherine and three-year-old Lucinda were at that moment. In a panic, she darted toward the backyard to look for them, and, unable to stop herself in time, tumbled right over the edge of the embankment. She flew through the air in something of an incomplete somersault and landed hard on her back.

As it turned out, Lucinda and Catherine were fine, but now Lynda was badly hurt. We didn't know it at the time, but she had fractured a vertebra in her neck. Screaming in pain, she lay flat on her back as little Lucinda, too young to understand what was happening, brought over a toy broom and tried to sweep the dirt off of her. As soon as I heard Lynda's cries, I ran out of the house and immediately set about trying to determine the extent of her injuries.

Our interpretations of what happened next neatly illustrate the difference between our personalities. As she tells it: "Chuck started hitting me with a stick in various places to see if I had any feeling. No gentle touch on the shoulder to say, 'Darling, you'll be all right'—just poking me with a stick!" She recalls that I then began ruminating about whether our health insurance policy was in place, and whether we would be able to find a doctor on Labor Day.

Of course, what I remember is hearing Lynda's screams and that terrible feeling in the pit of my stomach. The fear and the anxiety were all there, but my personality and my military training kept my mind on assessing the situation. I needed to quickly determine the extent of her injuries and the best, fastest course to obtain treatment. Underneath the cool reserve, I was an anxious young husband bending over his injured wife.

A year later, my mother-in-law got to see my response to a crisis first-hand when Lynda and I were visiting the LBJ Ranch with Lucinda and Catherine. It was a hot, bone-dry summer day, and we were spending some time outside at the pool. The girls were swimming in the shallow end with a babysitter nearby, and I was in the deeper part of the pool. Suddenly, Lynda's shrieks pierced the air, and I turned to see our two-year-old Catherine floating, motionless, face down in the water. My heart skipped a beat as I started toward her.

Lynda jumped into the water fully clothed, while I swam as fast as I could into the shallow end. When I pulled Catherine out of the water, her little body was cold and a sickly gray color, and she wasn't breathing. I put aside every other concern and focused on getting her breathing again. I instinctively began to squeeze her, trying to force the water out of her lungs. What I didn't expect was that water would come out of every orifice. As I squeezed, water shot out her nose, her ears, and her mouth—more water than I would have guessed a body that small could hold. Even a rubber band, which she had somehow gotten stuck up her nose, came out as I squeezed.

A Secret Service agent assigned to Lynda's father named Ed Nowland had heard Lynda's screams from the other side of the ranch house and raced over to help. President Johnson, who had been napping in the house, awoke at the commotion and came running out in his pajamas.

After what seemed an eternity of squeezing Catherine and alternating with Ed Nowland in giving her mouth-to-mouth resuscitation, we at last heard a weak, whimpering cry. Catherine was breathing again, but she hadn't taken a breath for the previous two minutes, and her little body was blue and shivering cold. I scooped her into my arms and took her straight into the nearest shower. I held her as warm water cascaded over her, bringing her temperature back up. Anxiously, we called a family friend at the Mayo Clinic in Rochester, Minnesota, who told us that, at Catherine's age, as long as she hadn't stopped breathing for more than five minutes, she shouldn't be at risk of any brain damage.

The next day, I had one more goal: to head off any fear she might have about the water. That afternoon, I held her hand and led her right back into the pool for a swim. And she was perfectly fine, happily splashing about with no apparent recollection of what had happened a day earlier.

Our daughters were remarkably resilient, and I would continue to be amazed at how quickly they would adapt to every move and change our family experienced.

IN THE SUMMER of 1970, after I had been back in America and heading up the PLC program for about a year, I started to focus on what might come next. Up to this point in my life, the right opportunity had always presented itself at the right time—graduating from high school, going to college, joining the military, and serving in Vietnam. With my Vietnam service behind me and my obligation to the Marine Corps fulfilled, I looked at the many avenues open ahead of me.

I certainly could have continued as an officer in the Marine Corps. I took enormous pride in being a Marine, and Lynda would have been very happy for me to continue on active duty. But I hadn't joined the Marines with the intention of making a full career out of the military. My marriage to Lynda was also a factor. The military, at its very core, should be a meritocracy, and I didn't want even the appearance of my having received any special treatment because of my marriage.

It seemed obvious to some that I would go into the Johnson family business—not politics, but broadcasting. Lynda's family had prospered in the broadcasting industry, which the Johnsons had been involved in for decades. But, being a bit proud, I felt I should make my own way. And while I admired and respected LBJ, I wasn't sure I'd be as happy working for him directly.

Of course, the president made no secret of his hope that I'd one day help run the family's broadcasting business. His least-disguised attempt to settle us into his Texas orbit came during a 1971 visit to the LBJ Ranch. Alluding to some unnamed errand for which he needed our help, he piled Lynda and me into the car and drove us through Austin, eventually pulling up in front of a four-bedroom house in a very nice neighborhood. "That could be yours," he suggested as we peered out the car windows. We looked at the house, then at him. A long moment passed.

"Thank you, sir," I said, "but we're not planning on moving to Texas."

I don't remember the president's precise response, but back at the ranch, he recounted the drive to his neighbor Harold Woods, summarizing it with the observation that I was an "independent bastard." I had no choice but to take that as grudging praise.

I considered several different options for what to do next. For a number of years, I had thought about going back to business school to get my MBA, particularly since I would be eligible for financial assistance from the GI Bill. I had enjoyed my undergraduate studies in business and thought that I could be successful in the field. But I was also increasingly intrigued by the idea of law school. While I wasn't sure I ever wanted to be a full-time practicing attorney, a great many of my personal and professional friends were lawyers, and I knew that a law degree could be useful in a wide range of careers. It seemed like a smart choice and the most appealing one that I seriously considered.

So, in the fall of 1969, I decided law school would be my next step. But I wasn't yet ready to make my decision public, so I took the Law School Admissions Test (LSAT) clandestinely and told almost no one of my plans. I applied only to the University of Virginia School of Law and was fortunate enough to be accepted. Lynda still jokes that I didn't even tell her until I'd applied, been accepted, and decided to go. Soon thereafter, we moved our family—including nearly two-year-old Lucinda and three-month-old Catherine—to Charlottesville, where I began law school in the fall of 1970.

When I enrolled, I resigned my regular commission in the Marine Corps and went on inactive duty status, becoming a part of the Marine Corps Reserve. It was important to me to at least stay in the inactive reserve, because if America were to get into another war, I wanted to be eligible to go back in. I was conscious that my resignation from active duty could be perceived by some as a repudiation of the Vietnam War, which was still ongoing. By staying on inactive reserve, I wanted to send the message that I was keeping the faith and that I was still committed, to the Corps and to the fight.

After almost a decade of active service, I also wanted to maintain a tangible connection to the Marine Corps, which had had such a dramatic impact on my personality, my career, and my life. In a way, I would bring the Marine Corps with me to law school, and to every role I would play for the rest of my life. No matter what job or title I held, I would always consider myself a Marine first.

9

Larger than Life

IN THE PREDAWN hours of April 7, 1972, Lynda and I were suddenly awakened by a commotion on the top floor of our Charlottesville split-level. We'd been sleeping downstairs in the guest room because Lynda's parents were visiting from Texas, and we'd offered them the larger, more comfortable master bedroom upstairs. Clad in our pajamas, Lynda and I rushed up the stairs to see what was happening. Lynda's father had suffered a heart attack. A Secret Service agent who had been on watch jumped in to tend to the stricken former president and call for an ambulance.

Within minutes, a volunteer rescue squad arrived and scrambled to stabilize him. Lynda's father was whisked to a nearby hospital, where he spent the next few days in intensive care while his condition stabilized. By this point in his life, my father-in-law had already suffered several heart attacks, mostly minor, but at least one that was very serious, prompting him to harbor a dark certainty that his days were numbered. His own father had died at age sixty after a series of heart attacks, and LBJ never thought he'd live even that long. His decision not to run for another term as president in 1968 was partly due to the fact that he didn't believe he would last another four years. Several years earlier, he'd even requested an actuarial study of his life expectancy, which concluded that he would die at age sixty-four. As we sat with him in the Charlottesville hospital, LBJ's sixty-fourth birthday was only four months away.

Despite his condition, President Johnson's stubbornness was undiminished, as Hal Rothman described in his 2001 book *LBJ's Texas White House:*

> Certain he was going to die, Johnson browbeat Lady Bird and his physicians until they grudgingly allowed him to fly home in a few days. The hospital director opposed the idea. Johnson insisted that when he departed life he do so from his beloved Texas and defied the leaders of the institution. Some accounts offer the mythic scenario of the director of the Charlottesville Hospital rushing to prevent John-

son's departure only to find an abandoned wheelchair in the hospital parking lot.[1]

Lynda's father had always enjoyed and found comfort at his Texas ranch, but in the four short years of his postpresidency, his homecoming had been bittersweet. He loved managing important affairs, and it was clearly frustrating to him to go from Oval Office meetings to kitchen-table updates on his small herd of cattle. Still, he kept his ranch hands jumping as though they were on call at the White House. Once, while driving around the ranch with my father-in-law, I heard him radio to his foreman, the long-serving and loyal Dale Malecheck: "Dale!" he boomed. "There's a heifer over here that's looking a little peaked; better come on over and take a look." And Dale came running.

Whenever Lynda and I visited the ranch, we engaged in a handful of favorite rituals. We'd take a ride in his spotless white Lincoln convertible and stop at a special hilltop outlook and park the car. He'd call back to the Secret Service car that always followed discreetly behind, and a few minutes later an agent would bring over drinks. There must have been a cooler in their car because the drinks never failed to be refreshingly chilled. LBJ's drink of choice was Cutty Sark scotch whiskey, and the Secret Service detail (as did anyone who knew the president well) always kept a bottle stocked. Cool drinks in hand, we would sit on the hill facing east and watch the exotic species of deer and other animals the president had brought in to stock the ranch. Or we'd sit facing west at dusk and watch a magnificent, fiery-red sunset over the Hill Country.

If LBJ was feeling social, we'd go visit cousin Oriole Bailey, who lived a hundred yards or so down the road from the ranch house. She was deaf as a post, and by this point his hearing wasn't much better. The two of them would shout amiably at each other, neither actually hearing what the other was saying. But they seemed to enjoy their exchanges just the same.

In these few years of reduced activity, his health declined visibly. Believing in the inevitability of his own mortality, he'd started smoking again and stopped cutting his hair, which grew long and white. He constantly sucked on nitroglycerine pills in an effort to keep his ailing heart in a stable rhythm.

Lynda, Luci, and their mother feared constantly for him. Lynda's mother thought often of the portrait of President Franklin Roosevelt by Elizabeth Shoumatoff that depicts a wan, exhausted man suffering the final effects of several maladies, including atherosclerosis and congestive heart failure. Shoumatoff was in the midst of the sketch when Roosevelt complained of pain in his head and collapsed with a cerebral hemorrhage. He died the next day. The portrait remains unfinished, the face and neck complete but the torso only sketched in. Mrs. Johnson did not want LBJ to end up like Roosevelt, crippled by health problems brought on by the immense stress of the presidency.

In many ways, Mrs. Johnson was the perfect foil to her husband—as low-key and poised as LBJ was loud and emotional. While the president always liked to have people around him, Mrs. Johnson was just as happy reading a book alone as she was at a gala.

Physically, Mrs. Johnson was small and unassuming, but in so many ways she was solid as a rock. Mrs. Johnson was a southern lady to the bone, and I never saw her act, even in private, in any way that Emily Post wouldn't have approved. I didn't think of calling her anything but "Mrs. Johnson," any more than I would have called my own parents by their first names. I don't think that I ever saw her unruffled or emotionally distraught. But at the same time, she was unfailingly warm and caring, always asking after the neighbor who had been sick or staff member who had just had a baby.

With both an associate degree and a bachelor's degree, with honors, in history, Mrs. Johnson was very well educated—especially for a woman of her day. Throughout her life, she was always intelligent and informed, though she wasn't as political as her husband. The two had different kinds of intelligence. For instance, if you had a speech that you wanted someone else to read, you might take it to LBJ for political analysis or emotional impact, but you would take it to Mrs. Johnson for substantive feedback.

Her intelligence was also practical. Mrs. Johnson had been taught finance by her uncle Claude Patillo, for whom she'd been named, and she became very proficient at it. Though this was mostly before my time, Lynda has always said that her mother had very effectively overseen the running of the radio and television stations that the Johnsons owned. Throughout Lynda's childhood, she remembers her mother traveling from Washington, D.C., back to Texas every month to review sales reports and consult with Jesse Kellam, who ran the day-to-day operations. When Lynda went to work at the station in Austin over the summer, she was called "Mrs. Johnson's daughter" by the staff, even though her father was a sitting senator at the time.

Mrs. Johnson's facility with the business also came from her self-reliance. After her mother died when Mrs. Johnson was five, my mother-in-law was raised by a father who owned a general store and didn't know a lot about raising a little girl, so she learned to trust her own judgment and do things for herself. She once told Lynda of the time when, at age fifteen, she drove her father's car by herself from Karnack, Texas, to Alabama to visit relatives. Lynda, horrified, asked her mother, "What would have happened if you had broken down?"

"Oh darlin'," Mrs. Johnson replied, "somebody woulda picked me up."

This independence served her well with a husband as busy and as demanding as LBJ and the obligations of serving as wife to the vice president and then president. Even with the constant travel and hectic schedules, Mrs. Johnson always seemed perfectly content to go wherever or do whatever was required for her role as both wife and First Lady.

For some people, it would have been hard to follow in the footsteps of a First Lady as impeccably stylish and iconic as Jacqueline Kennedy, but Mrs. Johnson was completely unruffled. She was always dressed appropriately for every occasion but was totally unconcerned about fashion. Once, when my mother-in-law was asked about Mrs. Kennedy's pillbox hats, she replied characteristically that it was "what was in Mrs. Kennedy's head that was important, not what was on her head." Mrs. Johnson's lack of concern for fashion sometimes frustrated President Johnson, who used to say that he wanted her to "sell for what you're worth." But she would just smile and keep doing what she had been doing. She did have a sense of humor about her looks—she used to joke, "If I had known that I would be First Lady, I would have gotten my nose fixed!"

Mrs. Johnson did have worries, but she was especially good at overcoming them. When her husband first got into politics, Mrs. Johnson was terrified of public speaking, so she went to a public speaking class and learned to be a very good public speaker. Though she was scared of flying in small planes, particularly in bad weather, Mrs. Johnson simply "screwed her courage to the sticking place," as Lynda likes to quote from Shakespeare, and flew all over the country. I always appreciated this calm practicality in my mother-in-law, and we would, more often than not, see things from the same levelheaded perspective.

Lynda was always awed by her mother's ability to calmly conquer challenges. In many ways, Lynda took after both of her parents—passionate like her father and intelligent and independent like her mother. Lynda and her mother were always very close, and their relationship was much more like one of best friends than it was of mother and daughter. Mrs. Johnson used to say that "the greatest thing that you can give somebody you love or care about are memories," because "nobody, not even the richest person in the world, got more than 24 hours in a day." The giving freely of your time was always the most coveted gift of both my father- and mother-in-law.

WE CELEBRATED CHRISTMAS of 1972 at the ranch. Two days later, on a gloomy December day, the whole family, including Lynda's parents and Luci's family, had just gathered for an intimate lunch. About halfway through the meal, however, LBJ got word of a terrible bus accident in New Mexico the night before which had left nineteen dead, many of them Mexican American teenagers who attended Crockett High School in Austin.

At this point, it was generally understood that President Johnson's next heart attack would almost certainly be his last, and travel was clearly not recommended. But as soon as he heard about the accident, he announced he was going to Austin to be with the families of those children, despite his doctor's protests. I'll never forget his response: "These are my people," he declared. "They were there for me when I needed *them,* and they need *me* now, and I'm going to go." That was the final word. The *Austin American-Statesman* later reported on the services, which were attended by more than five thousand people: "Fourteen caskets lined the front of the auditorium, and former President Lyndon Johnson and his wife, Lady Bird Johnson, were among the mourners."[2] To LBJ, that was where he needed to be.

Those who didn't know President Johnson sometimes spoke of him as a pure politician, a man for whom the game of power was the be-all and end-all. Though it's true that he was a consummate politician—he knew how to play the game, and he played it aggressively—it's also true that his reaction to the bus accident illustrates another, perhaps more important, side of a complex man. He wasn't going to comfort the families in order to garner votes. He was just an old man who wanted to offer whatever comfort and support he could to those who were grieving.

On that same December 1972 visit to the ranch, LBJ laid out his plans for his own funeral—where he wanted to be buried, who he wanted to deliver his eulogy, and even where he wanted people to stand. In fact, he took all of us down to the family cemetery so he could point out the precise spot, under a tree, that he'd picked out. He'd also tended to just about every worldly affair he could think of, getting his estate in order, selling KTBC (the television station he and Mrs. Johnson had owned since 1943), and finalizing other complicated business transactions.

Only a few weeks later, on January 22, 1973, as I was changing into athletic clothes to play a league volleyball game, the phone rang in our Charlottesville home. Lynda's father had passed away after a massive heart attack. True to the actuarial table, LBJ was sixty-four years old.

It was late afternoon when we got the news, and within the hour we got a call telling us that President Nixon was sending a plane to take us to Texas that evening.

When we arrived at the ranch, the scene was emotional and chaotic. President Johnson elicited deep emotions in people, and those who loved him did so deeply. Though his death wasn't a surprise, it was still a devastating blow for everyone who gathered at the ranch. Some seemed dazed. Others tried to distract their grief with useful projects. Even foreman Dale Malecheck, whom I'd always thought of as the consummate tough, grizzled old cowboy, had completely fallen apart, sobbing unabashedly in the living room.

Amid the grief, there were tasks that needed to be taken care of, including ensuring the preparation of the president's remains. I was the family member designated to look upon him last and ensure that he was laid out as he had wished. At an Austin funeral home, I was escorted to his casket. Gazing down on Lyndon B. Johnson in death, I was struck by how stark the contrast was between the vibrant, energetic man I'd known, and the pallid body now lying before me. The funeral home had done its job well, but the president looked so empty in death that I was glad that the family had decided to have a closed casket for the services. He had been too vital a man to be remembered in any way but alive.

President Johnson's body first lay in state for a day at his presidential library in Austin. The next morning, Lynda, the family, and I accompanied the casket on President Johnson's final journey to Washington, aboard the Boeing 707 that served presidents from John F. Kennedy to George H. W. Bush as Air Force One. It was on that same plane, nine years earlier, that LBJ had taken the oath of office on the tragic day President Kennedy was assassinated.

President Johnson's body lay in state in the Capitol Rotunda. First, official Washington paid their respects—cabinet officials, congressional leaders, and political colleagues, followed by the military. Then the Rotunda was opened to the general public as an honor guard stood in a circle around the flag-covered casket, remaining, in shifts, throughout the nightlong vigil. Members of the family took turns standing at the foot of the coffin, greeting members of the public who came to offer their condolences. I think the president would have been pleased by the public response. More than thirty thousand citizens, the overwhelming majority of them the hardworking, average Americans for whom he had toiled and cared so deeply, streamed through the Rotunda to pay their last respects.

The following morning, on a warm, sun-drenched January day, President Johnson's body was borne down the aisle of the National City Christian Church in Washington, D.C., by an honor guard, who placed the casket on a red velvet catafalque. As the honor guard turned to leave, "a young black Marine who had carried the casket marched stolidly back down the aisle with a single line of tears running down his face."[3]

We left the funeral service and drove to Andrews Air Force Base to fly back to the ranch, where President Johnson would be buried in his beloved Hill Country. When we entered the living room at the ranch, we found it full of family members sharing memories, telling stories, and supporting each other. The day was bleak, bone-chilling, and it had been raining steadily since the night before, so Tom Johnson (a former aide who was no relation) lent me a black raincoat, as I had left mine in Charlottesville. Many people had flown out from Washington to be at the burial, and they filed through the living room, where someone had to put down a big plastic mat over the carpet to try to contain the water and mud tracked in by the mourners. Mourners of all kinds crunched their way through the living room, and the cowboy boots of local friends and neighbors mixed with the polished black oxfords of state and national officials. Ethel Kennedy, the widow of Robert Kennedy, made the trip out to the ranch, putting behind her all of the animosity that had built up between her husband and President Johnson. So did newly sworn-in Senator Joe Biden, who had lost his first wife and his daughter in a car crash only the month before. Lynda and I were touched that so many made the trip halfway across the country to honor her father's memory.

Everything was orchestrated according to President Johnson's instructions. Standing beneath the tree he had chosen as his final resting place,

Dr. Billy Graham officiated the service, as the president had requested. It was an intimate and suitable ending for a man who had so loved surrounding himself with family and friends.

PEOPLE OFTEN ASK me what I thought of President Johnson. When I first met him, he was the president and I was a military social aide. Our relationship was very friendly and pleasant, but we were hardly intimates. Once Lynda and I became engaged, he, like any future father-in-law, started taking a more personal interest in me. We had some private conversations, though they were not easily arranged when he was head of state. The letters he sent while I was serving in Vietnam meant a great deal to me. When I returned from the war, he was out of office and had retired to a quieter life. But even in that short time that I knew him after his presidency, I never got out of the habit of calling him "Mr. President" or "sir."

His retirement from public life allowed him to enjoy more time with us and his young grandchildren. He loved bouncing them on his knee as he told stories, and his annual performances as Santa Claus delighted his grandchildren and remain legendary in the family. We still have home movies that resound with his distinctive "Ho, ho, ho!"

He was a man for whom I developed an enormous respect and was proud to call my father-in-law. He always treated me with generosity, and his wife, daughters, and grandchildren—who knew him as "Boppa" and Lynda's mother as "Nini"—with boundless love. Today, I enjoy being called "Boppa" by my own grandchildren.

Although he was my wife's father and my children's grandfather, President Johnson always felt larger than life to me, a man whose passions and beliefs, and the manner in which he expressed them, were as expansive and intense as those of any other human being I have known. As many biographers have noted, the president was far from perfect. In this, he was no different from many of the great political and social reformers of our nation's history, none of whom were without faults. Lyndon Johnson was complicated and mercurial, capable of being overbearing one minute and compassionate the next. His assessments of both his political allies and enemies were brutally frank, earthy, and usually dead-on. He loved to play practical jokes, and he always wanted to be surrounded by friends. Mrs. Johnson quickly learned to be prepared for any number of last-minute dinner guests, any night of the week. One of his favorite games was to get his dog Yuki—a little mongrel that Luci had rescued from a gas station years before—to bay. The two of them would throw their heads back together and howl in gleeful unison, startling the livestock and housekeepers alike.

Saying "I'm sorry" seemed to be impossible for this proud man, but when he realized he'd been unfairly tough on a subordinate, he would smother him or her with gifts in an unspoken gesture of atonement. And LBJ always shopped in large numbers. If he bought one designer dress for a chastened secretary, he would buy the same one for every other female in the office, regardless of personal styles or preferences.

Notwithstanding President Johnson's quirks, he was a master politician who used his talents—his intimate knowledge of every member of Congress and his unrivaled powers of personal persuasion—to make the country a better place for the disadvantaged. He was able to get passed a flood of landmark legislation that may never be matched by a single president again.

Shortly after taking office following the assassination of President Kennedy, President Johnson made the politically perilous decision to push for civil rights legislation that had been stalled in Congress for months. When told that he shouldn't waste political capital on a civil rights bill that had little hope of passage, the president said, "Well, what the hell's the presidency for?"[4]

Though President Johnson was not on the same oratorical level as, say, Winston Churchill, John F. Kennedy, or Martin Luther King Jr., on a few distinct occasions, he rose beyond expectations, particularly when speaking about civil rights, where the genuine passion of his remarks ran deep. His 1964 State of the Union address is one of his best-remembered because the president declared an "unconditional war on poverty" and took a firm stand against discrimination: "We must abolish not some, but all racial discrimination. For this is not merely an economic issue, or a social, political, or international issue. It is a moral issue, and it must be met by the passage this session of the bill now pending in the House."[5]

President Johnson's "Great Society" programs—his visionary effort to cast a safety net beneath the neediest Americans, with initiatives such as Head Start, Medicaid, and the establishment of the Department of Housing and Urban Development—have been broadly attacked as the epitome of the supposed fiscal irresponsibility and "big-spending liberalism" of the 1960s. Those who have leveled charges of fiscal irresponsibility are forgetting Johnson's southern roots. Fiscal conservatism has always been a prerequisite for political viability in Texas. By investing government money in programs that increased opportunity for the poor—through measures like education, food security, and health care—the War on Poverty legislation effectively gave Americans a hand up, while managing to be much more fiscally responsible than the programs are usually given credit for.

I developed enormous respect for the audacity of President Johnson's Great Society vision and his willingness to challenge the status quo on behalf of those in greatest need. Millions of people have seen their lives made better by my father-in-law's initiatives, and I believe that this commitment, even more than any specific program, should be his enduring legacy.

PART II

THE NEW DOMINION

ON A SATURDAY morning in the summer of 1972, I was having a midmorning coffee break at Duke Zeibert's Restaurant, an old Washington institution frequented by the city's movers and shakers. It wasn't my usual spot for coffee or my usual company. It just happened to be my turn, as a summer associate at Williams, Connolly and Califano, to spend a little time with two of the top guns: Edward Bennett Williams and Joe Califano. Both men were name partners at the firm, as well as prominent Democrats. Ed was treasurer of the Democratic National Committee (DNC), while Joe served as the committee's general counsel.

The three of us were talking when Zeibert himself came striding over to our table with a telephone (a courtesy he extended to only a handful of Washington's power elite) and said to Joe, "You have a call," as he handed him the receiver.

As Ed and I listened to Joe's side of the conversation, we became increasingly perplexed. It was someone from the DNC calling to tell Joe that the headquarters, located in the Watergate complex, had been broken into during the early hours of the morning. Five men had been arrested. The three of us exchanged bemused glances across the table—the whole thing sounded bizarre and foolish. Joe hung up the phone, and we speculated—what if someone in Nixon's inner circle knew about this? It hardly seemed likely at the time.

Two years later, following my graduation from law school and a yearlong clerkship on the U.S. Court of Appeals in Richmond, Lynda and I were moving back to Northern Virginia on August 9, 1974. As we drove north on Interstate 95, with six-year-old Lucinda and four-year-old Catherine playing in the back seat, we listened on the radio as Richard Nixon became the first and only president to resign his office.

We faced the grim news with mixed emotions. There's a common bond between First Families that develops under the intense spotlight of public life because few people can empathize with their unusual position. At the time of Nixon's resignation, there were only twenty-nine living members of First Families and no other living former presidents. The Nixons were closer to us than other First Families because of proximity—Nixon succeeded Lynda's father as president of the United States, and their daughters were only a few years younger than Lynda. We had become good personal friends with Julie Nixon Eisenhower and David Eisenhower, and remain so to this day. Lynda and I had attended Tricia Nixon's wedding to Eddie Cox in 1971 in the Rose Garden, where Lynda had danced with the president while I danced with First Lady Pat Nixon. We couldn't help but feel a certain sadness and compassion for the Nixon family during their time of trial.

Yet, for all our understanding for his family, President Nixon had clearly broken a bond of trust between the people and our elected representatives that would not be easily repaired.

It would have been easy, during that time of mistrust of politicians, to decide that I wanted nothing to do with the practice of government. But I believed that politics could be about service. I saw government the same way as my grandfather, Robert Woolley, when he wrote, in an unpublished manuscript housed at the Library of Congress, that "an American citizen's most important duty is to realize that politics—no matter how offensive it be to the sensitive, lofty nostril—is the science of government, and to delve into it; to know that this great-hearted nation of ours is humanity's beacon of hope; that our first business is to safeguard our government so it may continue, strong and free, to assist a prostrate world to its feet once more."[1]

10

Stepping into the Fray

ON AUGUST 15, 1974, less than a week after Nixon's resignation, the *Richmond News Leader* ran a story with the headline, "Challenge: LBJ's Son-in-Law Ponders Politics." It was more of a personality profile than a hard-hitting news piece, but the reporter intimated that I might have a future in politics, despite the fact that I had told him I had no plans to do so. "Robb . . . does not give the impression that he would enjoy the limelight," the story acknowledged.

The truth was that Lynda and I were happy that during my three years at law school—from the fall of 1970 to the spring of 1973—the public attention on our family had waned. We lived in a small house in the college town of Charlottesville, endeavoring to raise our daughters in as ordinary an atmosphere as possible. In some ways, this time was the closest thing to "normal" life we would ever experience. At that point, stepping into the public spotlight was not on my mind.

Following my graduation from law school, I was fortunate to land a clerkship with Judge John D. Butzner Jr. on the Fourth Circuit of the U.S. Court of Appeals, headquartered in Richmond, Virginia. Gentlemanly, scholarly, and highly respected, Judge Butzner was a broadminded man who always took a personal interest in his law clerks. In addition to imparting the finer points of the law, he taught me about everything from the architectural history of Richmond to the art of fly fishing. Judge Butzner became a mentor of sorts, and years later, when I was governor, he would bring his law clerks up to the Capitol to meet me, a gesture I found quite touching.

I enjoyed the work, and as a bonus I didn't have to worry about clients or billable hours. The position made me think that perhaps I could be content as a judge and live up to my childhood nickname, "the little judge." As it was, the yearlong clerkship would end up being a distinct highlight of my short legal career.

With our move back to the D.C. area in the fall of 1974, I became an associate attorney at Williams, Connolly and Califano, the firm where I'd been a summer associate during law school. Lynda and I were ready to settle into post–law school family life. We had previously purchased a plot of land on Chain Bridge Road in McLean, Virginia, and were building a home there. My new career as a lawyer was just getting started, but I found myself increasingly restless. Williams, Connolly and Califano was renowned for taking on difficult, high-profile cases, and it was often fascinating to work with their stable of top-notch attorneys. Yet, without really intending to do so, I found myself paying closer attention to politics in Virginia.

Virginia is a state that defies easy characterization, politically or otherwise. The state stretches from the Atlantic Ocean to deep in the Appalachian Mountains, and its southwestern tip pushes farther west than Detroit, Michigan. From the progressive D.C. suburbs, to conservative rural lumber towns along the North Carolina border, Virginia is a state of deep and persistent contradiction. The state was both the home of the capital of the Confederacy during the Civil War and, in 1989, became the first state to elect an African American governor. Even today, while home to some of the most successful tech companies in the country, a significant part of Virginia's economy is driven by agriculture. The state has never been easy to wedge into a single description.

In the early 1970s, Virginia's political landscape was equally hard to nail down. At the beginning of the twentieth century, the state government, dominated by conservative southern Democrats, enacted a series of Jim Crow laws that codified segregation, even enshrining it in the state constitution. By severely restricting suffrage in the state, the segregationist Democrats maintained power by controlling public offices at every level, from the local sheriff to the chief executive. In the 1920s, this political clique came under the control of Harry F. Byrd Sr., who was Virginia's governor from 1926 to 1930, and then served in the U.S. Senate for more than thirty years. Byrd ran the conservative, segregationist political operation that became known as the "Byrd Machine," the "Byrd Organization," or simply the "the Organization." The Byrd Machine continued to control the ballot box, suppressing African American votes, handpicking candidates, and holding state elections on odd-numbered years, ensuring that conservative state Democrats would never have to share the same ballot with their more progressive national Democratic counterparts.

At the same time, Virginia was the origin of several of the Supreme Court cases that chipped away at segregation. The cases that outlawed interstate bus segregation (*Irene Morgan v. Virginia*) and segregation at interstate bus terminals (*Boynton v. Virginia*), making it easier for people of color to travel anywhere in the country, began in Virginia. The aptly named *Loving v. Virginia,* which legalized interracial marriage, began with a couple in Caroline County. And one of the five cases that would become *Brown v. Board of Education* began in Prince Edward County, Virginia.

It was the response to *Brown v. Board* by the Byrd Machine that became what is known as "Massive Resistance." Making a stand opposing school integration, the Byrd Machine went to work, passing new state laws and policies to prevent integration by reassigning pupils, giving tuition grants, and, finally, closing down public schools that attempted to integrate. These policies were struck down by the court, and with much local resistance, Virginia's schools were slowly integrated, beginning in 1959.

Harry Byrd Sr. retired in 1965 and died a year later, and the Byrd political machine began to lose power. Virginia Democrats began attempting to mold a new post-Byrd party, but leaving behind a deeply entrenched segregationist past would be very difficult.

This shift came as the national political parties were changing, too. Against the backdrop of the civil rights movement, 1960s counterculture, and an increasingly unpopular war in Vietnam, the national Democratic Party embraced civil rights and became more vocally antiwar. Southern segregationist Democratic voters, previously a part of FDR's New Deal Coalition, began shifting over to the increasingly conservative Republican Party. Virginia, which had previously been a Democratic stronghold for presidential candidates, went for Richard Nixon in 1968 by more than ten percentage points. In the contest for the Virginia governorship, the election of moderate Republican Linwood Holton, who opposed Massive Resistance, in 1969 ended an eighty-four-year uninterrupted hold on the office by Democrats. The exodus of moderate voters from the Virginia Democratic Party was accelerated by George McGovern's failed 1972 campaign for the presidency. McGovern's declaration that he would "crawl on my hands and knees" to Hanoi in order to secure the release of POWs struck a sour note with many Democrats, including me. A Democratic presidential candidate wouldn't win Virginia again until Barack Obama, four decades later.

By the early 1970s, Virginia's Democratic Party was at a crossroads over whether it would stick to its conservative past or step into line with the more liberal national party. The bad news for Democrats was that its influence was waning and its direction was unclear. The good news was that the situation, as dire as it was, provided both the impetus and opportunity to reform the party.

My own politics at the time were no more clear-cut than those of my state. My parents had each come into their marriage belonging to different political parties and religions—my father was a Presbyterian and a Republican, and my mother was an Episcopalian and a Democrat. They decided for practical reasons to agree on one of each, so my siblings and I were raised Republican and Episcopalian, though we were never particularly dogmatic about either. My parents later told me that by the 1964 presidential race, both had decided to become Democrats and had voted for President Johnson.

There are many elected officials who felt driven from an early age toward politics or made heroes of the political idols of their youth. This was not true in my case. Even if they were being particularly flattering, I don't think that my siblings would ever say that they "always knew" that I'd run for office.

I had been elected as class president in the tenth grade, and as a student senator at the University of Wisconsin. But these were less political races than they were popularity contests, and neither role had many actual duties. If there is something to be taken from those experiences, it is that I enjoyed the challenge of leadership.

As an active-duty Marine Corps officer, I hadn't been particularly political, but my experiences speaking on college campuses in 1969 and 1970 as head of the Platoon Leaders Class (PLC) program had an impact. As the *Washington Post* reported in 1981: "It was as a result of his experiences talking to antagonistic college students that Robb began to think about politics. He said he got a visceral feeling that he could 'bring people together and develop a sense of personal respect and communications.'"[1]

Of course, when I married Lynda, I was exposed to politics in a whole new way. And while my political views were certainly affected by my father-in-law, I was influenced by a number of different people. One politician I had always admired was Senator Henry "Scoop" Jackson, who served as a representative and then a senator from Washington State from 1941 to 1983. He was a Democrat who was liberal on social issues, a staunch supporter of civil rights and protecting the environment, but tough on national defense and fiscal responsibility—positions that aligned with my own long-held views.

I admired the way that Jackson put his own values ahead of party politics. As my friend Senator John McCain, who served as a military liaison officer to Jackson before entering politics himself, said in his last book, *The*

Restless Wave: "Scoop Jackson's opposition to Soviet tyranny and aggression, and his support for the world's oppressed, made him as much of an irritant to Jimmy Carter's administration as he had been to the governments of Richard Nixon and Gerald Ford. Scoop had his convictions, he believed in America's mission, and when it came to acting on his beliefs, he didn't particularly give a damn which party was in power. America's ideals came before party loyalty for him."[2] Jackson would become something of a guiding star for me in politics, and I would proudly call myself a "Scoop Jackson Democrat" for many years to come.

I'd taken two small steps into a slightly more political and public realm while I was in law school. The first was when I was elected as president of the Student Legal Forum. My principal responsibility was to persuade provocative leaders in the fields of law, government, and the media to address the university community and stimulate discussion of current issues. In the most recent years, the Forum had hosted only a handful of speakers each year, but this was the twenty-fifth anniversary, and I set my sights on procuring twenty-five thought-provoking speakers.

The final roster of speakers was varied. We had Vice President Spiro Agnew, former vice president Hubert Humphrey, future vice president Nelson Rockefeller, future president George H. W. Bush, sitting Supreme Court justices Earl Warren and Thurgood Marshall (both off the record), legendary reporters Walter Cronkite and Howard K. Smith, civil rights activists, and prominent members of Congress from both sides of the aisle.

The night that stuck with me, however, was hosting Allard Lowenstein, an energetic and provocative former one-term congressman, known as the leader of the "Dump LBJ" movement. Some may have thought it was odd for me to invite him—especially since LBJ was still living at the time—but in fact, the former president expressed enthusiasm for my choice. Even at the dedication of his own presidential library, my father-in-law said that he hoped that his administration would be presented openly and frankly— "with the bark off."

After his speech to the crowd in Charlottesville, as I walked Lowenstein to his car, he turned to me unexpectedly and said, "Let's go to your house and have a drink." Lowenstein intrigued me, so I agreed, and we spent an unexpectedly pleasant and entertaining evening discussing life and politics over a couple of beers in my Charlottesville kitchen. By the time we parted ways in the early-morning hours, I felt like we had developed an unusual bond. In fact, when he ran again for Congress in 1974, he asked me to cut a commercial for him, and I did, with a pitch I could make in good conscience: *Congress couldn't function with 435 Al Lowensteins, but having one to keep us on our toes would be healthy.*

Each of the twenty-five speeches of the Student Legal Forum drew sizeable crowds, and my role as a kind of master of ceremonies increased my public profile and left me with a certain political credibility, serving as a "coming out" of sorts.

My first experience with a political campaign came around the same time, in the fall of 1972, when a classmate named Jack Young happened to give me a *Law Review* article about Virginia's Senator William Spong Jr. With large tortoiseshell glasses and a low-key speaking style, Spong seemed to relish his lack of sparkle, once describing himself as a "low-visibility" senator.

Spong took a principled stance supporting busing as a tool of public school integration at a time when, in the wake of Virginia's Massive Resistance, integration of public schools was still a very contentious issue. In 1966, Spong's Democratic primary victory against Senator A. Willis Robertson (father of future Christian televangelist Pat Robertson) was the first defeat of the Byrd Machine in Virginia.

The *Law Review* article that Jack Young gave me described Spong's approach to two controversial Supreme Court nominations by President Nixon: Clement Haynsworth and G. Harrold Carswell. What struck me wasn't so much Spong's positions but his approach. He had taken each nomination on its merits and, through careful argument, not political calculus, had come to a decision independent of his party's line. It was exactly what I thought we needed in government. So, I decided to pitch in on Spong's 1972 reelection effort by ghostwriting a number of op-eds in the local and student newspapers.

Spong's Republican opponent focused his attacks on Spong's progressive social positions, running racially charged radio ads in rural areas attacking Spong relentlessly on the busing issue. Unfortunately, there was enough lingering opposition to civil rights in Virginia at the time that the tactic worked, and Spong was defeated in 1972.

Two years later, while working at Williams, Connolly and Califano, I decided to make another foray into politics by joining the Fairfax County Democratic Committee. It was the best way to meet local activists, pay some of my dues at the grassroots level, and better understand the inner workings of the party. A short time later, I won my first elective race since my university days: a spot on the State Central Committee, the state party's governing body.

By 1976, I was spending my nights and weekends on political pursuits—State Central Committee sessions, candidate meet-and-greet events, and local meetings—but I was still working full-time at Williams, Connolly and Califano. After two years with the local party, I found myself increasingly intrigued by the possibility of running for office.

IN THE SUMMER of 1976, I made plans to attend the state Democratic convention. A longtime White House photographer for United Press International and a friend from my days as a White House military social aide, Roddy Mims, said to me: "Governor [his nickname for me], let me come along to the convention. I'll show you how we can get something started." I wasn't the only friend Roddy called "governor," but I did think it had a nice ring to it.

At the convention, Roddy trailed me with his cameras everywhere I went. I still hadn't met many of Virginia's delegates and party activists by that point, but when I came up to shake their hands with a photographer snapping pictures of my every move, it certainly made an impression. Roddy took photographs of me with hundreds of delegates. He knew that little gesture would create buzz, boosting my visibility, and, ultimately, my candidacy.

Elected office was a type of public service that I felt confident that I could be good at—leading efforts to solve people's policy problems. The appeal was squarely in the service element rather than the rough-and-tumble of politics. And at some point during my courtship by Virginia Democrats, like an athlete who's just joined a new team, I grew more and more enthusiastic about the possibilities for change in our state. I felt a sense of challenge and potential satisfaction at what leading Virginia might bring. In the end, running for office seemed like the natural next step.

Aiming for a local office, such as a position on a school board, would have been the conventional choice, but my competitive nature drove me to seek something bigger: I eventually wanted to run for governor. In order to get there, I planned to run first for lieutenant governor.

That year, the office of lieutenant governor had no clear and deserving heir apparent, but I made sure that, before I decided to run, I met with the two other serious potential Democratic candidates—State Senators Hunter Andrews and L. Douglas Wilder. I told them each bluntly, "If you plan to run, I won't." Both said they had no plans to run in the upcoming cycle and graciously deferred.

Lynda, however, was less enthusiastic about my foray into elective politics. She knew that a career as a politician would open up our lives to public scrutiny in a way that a career as a lawyer, a businessman, or a Marine never would. Lynda had been in the public eye for most of her life, knew the toll that it had taken on her father and family, and she was understandably anxious about the prospect of inviting the glare of that often withering spotlight back onto our family. My decision to run was a big adjustment for her—in a married life where, admittedly, she was already making more adjustments to suit me than the other way around.

In August 1977, *People* magazine ran a three-page story with our fairly frank comments about the situation. Lynda, whom they described as "painfully rethinking her whole life," said: "It's fine for me to have a career, but I should have my career wherever he's living and make sure I have dinner ready. And of course, I'll go to the PTA and get the two children to school."[3]

Lynda knew the stresses of the campaign. "I knew the long hours, I knew the stress level, and how hard it was on the children," she said later.

Amusingly, the article also related that "grandma Lady Bird Johnson is of the old school and more supportive of Chuck than of her own daughter."[4]

Ultimately, in spite of all of her reasonable and understandable reservations, Lynda had faith in my ability to do the job. Lynda was an essential support in every campaign I ran in—she was, after all, the daughter of President Lyndon Johnson, a political titan, and Lady Bird Johnson, the first First Lady to actively campaign with her husband. At events where I was scheduled to speak, Lynda would visit every table and work the crowd like the seasoned professional that she was.

"I'm really shy," she'd later admit, "but I knew you have to go out and grab people and introduce yourself."

Lynda knew that I had a deeply ingrained disdain for self-promotion, which, in a system that involves a lot of self-aggrandizement, was a sizeable handicap.

"I could say things about him that Chuck couldn't say about himself," Lynda later said. "When all was said and done, although I wouldn't have chosen for Chuck to go into politics, I supported his decision because I thought he'd be a good public servant."

At least that assured me that I'd get her vote.

At the very end of 1976, during the political news void between Christmas and New Year's Day, I sent out a short press release to formally announce my candidacy for the Democratic nomination for the office of lieutenant governor of Virginia.

Almost immediately, one opponent dubbed me an "Instant Virginian." Although my ancestors had a long and politically active history in Virginia dating back to the 1600s, to many in the state I was still an outsider because I had been born in Arizona and had actually only lived in Virginia for a few years as a teenager and again as an adult.

To establish my bona fides, Lynda compiled an extensive family tree for the race. I didn't realize just how entrenched in Virginia history my family had been until Lynda turned up direct Virginia forebearers who had fought in the Revolutionary War and the Civil War and even several politicians. It turned out that my paternal great-grandfather, James Robb, had fought for the Union army and was wounded in the Battle of Cold Harbor outside of Mechanicsville, Virginia, while I also had ancestors who fought for the Confederacy. Through my paternal grandmother, I'm descended from the Lewis family, a prominent early Virginia family that included Revolutionary War commander Andrew Lewis. Lewis commanded the Virginia forces at the Battle of Point Pleasant, where his niece's husband and my fifth-great-grandfather, Captain John Frogge, was killed in what is considered by some to be the first battle of the Revolutionary War.

The story of my mother's family in Virginia went all the way back to the 1600s, when one of my direct forebearers, Arthur Allen, served as speaker of the House of Burgesses in Colonial Williamsburg.

A few generations later, George Alfred Trenholm, my maternal great-great-grandfather, was a successful shipping magnate who cut a wide swath through the seaport society of Charleston, South Carolina. Trenholm served as the second secretary of the treasury for the Confederate States of America from July 1864 until April 1865 and owned a merchant firm with sixty ships that served as blockade-runners during the war, surreptitiously delivering supplies for the South through the Union blockade of southern ports. Described by contemporaries as tall and handsome, Trenholm was a dashing figure, and it is widely believed that Rhett Butler, the character in *Gone with the Wind,* was based on him.

My family was descended from these Allens, Trenholms, Howards, de Graffenrieds, Lewises, and Robbs whose houses, gravesites, birthplaces, and battlefields were sprinkled across Virginia. We even wrote up a list of all of the counties with connections to my family so that Lynda and I could point them out when we were speaking in the area.

On the trail, I found myself repeatedly reciting the list of my Virginian ancestry for reporters or using a line that my mother, who had been born in Fairfax, Virginia, suggested herself: "Well, I'd like to have been born here, but at the same time I felt I should be with my mother!"

There were also advantages to my "outsider" status. I was not tainted by the legacy of segregation in Virginia politics. For decades, the state's seg-regationist Byrd political machine required candidates to toe their line in order to win the Democratic Party's nomination. But now, in the late 1970s, the ground had begun to shift. Having entered Virginia politics after the power of the Byrd political machine had waned, I didn't have a track record with the party's segregationist past—which had now become a liability for more seasoned politicians.

I enjoyed high name recognition among the voters, but my notoriety was a double-edged sword. Some remained unhappy with LBJ's still controver-sial legacy of the Vietnam War and his efforts to promote civil rights in the South. This was especially tough in Virginia, where questions regarding civil rights were just as troubling as those regarding the war. And in the Old Dominion, "the war" could refer to either Vietnam or the Civil War. A poll taken prior to the campaign showed that voters were two-to-one negative on my Johnson connection.

On the other hand, my status as a minor celebrity did give people a peg upon which to hang their recollections of me. If I managed to leave a good impression in a speech or one-on-one encounter, my name recognition gave me a better chance of being remembered positively at the polls. In a way, I benefited from a combination of the name recognition and *lowered* expectations thanks to mixed feelings about President Johnson.

I made it through a tough primary election against two members of the Virginia House of Delegates: Richard S. "Major" Reynolds, scion of a respected Virginia family, and the more liberal-leaning Ira Lechner. My Republican opponent in the general election was Joe Canada, a two-term state senator from Virginia Beach. Joe was a big, friendly lawyer, more of a good old boy than a policy wonk. I knew he'd be a tough opponent, and the current state of the Democratic Party wasn't going to help.

The Democratic slate that year highlighted the deep divisions in the post-Byrd Virginia Democratic Party. Our gubernatorial nominee, former lieutenant governor Henry Howell, was adored by the more liberal base of the party, while our nominee for attorney general, Ed Lane, was a die-hard conservative and a favorite of the old Byrd political machine. So, the Democratic ticket in the general election for statewide office in Virginia in 1977 was a liberal (Howell), a moderate (me), and a conservative (Lane), leading Howell to quickly dub it the "Rainbow Ticket."

I hit the general campaign trail with vigor, traveling the state with my family and campaign staff in a van dubbed the "Chuckwagon." My family was unquestionably a major asset on the campaign trail. Our daughters Lucinda and Catherine, by now nine and seven, enjoyed getting into the action, wearing T-shirts with the message, "Win or Lose, We Get Our Daddy Back," and making posters. Catherine ended up painting the simple slogan "Vote for My Daddy" on a poster after "lieutenant governor" proved too much for a seven-year-old to tackle.

Lynda crisscrossed the state with and without me. At one campaign stop, she was being driven to a parade in Louisa County by my loyal aide Ben Dendy. Ben was only nineteen years old at the time, a political wunderkind who, though he was young, still had more political experience in Virginia than I had at the time. Ben hadn't yet graduated from college, but he was determined to do the job, so he took a year off to work on the campaign.

The plan was for Lynda to ride in the Louisa County parade with an important local supporter, but Ben got lost in the countryside, they fell behind schedule, and the parade started without them. Undeterred, Ben drove right across a cornfield to catch up with the tail end of the parade. They taped a campaign placard on the side of his VW Bug, Lynda hopped on the hood of the car, and the two of them drove along, bringing up the rear of the parade. The people loved it, applauding my hard-charging wife around every bend in the road.

Lynda's mother very graciously agreed to make campaign appearances for me as well, traveling up from Texas several times during the campaign season to help out. She also gathered a group of some of her old friends — mostly other wives of U.S. senators — in the living room of our McLean home and, over cookies and lemonade, wrote personal notes inviting Virginia notables to some of my fundraisers.

Predictably, there was some backlash against the "star quality" of my campaign, as some Republicans criticized both up-and-coming Virginia Republican John Warner — who'd recently married actress Elizabeth Taylor — and me for "famous-wife syndrome."

My crucial support wasn't just from big names, though. Even organized labor, which was troubled by the pro-business leanings Ed Lane and I espoused, ended up reluctantly endorsing the Democratic ticket with the less-than-enthusiastic comment, "They may be turkeys, but they're OUR turkeys!"

The most personally meaningful demonstrations of support came from two retired Marines with whom I'd served—Sergeants Major Elmer Koren and J. J. Carroll. These men, who did not know each other, each independently reached out to my campaign and offered help. Koren and Carroll had been senior enlisted Marines (noncommissioned officers) when I was a younger commissioned officer. Koren had been a first sergeant in my ROTC program at the University of Wisconsin, and Carroll had served as my company first sergeant in Vietnam. Officers in the military are senior in rank to noncommissioned officers, so it isn't uncommon for relations between upstart young officers and older noncommissioned officers to be a little strained. During our time serving together, I had tried to be highly respectful of each man's skills and knowledge, and, as a result, my relationships with Sergeants Major Koren and Carroll had always been good. But I never expected that these two nonpolitical men would voluntarily enter the political arena to publicly endorse me and hold events for me in their neighborhoods. Carroll even cut a short TV commercial for the campaign. Despite many more high-profile endorsements, earning the support of my fellow Marines in my very first bid for public office was one of my proudest moments.

By the fall of 1977, the campaign was in high gear, and the schedule was occasionally hectic to the point of absurdity. There were naturally times when Lynda and I didn't see each other for several days, as we split up to cover as much of the state as possible. We tried to talk by telephone every night, but, before cell phones, that meant we had to plan to be near a stationary telephone while we were on the road.

In late September, our paths did cross in the small railroad town of Crewe, Virginia, where Lynda was scheduled to attend the annual dinner meeting of the Southside Electric Co-Op in the evening and I was set to address the business meeting the following morning.

I began my speech the next day by declaring, with an ear-to-ear grin: "Happiness is unexpectedly getting to spend the night with your wife on the campaign trail!" Nine months later to the day, our daughter Jennifer arrived, our third child in a planned family of two. For a while after Jennifer's birth, the motel where we had spent the night even displayed an amusing commemorative plaque in the room in which we had stayed.

NOVEMBER 8, 1977, was a tough day for Virginia Democrats. Henry Howell lost to John Dalton in a landslide, the third Republican gubernatorial victory in a row. Our Democratic nominee for attorney general, Ed Lane, lost to up-and-coming Republican state senator Marshall Coleman. But when the votes were counted, I'd been elected lieutenant governor by eight percentage points—a margin of almost one hundred thousand votes. The biggest surprise was how many Virginians chose to split their ticket—vote for two different parties for statewide elected officials—which made my victory possible.

On Inauguration Day in Richmond in January 1978, I stood on the platform above the Capitol steps wearing the traditional dark morning coat and top hat. Though I may have looked as somber as an undertaker, I was excited to be sworn into office for the first time.

By the time we left the last inaugural ball that night it was well past midnight, but we drove straight from the festivities to our home in McLean, two hours north. We'd received news that our old friend, former vice president Hubert H. Humphrey, had died that morning, and we wanted to make sure we would be able to attend a memorial service at the Capitol in D.C. early the next day.

Humphrey had served as vice president to Lynda's father, and both Lynda and I had liked and admired him for years. Nicknamed the "Happy Warrior," Humphrey was loquacious and energetic, a man of indomitable spirit.

When I was serving as president of the Student Legal Forum at UVA Law School, Humphrey had given the most stirring speech of the year. Drawing an overflow crowd, he contrasted his vision of America with that of then president Richard Nixon, closing with the lines of poet Carl Sandburg: "I see America, not in the setting sun of a black night of despair ahead of us. I see America in the crimson light of a rising sun fresh from the burning, creative hand of God. I see great days ahead, great days possible to men and women of will and vision."[5]

The last time Lynda and I had seen Humphrey was at our home in McLean a few months before his death. The weather couldn't have been nicer, so before heading inside, he and I stood in our driveway talking and reminiscing until Lynda finally asked us to step in for lunch. Humphrey had been ill for some time and was undergoing treatment for bladder cancer, but he clearly yearned to run for the Democratic presidential nomination one last time. Even as his body was failing him, his heart never faltered, and I could see the passion and raw emotion he radiated. Sadly, Hubert Humphrey would never have another chance to run for office.

When we arrived at the U.S. Capitol that Sunday for the memorial service, Lynda and I joined her mother at a small gathering of mostly past and present First Family members and congressional leaders. We arrived at about the same time as the Nixons, and I soon found myself, completely by chance, in a conversation with former president Richard Nixon and his former secretary of state, Henry Kissinger. Because I was not an intimate of either man, I didn't expect our conversation to be anything more than pleasantries and reminiscences about Humphrey. As we began to talk, however, it seemed apparent to me that the other two men hadn't had a meaningful face-to-face conversation since Nixon had resigned the presidency in 1974. In the interim, much had been said in the press about both men and their complex relationship during a troubled presidency.

As I stood between the former president and his former secretary of state, who were engaged in an unusually stilted dialogue and using me as a buffer for their mutual discomfort, I thought about how even those who have reached the height of political power are still, inevitably, human.

A short time later, we filed into the Capitol Rotunda. The memorial service for Humphrey was fittingly moving, particularly for Lynda, who had made a point of finding Humphrey campaign paraphernalia and wore a green and white scarf decorated with his emblematic "HHH." Vice President Walter "Fritz" Mondale, not known as an inspiring orator, delivered a touching eulogy for his former mentor that echoed through the Rotunda and ended with words I would never forget: "He taught us all how to hope and how to live, how to win and how to lose, and in the end, he taught us how to die."[6]

I didn't agree with Hubert Humphrey on all of his policy positions, but I was in awe of his commitment to stand up for them, whether or not they were politically convenient. I will never be mistaken for Hubert Humphrey, either in substance or in tone. But I did hope, as I stood there on my first full day as an elected official, listening to the eulogies for this great man, that I could bring to my new career even a fraction of his conviction.

11

A Future Worthy of Her Past

A LITTLE OVER three years later, on May 30, 1981, at the state Democratic Party convention in Virginia Beach, former governor Colgate Darden officially placed my name into nomination to be the party's candidate for governor.

For me, Darden's participation was nearly as meaningful as the nomination itself. Darden was a true living link to Virginia history. Urbane and intellectual, with the genteel manners of an earlier age, Darden possessed formidable political skills, yet he radiated warmth and a complete lack of arrogance that rendered him very approachable. I admired him because, like Bill Spong, he was not a great orator or charismatic figure but a principled, dedicated public servant and an honorable citizen to the core. In short, he was a class act.

Though he had been retired from politics for more than three decades, I had visited Darden often during my term as lieutenant governor. I had benefited enormously from his sage counsel, and he became something of a political mentor to me as we talked endlessly about Virginia and its current political situation. Spending a few hours with Colgate Darden was like taking a whole course in Virginia's history. Despite his physical frailty at age eighty-four, his mind was as sharp as ever, and he counseled me to keep working to enlarge our party's vastly diminished tent.

When Governor Darden came out of retirement to place my name into nomination at the convention, it felt like an old-guard blessing, a kind of laying on of hands that sent a strong signal to a rejuvenating Democratic Party. His gesture was made even more poignant by the fact that it ended up being his last public appearance. One week after the convention, Colgate Darden died of heart failure. I wouldn't have his wise counsel to draw upon if I did become governor, but I would never forget the lessons he had taught me.

FOR ANYONE WHO even remotely followed Virginia politics, it had been clear since 1977 that I planned to run for governor in 1981.

In Virginia, the role of the lieutenant governor, in which I had been serving for the previous three years, was similar to that of the vice president of the United States, in that it doesn't have much constitutional or statutory authority. As one columnist so eloquently wrote, "The lieutenant governor in Virginia doesn't have the power to lead a troop of Boy Scouts on a 14-mile hike." It was said that the lieutenant governor's primary duty was to inquire every morning about the governor's health.

This was a $10,500-a-year, technically part-time job with limited duties: preside over the Virginia Senate during the two months of the year that it was in session, cast tie-breaking votes when the Senate deadlocked, and succeed to the higher office if anything renders the governor unable to complete the term.

This point was driven home when I learned, after the election, that the administration wasn't planning to allot the lieutenant governor an office big enough to house my staff. So I took over a square three-story red-brick structure standing in the corner of Capitol Square called the Bell Tower, which had been previously used, among other things, as an arms depository and a fertilizer storehouse. We barely fit inside the tiny, spartan space, and there was no bathroom or running water, but it was close to the Capitol and had a kind of old-fashioned Richmond charm.

Though the lieutenant governorship brought with it little official room for building a political or policy platform, serving in that role gave me good practical political experience and relationship building. But I may not have gotten off to a very auspicious start the first time that I presided over the Virginia Senate. Using a gavel that Lynda had had specially made for me, carved from the wood of a 175-year-old oak tree that had recently fallen at Arlington House, I opened the Senate and bellowed procedural statements that I had been studying since my election in November. However, when the Senate proceedings reached a pause, and I should have announced a "recess," I instead boomed out, "The Senate will stand at ease!" The senators had a good chuckle at my expense. In the end, presiding at the State Capitol allowed me to get to know the many personalities and power brokers on the Senate floor and around it—the formal and informal networks and relationships that together created a lawmaking body.

Graciously—and no doubt to the dismay of some of his party's faithful—Governor John Dalton also invited me, a member of the opposite party, to attend cabinet meetings, an experience that allowed me to study the personnel management and daily tasks of the governorship up close. I could evaluate departments in action and see firsthand how the sometimes in-scrutable gears turned in the governor's office.

By the time that I stepped into the office, the post of lieutenant governor had been increasingly seen as a potential stepping-stone for those interested in running for governor. And the lieutenant governor was often in compe-tition for that office with the attorney general, a full-time position that has a much more substantive, and higher-profile, role as the state's chief lawyer. Virginia's then attorney general, Republican Marshall Coleman, quickly emerged as my primary rival for the office of governor. Governor Dalton had done an admirable job but was limited by the state's constitution to a single term.

Coleman—a tall, trim, fair-haired politician with an occasionally bit-ing wit—began his political career as president of the student body at the University of Virginia, later rising to prominence as a relatively progressive "Mountain Republican" in the Virginia Senate. He had a whole catalogue of attractive qualities: a winning personality, a sharp intellect, and a young family.

Coleman was especially strong in 1981, in the first year of the feel-good Reagan Revolution. Virginia's Republican Party was robust and upbeat, still riding the coattails of the Reagan victory and the twelve straight years of Republicans holding the governorship in Virginia. They also held one of Virginia's two seats in the U.S. Senate (the other was held by Harry Byrd Jr., who was now an Independent) and claimed nine of the then ten Virginia seats in the U.S. House of Representatives.

Finally, Coleman would enjoy the support of the outgoing Republican governor, which would translate into significant financial backing and votes in November. By most objective criteria, Coleman entered the race as the favorite.

As political pundits were quick to point out, Coleman and I were also similar in many ways: we had both served in the Marine Corps, we were the heirs apparent of our respective political parties, and we were relatively young. On Election Day, Coleman would be thirty-nine years old, and I would be forty-two—both young enough to become the second-youngest Virginian to hold the state's highest office, behind only Thomas Jefferson. Our apparent similarities were so great, in fact, that the punditry took to calling us "Tweedledum and Tweedledee."

While Coleman may have been seen as the front-runner, I wasn't starting off from a bad position either. Perhaps the biggest advantage I had coming into the race was still name recognition, which gave me a critical opening to better introduce myself to the public and create a positive impression. But I could also point to my efforts as lieutenant governor to promote education, economic development, and tourism. My work with organizations such as the Virginia Forum on Education, which I helped to found and then served as its chairman, gave me the opportunity to discuss challenges with the state's leaders in education and hone my policy goals on the topic. My work allowed me to travel all over the state, meeting constituents and developing a deeper understanding of the specific challenges of Virginia's diverse regions.

Additionally, my tenure as lieutenant governor had given me the opportunity to rebuild confidence in the Virginia Democratic Party and broaden the definition of a Virginia Democrat. As the highest elected official in my party in the state and de facto head of the state party, I believed that I had a responsibility to attempt to bridge the widening gap between the party's more conservative and more liberal wings. Not long after assuming office, I had put together an informal commission aimed at finding a strategy to improve the Democratic Party's fortunes in Virginia, headed by the politician who had so impressed me a few years earlier—former U.S. senator Bill Spong.

After months of research (and rounds of drafting executed principally by my extremely capable chief of staff, Stewart Gamage) the Spong Commission publicly released its report calling for the Virginia Democratic Party to move beyond catering to individual constituencies and toward a political agenda that addressed the needs of a broader section of Virginians. The report also called for a new party leader who was committed to taking our party in a new direction. Within a year, the Virginia Democratic Party had a new chairman, a new governing charter, and a new lease on life.

The new direction of the party fit well with my own nontraditional stances as a nondogmatic progressive Democrat. Liberal on social issues but fiscally conservative and supportive of a strong national defense, I didn't fit the mold of the national Democratic Party, and I could credibly reach a broad base of Virginians.

My position as a nontraditional Democrat put Coleman in a particularly tight spot. In 1977, he had run successfully for attorney general against Ed Lane, an old-school conservative Democrat. In that race, Coleman ran to Lane's left, boasting of a progressive record on civil rights, labor, education, and environmental issues. But the label of "liberal Republican" created a real challenge for Coleman in 1981, when his party had grown increasingly culturally conservative, and he was running against a more moderate Democrat. Worried about the implications of this perception, Coleman's most important Republican financial backers compelled him to switch gears and try to run against me from the right, a decision that would haunt him for most of the campaign.

But, in order to capitalize on the perception that Coleman had shifted positions for political expediency, I would need voters to trust me—a Democrat—as their alternative. My previous four years as lieutenant governor helped to establish me as a "known quantity" and showed voters that putting a Democrat in a statewide elected office did not bring the state government to a crashing halt. It also helped that I was not, as a politician or as a man, a particularly bombastic person. Virginians might have been scared off by a passionate orator, but my more establishment style and demeanor felt relatively safe. Politics is, after all, ultimately personal, and I had to meet a likeability bar before they felt comfortable voting for me, whatever party I belonged to.

As my campaign for governor got underway, I reached out to leaders and organizations representing the old guard that could lend an air of passing the torch without promoting the old segregationist policies that I was determined to bring to an end. I was pro–civil rights and against segregation—period. I won the critical support of such leaders as Elmon Gray, Roy Smith, and a nonpartisan group organized by independents and disenchanted Republicans who called themselves "Virginians for Robb." Continuing the theme of passing the torch, we chose an expression that struck a nice balance between tradition and progress: "For a future worthy of her past."

There was also an important constituency that I knew I would have to work hard to win over: the African American community. Though African Americans in Virginia almost always voted overwhelmingly Democratic, there seemed to be a lingering uncertainty about me, partly because I still had no documented record of any significance on civil rights. Luckily, I was aided by a trailblazer in the African American community.

Then the highest-ranking African American officeholder in the state, State Senator Doug Wilder was a fascinating figure in Virginia politics. The grandson of slaves, Doug had a street-fighting political style that reflected the struggle he'd faced in the political arena. He possessed a combination of political savvy, volatility, and intellect, and he had an instinctive knack for delivering the incisive remark that could cut a political opponent—or ally—to the core. Doug was a force to be reckoned with.

During my time as lieutenant governor, despite a few minor skirmishes, Doug and I developed a rapport and worked together well. I understood that Doug was passionate and outspoken, whereas I was much more buttoned-down and conventional. Though our styles were very different, we shared a mutual respect. I sought out Doug's support and friendship early in my political career, and for the better part of a decade, he and I had a good working relationship.

In my 1981 race for governor, Doug stepped in to help convince African American community leaders to formally endorse me, sending a signal to African American voters that I was worth taking a chance on.

With the support of important leaders in both the moderate and liberal wings of my party behind me, my next step was to explain my views to all Virginians. They weren't used to a Democrat who believed in both civil rights and fiscal responsibility, and I ran the risk that they would think I was pandering for votes. My reluctance to offer simple sound-bite responses on complex issues sometimes got me into trouble. Some felt that I had a tendency to waffle, when my goal was actually to understand both sides.

"A Robbian sentence . . . can be something to behold," wrote influential political columnist George Bowles. "Between the subject and predicate, the tortured trail of verbiage may lead the listener through a bewildering maze of qualifications, modifiers, parenthetical observations and illustrative digressions. His syntactical meanderings leave reporters gasping for breath and grasping for meaning."

I needed to show Virginians exactly where I stood. I saw my chance with our first gubernatorial debate in the spring of 1981, where I immediately took the offensive to draw a strong contrast between Coleman and myself on consistency.

I began by thanking the sponsor for "the opportunity to clear up some misunderstandings." With that, I turned to my opponent and said, "My good friend Marshall Coleman has said he has not always known where I stood."[1]

I proceeded to tick off my "for or against" positions on twenty-three hot-button issues such as tax cuts, the Equal Rights Amendment, and balancing the state budget. The list was by no means a litany of popular positions, and I admitted to the crowd that I was sure I would "offend everyone here with one of them."[2] Even though they were controversial, taking a clear position helped establish me as dependable and countered my lack of legislative history or public accomplishments.

Coleman, on the other hand, struggled throughout the debate to explain his shifting positions on the issues. Beads of sweat formed on his brow, and even he didn't appear to fully buy his own spin.

I kept up this theme throughout the campaign, trying to make sure that I stayed absolutely consistent in my positions. Liberal and conservative groups would get the same answer: I believed in reining in government spending, but I also believed in funding important social programs, such as education, and I would fight for higher teacher salaries. Knowing that I would stand by my convictions let voters know that they could trust me, even if they didn't agree with me on every point.

Meanwhile, I had to keep up the momentum in the campaign. I had a solid team behind me, led by the steady hand of my campaign manager, David Doak, who would go on to become a successful national media consultant. Doak was especially good at working with the various stakeholders, supporters, and advisors on the campaign, making them all feel listened to and keeping the train moving forward toward Election Day.

My family also played a critical role on the trail. I had been concerned that our daughters might not be as excited for this campaign because winning would mean some major adjustments. The governorship was a full-time position that would mean a move for the whole family to the Governor's Mansion in Richmond, where they would have to make new friends and attend new schools. Like most young children, though, our daughters had the gifts of optimism and resilience, and were ready to make plans for their new home even before the race began. Jennifer, who was then three, remembers that for a while she thought my name was "Chuck Robb for Governor."

Lynda convinced her mother to again campaign for me by reminding her, in a loving way, that "I campaigned for your husband—now I want you to campaign for mine!" Mrs. Johnson graciously agreed to make several appearances, but even more importantly, she spent time looking after her three granddaughters so Lynda could join me on the campaign trail.

Lynda continued to be the best weapon in my arsenal. While I was serving as lieutenant governor, she had taken several of her own steps into the public eye. In 1979, she accepted an appointment by President Carter to chair the President's Advisory Committee for Women, replacing Bella Abzug, the outspoken New York congresswoman and feminist. Lynda proved to be a brilliant choice to lead the commission: she could express her support for the Equal Rights Amendment without being accused of opposing motherhood since she'd just given birth to our third child.

"I want to be a bridge between some of the women who've been very active and some of those who haven't been identified as being involved," Lynda said when she took the position.[3]

Some of my advisors worried that my wife's involvement as a women's rights advocate might hurt me in conservative Virginia, the only southern state Carter failed to carry in the 1976 election. But I wholeheartedly supported Lynda's work on issues such as women's health, education, and the ERA, and some electoral math wasn't going to dampen that support in the slightest.

On the trail in 1981, Lynda traversed the back roads of Virginia, going to a lot of the places where my own appeal might have been more limited. Virginia was a very courteous state, and even someone who might not agree with me wouldn't dream of being mean to a lady. Many of these voters had grown up watching Lynda in the White House, and a great many had watched our wedding on national TV only thirteen years earlier.

Lynda managed to gain support even from those skeptical Virginians who still viewed me as an interloper, despite my deep ancestral roots, by once again tapping into the Robb family genealogy. She found ancestors of mine buried in almost every cemetery in the Commonwealth to reinforce my Virginia pedigree.

I didn't fully appreciate at the time all of the ways that Lynda was helping our campaign. She had learned the lessons well from her own mother, who, when asked what she did to help her husband get elected, said, "I went behind him all the time and said, 'Thank you!' to all his staff and supporters." Thankfully, Lynda did the same for me.

Running with me were two solid candidates: Richard "Dick" Davis for lieutenant governor, and Gerald "Jerry" Baliles for attorney general. Importantly, the three of us agreed on the major issues, so we could run as a closely linked ticket without having to explain away our differences. It reinforced the image of the Democrats as solid and trustworthy and gave voters no reason to split their ticket.

As expected, the race went right down to the wire. Both Coleman and I expressed confidence leading up to Election Day, but I knew that, realistically, the tally could go either way.

At just after midnight on the evening of November 4, 1981, I made my way down to the ballroom of Richmond's Hotel John Marshall, where I had announced my candidacy nine months earlier, took the podium, and faced the cheering throng. The results were in: I had been elected governor of Virginia with 54 percent of the vote to Coleman's 46 percent. Coleman was apparently so confident that he would win, he joked in his concession speech, that when the results came in and I had won, he thought that the numbers must have been reversed.

I had won with the support of both liberals and conservatives, and a significant margin came from moderates. In progressive Northern Virginia I was favored by as much as two to one, and statewide I won an overwhelming majority of the African American vote.

In many ways, politics is about the right combination of qualities at the right time. Four years earlier, I may not have been able to convince Virginians to vote for a Democrat for governor, but in 1981, I fit the bill. I was progressive on civil rights at a time when Virginia was trying to break free of its segregationist past, and conservative on fiscal issues when the country was concerned with reining in government spending. I was strong on national security in a state with deep ties to the military. I brought together two different sides of the Democratic spectrum that were willing to overlook disagreements to vote for someone they thought would move Virginia forward.

It was surprising enough that a Democrat had won the governorship, but when the results came in, it turned out that we had done something that had seemed impossible: we had swept all three statewide offices. In the four years since Henry Howell had lost in a landslide, and after a dramatic party upheaval that pitted the liberal wing against those hoping to broaden our base, we had managed to rejuvenate the Virginia Democratic Party.

At the Hotel John Marshall, with Lynda and our girls at my side, I leaned into the microphone and shouted the first words that came to mind, a phrase from the old *Jackie Gleason Show*—"How sweet it is!"—and the crowd went wild. Jennifer, however, who was just three at the time and up well past her bedtime, put her little head down on the podium, and the crowd roared.

It was hard not to feel, at that moment in time, that we were on the cusp of a new era in Virginia politics. Just how far we could go was anybody's guess.

12

No Higher Honor

ON THE MORNING of January 16, 1982, I woke at 6:45 a.m., had my usual breakfast—orange juice and raisin bran—in my Richmond apartment, and headed, for the last time, to my cramped lieutenant governor's office to return a few calls. I met up with my family at St. Paul's Episcopal Church for the traditional preinaugural service, then returned to my apartment to change into formal attire and hurried to the Hotel John Marshall for a reception. I didn't realize until I reached the hotel that the vest of my morning suit didn't easily fit over a new addition: my bulletproof vest. It was the first time that I had worn body armor since I was in combat in Vietnam. Today, I was wearing it under very different circumstances. This was the day that I was to become the governor of Virginia.

By the time of the ceremony, I was actually grateful that my new state police security detail had asked me to wear the bulletproof vest because it served as an extra layer of protection against the bitter cold of the 26-degree weather during the outdoor ceremony at the Virginia State Capitol. Unfortunately for me, I had made a decision not to wear the overcoat and top hat traditionally worn by the incoming governor in an attempt to symbolize a changing of the guard. I also knew that I looked silly in a top hat. And I may have broken the spell—no governor since has worn a top hat to his inauguration.

Spectators did anything they could to keep warm, many wearing multiple layers of long underwear under their suits and dresses. Alice DuBois, a hearty seventy-year-old supporter, told the *Washington Post* that her guard against the chill was "a slug of Geritol and a bottle of bourbon."[1]

The United States Marine Drum and Bugle Corps made a special trip to Richmond to lead my inaugural parade, but the cold was so intense that many of the instruments simply didn't play. Clarinetists walked in front of the parade stand miming the "Marines' Hymn" while the horns made up the difference.

I stood up to the podium to take the oath of office as Lynda held the Bible, the same Bible that Lynda's mother had held for President Johnson when he was sworn in back in 1965. Virginia Supreme Court chief justice Harry L. Carrico stood across from me to administer the oath. The crowd hushed.

"Place your right hand on the Bible with your right hand raised," Justice Carrico said. The crowd broke into laughter at the error.

I smiled and quipped, "We should have practiced this more." The crowd got another chuckle as I placed my left hand on the Bible and raised my right. Less than two minutes later, I was governor.[2]

THAT EVENING, LONG underwear was traded in for tuxedos and gowns, and the Richmond Coliseum was transformed from a sports arena into a gala ballroom, filled to capacity with a cheerful mob of more than ten thousand excited supporters and friends. The dance floor was packed. I shook hands, posed for pictures, and danced with Lynda in a spotlight that made her red dress sparkle. For the first time, I got to dance with all three of our daughters, though I mostly carried Jennifer, who was then only three. The room hushed when I stepped onstage, but when I promised not to give another speech, the crowd erupted in cheers. After twelve years of Republican rule, the Democrats felt they deserved a real party.

The next morning, I woke up for the first time in the gubernatorial mansion and could feel the clock ticking. Since a Virginia governor may not succeed himself, I had only four years to fulfill the promises that I had made. I had a duty to the people of Virginia, and I wanted to get out of the blocks in a hurry. As I told a reporter shortly after my election, winning the campaign was just "a necessary prerequisite. The test isn't getting elected, the test is being governor."[3]

In my inaugural address, I had laid out the priorities for my administration: education, economic development, and fiscal responsibility. I was following the sage advice of Stewart Gamage, my chief of staff as lieutenant governor, to "keep it simple, keep it clear, and don't take on more than two or three things." Despite my best efforts to be succinct, my mother told the Washington Post that the speech was "good, but a little long."[4]

Before I could tackle those priorities, the first thing I needed was a top-flight team. During the transition period—the two months between Election Day and the inauguration—I was able to put together a highly regarded cabinet, a team of experienced advisors, a first-rate staff, and a comprehensive, three-hundred-page transition plan. The architect behind the plan was a staff member who had joined my team partway through my term as lieutenant governor and would soon become my chief of staff and right-hand man: David McCloud.

Standing a little over six feet tall, David was the picture of intensity around the office, but his droll wit and lilting Southwest Virginia accent smoothed over any rough edges. He was also a workhorse with an encyclopedic knowledge of the workings of state government who relished being an insider in the political game. David had previously been at Virginia's Department of Personnel and Training, and he actually took a considerable pay cut to come work for me. David took on something of an enforcer role, which freed me to concentrate more on political leadership. He had a laser focus on the success of our initiatives, wasn't particularly concerned with how he was perceived personally, and was unwaveringly loyal.

In addition to David, I was joined by the rest of my crew from my lieutenant governor days. Stewart Gamage wanted to stay up in the Northern Virginia area, so she became head of my Washington office. Ben Dendy came over to be my special assistant for constituent affairs and a member of the legislative liaison team. Ben had finished his degree at the University of Richmond (and been inducted into Phi Beta Kappa) while also working full-time on my staff in the lieutenant governor's office. Ben knew the General Assembly so well that David used to jokingly call him "my French friend, Count de Vote." Laurie Naismith had joined my staff in the lieutenant governor's office and proved to be an almost impossibly upbeat— and proficient—force on our team. She began the gubernatorial term as secretary of the Commonwealth, a role that Ben would take on toward the end of my term.

A critical member of my staff since my first day as lieutenant governor was Pat Mayer. I had known Pat since her husband had served with me at Marine Corps Barracks at Eighth and Eye while I was barracks adjutant. Pat was a formidable and constant presence on my team throughout my career— she would stay with me in each office or law firm until 2013. Her meticulous filing systems kept my lieutenant governor office, and every subsequent office, well organized, and her warmth set the tone for the office atmosphere.

I added some new faces on the gubernatorial staff as well, including Tim Sullivan as executive assistant for policy, Judith Johnson as cabinet assistant, and Charlie Sydnor as historian and speechwriter. An exceedingly bright young woman named Susan Albert (later known as Susan Carr) went to work on my gubernatorial campaign the day after she graduated from the College of William & Mary, probably not realizing at the time that she would join my staff in the governor's office and continue to work with me in various roles for the better part of the next two decades.

I also brought on an experienced, knowledgeable, and highly respected press spokesman, George Stoddart. Alongside David McCloud, George was one of the few staff members that I relied on to represent me to one of my trickiest constituencies: the media. George had a sly sense of humor that helped to cut the tension during tough situations and long, grueling days. George had been a reporter, which gave him both professional insight into what the press were looking for in writing a story, and the contacts to gather information from the source. Before walking into a press conference, George could predict, with almost uncanny accuracy, the first few questions that would be asked and the stories that were behind them.

George's abilities were indispensable to me because I was under a level of scrutiny, as governor, that I had never faced before. There was now a cluster of full-time reporters whose beat was, in essence, everything I did. And if I didn't do anything newsworthy on a particular day, they would need to find something to fill those dreaded blank spaces in the newspaper.

Our relationship with the media was generally amicable. The capital press corps was full of impressive reporters such as Don Baker, George Bowles, Margaret Edds, Marge Fisher, Joe Gaitins, Ernie Gates, Ruth Gersh, Eugenia Halsey, Mike Hardy, James Latimer, Charley McDowell, Robert Melton, Jeff Schapiro, Tom Sherwood, Tyler Whitley, George Wilbur, and many more. They were tough and thorough but fair. They already knew George, and they came to know me in time. If we learned of the potential for an erroneous story, George or I would generally be accorded an opportunity to clarify facts or have the administration's views heard before the story snowballed into something larger.

Our administration's relationship with the General Assembly was just as critical. Ben and David were my primary conduit to the legislative body, which we needed on our side in order to get our priorities written into law. Though both the Virginia House of Delegates and Senate were under Democratic control during my administration, the complexity of Virginia politics meant that it was never that simple. At this time, the Virginia legislature was run almost entirely on relationships and comprised some of the most colorful characters in the state. During the legislative session, David McCloud would chair a daily 9:00 a.m. meeting with key staff and any cabinet secretaries who were testifying before committees that day. The discussion ranged from where our legislation was hitting problems to who was kicking up dust. I was always impressed at how masterfully David, Ben, and a small team—including Phil Abraham, Jordan Goldman, Tim Sullivan, and Richard Dickerson—handled the incredibly complex maneuvering necessary to convince and wrangle the many larger-than-life personalities in the State Capitol.

In the Senate, our Democratic majority was split down the middle between an establishment faction and a more maverick block. The establishment was led by the formidable Senate Majority Leader Hunter Andrews. A forceful leader and superb orator with an encyclopedic knowledge of the law, Andrews had a "lilting Tidewater accent and regal bearing," and was described by another senator as "sharp as a tack and . . . mean as a mad dog when he needed to be."[5] Hunter was someone whose respect had to be earned, but it was worth earning. Hunter's group wasn't defined along ideological lines, so it included some of our more conservative allies, such as Senators Elmon Gray and Howard Anderson, as well as our more liberal allies, like Senators Joe Gartlan, Clive Duvall, Ed Holland, and Stanley Walker. Another base of power lay in the formidable Senator Ed Willey, who was president pro tempore of the Senate during my gubernatorial administration as well as chairman of the all-important Senate Finance Committee, a position that made him the holder of the purse strings. Willey had been in the Senate for nearly thirty years when I became governor and could even keep Hunter Andrews on his toes if he wanted to.

Not everyone in the Senate was an elder statesman, however. Senator Dick Saslaw had been in the Virginia Senate for only two years when I was elected governor and had served in the House for four years before that. Despite his relative youth, Saslaw was a good gut-level fighter on important issues and always a key ally.

Perhaps the most interesting character in the Senate wasn't even a senator. Jay Shropshire was the clerk of the Senate, giving him responsibility for the administrative workings of the Senate and placing him in the middle of Virginia state politics. Jeff Schapiro summed him up in the *Richmond Times-Dispatch*: "[Jay] was probably born with a telephone in his hand. During a campaign, Shropshire could work the phone as Liberace would a piano. You could count on Jay for a juicy tidbit. For him, gossip was the coin of the realm."[6]

On the other side of the State Capitol, the House of Delegates was largely run by House Speaker A. L. Philpott, the epitome of a conservative rural Virginia Democrat. Though he was once a segregationist, Philpott would later go on to endorse the state's first Black lieutenant governor. With a re-markable memory and a thorough knowledge of the state legal code, Phil-pott was a formidable fighter whom you wanted on your side. Philpott was crusty and sometimes a hard sell, but we could usually bring him around in the end.

One of Philpott's closest allies was a tougher nut to crack. Delegate Ted Morrison, who became chairman of the House Finance Committee in 1983, was profiled in the *Washington Post* under the headline, "Virginia's Bill Killer."[7]

We also had some natural allies in the House of Delegates, including Delegates Dick Cranwell, who had been an early supporter, Dick Bagley, Tayloe Murphy, and Chip Woodrum.

Delegates Al Smith and Alan Diamonstein—who was also the chair-man of the Virginia Democratic Party during my administration—were allies who turned into very good friends. The two were together so much that they were sometimes referred to as "Big Al and Little Al," even though they weren't that different in size, and I could never really figure out which was meant to be which. Along with Bill Thomas—a very bright lawyer and political strategist—the trio formed the core of my informal "Kitchen Cabinet." Many Sunday evenings during my administration, David Mc-Cloud would convene the group, and we'd spend hours sitting on the liv-ing room couches in the Governor's Mansion, talking through legislative strategy and lobbying tactics. Over time they became a part of our extended family, and their wives—Suzanne Thomas, Margarette Smith, and Beverly Diamonstein—also got in on the act. Suzanne, Margarette, and Beverly were truly indispensable, spending an untold number of hours organizing fundraisers, hosting events, and serving on boards—Beverly on the board of trustees of the Virginia Museum of Fine Arts, Margarette on the Virginia Commission for the Arts, and Suzanne on the State Board of Education.

I was fortunate to have a team of people around me that was highly com-petent and dedicated. There was always a strong bond of comradery among this group of friends, family, and staff members. Many were working very long hours together, some helping out after their own full-time jobs. Many of them, either formally or informally, stayed a part of the "family" for my entire time in public service and long after my retirement, which is some-what unusual in the ever-changing realm of politics. I expected a lot of my staff, and I wasn't always the easiest or most laid-back person to work for, but I was proud of their ability to deliver, day in and day out.

In the governor's office, we quickly learned that there was no typical day and that the only thing that didn't change day to day was the pace—it was always hectic. The schedule could start out perfectly balanced, but last-minute requests for meetings, emergencies, or crises would inevitably wedge their way in.

David McCloud summed up the intensity and unpredictable nature of the office one day in early 1983. I was planning to hold a small press conference that day to announce a friendly wager between myself and the governor of Florida, Bob Graham, on the outcome of the upcoming Washington Redskins–Miami Dolphins face-off in the Super Bowl. The nickname of Washington's offensive line for the team at the time was "the Hogs," so my wager was a pig named Josephine. The governor's offices were set up in a way that visitors could go directly from the outer hallway into David McCloud's office, and then, if seeing me was their objective, pass through to Pat Mayer's desk in front of my office. It was a convenient way for close allies to come speak with David or me without going through the public reception area, and David could still serve as a gatekeeper. On this January day, David happened to be in his office lobbying a junior legislator on a labor bill. David could get very intense in such discussions, using his full size and a good deal of passion to sway his listener. He was at the height of making his case when his door swung open and two of his colleagues ran through, wrangling a squealing pig. Josephine was apparently in no mood for the press conference and putting up quite a fuss as she was hustled in the back way. David and his guest just stared in silence for a moment, before David apparently burst into laughter and said, "This is the craziest damn place I've ever worked in."

My day at the office usually started after breakfast at the Executive Mansion, when I would walk to my office in the Capitol Building through the tunnel that connected the two buildings. I would make my way through a packed schedule and leave the office in the evening for either an official engagement or dinner with my family. I'd usually come back to the office in the late evening—one of my more productive work times because there were fewer distractions—and work until an hour or two past midnight. Then I'd retire to the residence and start all over again the next day.

Though I had been the one to accept the title, my family also took on the many new responsibilities and trappings of the role. On Inauguration Day, when Lynda and I reached our new home for the first time as the governor and First Lady of Virginia, I picked her up off her feet to carry her over the threshold. Together, our family would live for the next four years in a temporary home that was open for public tours, try to plan time together as a family between schedules that were timed down to the minute, and face the attention of a determined press corps.

Our daughters handled the situation with surprising aplomb. Once again, I credit Lynda's parenting skills for raising daughters who are both aware of the impact that they can have and unaffected by the spotlight. The pressures of constant press attention during formative years can be very tough, and our daughters had the benefit of a mother who understood that all too well.

I tried to make a point of being home for dinner with my family every night, unless an unavoidable commitment got in the way. I didn't get to spend nearly as much time with my daughters as I would have liked, but it was certainly better from their perspective to live in a house right next to their father's office rather than a hundred miles away in Northern Virginia, as they did for my time as lieutenant governor. Sometimes they took it upon themselves to visit me in the Capitol in the evenings. Catherine, in particular, used to roller-skate through the tunnel to stop by my office. If I wasn't at my desk, she was known to leave little notes signed from the "Secretary of Fun."

This was the new life that we had stepped into when I became the chief executive of the Commonwealth of Virginia. I was grateful that our family was a cohesive and supportive team, and we faced both the challenges and triumphs of those four years together.

13

The Democracy of Opportunity

ONE OF THE first pressing issues we faced when Lynda and I considered the move to Richmond was the question of where our two older daughters would attend school. We knew that it would be a very public statement—our decision to send Lucinda to a public elementary school in McLean had warranted a whole article in the *Washington Post* a full three years before I even ran for public office. Now, as governor of the state, education was one of my top priorities.

"The hour has come, the urgency is acute, for us to do whatever we must to reclaim for Virginia national pre-eminence in education," I had said at my inauguration. "No other effort will have as profound and lasting an impact on our future."[1]

My commitment to public education had made the choice of whether to send our children to public or private schools into a political statement, as well as a choice for our family. As we were making this decision, Lucinda, who was then thirteen years old, and Catherine, then eleven, to their enduring credit, came to me and volunteered for the experience of public school in Richmond. I suspect that Lynda put them up to it, but they were truly more than willing, and I appreciated their sensitivity on the subject, especially for young ladies not yet in high school.

In the end, Lynda and I decided that they'd be getting a solid education in the public schools in Richmond, and they'd also receive something more. We didn't want the girls to grow up in the kind of bubble that only admitted individuals of similar backgrounds. As the granddaughters of a U.S. president, as well as the daughters of the sitting governor, raised without material concerns, they could easily have entered adulthood without ever leaving that bubble. We wanted them to have a wider experience and become more well-rounded citizens.

I wasn't the first Virginia governor to make this choice. In 1970, Governor Linwood Holton, a progressive Republican, enrolled his four children—including Anne Holton, who later served, in two different administrations, as Virginia's First Lady and secretary of education—in Richmond's predominantly African American public schools during the height of Massive Resistance. His decision was one of the most important and courageous actions taken by any Virginia governor in the twentieth century.

Like Governor Holton, I saw education as essentially a civil rights issue, and I had ambitious goals for increasing access to learning in our state. As Thomas Jefferson—also a former governor of Virginia—said, we should "in education dream of an aristocracy of achievement arising out of a democracy of opportunity."[2]

To achieve that dream, we'd need to address the disparity of opportunities between affluent and poorer regions in the state. We needed to fix a system in which a high schooler living in Northern Virginia could expect a top-notch education, whereas one living in the rural Appalachian region might have to travel to another county in order to take calculus or Advanced Placement (AP) classes.

With the help of my secretary of education, John Casteen, and superintendent for public instruction, S. John Davis, and building on my work with the Virginia Forum on Education as lieutenant governor, we set to work. Part of our strategy was to highlight a few new flagship programs that addressed existing gaps in Virginia's education system. One such program was designed to give students in small, rural high schools the opportunity to take advanced classes or a more specialized subject, such as Latin or engineering, by offering instruction and coursework via interactive electronic classrooms that utilized the television and audio technology of the day. We started the project—one of the earliest of its kind—out of the newly formed Governor's Center for Educational Innovation and Technology at Varina High School in Henrico County near Richmond. And so, the Varina Project for Distance Learning was born.

Another of our flagship programs was the creation of several new Governor's Schools across the state, including the now internationally known Thomas Jefferson High School for Science and Technology in Fairfax County, commonly known as "TJ." Specialized public magnet schools like TJ that offer advanced coursework for exceptional students have become cornerstones of Virginia education.

We were very proud of these programs, but the bigger challenge to Virginia's education system was teacher salaries. In 1981, Virginia's teachers' salaries had sunk to thirty-second in the nation. We couldn't expect to attract the most talented teachers statewide if we didn't pay competitive salaries. We couldn't turn to the federal government, where a half billion dollars in federal cutbacks were threatening the very existence of national education funding. So the money would have to come from the state.

On first blush, it would seem that, as Democratic governor, it would be an easy task to get any legislation that I wanted through the General Assembly, where Democrats had a significant majority in both houses. That, however, would be neglecting the complex nature of Virginia's state parties. Because of its history as a southern conservative party, many of the state legislators who were nominally Democrats were vehemently opposed to some of my objectives and would quickly switch sides on any issue that they thought "too liberal." I was pointedly reminded of this once, when one Democratic state senator, after hearing out my proposal for some progressive legislation, looked me in the eye and said: "Be careful now. We may be Democrats, but you know that we can always be Republicans." So I couldn't expect a legislative rubber stamp.

And when it came to the budget, I also couldn't expect an easy fix. When my chief of staff, David McCloud, first showed me the state budget chapter in the transition plan, he had joked, "Once you read that chapter, you won't want to be governor anymore." In 1982, Virginia, like the rest of the country, faced a deepening recession, inflation, and growing unemployment, and I knew that resolving the state's looming fiscal imbalance would be one of my biggest challenges. I also knew that it was the key to getting any of my other priorities accomplished. Progress in other areas, such as education and economic development, simply couldn't happen without state funding. If we were going to provide a better future for Virginia, we'd need to find a way to tighten our belts.

I don't remember a time when I wasn't frugal. Fiscal responsibility had been a major plank in my campaign, largely because it is a fundamental part of my personality, instilled while I was young. My parents were practical people, never extravagant. My three younger siblings and I knew that our parents' families had each been prominent and well-off in the 1920s but had suffered heavy financial losses during the Great Depression. But my siblings and I didn't know until much later the extent of the financial troubles that stemmed from a single terrible snowstorm in the Arizona desert.

It started when my father, who had spent almost twenty years working his way up in the airline business in Phoenix, Arizona, let his adventurous spirit take over. It was 1947, and my father and mother made the decision to put his career on hold to run a dude ranch in Patagonia, Arizona, called the Circle Z Ranch. After a successful year running the ranch, my parents signed on to lease another dude ranch, the Hacienda Los Encinos, or "Home of the Oaks" ranch, in nearby Sonoita.

Southern Arizona, with plentiful sunshine and dry weather, was a paradise in the winter for people who wanted to escape the harsh northern climate, and business was generally good. It was certainly an outdoor paradise for a nine-year-old boy who enjoyed riding horses and learned to rope cattle. But in early 1949, it snowed nearly every week for two months straight. It was the first time that I'd ever seen snow, and it looked so incongruous out there in the desert, piled on top of the great saguaro cacti.

Although the snow may have been beautiful, it was a disaster for the dude ranch, and for my parents. Water pipes froze, and the power went out. Most of the guests ended their reservations early or canceled altogether. Only a few hardy souls stayed on, most notably one businessman who took it upon himself to poke holes in the swimming pool ice and draw water to flush the toilets. The ranch, which had always operated on a narrow margin, now had no chance of making a profit. My parents had to take a significant financial loss, far more devastating than they would ever let on to their children.

Suddenly, faced with a mountain of debt and a failing business, my father made what must have been painful, humiliating trips to each of his creditors to arrange payment plans for the money they were owed. My parents would spend the next thirteen years—from 1949 to 1962—paying off debts from that bleak winter. The difficult recovery had a profound effect on my father—it dampened his adventurous spirit. When he reluctantly gave up the dude ranch business and returned to the airline industry, he found himself working under men he'd hired a few years earlier.

To their credit, my parents managed to keep their children from the worry of the financial situation. I wasn't aware of all their corner-cutting, but I knew that they had to sell some of the heirlooms they'd inherited from both sides of the family to make ends meet. My parents always insisted that we live "properly" and upheld standards that would have made Emily Post proud. Sunday dinner meant dressing up and sitting down together at a table where the silverware was freshly polished. At the same time, they encouraged us to live frugally and to get summer jobs as soon as we were old enough.

When I was ten, I began to sell newspapers on the street corner near our home. Though I clearly couldn't have made much money that way, my father kept close track of the amounts that I, and later my siblings, contributed to the family finances. After his death, we discovered a brown file folder labeled "Boys Work Record." In it, my father had meticulously recorded all credits and debits to our "accounts," even calculating interest, with the intent of paying us back when the family was out of debt.

It was far from a hardscrabble upbringing, and we never felt denied the necessities, but it instilled a strong sense of fiscal responsibility that remains with me to this day. I put those values to work in my life and in public policy.

As governor, my frugality became almost legendary. I flew economy class on state business and was constantly flipping off lights in the Governor's Mansion to save on electricity. One editorial cartoon showed me mailing myself in a box at the post office to save on travel. Even the meals at official Governor's Mansion events were economized. Beverly Diamonstein joked that when official guests came to the mansion for dinner, "they'd eat beforehand." When one lunch ended with the presentation of Virginia-shaped cookies for dessert, my secretary of administration and finance, Wayne Anderson, inspecting the small wafer, grumbled: "We're just lucky he's not the governor of Rhode Island!"

I was quite content to be caricatured as a cheapskate. Fiscal responsibility isn't anybody's idea of a good time, but it was sorely needed. Virginia faced a revenue shortfall of hundreds of millions of dollars during the early 1980s. I intended to not only balance the state's budget but find necessary funding for our priorities.

I sent a clear signal with one of my first acts as governor: an executive order that placed a hiring freeze on state employees for the first three months of my term and capped the overall number of state workers during my term at the level it was when I took office. My goal was to keep the state government lean, but not by massive layoffs or furloughs. Through natural attrition and conscientious hiring, we ended my term with fewer state employees than at the beginning.

The most important efficiency measure during my term was our unique "level funding" process. When I first met with my cabinet officers, I told them: "We're going to begin by giving you the same number of dollars you had last year. I want you to tell me how you can do your job and provide all the essential services your departments are providing now, without any increase for inflation."

It was not at all a vague proposition—we developed a written agreement with each cabinet member that had very clear and specific expectations laid out at the beginning of our administration so that there would be no confusion. Cabinet officers in turn sent the same message to the agency and department heads under them.

It wasn't easy. I recall one of my department secretaries coming to me at the start of this belt tightening and saying that he simply could not run his programs without a second assistant secretary, which was not allocated in the level budget. I was sympathetic, but confident that he could find a way to run the department within the resources allocated. To my immense satisfaction, the secretary performed admirably—without the additional staff.

The belt tightening that resulted was beneficial for everyone: government officials learned to make do with fewer assistants; programs were streamlined or eliminated; and the savings were passed along to public programs. We couldn't launch major new initiatives that had a huge price tag, beyond the initiatives in education and economic development that we'd already set in motion, but we kept trimming and redirecting the money we had, without imposing new taxes or debts on the state.

"Government must now decide how to do more with less," I'd said in my inaugural address—and I meant it.

The next year, as the national recession continued, I recommended further cutbacks to programs and agencies, as well as salary freezes. But, as I told the General Assembly in my State of the Commonwealth address of 1983, "even in periods of austerity . . . there are investments state government can and should make to stimulate business expansion, to generate additional tax dollars, . . . to help those of our citizens who most need help, and to promote projects that directly affect our future in education and economic development."[3]

I promised the General Assembly that if we made these cuts we wouldn't have to reduce the salaries of state workers, shorten the workweek, resort to general layoffs, or increase taxes.

"As a consequence," I said, "we will also remain among the dozen states with the lowest tax burden in the nation and one of only 10 states in the country that still enjoys a AAA bond rating."[4]

The following year, as the economy was beginning to improve, I urged the legislators during my January 1984 State of the Commonwealth speech to maintain the austerity and "not to raise taxes, not to borrow for a bond issue, and not to spend any of our reserve fund."[5] I didn't want the return to prosperity to mean a return to the old ways of ballooning budgets, a state in debt, or mindless taxation.

By my January 1985 State of the Commonwealth address, I was able to announce a surplus that was expected to reach $238 million for the next fiscal year, leading to increases in education funding, teacher salaries, Medicaid, aid to dependent children, care for the elderly, child abuse programs, and transportation, as well as pay raises for state workers. By the end of my administration in January 1986, Virginia's elementary and secondary teachers, and state college faculty, were the highest paid in the South and would soon reach the national average.

Politics may be about promises, but governing is about making tough choices. Sometimes it is the governor's job to make a choice that makes people unhappy, even his party faithful. By making our administration do more with less, we showed that we could balance a budget while in a recession and still increase funding for public education. We showed that not only could a Democrat get elected in Virginia, but a Democratic administration could run the state as well as any other in the country.

14

The Aristocracy of Merit

ONE DAY, A group of legislators came into my office in the Virginia State Capitol. They were there to complain about my new secretary of commerce and natural resources. Their objection? "Betty Diener swears."

I hadn't been expecting this particular grievance, but I grasped their unstated meaning, and so I paused briefly before responding, "Don't men swear?"

The legislators said that it was different because Betty Diener was a lady, and this was Virginia. I let their answer hang in the air for another moment.

"I didn't hire her to be a lady," I said. "I hired her to be secretary of commerce."

It was not a long meeting. The lawmakers' grievance wasn't expected, but it also wasn't all that surprising. My administration was transforming government in a way that the old guard didn't always like. Times were changing, and Virginia was behind the curve. Slavery, segregation, Massive Resistance to school integration, and a painfully slow evolution in other areas of human rights and gender equality were all part of Virginia's history, but I was determined to make sure that they didn't shackle its future.

Before the term of my predecessor, John Dalton, no woman or African American had ever served in a Virginia governor's cabinet. Dalton had broken that indefensible record in 1978 by appointing Dr. Jean Harris, a Black woman, as the secretary of human resources. But I wanted to do more. Black Virginians and women had previously been relegated to roles in welfare and social service agencies. They had served as secretaries and support staff but rarely as the boss. I wanted to break these molds.

I hoped to make our administration more representative of the state than ever before. I aimed to promote qualified African Americans, women, and other historically underrepresented groups to prominent state government positions that had been dominated primarily by white men. I could set a precedent that would be almost impossible to reverse, even if it ruffled a few feathers.

My plan was to make Virginia's government more representative without fanfare, putting forward name after name of qualified women and minorities for the many positions that I had the power to appoint. For higher-level appointments, I worked hard to build support and mollify potential opponents before announcing my appointees publicly.

To my fellow Virginians, I might not have seemed like the obvious person to make the case for increased diversity in the state government. I didn't have the personal experience of having been discriminated against that often shapes guardians of civil rights. But for me, civil rights was a question of fairness. Since my childhood days as a "little judge," there had been no question in my mind that treating anyone differently on the basis of race, gender, or other immutable differences was simply unfair and wrong.

I had seen the injustice of public school segregation in Virginia at fifteen, when our family moved from Ohio to Virginia because of my father's job. It was the fall of 1955 when I began my junior year at Mount Vernon High School in Alexandria. This was a year after the landmark *Brown v. Board of Education* Supreme Court decision, but because of Massive Resistance, schools remained separate and unequal.

On the first day of school, I vividly remember riding on the school bus through a neighborhood called Gum Springs. The area was only a couple of miles or so from my house but so different from my own more verdant suburban neighborhood. Gum Springs was then a downtrodden, unpaved enclave of African American families that lay about halfway between my home and the school. It was founded by a former slave of George Washington's and became a sanctuary for freedmen and runaway slaves. But, more than 150 years later, the community hadn't received the modern conveniences that the nearby white neighborhoods had.

I was confused at first about why our bus didn't stop in this neighborhood, which was clearly on the way to our school. I soon realized that our school bus would never stop for the kids in Gum Springs because they were not white.

Mount Vernon wasn't the first all-white school I'd been sent to as a child, but my previous schools had been located in the generally less diverse areas of Arizona and rural Ohio in the 1940s and 1950s, where the African American population was virtually nonexistent. I hadn't, in my then short life, been confronted yet with the prospect of passing by African American children who lived within my school district. This was different. Every day that our bus drove through Gum Springs was a stark reminder of the state-sanctioned prejudice that was then enforced across Virginia and the South.

I knew it wasn't right, but as a teenager in 1955, I didn't think that there was anything I could do about it. No one at my high school, and certainly no one with any authority, seemed opposed to the practice. It wasn't until I got more involved in the body politic as an adult that I understood the full impact of discrimination and the forces behind this fundamentally unjust system.

When I was elected governor of Virginia, I knew that I needed to use my opportunity to advance the representation of our state's many highly qualified women and African Americans whenever possible. Betty Diener, who had a doctorate from Harvard in business administration and was the dean of the business school at Old Dominion University, was the perfect example of an extremely capable appointee who also served to break the mold. Diener entered an arena that had dealt only with courtly, white, southern gentlemen, and from day one she relished her role in shaking things up. The legislators who moaned to me about her language weren't wrong—a smart, salty-tongued, strong-willed woman, Betty tore through genteel Richmond like a tornado.

"I probably ought to be more dainty," she'd chortle, before letting loose a blue streak. Though she would be the first woman to serve in her position, she seemed more likely to intimidate the rest of the cabinet than the other way around. Betty, aided by her very capable deputy, Maria (Keech) LeGrand, deftly managed the twenty-two state agencies and four thousand employees under her purview.

Another appointee that surprised the establishment in more ways than one was my choice for secretary of transportation and public safety. The position had jurisdiction over the state police and state prisons—institutions historically associated with the oppression of minorities—and had been mostly filled by tough former law enforcement types who spoke the language of force. I felt it would send a strong signal to appoint Frank White, an African American former civil rights lawyer who had worked for the NAACP Legal Defense Fund. Soft-spoken and nattily dressed, he relied on the power of words and persuasion rather than intimidation, and was as buttoned-down and courtly as Betty Diener was boisterous.

In 1983, I also got an unusual opportunity to add a fresh face to Virginia's highest court. More than fifteen years after Thurgood Marshall was appointed to the Supreme Court of the United States, the Virginia Supreme Court still hadn't had either a woman or minority appointee. Unfortunately, Virginia Supreme Court seats were nominated and appointed by the General Assembly, not the governor. But in 1984, the Virginia Senate and the House of Delegates each nominated its own white male for a seat on the court, and neither body would yield to the other. This left the decision in my hands—a chance to advance the cause of civil rights immeasurably with a single act. It was clear to me that it would be politically easier to appoint a woman, and it was possible that the General Assembly would even do so in the next decade or so. The appointment of an African American, however, would take them much longer. And it would be a harder road for me, but it would crack the door open so much wider.

To fill the post, I chose a thirty-two-year-old lawyer named John Charles Thomas. A graduate of the University of Virginia School of Law and the first Black lawyer at the prestigious law firm of Hunton & Williams, Thomas boasted impeccable qualifications, but I still took pains to head off any possible opposition. I worked behind the scenes with leaders of Richmond's entrenched legal and business establishment to ensure that they would publicly endorse him, or at least not oppose him. Fortunately, this preliminary effort paid off, and there was no public dissent when Thomas's nomination was officially announced. In fact, the only question raised was his age, as reporters pointed out that he had graduated from law school only eight years earlier. Off the cuff, I responded, "When I was eight years out of law school, I was elected governor!"

The press seemed satisfied with that answer, and it wasn't raised again. Thomas was formally sworn in shortly thereafter, becoming the first African American to sit on the Supreme Court of the Commonwealth of Virginia.

The following year, I was given another prime opportunity to make a high-level appointment, this time to the Virginia State Corporation Commission. The commission, which regulates Virginia's various corporate entities, is one of the most powerful yet least well-known bodies in the state. The General Assembly usually selects the commissioners, but, as with Thomas's seat, the House and the Senate couldn't agree on a candidate, putting the appointment in my hands. When I called Tom Moss, the majority leader in the House of Delegates, to tell him about my pick to fill the vacancy, Tom responded without hesitation, "Who is she?" He was right—*she* was Elizabeth B. Lacy, the first woman to sit on the State Corporation Commission. It is safe to say that my efforts to make Virginia's government representative of all of its citizens were, by this point in my administration, well known.

The opportunities to appoint Commissioner Lacy and Justice Thomas had come to me through fortunate coincidences. But appointing women and minorities to fill thousands of posts throughout the state government took steady effort. During my first year in office, I had to fill more than 1,300 appointments to state boards and commissions. There were thousands of candidates to find and vet in a state where minority candidates had previously been left out of the process. Laurie Naismith, my secretary of the Commonwealth, had the task of keeping the files of hundreds of qualified candidates on hand for my review. Finding qualified women and minority applicants for all levels of positions was not a challenge at all—people had been waiting for decades for these opportunities—but screening the candidates and filling so many positions was a logistical challenge.

I enlisted then state senator Doug Wilder to serve as an unofficial ambassador to the African American community, helping me to find and screen potential appointees. The screening process was a vital step because it was very important to me that every person who received an appointment was clearly qualified to hold the position and that no one could credibly claim that an appointee was brought in purely to meet a diversity goal.

One-third of my appointments in the first year of my administration were women and African Americans—far more than Virginia had seen before. Michael Isikoff wrote in the *Washington Post* after my first year in office:

> Robb has undoubtably [sic] broken the mold, naming blacks to previously all-white agencies ranging from the State Elections Board to the Alcoholic Beverages Commission. He installed a black legal aid lawyer from Hampton to chair a new black-majority Parole Board—a move that startled lawyers in Virginia's criminal justice system. His naming of Azie Taylor Morton, the U.S. treasurer under President Carter, as commissioner of labor and industry, one of the top regulatory posts in state government, stunned members of the state's conservative business establishment.[1]

Commenting on Morton's appointment, Betty Diener gave a typically frank quote: "A black female from Texas with a labor background—add that up and, My God!"[2]

EVERYONE HAS HIS or her own style of effecting change. Some people are bomb throwers, some are rabble-rousers, and some are inspirational leaders whose words stir revolutions. I respect those skills immensely, but they are not ones that work best for me. My style tends to be evolutionary, not revolutionary. I didn't make appointments just to shock the system. Instead, I carefully and sometimes quietly selected candidates who were unquestionably qualified—and happened to represent something new. In this slow and steady way, I hoped to fundamentally, and irrevocably, move Virginia forward.

15

The Long, Hot Summer

As CAREFULLY AS a chief executive might plan the priorities of an administration, there will always be those occasions that draw public attention away from painstakingly prepared announcements or throw a wrench into a meticulously laid-out schedule. There were unexpected occurrences throughout my administration, but the biggest by far was what happened during the long, hot summer of 1984.

On May 31, 1984, six death-row inmates broke out of the maximum-security Mecklenburg Correctional Center in an escape worthy of a movie plot. The six—James and Linwood Briley, Lem Tuggle, Earl Clanton, Derick Peterson, and Willie Jones—overpowered guards, taking some as hostages and dressing in the uniforms of others. Then, placing a fire extinguisher on a stretcher and covering it in a sheet, they managed to convince the guards on duty at the prison gates that the item on the stretcher was a bomb that they needed to remove from the prison grounds immediately. Incredibly, the guards fell for the ruse, and the six inmates were allowed to leave in a prison van. It was the largest death-row breakout in U.S. history.

Two of the escapees were recaptured nearby within twenty-four hours, but four remained at large. The two escapees who created the most anxiety were the break's organizers, the infamous Briley brothers. This pair of sociopathic siblings had made headlines across the state when they'd committed a string of brutal killings in Richmond in 1979. They were ruthless, violent criminals, and Virginians would not be able to sleep soundly until these brothers were back in custody.

The same week that the Briley brothers and their accomplices broke out of prison, a heat wave swept across Virginia, with temperatures reaching just a degree shy of the record set in 1899. As one resident told the *Washington Post,* "We're in a state of roast."[1]

Each day that the prisoners were on the loose, headlines blared: "Manhunt" and "Four Escapees from Va. Death Row Continue to Elude Police in 4th Day."[2] Each possible sighting led to police surrounding campgrounds, conducting house-to-house searches, and sealing off rural areas to search on foot with dogs. One by one, the escapees were found, until, after nineteen days on the lam, as I listened in on the FBI telephone patch, the Briley brothers were surrounded and captured in Philadelphia at the home of their uncle—while they were barbecuing chicken in the backyard.

The peaceable recapture of all six death-row escapees was a great relief, but it only highlighted some of the very real problems in Virginia's prison system. Overcrowding had overwhelmed an unprepared system. I had raised the issue in my very first State of the Commonwealth address in January 1982, supporting the construction of more prisons and the exploration of "means of punishment other than the incarceration of nonviolent offenders in extremely expensive correctional facilities."[3] But in the summer of 1984, the prison problem took on a life of its own as the June manhunt was followed by a string of smaller incidents.

Ten days after the Brileys' recapture, two other maximum-security inmates at Mecklenburg Correctional Center escaped while on a painting detail outside the prison.

"This simply can't happen again," I told reporters—but the summer wasn't over yet.[4] Those escapees were apprehended within eight hours, but within two weeks there was another escape. This time a prisoner serving life plus ninety-two years for abduction, rape, and robbery simply walked away from a work detail at the Baskerville prison camp in Mecklenburg County.

The prison system got another black eye when the independent investigation that we'd commissioned to look into the situation at the Mecklenburg Correctional Center concluded that the conditions there were "highly dangerous and at times 'unmanageable.'"[5] In response, five guards were fired, and I ordered ten-day suspensions without pay for the Mecklenburg warden and deputy warden. It was too little too late, however. On July 12, there was a prisoner riot at Mecklenburg in which fifteen people were injured. The uprising was quickly put down, but the stricter security measures implemented afterward made conditions in the facility even worse. Tensions at the prison, which had been building since the May 31 breakout, were finally reaching a crescendo.

On August 4, six prisoners at Mecklenburg staged a second riot using homemade shanks. They overran an entire cellblock and took eight guards—two of whom were injured—and a food service worker as hostages. They released the two injured security guards later that day. The inmates issued a list of fifteen demands, some enumerating alleged misconduct by the prison guards and "inhumane, cruel, barbaric treatment at the institution."[6] Coming a little more than a decade after New York's 1971 Attica prison riots, which lasted four days and ended with forty-three dead, I knew we had to get the situation under control as quickly as possible.

On the day of the riot, I was in St. Paul, Minnesota, acting in my capacity as chairman for a meeting of the Education Commission of the States, so I had to communicate with law-enforcement officials by telephone. The atmosphere in the cellblock was extremely volatile, and the rioters' ringleader had declared his intent to execute the hostages. We needed to make decisions quickly, but there was a range of opinions about how to proceed. While determined to regain control of the prison, I wanted to avoid any action that might trigger even more desperate acts or lead to bloodshed. We brought in a trained negotiator from the state police Bureau of Criminal Investigations and the head of the American Civil Liberties Union's (ACLU) National Prison Project. At the same time, we cut off all water and electricity to the prison facility to raise the pressure on the rioting inmates. The rioters and hostages were in for a long, miserable night.

There were several officials, including Frank White, the man I had hand-picked to oversee the police and the prisons, who argued that we should move slowly and negotiate with the prisoners. I was willing to permit discussions with the rioters, but only up to a point. I saw this as a potentially deadly siege situation, and I understood the risks that needed to be taken to bring the situation to a conclusion. I didn't specifically override either the local authorities or Secretary White, but I did let them know what I wanted to see happen and said that I would accept full responsibility for the consequences. I decided to give the hostage-takers a definitive deadline for surrender and a vivid understanding of what police action would be taken once the deadline passed.

The negotiator conveyed my ultimatum to the prisoners: If they didn't surrender by 7:00 a.m. the next day, the police would storm the building with orders to use deadly force. I chose 7:00 a.m. because I knew that the longer the siege went on, the greater the likelihood that lives would be lost. The lack of water and air-conditioning would make the prison stifling in the muggy August heat, and if we waited for midday, the inmates could have done something desperate. I also knew, based on my Marine Corps experience, that dawn was often the best time to act, as the prisoners would be tired and disoriented from the long, tense night.

Then, I upped the pressure even further by authorizing police SWAT teams and canine units to line up outside the prison. All the rioters had to do was look out the prison windows to see rows of heavily armed police and hear the dogs barking and growling in anticipation—a show of force designed to make the stakes very plain.

As the clock ticked toward 7:00 a.m. on Sunday, August 5, hundreds of officers massed outside the cellblock. This was it: the inmates had to release their remaining hostages and surrender or face possibly deadly force. The 7:00 a.m. deadline came and went with no sign yet of the prisoners or their hostages. The inmates could hear the barking of the dogs as the officers began to advance. We all waited to see what they would do next. Suddenly, a flurry of activity was taking place in the cellblock. At 7:04 a.m., the remaining hostages emerged from the building. My chief of staff, David McCloud, said that the short period of waiting for the officers to advance was "the longest four minutes I'd ever lived."

The siege had lasted nineteen tense hours, but it ended with relative success. Although all six hostages had sustained injuries, two of them serious, none had been killed. Some of the inmates later claimed they surrendered because they'd accomplished their goals in sending out their list of demands. But others admitted to having been cowed by the massive show of force outside the prison, especially by the ferocious sounds of the barking dogs.

As fate would have it, later that morning I was scheduled to appear on NBC's *Meet the Press* in my capacity as the chairman of the Education Commission of the States. Although I'd had no sleep, I decided to go ahead with the appearance. My weary face betrayed the tension of the last twenty-four sleepless hours, but when the first questions were about the prison riot, I was gratified to be able to report its peaceful conclusion.

A FEW MONTHS later, in October 1984, the saga of that hot summer continued when Linwood Briley was put to death. His brother James was executed six months later.

The Briley brothers were not the first prisoners put to death while I was governor. All four of the executions carried out during my term were difficult, but the first—of Frank Coppola in 1982—stands out most vividly in my memory. Not only was it my first direct experience with the death penalty, but it was also slated to be the first execution in Virginia in twenty years, after the Supreme Court's moratorium on the death penalty ended in 1976.

Coppola was a former police officer who had murdered the wife of a Newport News used-car dealer in the process of a robbery. Because he was white, there were no allegations of racial bias, and because he declared, of his own volition, that he would rather die than live in prison, it was psychologically and emotionally easier for me not to intervene. The Briley brothers were similar—not only had their crimes been heinous, but they admitted to committing them. Still, the burden of a life-or-death decision entirely within your ability to halt weighs heavily on your conscience, as it ought to.

I was not then opposed to the death penalty; I had thought that there were some crimes for which there was no other adequate remedy. But I also felt that it was a horrible thing for the state to put someone to death, and it should never be taken lightly. I thought that it was critical that the facts of the crime were essentially unassailable. For each of the four death-row cases that came up during my term, I asked for all the evidence to be sent to my office so that I could meticulously review the case before deciding whether to proceed. I remember sitting before stacks of briefs, reading the pleadings of both sides so that I could be absolutely sure.

More than anything, I abhorred the sentiments of some of the picketers who would show up outside the prison before every scheduled execution waving signs like "Let 'em fry!" I always found that kind of enthusiasm about the taking of another human life to be repulsive.

The sign-wavers were there in October 1984 as the hour for the execution of Linwood Briley drew near, and the condemned prisoner was strapped to the electric chair. Virginia law requires an open phone line from the governor's office to the death chamber. A corrections official standing in the death chamber followed procedure to the letter, calling to ask if there was "any objection from the governor to proceeding with the state's requirement to carry out the sentence." When the call came, I told David McCloud to respond that the governor would not intervene. We both felt the somber weight of the moment as it came and went.

In recent years, I've seen and heard more about the effect that an execution has on the family of the person executed, the loved ones of the victim, and the ripple effect it has on the community at large. When the state takes a convicted criminal's life, a larger price is paid, not just by the person executed, but by all of those affected by that individual. Though I once thought that there were some crimes so heinous that only capital punishment was appropriate, the human impact on all concerned and the possibility of a wrongful death sentence have now convinced me that the death penalty ought to be eliminated altogether.

IN THE JANUARY following the prison breaks, long after the weather had cooled, I prepared to deliver my 1985 State of the Commonwealth address before the Virginia General Assembly. The night before the speech, as I wrestled with the last rounds of edits, Stewart Gamage came into my office and saw me leaning against a doorsill in my shirtsleeves, my face drawn.

"What's wrong?" she said immediately.

I took a deep breath and sighed, "They are missing one at Spring Street."

Yet another prisoner had escaped. And though that escape didn't spark a terrifying manhunt, the long, hot summer of 1984 had played one last trick.

The next day, as I stood before the General Assembly, I tackled a wide range of issues affecting the state—announcements about the budget, pay for state workers, and education funding—but the headlines the next day mostly bypassed those issues and instead read, "Robb Takes 'Full Responsibility' for Prison Problems."[7] I never had any doubt that I would take responsibility for the failings of the prison system, just as I had taken ownership of the decision to advance on the Mecklenburg prison during the August riot. I had expected that people would hardly notice such an admission, because it seemed to me the only reasonable course for the chief executive of the state. I thought I'd at least have to take some heat on the prison issue from Republican lawmakers. But after the speech, I was startled to find that my admission had given me more goodwill than I expected—even among the opposite party.

"He admitted all his sins," said one Republican lawmaker. "I don't know what else to say."[8]

Even my mother, who had by then moved with my father to Hume, Virginia, called to tell me that she was proud that I had taken responsibility for the issue. This was not something that she did often, so I remember it with particular fondness.

THE PROBLEMS OF that hot summer of 1984 were not the only unexpected ones that I faced as governor, nor were they the only major issues to distract me from my planned agenda. Every day, week, and month of my four years something would threaten to drag us off our carefully planned course. These unexpected occurrences were never well-timed, and always added to an already full plate, but I understood that they came with the territory. I tried to maintain a cool head and a steady hand. In the governor's office, as in so many arenas, you don't always get to choose your battles.

16

Clean Sweep

ON THE DAY that Virginia would elect new statewide leaders in November 1985, the *Washington Post*'s respected political columnist Mark Shields penned an exceedingly generous column about my administration:

> Virginia's outgoing Democratic governor, Chuck Robb, will probably accomplish something that many more celebrated governors— Ronald Reagan of California and Nelson Rockefeller of New York among them—have tried and failed to do. In Virginia, Chuck Robb leaves as his legacy a record and a political environment that make likely the election of his party's nominee to succeed him. . . .
>
> [Richard S. (Major)] Reynolds, who had never been an ardent admirer of Robb (to whom he lost a 1977 primary) credits the governor with "changing the political atmosphere of the state." Through four years of successful leadership, Robb has been able, according to Reynolds, "to kill all the political boogeymen." . . .
>
> Those "boogeymen" were the fears aroused by the political ruling class, which warned that if "those people" (read women, blacks, outsiders who were not the Right People) were somehow to gain power, the pillaging of the civic temple and the raiding of the public treasury would inevitably follow. Through the quality of Robb's stewardship and the distinction of Robb's appointments, that myth has been routed. . . . So positive has been public reaction to that performance that Democratic candidates for lieutenant governor and attorney general, respectively a black man and a white woman, are given an even chance to become the first in each category to win Virginia statewide office.[1]

The most gratifying endorsement that an administration can have— besides its own reelection—is the election of its chosen successors. In 1985, we hoped to do just that. An election of a groundbreaking slate of candidates would not only endorse the many changes brought about by our administration, but it also would cement the progress we'd made in the Commonwealth.

To my surprise, my approval ratings in Virginia, according to some published polls, were slightly higher than President Ronald Reagan's the year after his forty-nine-state rout of Walter Mondale. But my approval ratings in my last year in office did not, by any means, make the 1985 election a sure thing for the Democrats.

The Virginia Democrats had not been idle over the previous four years. Working with party officials and energetic supporters, we had helped rebuild the state's Democratic Party from the ground up by maintaining its traditional constituencies—teachers, unions, minorities, and women—while enlarging the party's tent. We worked to attract open-minded business leaders who could see the value of Virginia shedding its old, stodgy ways and becoming a more attractive place for businesses. All that was left in 1985 was to choose our candidates to rally around.

Gerald (Jerry) Baliles, Doug Wilder, and Mary Sue Terry rounded out a truly diverse—and ambitious—ticket. If they could pull it off, Terry would be the first woman ever to hold statewide office in Virginia and only the second woman to be elected as attorney general in any of the fifty states, and Wilder would be the first Black man to win statewide office anywhere in the South since Reconstruction.

During my time as governor, Doug was serving as the only African American state senator and was a fellow night owl. On occasion, Doug would stop by my office late at night for a friendly chat. In one of these evening conversations, Doug indicated that he felt Virginia was finally ready to elect a Black man to a statewide office in 1985. I agreed wholeheartedly. When he announced that he would run for lieutenant governor, I was eager for a chance to support him.

Doug would have a hard road to statewide office. Regrettably, racial bias was still a factor in parts of Virginia, and he had never faced the electorate outside of his majority Black Richmond state legislative district. Republicans quickly dredged up the personal attacks that had been quietly trailing Doug through previous races in an effort to taint his historic candidacy.

Some political analysts predicted that Virginia wasn't ready, and that trying to elect both the first woman and the first African American in one election was too much for the state to handle. But I believed it was eminently possible, and I wanted to do everything in my power to make it happen. So, I threw myself into their election campaigns full-force—advising, advocating, campaigning, and fundraising.

To shift attention away from doubts about any one of the candidates individually, I encouraged them to campaign as a historic slate, "joined at the hip" as a single powerful movement. In my appearances all over the state, I painted the election as a personal challenge to Virginians to make history by electing the son of a truck driver (Baliles), the grandson of a slave (Wilder), and the daughter of two schoolteachers (Terry) to statewide office. I implored them to "rise to the occasion and cast a vote you can be proud of!" and called the slate "a vision of Virginia's future."[2]

By shifting the debate in this way, I hoped to turn a potential negative—the discomfort some Virginians felt about the "unconventional" slate of candidates—into a positive feeling of taking part in a history-making election. In the final days, the polls showed the races coming down to the wire. I joined the candidates in a two-day marathon of rallies and events in every corner of the state, telling Democrats that we were "facing a 'rendezvous with destiny.'"[3]

ON ELECTION NIGHT, I invited all three candidates and their families to dinner with us at the Governor's Mansion, which was buzzing with an air of excitement and anticipation. We planned to all go together to the victory celebration at the Hotel John Marshall when the results came in. Mary Sue's victory was declared first and Jerry's soon thereafter. But as the evening wore on, the results in Doug's race remained uncertain. Jerry and Mary Sue were, understandably, anxious to give their victory speeches in time for the eleven o'clock news, but I urged them to hold off until Doug could join them. Our ticket ran together as a team, and we should claim victory as a team.

Finally, the verdict was in: Doug Wilder had won. It was an amazing night. Virginia's Democrats had done it again. Not only had we swept the top three statewide offices for the second election in a row, we'd made history doing it. As we entered the hotel's ballroom and all three newly elected statewide officials took the stage, it was clear to everyone in the room that something very special had happened in Virginia that day.

Our Democratic slate's 1985 clean sweep in Virginia made headlines and surprised political strategists all over the country, with observers heralding the results as everything from "a crowning victory" to "the death of Jim

Crow." Pundits debated how Virginia Democrats had managed, in a traditionally conservative, majority-Republican state, to lift themselves out of seemingly perpetual electoral futility to two statewide sweeps in a row.

A particularly insightful perspective came from my 1981 gubernatorial opponent, Marshall Coleman: "Republicans this time didn't have the scare tactics they could use in the past. . . . It was no longer credible to say that if the Democrats win, it would be the end of the Virginian way of life."[4]

WHEN I HANDED the keys to the Governor's Mansion to Jerry Baliles on January 11, 1986, it was a triumphant moment. We'd worked hard, and the voters of Virginia had elected the three people who were most likely to carry on the priorities of our administration.

I admit that I was not altogether excited, however, to leave the Governor's Mansion. My family had all been very busy in Richmond, but with my office in the State Capitol connected to our home by an underground tunnel, I got to see my family more than I ever had before, and I was home for dinner almost every night. All three of our daughters were still at home until the last year of my term, when our eldest, Lucinda, went away to school. For us, the Governor's Mansion had, in fact, felt like home.

Serving as Virginia's chief executive also fit my personality to a T. It allowed me to exercise my penchant for order, discipline, and efficiency. I liked being able to tackle problems directly and see real change happen over the course of just a few years. I enjoyed the experience of being the state's chief executive officer, responsible for its successes and its failures. My experiences as governor had been as varied as they were busy, and it was both an incredibly challenging and rewarding experience. If not for Virginia's constitution disallowing consecutive terms, I would almost certainly have run for reelection.

While I didn't relish leaving a job that I particularly enjoyed, I was proud of the progress that we had made since that bone-chilling January day in 1982 when I took the oath of office. Despite starting our work in the teeth of the early 1980s national recession, the state had prospered with the creation of a record number of new jobs and the fastest rate of employment growth in its history.

Our administration championed economic development initiatives such as the Center for Innovative Technology, an agency designed to promote research at colleges and high-technology industries. Dulles International, a long-underutilized airport in the Washington suburbs, was now, as I said in my final State of the Commonwealth speech in January 1986, "the fastest-growing airport in America."[5]

We also raised both teacher salaries and student test scores, "helping make the state's schools 'first in the South.'"[6]

In an article published shortly before I left office, the *Washington Post* wrote: "Under Robb . . . state aid to education flourished and a decade-old trend of decreasing state support was halted. . . . [S]pending rose in three years by more than $700 [per pupil] and, fueled by the economic turn-around, is expected to go higher in the two-year budget Robb will submit in January."[7]

A far less sexy effort, but one of the most important, was the review of thousands of government regulations to make government more efficient. Betty Diener, my secretary of commerce, told the *Washington Post* that her agency alone "reviewed more than 35,000 regulations, eliminating almost 7,000 of them and simplifying about 8,500."[8]

We were also able to pass the Virginians with Disabilities Act, which protected against discrimination in employment, education, housing, voting, and places of public accommodation. Spearheaded by the very capable Jordan Goldman, the Virginians with Disabilities Act was a trailblazing piece of legislation, enacted five years before the Americans with Disabilities Act.

With all these successes, I was pleased to be able to say that Virginia was the only state in the nation not to impose a general tax increase. We were also the only state not to issue state bonds, which is an especially tempting move for many state governments. Issuing state bonds meant that the state government was essentially spending money that was lent to it by the bond holders and leaving the next administration with the task of paying it back—with interest.

In the more than three thousand appointments made during my term, we brought on board record numbers of highly qualified Virginians from previously underrepresented groups to serve as cabinet officers, department and agency heads, and on various state boards and commissions.

"In all," said the *Washington Post,* "Robb tapped more than 900 women and blacks to state courts, boards, and commissions—effectively showing that Virginia's revered conservative government would not come tumbling down if white men did not control everything."[9]

Standing on the grandstand in the brilliant sun as Mary Sue Terry, Doug

Wilder, and, finally, Jerry Baliles took their oaths of office, I knew we were turning the state over to very capable hands.

As one of my most trusted aides, Susan Albert, once said, "We had made so much progress in those four years that they would never be able to get it back to where it was."

Virginia was now irrevocably a part of the twentieth century.

PART III

NATIONAL EXPOSURE

AFTER THE 1984 presidential election resulted in the Democratic Party's fourth loss out of the previous five elections, I, along with several like-minded colleagues, was looking for ways to make our party more competitive on the national stage. One way was to reform the Democratic presidential nominating process, which had often forced candidates to be beholden to the parochial interests of the early-voting states such as Iowa and New Hampshire. For instance, Iowa's STAR*PAC, an antiwar political action committee, required that a candidate declare an extremely "dove-ish" stance on national security in order to win their influential endorsement. But such stances were often further to the left than the candidate's overall message and, most damagingly, out of step with much of the rest of the country. Al Gore was the only Democrat seeking the nomination in 1988 who had the courage to stand up to STAR*PAC, an impressive move that earned him my endorsement in the race—an endorsement that I hoped would send a message, even though Al was a long shot to get the nomination.

A few of my colleagues and I wanted to give a larger slice of the country greater influence in the presidential nominating process, starting in 1988, by creating a new configuration of the Democratic presidential primary elections that came to be known as "Super Tuesday." By holding multiple primaries and caucuses on a single day early in the nominating process, we hoped to compel candidates to address the most important *national* challenges that the next president would have to confront. This would—hopefully—leave the Democratic Party with a more electable Democratic candidate in the general presidential race.

Laws governing the timing of state presidential primaries and caucuses are made by the state legislatures, so we began meeting with state leaders across the country in an attempt to move up the voting days, state by state. In the end, some twenty states, most of them from the South, voted to hold their presidential primaries and caucuses on the same day: March 8, 1988.

On the night of the first-ever Super Tuesday presidential primaries, I had a full slate of interviews scheduled with the major networks, including ABC, NBC, CBS, and CNN. Because I was one of the main architects of

Super Tuesday itself, I was being featured in the coverage of the night, and a cameraman came to my office to take some footage of me walking through the hallways.

Walking ahead of the cameraman through a darkened hallway—it was long after everyone else had left—I turned to warn him not to trip over a potted plant near the doorway. I turned forward just in time to crash, face first, into a plate-glass door that was always open during regular hours. The next thing I knew, I was lying on the carpet, looking up at the worried face of my assistant, Susan Albert. On the plate-glass door behind her was a face-sized smudge.

Despite a slight concussion, a throbbing headache, and feeling a bit woozy, I went ahead with each of my scheduled interviews. Super Tuesday was simply too important for me to miss opportunities to promote the rationale behind it. I made it through all of my interviews, though I was unsteady enough to have to check in between each one with staff members watching on television to make sure that it wasn't coming through on-screen.

Looking back on it, that Super Tuesday was an encapsulation of my first steps onto the stage of national politics. With several other like-minded politicians, I approached some of the fundamental problems facing Democrats in a new way—a way that caused some ripples within the establishment—and established myself as a new kind of Democrat. But just when it looked like I had smooth sailing ahead, I ran headlong into obstacles that I never even knew were there. I moved forward, a little more bruised than before.

17

Sacred Cows

THE 1984 DEMOCRATIC National Convention was held in July in San Francisco. I was still in the third year of my gubernatorial term, and, as chairman of the Democratic Governors Association, I was invited to address the convention on the night of the official nominating speeches.

On the day of my speech, I met with my speechwriter, Charlie Sydnor, in my hotel room to go over what he'd written. We had discussed earlier what I wanted to say, but with the hectic schedule of convention week, we hadn't yet had a chance to go over the draft of the speech itself. True to form, the speech he'd written was very impressive.

"This is a great speech," I told Charlie. "Unfortunately, it's not the message I want to give to this convention." It was the kind of speech that is normally given at political conventions: critical of the other party, complimentary of our own, and filled with optimistic rhetoric.

I would never claim to be the easiest person to work for, and after all the careful time Charlie had poured into that speech, I couldn't blame him for what he did next.

"Okay, Governor," he told me. "Good luck with the new one." With that, he left the room, having no intention of starting over on a new speech.

I then turned to the other two staff members in the room: the head of my Washington office, Stewart Gamage, and my press secretary, George Stoddart. Dutifully, they pulled out notebooks and began scribbling as I tried to explain the challenge I wanted to lay down that night at the convention. Then they hurried into another room to start writing.

They worked frantically on the new speech, literally cutting out phrases and ideas from their pages of copious notes and carefully laying them out in the order they thought they should be presented. As the clock ticked closer to showtime, they were making great progress.

The old San Francisco hotel in which we were staying had no air-conditioning, so they'd opened a window to get a little fresh air in the stifling July heat. They had just finished laying out the pieces of their notes when someone knocked on the door and came into the room. The sudden cross-breeze picked up nearly all their little slips of paper off the bed and sent them flying out the window. Stewart and George rushed to the ledge just in time to see the speech floating away like confetti in the breeze.

George turned to Stewart and said, "Well, you'd better remember what was on those pieces of paper, because we've got to start all over again."

Working from memory and the few scraps that hadn't made it out the window, they managed to pull everything back together and wrestled my thoughts onto paper, now pinned firmly down with a desk lamp. With only minutes to spare, they rushed the speech over to the teleprompter.

The atmosphere in the convention hall on the evening of July 18, 1984, was restless. Walter Mondale was set to be nominated the following evening, but supporters of his main rival, Gary Hart, were waving campaign signs throughout the hall, and the two sides were chanting back and forth. The chair banged her gavel and called repeatedly for attention but was drowned out by the chants.

It was in this somewhat chaotic scene in front of a fractured party that I took the podium and gave what was probably the most important address of my career up to that point. I said to the delegates:

> It is not enough for us just to say what is wrong with Ronald Reagan, what is wrong with the Republican Party. . . . We have an obligation to say what we will do, and where we will take this country. . . . Our party has never been the party of the status quo. We have been the party of progress and change. . . .
>
> The Democratic Party, at its best, has asked the American people to take risks and make sacrifices, and to work together for the common good, and if we want to remain the majority party in this country, we cannot afford to cling to the ghost of a time now vanished.
>
> We cannot become a party afraid to say no—even to our friends. We must risk alienating, for a brief period, even some of the members of our great coalition, especially when narrow interests stand in the way of our national interests. We cannot continue to mortgage the future of succeeding generations.
>
> To our trade unions, we have to say yes to job security and fair wages, but no to protectionism and artificial barriers to competition.
>
> To our American businesses and their lobbyists, we have to say yes to innovation and the free market, but no to regulations that protect inefficiency and frustrate competition.

To our dedicated teachers, we have to say yes to higher salaries and increased respect, but we have to say no to practices that reward mediocrity and ignore the performance of our best.

To our sons and daughters, we have to say yes to educational access, but no to social promotions.

To the American people, we have to say yes to arms control, but no to showboat diplomacy.

To the Pentagon, we have to say yes to a strong national defense, but no to cozy contracts and weapons that don't work.

To the Republicans, we have to say yes to fiscal responsibility and a balanced budget, but no to denying women the full protection of our Constitution. . . .

If all of us will take the risk and make the sacrifices, we can prove to the American people that we are not only compassionate enough to care, but tough enough to govern.[1]

I knew I was taking a risk in publicly confronting some of our party's sacred cows. But I felt that the political hazard was far outweighed by the enormity of the problems in the Democratic Party.

It seemed to me, and to a growing number of other Democrats, specifically elected officials, that our party was being divided in two. One faction consisted of our party's elected officials—those who were directly accountable to the voters and constituents, and who were expected to answer for the campaign promises they'd made. The second consisted of core Democratic constituency groups—the "true believers" whose passions gave the party its soul, but who sometimes seemed unwilling to compromise, even when their demands might thwart workable alternatives and damage the party as a whole.

This second group dominated the national party, which was why many Democratic voters viewed the national party as beholden to a collection of special-interest support groups. While voters could sympathize with the plight of the poor and disenfranchised, they also wanted a party that represented their own interests, and they didn't believe that the Democrats were doing that. It was these promises to the party's sacred cows that needed to be challenged if Democrats were to provide the American people with a platform that they could truly believe in and that Democratic elected officials across the country felt that they could deliver. We needed to bridge the gap between what the very liberal constituency groups insisted on having and what the elected officials needed to provide to their constituents.

Over the next few days, the convention continued—Mondale was nominated for president and Geraldine Ferraro became the first woman ever nominated for vice president by a major party. The next morning, I attended the last event of the convention, a symbolic send-off of the newly christened ticket called, sometimes ironically, the Unity Breakfast.

I was standing with other elected officials on the small stage, awaiting Mondale's arrival and the beginning of the program, when a tall, barrel-chested, glowering labor leader came striding up. This bear of a man stood less than a foot from me onstage and poked his finger angrily into my chest. In my speech two nights before, he growled, I had insulted everything his organization and the Democratic Party stood for.

While I had carefully avoided "bashing" any particular Democratic support group, I had known that the speech would cause discomfort among some traditional constituencies. That was its point. That morning's confrontation with the labor leader meant that the message of my speech had been taken seriously. I had skewered a number of sacred cows, and now some of the herd was turning on me.

A few days later, I received a phone call from Senator Sam Nunn of Georgia, who had been intrigued by my speech and wanted to set up a meeting with a group of other like-minded Democratic elected officials. That first meeting included Senators Lawton Chiles (FL), David Pryor (AR), Dale Bumpers (AR), David Boren (OK), Al Gore (TN), John Glenn (OH), and Lloyd Bentsen (TX). Representative Gillis Long of Louisiana was the only member of the House to participate at that time, and I was the only governor. We all agreed that something needed to be done and that to do it we would need to expand the nucleus of our new group by recruiting some additional members.

The recruiting was made easier when the drubbing at the ballot box that November underlined the need for change in the party. Mondale's message and image never really came together. He backed nearly every interest in the Democratic Party and gained the endorsement of nearly every liberal group almost a year before he was nominated. But his platform appeared to be little more than a laundry list of each group's requests rather than a comprehensive plan for America's future.

"Unfortunately," said Mondale's former chief of staff, "the national party is seen as the sum of its interest groups."[2]

Too few voters could tell what he stood for, or what the Democratic Party stood for, and we were defeated in forty-nine states. Mondale won only his home state of Minnesota and the District of Columbia, securing just 13 electoral votes to President Reagan's 525. It was the most one-sided electoral defeat for any presidential candidate in history and the Democrats' fourth loss in five presidential elections.

After the thrashing, the Democratic National Committee (DNC) sought a new chair to lead the party into the future, while our small, still unnamed group of like-minded politicians began to come together. We tried initially to recruit our own candidate for DNC chair, but that didn't pan out. The party eventually nominated a former political aide to Senator Ted Kennedy, Paul Kirk, whom I liked and respected. But Paul and the DNC were wary of our group and how we might challenge the status quo.

I was frank with Paul and told him, just minutes before he was formally nominated to become chairman: "We're going to support you, but we're still going to form this group. We don't want anyone to feel threatened by it. We accept and respect the DNC's role, but we need for you to accept ours as well."

On February 28, 1985, Sam Nunn and I stood with several other Democratic leaders on Capitol Hill to announce the formation of the Democratic Leadership Council (DLC). The *New York Times* ran a front-page story with the headline "Dissidents Defy Top Democrats; Council Formed."

In defiance of the national party leadership, a group of Democratic officeholders from the South and West today announced the formation of an independent council to help shape party policy and rules. . . .

"We view the council not as a rival to any other party entity but as a way station or bridge back into the party for elected Democrats," said Representative Richard A. Gephardt of Missouri, who will serve as chairman.[3]

At the time, Dick Gephardt had not yet run for president and, as the incoming chairman of the House Democratic Steering and Policy Committee, was well-suited to be our first chairman. I also felt that it was important that, with our membership skewed toward the Senate, our first chairman should come from the House of Representatives, facilitating recruitment of House members and other state and local officials and drawing us away from an image as the "House of Lords."

This was also one of the reasons for our name. The name "Council of Democratic Leaders" had been suggested, but I thought that sounded far too aristocratic, so I recommended the "Democratic Leadership Council."

At our formation, the DLC had a small but extremely able staff in place. Al From, a staffer for Representative Gillis Long who had been executive director of the House Democratic Caucus and a deputy advisor to President Jimmy Carter, came on board as our director and our first professional staff member. A dedicated policy wonk, Al was gung-ho about our group's long-term goals but, at age forty-one and with a family to support, he felt he needed some security in case the DLC proved to be a "flash in the pan." So, I personally guaranteed Al's salary for the first year if he'd sign on, and years later he still enjoys telling people that his beautiful home and his kids' college education were the fruits of this risky venture. Al would eventually become president of the DLC and would lead the organization until his retirement nearly a quarter century later.

In the very earliest days of the DLC, we only had two other professional staff members: Will Marshall and Melissa Moss. The staff may have been small, but it was supercharged. Will became our "issues guru" and went on to found the Progressive Policy Institute in 1989, which served as the policy arm of the DLC. Melissa, our first finance director, was a one-woman dynamo with an unquenchable intelligence and enthusiasm who could charm the birds out of trees (and dollars out of Democratic wallets).

This team had a major task ahead of them: create a political organization from scratch. We weren't affiliated with any of the establishment organizations, which gave us credibility as an independent voice but also meant that we had to create our own platform and establish ourselves as a group with enough clout to be taken seriously. Our first goal was to build a membership base among elected officials large enough to merit a voice in the political process. And we had to do this while raising money, generating press, and coordinating with elected officials across the country in a time before email and cell phones.

Initially, our effort to launch the DLC got off to a somewhat rocky start. *Time* magazine speculated that we were simply "a vehicle for the 1988 presidential ambitions of some of its founders, including Robb and Gephardt."

But we took to the road, planning events across the country where local Democratic politicians were relieved to hear a message that resonated in their state more readily than the national party message. DLC events became popular with local press and our message quickly gained momentum.

My family sitting on a corral fence at Circle Z Ranch in Patagonia, Arizona, in 1948. *From left:* Wick, my father, me, David, my mother. (Larry Monahan)

In Arizona at age nine. (Robb Family Archive)

With my siblings, Wick (*back right*), David (*front right*), and Trenny (*front left*), and Grandfather Woolley. (Robb Family Archive)

My parents (*right*) and me at my graduation from the University of Wisconsin–Madison, with Captain Todd (*far left*). (Robb Family Archive)

Performing my duties as officer in charge of the White House color guard and military social aide, with President Johnson, Lady Bird Johnson, and Emperor Haile Selassie of Ethiopia in the background. (White House Photo)

Receiving a gag gift of my face pasted on the body of the Marine Corps commandant at a costume engagement party. (Michael A. Geissinger/White House Photo)

With Lynda, heading to the rehearsal dinner, surrounded by the press. (White House Photo)

Dancing with Lynda at an engagement party. (Robert L. Knudsen/White House Photo)

Standing with Lynda at the altar during the wedding rehearsal, with best man, Doug Davidson; matron of honor, Lynda's sister, Luci; and Reverend Canon Gerald McAllister. (Robert L. Knudsen/ White House Photo)

Lynda and her father share a moment during the wedding rehearsal. (Mike Geissinger/ Lyndon B. Johnson Presidential Library and Museum/NARA)

As newlyweds, Lynda and me walking through the sword arch after the wedding ceremony. (White House Historical Association)

Greeting Alice Roosevelt Longworth in the receiving line following the wedding ceremony. (White House Historical Association)

Cutting the wedding cake (with my sword) as Lynda's parents look on. (Yoichi Okamoto/ Lyndon B. Johnson Presidential Library and Museum/NARA)

Briefing the tank commander (*left*) on the source of enemy fire during a firefight in the "Arizona Territory" across the river from my command post in Vietnam. (Eddie Adams/AP/Shutterstock)

The daily ritual, up against some ammo boxes, whenever I was back at my company combat base in Vietnam. (Eddie Adams/AP/Shutterstock)

Communicating with my platoon commanders via radio during an operation near a Viet Cong village. (Eddie Adams/AP/Shutterstock)

Looking over an area during a sweep in May 1968. (Eddie Adams/AP/Shutterstock)

Directing movements of India Company via radio from a dike in a rice paddy as Viet Cong snipers open fire. (Eddie Adams/AP/Shutterstock)

My father-in-law listening to a tape that I had sent to Lynda from Vietnam. (Jack Kight-linger/Lyndon B. Johnson Presidential Library and Museum/NARA)

On the campaign trail in 1981. (Claude B. Smalts)

Campaigning with Jennifer in 1981. (Robb Family Archive)

"We should have practiced this more." Gubernatorial swearing-in with Chief Justice Carrico. (*Richmond Times-Dispatch*)

Celebrating my election to the Senate in 1988, with Governor Jerry Baliles (*left*), Lieutenant Governor Doug Wilder (*center*), and Attorney General Mary Sue Terry (*right*). (Robb Family Archive)

At a campaign event in 1994 with (*from left*) Lynda, Representative Barbara Jordan, Catherine, Cecilia (Mrs. Thurgood) Marshall, and Mrs. Johnson. (Mark Charette)

With Lynda, talking to President Clinton at a campaign event. (White House Photo)

With fellow Vietnam veterans in the U.S. Senate in 1996: (*from left, back row*) Bob Kerrey (D-NE), Chuck Hagel (R-NE), John Kerry (D-MA), John McCain III (R-AZ), and (*front*) Max Cleland (D-GA). (Kiley Cruse/*Omaha World-Herald*)

President George W. Bush announcing Larry Silberman and me as the cochairs of the WMD Commission in 2004. (Paul Morse/White House Photo)

With Lynda and our daughters, (*from left*) Catherine, Lucinda, and Jennifer. (Robb Family Archive)

In 2019, with Lynda and grandkids, (*from left*) Lawrence, Charlie, Madeline, Joshie, and Austin. (Robb Family Archive)

In November 1985, we convinced Paul Taylor, a rising star in political journalism, to join us on the road. When he arrived at an event in Greensboro, North Carolina, expecting the usual polite gathering, the room was so full that Taylor had to force his way in. He was blown away. Individually, he said, these politicians "would have trouble filling a firehouse."[4] But coalescing under the single banner and message of the DLC, we were becoming a movement.

A few weeks later, Taylor wrote in the *Washington Post* that "one year after the Democrats' 49-state presidential drubbing, these moderates seem poised to capture the soul of their beleaguered party."[5] We were starting to break into the national political consciousness.

Personally, the founding of the DLC marked a new phase in my political career: a clear move onto the national political scene. Up to this point, I had served in a few national and regional organizations and chaired both the Democratic Governors Association and the Southern Governors' Association, but they were mostly insider groups. The DLC was a much more public group with national party significance.

Following my term as governor, I'd accepted a position as a salaried partner at the highly regarded law firm of Hunton & Williams. My role there allowed me to serve in an advisory role to the firm, while keeping my hand in the political realm. So, after Gephardt's term as the DLC's first chairman ended in 1986, I agreed to serve as the next chair.

I had a condition for acceptance, however. Early on, the DLC was dubbed "Democrats for the Leisure Class" and the "Southern White Boys Caucus." The nicknames highlighted a serious concern: our original membership was largely made up of white southern males. Though this was primarily a vestige of the makeup of elected officials at the time, it was a priority of my chairmanship to recruit more women, African Americans, and other minority members into the DLC. I made a personal effort to recruit such iconic leaders as Mayor Tom Bradley of Los Angeles, Mayor Harold Washington of Chicago, former U.S. representative Barbara Jordan of Texas, and Mayor Henry Cisneros of San Antonio.

Another priority was to establish the group as more than a flash in the pan. In its first year, the DLC had successfully gotten its name on the map. In our second year, we needed to tell people what we believed. I decided to publicly solidify our principles through a series of speeches that laid out the positions of the DLC and challenged the conventional thinking about Democrats.

I began a speech in April 1986 at the National Press Club in Washington with a bold statement: "The New Deal consensus which dominated American politics for 50 years has run its course." I continued:

> A new political era is taking shape. In the new era, ideas are the currency of politics . . . and Democrats won't begin to win national elections again until we're competitive in the battle of ideas. Since the late 1970s, the Republicans have been on the intellectual offensive. They've appropriated themes that used to belong to the Democrats: keeping our economy healthy and our defense strong. Democrats need to reclaim these bedrock issues. . . .
>
> As we enter the new era, Democrats need to . . . reclaim our heritage as the party of national purpose, we need to issue the call for a renewed commitment to the ideal of citizenship in America.[6]

A few weeks later, I spoke again at Hofstra University's Presidential Conference on President Johnson. I broke with Democratic conventional wisdom, saying that the true legacy of President Johnson's Great Society was not its programs, but its willingness to experiment, to risk new departures, to seize the initiative. Then I called on Democrats to embrace that spirit in order to face the "new social dilemma": a bottom tier of society that had become trapped by poverty in a welfare system that did not help to lift them up.

At the time, many well-intentioned liberal social welfare programs created unintended and unfortunate incentives. Taking a minimum-wage job, particularly when combined with the cost of traveling to work or paying for child care, often meant a net loss of income compared to government benefits, trapping millions, I said, "in a tragic cycle of deprivation, disorder and dependency."[7] The fix, as I saw it, was not a half measure:

> I believe this nation needs to undertake a fundamental restructuring of our public welfare system. For me, the issue is not just cost. In fact, as an acknowledged fiscal conservative, I'd be willing to spend as much or even more than we do today if I could be confident that the money would go into a system that really works.
>
> We need a whole new approach to social policy. We need a social policy that fosters upward mobility, not one that freezes people in dependence and despair. We need a social policy that rewards self-

discipline and hard work, not one that penalizes individual initiative. We need a social policy that encourages families to stay together, not one that pulls them apart. We need a social policy that instills basic values, not one that simply yields to the laws of the street. Above all, we need a social policy designed to restore America's poor and dispossessed to full citizenship—to both the benefits and the obligations that citizenship entails.[8]

I criticized solutions on both sides of the aisle that had succeeded only in winning votes, not moving people out of poverty:

Drastically scaling back or dismantling public welfare programs—as some conservatives have suggested—is really no solution at all. Laissez-faire may be good economic policy but it's terrible social policy.

Yet we can't afford to perpetuate or simply expand a welfare system which clearly isn't working well enough and which, in fact, seems to be subsidizing the spread of self-destructive behavior in poor communities.

The prerequisite for any successful social policy has to be healthy economic growth. This isn't the time to get caught up in distributional politics—it's time to make the economic pie grow.[9]

This wasn't just an economic argument—I wanted to shine a bright light on what I had been hearing from many leaders in the Black community and what they saw as causing disproportionate poverty among African Americans. I wanted to start a conversation that would lead to real solutions instead of the ineffective political posturing of each party, which either demonized or pandered to the community in turn.

As a nation, we've got to come to grips with some uncomfortable truths. And we've got to end the conspiracy of silence that has inhibited frank public discussion of the new obstacles to black progress. . . .

It's time to do what a number of black leaders have started to do: focus on the causes and possible remedies to the epidemic of teenage pregnancy in poor communities . . . the disintegration of families . . . rising dropout rates and widespread illiteracy . . . and to appalling rates of crime and violence and imprisonment. . . .

By doing nothing in the face of these realities, the federal government has created a de facto social policy of welfare dependency for women and prison for men. . . .

A policy that relies primarily on prisons to handle social problems is costly, callous, and ultimately futile.[10]

A *New York Times* editorial titled "Hard Truths about Race" agreed with the premise of my speech and added: "Civil rights and welfare alone are not enough for the most disadvantaged of our citizens. The Democratic Party ought to be leading the search for new ideas. And Americans of every persuasion ought to join it."[11]

A few weeks after the speech, Al From was sitting at a dinner in Austin, Texas, next to former representative Barbara Jordan. At the dinner, Jordan turned to Al and said that she'd read my speech, that she'd "been waiting for a white politician all those years who would speak out about those problems," and that she wanted to be a part of the DLC.[12] I had been making an extra effort to recruit Jordan, who was an eloquent speaker, forceful advocate, and a titan in the African American community. We welcomed her into our organization, and, at our conference in Williamsburg, Virginia, in 1986, Jordan said: "We are not going to use government as the great master handout. We are going to use government . . . as the base, to help this developing partnership, to bring about this new social policy consensus. And we believe that in this country, freedom, duty, choice, responsibility, are all words which are inextricably interlinked."[13]

In the next year, the DLC, which was a 501(c)(4) nonprofit advocacy organization, invited Democratic candidates for the 1986 midterms to share their ideas at forums and policy conferences. These events gave DLC candidates a chance to address issues, like national security and fiscal responsibility, in a way that voters hadn't seen from Democrats in recent elections. Candidates who had previously run away from the label of "Democrat" were now embracing the moniker of "DLC Democrat," and the association appeared to be helping them.

WHEN I DECIDED to confront some of our party's sacred cows at the 1984 convention, I had hoped that it would lead to changes in our party, but I didn't realize it would turn into a new organization, of which I would later agree to become chair.

I stepped down as chair after a year because I felt that the organization needed a current elected official at its helm. The ideas were built on what was working on the ground with elected officials who were accountable to their constituents, and I thought that the organization's leader should reflect that. But I stayed active with the group for years to come because I believed in its fundamental mission to question the orthodoxies of the Democratic Party and find workable solutions for the American people.

As I began to emerge from my years as governor of Virginia and find a place on the national political stage, the DLC gave me a platform to experiment with new ideas, challenge old political assumptions, and help to reshape our national party.

18

Pandora's Box

IN POLITICS, SUCCESS can be just as threatening to our allies as it can be to our enemies. And animosity between former allies can run deep. After Democrats swept the Virginia statewide offices and I took on the chairmanship of the DLC, I was getting more attention on a national stage. At the same time, I was challenging a lot of the accepted norms of my party, something that rankled many Democratic supporters, elected officials, and their staffs.

In late November 1986, I returned from a long business trip to Europe and Asia. The trip was for Hunton & Williams, where I had been working since I left the governor's office earlier in the year. This should have been a quiet period for me—I had left office with high approval ratings, was not serving in elected office, and my work was not especially controversial. But almost before I could put my bags down, I got a call from my former gubernatorial press secretary, George Stoddart. I could hear from the tension in George's voice that something was wrong.

"Goldman has been talking about you again," George said.

While I'd been away, Paul Goldman, who had been Doug Wilder's campaign manager in his successful 1985 race for lieutenant governor, had delivered a speech in Williamsburg, Virginia. In the speech, Goldman said that during the 1985 election, "Virginia had its share of influential and powerful politicians whose politics were irreversibly molded by a mindset that was colored by the pigmentation of Doug Wilder's skin," and that those politicians had worked against Doug's election.[1] Although Goldman did not identify the politicians by name, Mike Hardy at the *Richmond Times-Dispatch* reported that "it was clear . . . that he was including, among others, former Govs. Charles S. Robb and Mills E. Godwin."[2]

This was not the first time that Goldman had made claims about my involvement in the race. Shortly after the election, Goldman had begun calling reporters around the state, "playing down" my role in Doug's victory.[3] Goldman thought that I was getting far too much credit and had decided, in his own words, to "set the record straight."[4]

"It's not anti-Robb," he told reporters. But, he continued, "we did not ride anyone's coattails."[5]

It wasn't clear to anyone why Goldman and Wilder would instigate an intraparty squabble after they had just won an important election that had received national attention. Don Baker at the *Washington Post* theorized that, "by getting the word out early that he won on his own, rather than on Robb's coattails, Wilder may be trying to separate himself from Attorney General-elect Terry," who was his presumptive competition for the Democratic gubernatorial slot in 1989.[6]

Whatever the motivation, Goldman's words particularly upset members of my staff, who had worked hard during their free time to support Doug's campaign through fundraising, press outreach, and briefing Doug on relevant issues. One staffer wrote to me, "I think that I can speak for your staff in saying that none of us really expected to get any credit or praise for what we did—we all would have helped no matter where we were or what we were doing—but we certainly didn't expect to get criticized or cause you to get criticized."[7]

I was not the only fellow Democrat whom Doug publicly criticized in the year following the election. In 1986, Doug began, without warning, publicly disparaging the policies of his own Democratic governor, Jerry Baliles, and decisions of the Democratically led General Assembly. On several occasions, Doug "broadsided" the governor, mostly on issues of corrections and transportation policy, two hot topics in Virginia at the time.[8] The transportation issue was especially egregious because Doug, as the lieutenant governor, had agreed to function as Baliles's "eyes and ears" on the important State Highway and Transportation Commission and had presided over a contentious special session in the Virginia General Assembly to debate the plan. After staying silent over the merits of the plan through the session, Doug had, without warning to the governor, publicly criticized the commission's work. Not only was Governor Baliles blindsided, but now Democratic state senators, who had just been through the bruising special session, felt, as one said, "'sandbagged' by Wilder."[9] Even politicians who agreed with Doug's criticisms were chagrined that he had waited until a week *after* the vote on the related tax increase to speak up. "It's mystifying," said one state senator.[10]

By October 1986, the *Washington Post* reported on Wilder's criticism of the Virginia General Assembly and governor as "the latest chapter in the political saga of what might be called 'Doug Wilder: His Own Man.'"[11]

Though many of Virginia's Democratic leaders, including Governor Baliles, were frustrated and angry, there was a reluctance to confront Doug because he was unpredictable and obviously willing to publicly go after members of his own party. But I felt that I couldn't let Doug continue with his erratic attacks without letting him know that it was harming his credibility with his political allies. I thought that it was important to stand up to Doug.

So, in November 1985, and again in August 1986, I wrote Doug two frank, detailed personal letters that confronted him on his actions and let him know that he was harming his relationships in the state. Letters may seem antiquated now, but in the mid-1980s—before email or mobile phones—it seemed like the most straightforward way to lay out all of the facts and have a written record of my concerns.

In the first letter, I reminded Doug of the scope of the commitment to his candidacy by both myself and members of my staff, the work we'd done on his behalf, and the history of our friendship.

"Your victory sent an extraordinarily positive message throughout Virginia and across the nation," I said, "and I urge you not to let your opportunity pass by or let the bright potential your victory represents go sour."[12]

In my second letter, I reiterated this sentiment, as well as serious concerns about how his treatment of his friends and allies, including Governor Baliles and other Virginia elected officials, was hurting his credibility.

"I am not talking about disagreements on policy matters or on individual issues where honest differences ought to be raised and discussed," I said. "What I am talking about are deliberate distortions and untruths, and the blindsiding of allies without at least trying to resolve differences first."[13]

I ended the letter by trying to impress upon Doug how important it was that we sit down and talk, since we'd always been able to work out differences well in person. I tried several times to get an in-person meeting with Doug where we could discuss this face-to-face, and my staff went back and forth with his, but to no avail. Though I fully expected my correspondence to start a conversation, Doug never responded to either letter. When I crossed paths with him at events, I would remind him that I was still waiting for a response. Doug would always say, "I'll get back to you," but as the months went by, that didn't happen.

By November 1986, when I took George's phone call about the latest round of public criticisms, my frustration was at a breaking point. I listened with disbelief to George recount what Goldman had said. It was one thing to claim that I was getting too much credit for Doug's win—that was, at least, a matter of some debate or perspective. But to claim that I worked *against* his election on the basis of race was both patently false and directly counter to my core ideals. What was worse, George pointed out that a whole new crop of reporters had been assigned to cover Virginia politics since the 1985 election, and they were reporting Doug's words as though they were facts, without any examination of what had happened in the campaign.

"These new reporters don't know the history," George said. "If you don't correct the record now, that will be the new record."

George wanted to release the letters to the press to give them a factual account of the previous year. I was reluctant, but I took his advice, and on December 3, 1986, George released the letters to the press. As I said to reporters, I could keep turning the other cheek, but eventually, "You just plain run out of cheeks."[14] Within hours, the whole state was buzzing with the news.

The next day, two dozen red roses were delivered to my office from a longtime Democratic activist, along with a note to thank me for standing up to Doug for what he'd done to Jerry, me, and his other longtime political allies.

Doug immediately condemned the letters' release, calling it, in one of his better plays on words, "an act of incontinence." But my letters had raised serious questions, so Doug now faced intense public and media pressure to do something to put the matter to rest. "The honeymoon is over and controversy is engulfing Lt. Gov. Douglas Wilder," began one article.[15] Within a week, Doug arranged a meeting with me.

On December 17, 1986, Doug came to my home in McLean. Though we had agreed to keep the meeting private, a gaggle of cameras and media materialized outside at the end of our driveway. Lynda sent a plate of homemade fudge out to the freezing reporters, and later, when leaving the house with one of our daughters, told them, "You know, when the governor says his schedule is private, that's what he means."[16] The press readily ate the fudge but declined to leave.

Inside, Doug and I sat together at the dining room table for nearly three hours. Doug argued vigorously against some of the points I'd raised in my letters, insisting that I should publicly renounce them. Doug was an excellent debater, and with his combination of charisma and chutzpah, I believe he expected me to give in.

I was happy to quibble over tactics, but I stood by the letters, which were entirely factual. I also wasn't interested in making things any more difficult for him and didn't feel any need for meaningless displays of power. I just wanted what I'd wanted all along: for Doug to stop making erroneous remarks, and for any talk of a "feud" between us to be ended. Doug finally agreed, and the two of us stood at the table and shook hands.

There was one remaining roadblock: the reporters who were still camped out at the end of our driveway. I knew that Doug wouldn't want to face them just yet—he was leaving the meeting with no concessions from me to announce, and he'd agreed not to criticize me anymore for having written the letters. I was sensitive to his predicament and offered him a quieter, if unorthodox, way to get past the media scrum.

A few minutes later, Doug left through our back door, which faces the Potomac River. He worked his way in the dark along the steep hillside to our neighbor's house, where I had arranged for his car to pick him up. It took the press about four hours to finally catch up with him, and by that time he was able to control the dialogue, merely acknowledging that we'd had a good meeting and leaving it at that.

We issued a joint statement later that night that offered "a glimmer of friendship," according to the *Washington Post*. The reporter added that "there was no word on whether fudge would be provided to reporters attempting to cover the men's future summits."[17]

So far, the so-called "feud" with Doug Wilder had been the only ripple in my otherwise relatively tranquil time out of political office. For my part, I was glad that we could put the whole thing behind us. I always liked Doug personally, and I appreciated his political abilities. Doug had faced and overcome far bigger challenges than I had, and I respected that. I thought it was important, in this case, to set the record straight, but I didn't enjoy this kind of personality-driven politics. I believed, or at least hoped, based on my experience in the political arena in the 1960s, 1970s, and early 1980s, that serious political reporters would ultimately be more interested in the issues than in chasing down schoolyard barbs between grown men. I wanted to avoid any more personal attacks and focus instead on legitimate policy issues.

19

A New Challenge

I NEVER IMAGINED myself hitchhiking in Europe, but there I was, the former governor of Virginia, standing on the side of the road in Belgium in a suit and tie, with my thumb out.

I was on another trip for Hunton & Williams, this time with Mike Barr, a partner at the firm and head of the Washington office. We were scheduled to meet with the secretary general of NATO, Lord Peter Carrington, at the organization's headquarters on the outskirts of Brussels. We'd hired a car and driver to take us to the meeting, but the car broke down well outside the city. With cell phones not yet an option, and no town in sight, we had no way of contacting NATO headquarters or calling for another car. So, Mike and I did the next best thing: we stood on the side of the highway and tried to flag down a ride.

The first vehicle that pulled over to offer help was a large commercial truck filled, as it turned out, with kiwifruit. Mike and I explained our dilemma to the driver as best we could—neither of us were proficient in any of Belgium's principal languages—and he graciously invited us to hop into the cab. A short time later, we pulled up to the checkpoint of the heavily guarded NATO compound. Mike and I climbed down from the cab of the truck in our suits and ties and carrying our briefcases, and walked over to the guards, who met us, unsurprisingly, with a considerable amount of skepticism. After several slightly confused phone calls between the sentry post and the secretary general's office, however, the guards stopped their snickering, snapped smart salutes, and escorted the two Americans from the fruit truck into the headquarters.

DURING THE THREE years after my term as governor, international travel became a mainstay of my schedule and allowed me to spend more time on issues involving international relations.

My interest in international relations had developed slowly over many years. As a child, my only contact with foreign lands was to travel with my father in our family car from Arizona just across the border to Nogales,

Mexico, where he'd buy the alcohol for the dude ranch my parents were managing. Customs allowed him to bring over a certain amount of liquor per person, regardless of age, so he would bring me along to double his allotment.

Like many other young American men and women, I first truly saw the world in the uniform of the United States military. In the summer of 1958, following my freshman year of college, I arrived at the Norfolk Naval Base in a midshipman's uniform for my "3rd class cruise," a NROTC training exercise in which midshipmen live and work essentially as enlisted personnel. I was assigned to the USS *Harlan R. Dickson,* which had scheduled ports of call in Spain, Norway, and the Netherlands.

In the next ten years, as an officer in the United States Marine Corps, I got to visit many different countries—from Sardinia, to Haiti, to Malta, to Vietnam. After active duty, much of my international travel would continue to be in an official or semi-official capacity. In the mid-1970s, before I was elected to a political office, Lynda and I had the opportunity to travel with her mother to some of the world's most interesting countries at the invitation of their leaders. Everywhere we went, Mrs. Johnson was so beloved that she was often treated like a visiting head of state. We were the guests of Shah Mohammad Reza Pahlavi of Iran and enjoyed tea with former prime minister Golda Meir at her Tel Aviv apartment. Prime Minister Meir was such a magnetic person that even Mrs. Johnson's Secret Service agents asked for a picture—something that Lynda and I had never seen them do before and have never seen them do since.

By traveling with Mrs. Johnson, Lynda and I got to participate in international diplomacy in a very up-close and personal way. The Israel trip itself did much to increase my interest in foreign relations. I had read a lot about the country's complex international situation, but I got a deeper perspective when Prime Minister Yitzhak Rabin took me on a personal tour of the Golan Heights, a strip of disputed high ground between Israel and Syria. I could see why the terrain of the Heights made it such a tactically important area. And as we walked over the Heights, Rabin discussed the complex relations between Israelis and Arabs in the area. Seeing the terrain and speaking to Rabin, I got a much more thorough understanding of the regional conflict—the internal political pressures faced by the Israeli prime minister as well as the external security concerns—than I did in all of my reading on the topic.

In 1979, while I was serving as lieutenant governor, I led a delegation, under the auspices of the American Council of Young Political Leaders (ACYPL), to the People's Republic of China. This was my maiden voyage into diplomacy where I was at the helm, and I thoroughly enjoyed the experience.

When I became governor of Virginia, I went on trade missions and foreign delegations designed to generate foreign investment and job creation in the Commonwealth. There was a fair amount of diplomatic work, but the focus was primarily on economic issues rather than international relations.

When my term as governor ended, I began to travel overseas more frequently, both for my law firm (such as the trip in Belgium) and at the behest of pro-democracy organizations. I was able to secure meetings with foreign leaders largely because, as a former governor who had left office with promising approval ratings, there were intimations that I might run for higher office, and developing a relationship was seen as beneficial. I'm sure it also helped that I was the son-in-law of President Johnson, a towering figure on the international stage who had passed away only fifteen years earlier.

Peter Hardin at the *Richmond Times-Dispatch* noticed my busy international travel schedule in April 1987:

> In Japan two weeks ago, he met with Prime Minister Yasuhiro Nakasone.
>
> In Central America recently, he conferred with President Jose Napoleon Duarte of El Salvador, President Oscar Arias of Costa Rica, and President Jose Azcona of Honduras.
>
> In West Germany last year, he met with Chancellor Helmut Kohl, Foreign Minister Hans-Dietrich Genscher and Finance Minister Gerhard Stoltenberg.
>
> He has huddled with Soviet "refuseniks" in Moscow and listened to wounded Contra guerrillas at a hospital in Honduras. He has discussed international issues with NATO Secretary General Lord Carrington and visited with French Prime Minister Jacques Chirac at a recent embassy function here.
>
> And he has talked about trade, arms reduction and terrorism to audiences in Tokyo; Latvia in the Soviet Union; Bonn, West Germany; and in the United States.[1]

I was, as Hardin put it, "quietly schooling" myself in foreign affairs — broadening my knowledge about America's relationships abroad.[2] Overall, I visited more than thirty countries in the three years after my term as governor. The countries were frequently not stable democracies, and I would meet with leaders to listen to them discuss their challenges, while promoting democracy and basic human rights—sometimes referred to as unofficial "track II" diplomacy.

One of the most memorable such trips was to Angola to meet with guerilla leader Jonas Savimbi, the head of UNITA, the insurgent movement that was supported by the United States. (Eduardo dos Santos, head of the Soviet and Cuban-backed Communist government, had declined to meet with me.) In order to reach Savimbi's command post, hidden deep in the jungle, we were given instructions to meet at a base camp, where we were provided tailor-made UNITA uniforms to wear and shown to our transportation: a rather precarious-looking Beechcraft King Air propeller plane, which I assumed had been procured by the CIA. We boarded the plane after sundown and flew under the cover of darkness to evade the government's forces. We flew as low as possible, just above treetop level, with no exterior lights and no communication systems running. At one point we were flying so low we could see a herd of elephants in the moonlight on the grasslands just below us.

As we neared our destination at a prearranged time, uniformed UNITA rebels emerged from their foxholes to light smudge pots to outline the makeshift runway so our pilots could see where to land. We met with Savimbi in his command post from midnight until 5:00 a.m., discussing his strategy to defeat the Communist forces. Then we hurried back to the airstrip to leave the same way we had arrived, before sunrise exposed our flight path.

On trips like the one to Angola, I gained invaluable firsthand knowledge of many hard-to-reach nations and was able to develop relationships with many foreign leaders, even several who had a loose or tenuous relationship with the United States government.

However, there were very few arenas in which I could continue to pursue this policy area. To have a hand in affecting international relations and national security policy, I'd need to serve in the executive or legislative branches of the federal government. With a Republican president in office in the mid-1980s, my chances of being offered a cabinet position were slim. So, once again, I began to consider another run for office—this time, the U.S. Senate.

The decision to run seemed like a natural one. I knew by then that, though I was privileged to work at a highly regarded law firm with very talented people, the life of a practicing attorney in a large firm did not fully engage me in the same way that public service did.

Running for a second nonconsecutive term as governor of Virginia in 1989 had also been a possibility, and an appealing one, since I had found my first term both challenging and rewarding. But going back to the Governor's Mansion felt a little like trying to go home again—a step backward that had little chance of living up to expectations.

Of course, the other office that I was rumored to have had interest in for years was the presidency. When asked, I would say only that the speculation made it more likely that people would return my phone calls. But I also avoided making trips during this period to Iowa or New Hampshire—trips that might have unintentionally signaled a run I didn't plan to make. In truth, I never intended to be a presidential candidate.

For one thing, I didn't fit the mold of a traditional Democrat. In foreign affairs, I was more hawkish than the Democratic base at the time. On fiscal matters, I was more conservative and willing to cut programs that were considered sacrosanct by the Democratic establishment. These positions had made me a strong candidate in Virginia but would be huge liabilities in a national Democratic Party nomination contest, which too often required candidates to meet certain party litmus tests. Unfortunately, for someone who didn't always fall in line with his own party's base, that meant a primary nomination would have been practically impossible.

Additionally, I wasn't temperamentally well-suited to making the type of overly optimistic campaign promises increasingly necessary in presidential nominating contests. This would make it hard for me to tell Americans two things: where I wanted to take the country, and how I proposed to get there. Trying to wedge my vision for America's role on the international stage into a campaign sound bite took me into territory in which I was not comfortable—having to say one thing to get elected and do something else to govern. I had developed a point of view on foreign policy based on my many meetings with foreign leaders and my view of America's role in the world. However, translating this view into a succinct piece of campaign rhetoric would have made it too simplistic to fit into every complex international conflict that America might encounter over the following four years. In my previous campaigns, I had insisted on keeping our goals realistic and giving honest (and sometimes unpopular) opinions on a policy or situation. I had always tried to underpromise on the stump and overperform in office—not an easy way to win any election, and particularly a presidential primary. I knew in my heart that I couldn't create a vision optimistic enough to excite the electorate without making promises on which I didn't believe, in good conscience, that I could deliver.

Just as importantly, I simply didn't have the necessary fire in the belly to endure a long, brutal, high-profile campaign. I had had the uncommon experience of being a firsthand witness to the toll the office could take on a president's health, heart, and soul—and the cost to their loved ones. Lynda, I knew, still bore scars from the vitriol she and her family faced during her father's time in the White House. Her father left office exhausted and prematurely aged, and he died just four years later, without getting the joy of watching his grandchildren grow up. I didn't want to put myself or my family through that experience.

While I didn't plan to run for president, I was interested in the U.S. Senate seat up for election in Virginia in 1988. I would have to challenge the Republican incumbent, Senator Paul Trible, who was expected to run again. Trible was only forty years old, just finishing his first term, and had already raised more than $1 million for his reelection campaign. But polls in the summer of 1987 showed that, in a head-to-head matchup, I'd have a distinct advantage. Then, in September 1987, I was at an event in Hopewell, Virginia, when a TV reporter came up to me, camera rolling and microphone in hand, asking for comment on Trible's announcement that he wasn't going to seek reelection. I'm told my expression of disbelief—captured on camera—was apparent. Trible's decision caught virtually the entire political establishment off guard.

Within a week of Trible's surprise announcement, I received private phone calls from two prominent Republicans—my 1981 gubernatorial opponent, former attorney general Marshall Coleman, and U.S. congressman Stan Parris—each asking if I intended to run for Trible's Senate seat or make another run for governor. When I replied that I was only considering the Senate, each thanked me and immediately accelerated their plans to seek the Republican nomination for governor in 1989, where they would later be joined by none other than former senator Paul Trible.

On Tuesday, November 10, 1987, I stood in front of a bank of microphones at the Richmond headquarters of Hunton & Williams to announce my intention to run for the U.S. Senate.

The morning of my announcement was jubilant—I was declared the front-runner for a seat in the U.S. Senate. But that same day we received some devastating news. George Stoddart, my brilliant and dedicated press secretary throughout my gubernatorial years, had a brain tumor. I had relied on George's savvy advice to weather crises and to promote my state priorities throughout my administration. George's relationships with individual members of the press combined with his outstanding instincts to give me a road map through even the toughest terrain. He understood what reporters wanted, what their editors needed, how to give it to them, and whether to steer clear.

After the press conference was over, I went to see George at his home. True to form, he was upbeat about his prospects. Unfortunately, the prognosis wasn't good, and he was too sick to return to work. As the election drew closer, I felt his absence, both as a colleague and a friend. I often found myself missing the levity of his presence in our office and the counsel I had come to rely on. It was then—in this next chapter in the public eye—that I could have used his help more than ever.

But it was not to be. George fought his illness valiantly for the next year. We were robbed of his vitality, insight, and advice when the tumor took his life in September 1988. George's death was a staggering blow to me personally and to the many others who had known and loved him.

MY OFFICIAL SENATE campaign launch was on April 7, in front of a flag-waving crowd of hundreds of supporters on the steps of the Virginia Capitol. The mood was ebullient. Thanks to a few good friends—principally Al Smith, Alan Diamonstein, and Bill Thomas—my fundraising had already proven effective. My statewide approval ratings remained high, and I had a popular record from the governorship and the DLC chairmanship on which to run. Expectations were so high as we kicked off the race that I had to warn my supporters not to think of it as "a cake walk."[3]

But we still didn't know who my Republican opponent might be. Finally, at the Virginia Republican convention in June, the GOP made an unexpected choice: a Black Baptist minister named Maurice Dawkins, a former civil rights activist, Washington lobbyist, and skilled orator. Taking the stage at the convention, Dawkins extolled Christian, conservative values and denounced me in a speech that so electrified the many uncommitted delegates that he managed to capture the Republican nomination on the first ballot. According to the *Washington Post*, whatever Dawkins lacked in experience or fundraising potential, he "tried gamely to make up for it in exuberance, bobbing on the balls of his feet on the convention stage as he pledged to take a political 'baseball bat' to his Democratic rival."[4]

Dawkins was the first Black U.S. Senate candidate from either party in Virginia and seemed to offer Republicans a chance at winning over a substantial percentage of the Black vote, which was traditionally a Democratic voting bloc in an otherwise overwhelmingly Republican state. As a relatively unknown candidate, however, he would need more than that to beat me in the fall. He was determined to use his baseball bat, and he came out swinging.

Once his campaign was underway, Dawkins and Virginia Republican operatives began playing up every rumor about me he could find, implying all kinds of nefarious activities without once offering any proof. During our debates, Dawkins focused almost entirely on personal attacks rather than addressing any issues of real substance. The coverage in the *Washington Post* of our second debate began with the ominous line, "Virginia's U.S. Senate campaign grew nastier today."[5]

His campaign ads painted me as nothing short of criminal, and his campaign produced a brochure titled "The Chuck Robb they don't want you to know about!" Even Republican senator John Warner criticized Dawkins's ads for being over-the-top.

The irony was that the personal attacks and dirty tactics had very little effect on Election Day. On November 8, 1988, I won election to the U.S. Senate in a landslide. With 71 percent of the vote, I ended up with a greater vote total than any previous candidate on the ballot in any election, state or national, in Virginia's history. This lopsided victory was in spite of the fact that Republican George H. W. Bush had defeated Michael Dukakis in Virginia for the office of president on the same ballot with 59 percent of the vote to Dukakis's 39 percent. So once again, a large number of Virginians who had voted for me had also voted for a Republican at the top of their ticket.

I was gratified that so many Virginians had put their faith in me and was looking forward to a whole new and energizing challenge. I was finally headed to the U.S. Senate and happy to put the nastiness of campaigning behind me.

20

The Most Exclusive Club

ON JANUARY 3, 1949, Lynda and her mother sat in the gallery of the United States Senate. They heard the secretary of the Senate call then senator-elect Lyndon Baines Johnson's name and watched him stride down the aisle alongside his state's senior senator. They saw Senator Arthur Vandenberg, his right hand raised, administer the oath: "Do you solemnly swear that you will support and defend the Constitution of the United States?" And they heard the confident, proud response: "I do."[1]

Mrs. Johnson remembered the day as a blur of confusion, with senators and their families hurrying in and out of the Senate chamber and to various events. Lynda's recollection of the day was even more limited: "I was 4 years old and I don't remember a word."[2]

Forty years later, to the day, both of these indomitable women stood in the Senate chamber once again, this time surrounded by our three daughters, my parents, and other members of the Johnson and Robb families. When the secretary of the Senate called my name, I walked down the same aisle, escorted by Virginia's senior senator, John Warner, between the same rows of the desks where once sat Senate greats—Webster, Dirksen, La Follette. I stood before the dais, framed in marbled columns, and took the oath. When I said, "I do," the Johnsons and Robbs in the gallery gave a standing ovation. It was always a boon to have that stalwart team in my corner.

After the ceremony in the Capitol, Lynda and some of my staff had planned a reception to properly thank family, friends, key supporters, campaign workers, and Democratic committee members at Washington's Union Station. Our small group of family members walked the two blocks to the party, expecting to enjoy a warm reception and a cheerful reunion with friends and supporters. When we entered the station's cavernous vaulted atrium, we found a virtual pep rally. More than three thousand people had poured in by car, bus, and train from all across Virginia, a far greater turnout than we expected. Guests were spilling out of the room we'd reserved, and into the station's vaulted Main Hall. Al Smith, my friend and advisor, told the *Washington Post* that day, "What started out as a little ice cream social sort of got out of hand."[3]

The enthusiasm was especially sweet for Lynda and me. Though I had won by a very lopsided margin, it had been a brutal campaign full of the kind of personal attacks that I abhorred. We were relieved to be able to finally put it behind us.

WHEN THE CEREMONIES and the celebrations were over, my days were filled with an endless list of details to complete the organization of my Senate office, staff, and duties. Given my policy interests, I would have liked to have started out on the Armed Services and Finance Committees, but my senior colleague, John Warner, was already on Armed Services, and there were no vacancies on the Finance Committee, so I was happy to get assigned to the Foreign Relations Committee, the Budget Committee, and the Commerce Committee, which would touch on the areas of foreign relations and fiscal responsibility.

Majority Leader George Mitchell also knew that I was interested in playing a leadership role in the Senate hierarchy, but I wasn't a good fit for a position such as party whip, where I would be required to advocate party positions on issues I did not necessarily agree with. So, in my second year in office, George appointed me to chair the Democratic Senatorial Campaign Committee (DSCC), where it was my job to get Democrats elected to the Senate in 1992 by raising money and providing campaign support. While I'd support all kinds of Democrats across the country, I also took on the role with the personal goal of electing more female Democratic senators. At the time, there were only two female senators, Nancy Kassebaum (R-KA) and Barbara Mikulski (D-MD). But we had an impressive slate of women planning to run in the 1992 election cycle, and I was looking forward to helping them. I readily accepted the responsibility and the additional time commitment of fundraisers and strategy meetings across the country.

My schedule was quickly packed. The Senate's chaotic rhythm was difficult to adjust to. In comparison to the sometimes glacial pace of actually passing legislation in the Senate, a senator's day-to-day schedule can be brutally fast-paced. Frustratingly, as a relatively junior senator, you have very little control over when your meetings, hearings, events, and votes are scheduled, because much of it is subject to decisions made by the Senate leadership. It's impossible to develop any real routine, and there's no such thing as a typical day.

My hectic and unpredictable schedule made me a frequently absent father and husband, but Lynda, as she always had, carried the bulk of the load at home. By that time, our two eldest daughters were in college—Lucinda at Princeton University and Catherine at my law school alma mater, the University of Virginia. I'm proud to say that all three of our daughters would eventually graduate from highly regarded institutions of higher learning— Catherine would go on to get her J.D. from the University of Texas at Austin School of Law, and Jennifer would later attend Duke University. But when I was elected to the Senate, Jennifer was still in middle school. Whenever possible, I would take the time to get to her soccer or field hockey games, standing behind the goal to watch our daughter play goalkeeper from her vantage point. Lynda, of course, never missed a game. I was particularly lucky to have a partner who could step in and, in truth, fill both parental roles, while I tried to fill the role of "senator."

Because I represented Virginia, a state so close to Washington, I had more requests for meetings with constituents and interest groups than senators from more geographically distant states, and, as a result, I spent many evenings working late. For my first few years in the Senate, I was almost obsessive about not missing votes, no matter what time of day or night they might occur and no matter the topic. For a while, I had one of the longest streaks of not having missed a single vote in the Senate. Even when I was away from Capitol Hill on a day that votes were being held, I would faithfully keep my Senate pager on hand (in the days before cell phones) and respond to its beeps by excusing myself from meetings or events to return for a vote. But finally, in my fifth year, I raced back to the floor just after a vote closed, and my streak was broken. As my staff could attest, I was less than pleased at the time, but soon after, I saw how unimportant the streak had been. I still made a point of making it to every vote that I possibly could, but I was a little less fanatical about it.

Most meetings were packed into narrow time slots, and topics frequently jumped dizzyingly from one meeting to the next. In the span of an hour, I could have three different meetings to discuss totally unrelated topics, which may or may not have had anything to do with my own legislative priorities. With so many diverse issues vying for a senator's attention, it's simply not possible for one person to have the requisite knowledge about every single topic that might come before the Congress, a fact that makes legislative aides and other staff members indispensable.

Luckily, I had a truly first-rate team, starting with my right-hand man,

David McCloud, who returned as my chief of staff—the role he had played while I was governor. David would be a steady presence during my first few years in the Senate.

Right outside my office sat my primary gatekeeper, Pat Mayer, who served as my assistant and de facto mother confessor of the whole office. With a steady hand, Pat filled her role, which was so crucial as to defy definition, as she had since my time in the lieutenant governor's office.

Another constant was Susan Albert, who had started in my gubernatorial office, stayed on as one of my assistants through the years at Hunton & Williams, and now joined the Senate staff. Incredibly hardworking and unflinchingly loyal, Susan had many different roles over the two decades that she worked with me, all of them essential to the smooth running of the office.

In addition to Susan and Pat, there was a vital crew of staff members that stayed with me for all twelve years in the Senate: Peter Cleveland, Jim Connell, Anne Geyer, Debbie Lawson-Goins, Matt McGowan, Jim O'Quinn, and JoAnn Pulliam. We were also joined along the way by some other very able staff members, including Kim Anderson, Rob Braziel, Christine Bridge, William Clyburn, Brian Cohrs, John DiBiase, Sheila Dwyer, Julius Hobson, Bryce Hunter, Jennifer Ney, Wyatt Shields, Julia Sutherland, Sandy Thomas, Bobby Watson, and Peggy Wilhide.[4]

Kerry Walsh Skelly was a rising star at Hunton & Williams when she volunteered to help during my Senate campaign, and after the election I hired her as my new legislative director in my Senate office.

David McCloud brought in Steve Johnson, whom I hired as press secretary. Steve wasn't really a "political animal" and hadn't worked on a campaign, though he had been a reporter for several years and had even written his doctoral dissertation at the University of Virginia about my governorship.

These bright, dedicated members of my staff were only a few of many who added their talents to my Senate office during my tenure. For both Lynda and me, these individuals, who dedicated so much of their time and industry to my efforts, became an extension of our family. They created an office filled with diligence and comradery that was free of the internecine squabbling of some political staffs. I didn't realize until much later that it is rare to have as little staff turnover as my office experienced during my time in both state and federal government. Several members of my staff were with me through multiple terms and even multiple offices. Most of them have remained close friends to this day. Much to my enjoyment, we had a few interoffice marriages. During my time in the Senate, I was even asked to be best man by a former member of my staff who was still very much a part of the "family"—Ben Dendy. I was happy to serve, but I also knew that I'd be flying back to the United States from Russia on a Senate trip the same day as the wedding, so I made sure that Ben had a backup.

It was this team that stuck with me through some very tough times, and I could never adequately express how grateful I was to them for their loyalty and dedication.

I would come to rely on the support of this crew in the unfamiliar environment of the Senate. Unlike the governorship, the Senate did not fit with my natural tendency toward clear chains of command and organization. In that way, I took after my father, who was organized even in his final acts. In early 1995, when my father was in his late eighties, my mother was no longer able to care for him in their home, so he moved into a nursing home. He began immediately to start getting his affairs in order—making a new will, updating his records, and the like. Then he carefully filled out an absentee ballot for an upcoming election, put it in an envelope, addressed and stamped it, and set it out to be mailed. When that was complete, he lay back on his bed and died quietly on October 17, 1995, at the age of eighty-seven. When I went with my siblings to help clear out his things, we found them already neatly arranged, boxed, and ready to be taken away.

I completely understood my father's inclination to have everything in its place. I appreciated well-ordered systems, and I liked to be able to see the whole board, to make judgments with all the information in front of me. I'd been able to do that as governor, where final, passed legislation was sent to my desk for a signature or veto.

It was very different in the Senate, where a single senator's vote on any given bill, some of which are hundreds of pages long, was only one step in the lengthy and arduous process of making a law. Because there were several votes on a bill—to get it out of committee, to bring it to the floor for discussion, to end discussion, and so on—long before it reached final passage, there were many stages at which a bill could change fundamentally. It could be hung with amendments (sometimes so many that it was called a "Christmas tree bill"), be stripped of all impact by rewrites, or it could change significantly when the House and Senate versions were reconciled in a conference committee. A vote at any stage doesn't give a senator any real control over the end result, merely a voice on the particular action on the proposed legislation at that time.

Before I had even taken the oath, I could see that it might be a challenging adjustment. In November 1988, Senators Daniel Inouye, J. Bennett Johnston, and George Mitchell were in the process of lining up support among Democratic senators for the position of majority leader. As a new senator without previous ties to any of the candidates, I was assiduously courted by all three. Senator Inouye even offered the Senate desk once used by then senator Lyndon Johnson—a nice ceremonial prize for any up-and-coming politician hoping to follow in LBJ's footsteps. While I found the whole process fascinating, it wasn't how I wanted to choose a leader. I met with all three candidates, and after consulting with my staff and other Democratic senators, I decided to vote for Mitchell, who, I felt, had the most compelling leadership skills and experience to succeed. But I didn't make my support contingent on a special favor, which I was later told struck Mitchell's office as odd.

When I sat down for the first time on the floor of the Senate, it was behind one of the Senate's beautiful mahogany desks, but it wasn't LBJ's. I don't know who got LBJ's former desk that term—I simply accepted the next available desk.

21

Distant Lands, Faraway Lives

MY WORK ON the Foreign Relations Committee was one of the most fascinating parts of my time as a United States senator, but it was also one of the most time-consuming. Understanding the nuances of the political, cultural, and social conflict in a foreign country was difficult and complex, but it was absolutely necessary when we were making decisions about how such conflicts would affect U.S. foreign policy. In order to better understand such situations and the major players involved, I traveled frequently on Senate recesses to countries experiencing political or social upheaval.

When I began my first term in the Senate, America's most important international relationship was with the United Soviet Socialist Republic (USSR). In January 1989, the Cold War was still in progress, the USSR was intact, and the Berlin Wall separated democratic West Germany from Communist East Germany. But there were signs of change in the air. Since becoming general secretary of the Communist Party of the Soviet Union in 1986, Mikhail Gorbachev had been enacting reforms that loosened the grip of the government, allowing non-Communist parties to participate in elections for the first time. To help revive the stagnant Soviet economy, Gorbachev sought to improve Soviet relations with the rest of the world, broaching relations with the West for the first time in decades.

Entering the Senate during this period gave me the opportunity to deal with international questions at a time of great change and uncertainty. With the benefit of hindsight, the fall of the Soviet Union and the independence of former Soviet states seems like the natural outcome. But, at the time, there was little telling how the Soviets loosening their control over their satellite countries would affect peace and stability throughout the world. Without control from the USSR, satellite countries could be left with power vacuums, leading to ethnic strife, regional feuds, and leadership struggles.

One of the countries left with an uncertain future was Poland, and in 1989 we watched apprehensively as the country took its first steps away from Soviet control, which it had been under since before the end of World War II. In June 1989, Poland held its first free and open election since the war, and Polish voters defied their former oppressors by electing a non-Communist majority to parliament. In the past, this action would have been met with Soviet tanks swiftly rolling over the border at the Fulda Gap from the east. But as the summer wore on, this didn't happen, and everyone was waiting to see who would make the next move.

Senator Alan Cranston (D-CA) planned a fact-finding congressional delegation to Poland in August 1989 and invited me to join. This was not my first trip behind the Iron Curtain—I had visited several Eastern Bloc countries and had even been to Moscow at the height of the Cold War. On one trip before I was in the Senate, I was given a tour of the new, unfinished U.S. embassy, built by the Soviet government. It was an unusual tour due to the fact that the U.S. government had discovered that the Soviets had installed eavesdropping devices in the permanent superstructure of the building, inside concrete floors and steel columns. At the time of our visit, our intelligence agencies didn't want the Soviets to know that the United States knew about the bugging, so when we reached the bugged section of the building, the tour was conducted in complete silence. The State Department officer leading our tour had to write everything out for us on a notepad. It turned out that the eavesdropping devices were so cleverly and deeply hidden in the structure that they couldn't be removed without complete demolition.

During that trip, Moscow under Soviet control had a quiet feel, and there was a pervading awareness of government presence. That omnipresent Soviet control meant that we were assured total security and more freedom of movement—we could have ridden around on bicycles without fear because the government wouldn't have let anything happen to prominent visitors. Ironically, it was in the countries that were friendly to the United States, the democratic countries where the citizens had more freedom of movement, that we had to use evasive driving techniques.

When our delegation arrived in Warsaw in August 1989, it was immediately apparent from the atmosphere that this was no longer a city in a strictly controlled Soviet state. It had an electric feel that was lacking in Cold War Moscow. The newly formed anti-Communist government had yet to choose a cabinet, or state publicly whether the Communists would have any part in it. There were worries that excluding all Communists from the government could provoke vocal or even violent blowback, from within the country and without. The new government's next steps could have destabilizing consequences.

Over three days, we met with leaders on both sides—the deputy to the previous Communist parliament, the head of the new victorious party, the sitting Soviet-backed president, and the foreign minister. We questioned each on how the multiple groups, factions, and power brokers could react to a variety of possible next steps.

Watching the situation from Washington, D.C., it could seem as though the new Polish leaders were being indecisive, or even dishonest, because their statements on building the new government were changing weekly. But as soon as we began talking face-to-face, it became clear that the political situation on the ground was shifting rapidly, and that the outcome was, indeed, far from certain.

We spent the most time with Lech Walesa, the chairman of Solidarity, the trade union that had become an activist movement and was now the leading political party in the non-Communist coalition. We were eager to meet Walesa and pleased to find that he seemed very much to live up to his image. His personality was colorful, and he gave the overall impression of a natural leader who was invested in moving Poland beyond its Soviet-controlled past. It wasn't until many years later that Walesa would be accused of having been a Soviet collaborator in the 1970s, a charge that he denied.

We also met with President Wojciech Jaruzelski, a former general in the Polish army who had led a repressive Soviet-backed military state for nearly a decade. I was anxious to see how he, and therefore his Russian backers, would handle the recent parliamentary elections.

When we met with Jaruzelski, our discussions were careful and littered with the language of diplomacy. Consistent with my briefings and the actions of his ruthless regime over the last decade, I found President Jaruzelski to be a model of a military dictator and Soviet puppet. What I found interesting about the discussion was that the president did not appear, in my estimation, to be the type of megalomaniacal dictator who would do anything in his power to retain control of Poland after having lost the popular election. He seemed to be more of an apparatchik, a tool of the Soviet Union, and not an ideologue. If Gorbachev was indeed serious about allowing free elections in Poland, I didn't believe that the Polish president would stand in the way.

It was a subtle but very important difference that would not have been evident without a face-to-face meeting. Small cues—like which leaders are protected by a well-ordered guard, whose guards were smartly dressed, and whose offices have been stylishly decorated—can tell you who holds the real power in the country.

These same types of cues would be very much in evidence on a trip to Liberia in 1991. I visited Liberia on a congressional delegation (CODEL) led by Senator Paul Simon, who chaired the Senate Foreign Relations Subcommittee on African Affairs. We were scheduled to meet with President Amos Sawyer, but we noticed on the flight there that we didn't have a meeting with the Liberian warlord Charles Taylor, the opposition leader. As a rule, when I visited a foreign country, I tried to meet with both the ruling and opposition leaders.

At this stage of the bloody ethnic conflict in Liberia, Taylor claimed to oppose a government under President Sawyer that had come to power through a coup d'etat and held that power through fraudulent elections. Neither side had the clear-cut moral high ground, and the war crimes for which Taylor would later be indicted by the World Court were still years away.

Our embassy representative in Monrovia couldn't set up a meeting with Taylor because we had no diplomatic relationship with the rebels, but we decided it was worth going outside of the support or protection of the U.S. State Department. So, my military liaison, Terry Paul, went out in the street, looking for a connection to set up a meeting. This was something of a specialty of Terry's, who had that rare mix of geniality and tenacity that could talk almost anyone into any harebrained scheme. An experienced Marine Corps officer with an infectious southern drawl, Terry was a mainstay of my international travel in the Senate. Somehow, he managed to set up a meeting with Taylor.

Senator Simon was not interested in joining us in this off-schedule excursion. So, Terry and I piled into a car driven by a supposed member of Taylor's group. We were joined by another mainstay of my Senate travel, Peter Cleveland. Peter, my aide on the Foreign Relations Committee and himself the son of a U.S. ambassador, was young, bright, quick on his feet, and ready to travel. The team of Terry and Peter was a major asset on any trip.

The three of us set off into the jungle, stopping at a great number of imposing checkpoints, many of them armed by what looked like nine-year-old boys, wearing helmets and carrying assault rifles. Once we were past their first checkpoint, traveling deeper into rebel-held territory, our safety was effectively in the rebels' power.

After about a half hour, we stopped in front of a suburban split-level home in a small clearing surrounded by dense jungle vegetation. Taylor's jungle hideout appeared as if it had been magically transported from an Ohio subdivision and materialized in the middle of the Liberian civil war. We walked into the house, slightly concerned that this surreal slice of Americana couldn't possibly be the headquarters for a notorious warlord. We sat down in the living room, and, after some anxious waiting, in came Taylor, greeting us as guests.

The conversation was animated but cordial. Taylor, who had graduated from Bentley College (now Bentley University) in Massachusetts, spoke fluent English. We were acutely aware, however, of the man who stood behind Taylor throughout, unmoving and expressionless: a burly six-foot-ten-inch security guard with a gleaming .45 revolver on his hip.

I told Taylor that the U.S. Congress was paying attention to the impact of the ongoing conflict, which had resulted in the killing, maiming, and terrorizing of hundreds of thousands of his countrymen. Taylor responded that he was fighting to rid his country of what he viewed as an oppressive regime. He saw his fight as completely justified, and the collateral casualties of that fight to be unfortunate but unavoidable.

The conversation with Taylor lasted several hours, by the end of which Terry, Peter, and I were more than ready to leave. I thanked Taylor and said that it was time we got back to Monrovia. But Taylor had one more surprise up his sleeve.

"Oh, no no no," Taylor said, in his most hospitable voice. He was very smooth, and his personal demeanor could be disarming. "You must stay for lunch."

I tried to beg off. We had appointments to keep and a schedule to get back on. I tried every excuse I could think of as Terry, Peter, and I inched toward the door.

"Oh, no," Taylor said, "I have refreshments!"

At that, he clapped his hands loudly and out from the kitchen came a bevy of young Liberian women carrying silver trays laden with cans of Colt 45 malt liquor.

We managed to get out the door without partaking and headed back through the jungle toward Monrovia.

The impression I got of Taylor was that of a very well-reasoned and well-organized military leader, not a madman or a thug. He was charming in a somewhat threatening way, and I could see immediately how he instilled both loyalty and fear in his followers.

But the journey itself had also been enlightening—we had traveled through relatively orderly security checkpoints in the region held by Taylor's forces, and the fact that Taylor had shown up at the appointed time and place revealed a certain level of organization in the rebel camp.

The subtle cues of atmosphere that you can pick up only in person were especially important in countries where the situation was far from straightforward. Few countries were as complex as Cambodia, a country on which, as chairman of the East Asia Subcommittee of the Foreign Relations Committee, I was particularly focused.

When I came to the Senate in 1989, the situation in Cambodia was unstable and uncertain. The puppet government was controlled by Vietnam, which was itself controlled by Soviet-backed Communists. In opposition, the former royalists were allied with the overthrown former government of the Khmer Rouge, the brutal regime led by Pol Pot, whose reign was marked by the systematic killing of more than 1.7 million Cambodians, now known as the Cambodian Genocide. The situation was made more confusing in the West because we had had so little direct government-to-government contact with Cambodia or its various leaders for many years.

When I made my first trip to the country in February 1990, peace talks were at a standstill, and I was particularly aware of the military and humanitarian implications of failure. America obviously had no interest in getting drawn into another protracted military conflict in Southeast Asia. At the same time, we were wary of what a Communist-controlled Cambodia could mean to American interests in the region. And the world now knew about the Khmer Rouge's "Killing Fields," and could not stand idly by if the country fell back into Khmer hands.

On the first day, I hopped between the base camps of the two major combatants by helicopter, meeting with commanders and observing their troops. To my surprise and relief, both camps were trim, neat, and well-ordered. The guards had proper uniforms and weapons that appeared functional. There were no assault rifles held together with duct tape, or bands of undisciplined troops roving in and out of the camps at will. In person, all signs pointed to two sides with the means and intention of restoring order and following the terms of a peace agreement. They also appeared positioned to return to a state of war should the peace talks break down.

The next day, I flew into Phnom Penh. Very few Americans had seen the streets of Cambodia's capital for decades, and few photographs of the city had made it beyond Cambodian borders. The impression that I got riding through the streets couldn't have been captured by still images anyway. Despite the scores of Cambodians on the streets, traveling to work and conducting their daily business in local shops, the sense I got was one of emptiness. The population felt sparse, and everyone we saw in the street seemed to be conducting their business as quickly as possible before they could duck back out of sight. More than any Senate briefing, this twenty-minute car ride through Phnom Penh made it clear that the people of Cambodia carried on with the banalities of everyday life in an environment of fear. The other striking sight was the lack of cars—our vehicle was surrounded by Cambodians riding bicycles and scooters, sometimes carrying entire families on the tiny frames, but very few automobiles. This was the surest sign for me that the Cambodian economy was woefully underdeveloped, and its people were suffering from the years of war and isolation.

I met with the major leaders, including Prime Minister Hun Sen, who embodied the complex nature of the conflict. Hun Sen had been a battalion commander in the Khmer Rouge regime, but he fled to Vietnam during internal purges, led a rebel army, and was now the prime minister of the Vietnamese-backed puppet government. The sense I got from Hun Sen was that he understood power and his moves were calculated to convey and maintain his own authority amid a very unstable situation. I met with Hun Sen at least three times over the years, and his manner never relaxed. He had a glass eye, which he would remove and clean during our conversation in what appeared to be an attempt to put us ill at ease and demonstrate his dominance. At our first meeting, Hun Sen's aide approached me in the holding room just before I was to go in to see the prime minister.

"The prime minister is not wearing a tie," the aide said. "You need to remove yours."

"I would prefer not to remove my tie," I responded calmly. "The prime minister is welcome to not wear a tie."

The aide looked flustered and tried to insist, while I remained calm and polite, but firm. When he had exhausted his arguments, the aide excused himself and left the room. A short time later, he returned—I could see Hun Sen, with my tie on. It was all a power game that I don't think the prime minister was accustomed to losing.

Despite his stern countenance, my first meeting with Hun Sen went reasonably well. We discussed the fragile state of the country but also broached the thorny topic of the missing remains of U.S. servicemen. More than two thousand military personnel were still listed as missing in Southeast Asia during the Vietnam War, and, at the time of my visit, we had not retrieved any remains from Cambodia. There had recently been hints of progress, so I brought the issue up with Hun Sen when we met and provided him and other Cambodian officials with information on missing military personnel. It was a humanitarian breakthrough when the Cambodians agreed, several months and much correspondence later, to allow an American identification team to examine what were believed to be the remains of eighteen of our missing servicemen. Since this initial breakthrough, the remains of dozens of American service members have been identified and repatriated.

During my trips to Cambodia, I also met with the leader of the royalist faction, Prince Sihanouk. Sihanouk, a colorful little man with a tiny white dog, had been resolutely supporting the resistance movement from exile in Beijing for many years, but he was essentially dependent on China's support. Sihanouk maintained the trappings of an absolute ruler, requiring that his court follow intricate rules of deference, which he demanded even from his own son, Prince Norodom Ranariddh, a grown man and secretary-general of the royalist political party. I was surprised when I saw Ranariddh enter Sihanouk's presence on his knees and exit in a crawl without turning his back to his father. It was a demeaning gesture, which I thought demonstrated Sihanouk's insecurity in his own power and leadership.

The one thing I took from all of the Cambodian leaders was an insistence that the future of their country should be self-determined—though that was the extent of their agreement. As I wrote in an op-ed piece in the *Washington Post* after my return, I came away from these meetings convinced that "these divisions are so vast that the Cambodians on their own will not be able to forge a workable solution that does not involve ongoing bloodshed."[1] After a trip spent face-to-face with the Cambodian leaders, troops, and citizens, it was clear to me that intervention on the part of the United Nations was needed to guarantee that the country didn't slide right back into civil war.

In 1991, after two years of negotiations, the Paris Peace Accords were signed. By the time I returned to Cambodia in 1993, their first democratic elections had recently been held, under the watchful eye of the UN, and the newly elected leaders were putting together a democratic government from scratch. "Piece by piece," I said in my report from the trip, "the Cambodian jigsaw puzzle appears to be coming together."[2]

But there was still a piece missing. The Cambodian people had been through a terrible trauma during the Khmer Rouge regime: their fellow countrymen were responsible for as many as 1.7 million deaths, over 21 percent of the population. During my first visit to Cambodia, I was taken to the Tuol Sleng Genocide Museum—a former prison that had been turned into a chronicle of the genocide, told through the stories of the people who lived, were tortured, and died at the site. In one of their most moving exhibitions, the museum re-created the inside of each stark, tiny cell and put a picture of its occupant—all of whom had been tortured and the vast majority murdered—at the head of the bed. The museum left a visceral impression of the genocide that raw numbers could never have achieved.

A mass genocide of this scale could not go unpunished. We had said "never again" once already in my lifetime. Without justice, or at least an honest and open airing of what happened and who was responsible, it would be too easy for retribution and resentment to tear the country apart again.

In 1994, I advocated for State Department funding of a Cambodian genocide project that would gather information and "train contemporary Cambodians how to use the information to build a legal case" against Khmer Rouge leaders such as Pol Pot, who was then still at large.[3]

A relatively modest amount of funding was eventually allocated for the genocide project, and researchers at the State Department and Yale University began combing through the Khmer Rouge's disturbingly extensive files of mass death. In 1997, the Cambodian government established the Extraordinary Chambers in the Courts of Cambodia, commonly known as the Cambodia Tribunal or Khmer Rouge Tribunal. The work was slow, but a few senior members of the Khmer Rouge were eventually charged and convicted of crimes relating to the genocide. Unfortunately, Pol Pot died under house arrest before he could face an international tribunal.

MY RETURN TO Cambodia in 1993 was a part of a grueling ten-day sprint across Southeast Asia during the August Senate recess that included meetings with leaders in seven countries. Following my meetings in Cambodia, I continued on to Vietnam, where, as I later wrote in my trip report to the Senate Foreign Relations Committee, my visit "began on an inauspicious note."[4] I arrived on the tarmac in Ho Chi Minh City (formerly Saigon) carrying a box of medicine destined for Dr. Nguyen Dan Que, a jailed pro-democracy advocate. Dr. Que was an endocrinologist who had been speaking out against human rights violations under the repressive regime and was then serving a twenty-year sentence in a Vietnamese prison for "subversive activities."[5] Dr. Que's brother happened to live in Northern Virginia, and I had been following his case for some time.

After months of wrangling between the government and my diligent staff, I had been granted permission to meet with Dr. Que and deliver a box of needed medicine for the chronically ill doctor. Under the auspices of a humanitarian mission, it was a gesture of goodwill that the Vietnamese government had allowed the meeting.

However, when I arrived in Ho Chi Minh City, I was met on the tarmac by a stone-faced Vietnamese Foreign Ministry official who told me that my meeting with Dr. Que had been canceled by the government, with no explanation.

I remember expressing my displeasure forcefully and telling the official that this would not improve relations between our countries. I don't remember raising my voice, but Peter Cleveland said later that he had never seen me so angry before.

I thought that the Vietnamese had missed an important opportunity to signal clear progress in their relations with the United States, and their skittishness gave me an insight into the government's insecurity. Confident governments don't make last-minute changes or deny simple humanitarian needs. As I said in my report: "I departed Vietnam with great concern about its internal security apparatus and methods and broad denial of individual liberties and freedoms."[6]

At the same time, my meetings with Vietnamese officials over the next two days were some of my most rewarding of the trip. We left Ho Chi Minh City without stepping off the tarmac and reboarded our aircraft to fly south to Da Nang. There, Peter and I boarded a helicopter to tour by air the area outside Da Nang where, as a Marine captain, I had led India Company 3/7. With the trusty maps I had brought back from my tour in Vietnam spread in my lap, I poked my head between the two pilots, directing them in dizzying turns over the same hills and valleys where India Company had fought twenty-five years before.

Later that day, when I met with Vietnamese officials who had fought on the other side of that conflict, I was pleased to tell them about my tour of the old battlefields, once again full of rice paddies. I told them simply that I fought there, my men had died there, and that I respected the determination of our opponents. They seemed to return the sentiment, and it was a good conversation between officers who had once been enemies.

It was a very human moment, and one that I appreciated because it can be too easy, especially in politics and war, to dehumanize the people of foreign nations. When I served in the Vietnam War, we tended, quite naturally, to view enemy soldiers as Communists to the core, fighting to impose Soviet ideology at all costs. But the prisoners that we took, both Viet Cong and North Vietnamese Army (NVA), weren't shouting Communist slogans and turned out to be fairly normal human beings. Usually, when we went through the pockets of a captured or killed enemy fighter, looking for plans or other intelligence, we would find pictures of children, wives, and families that looked an awful lot like the pictures that we were carrying around in our own pockets. In the end, the enemy soldiers were not always the boogeymen that they were made out to be. Despite cultural differences and barriers of language, custom, and religion, what I found in all of my international travels was a multitude of similarities.

22

Issues of War and Peace

ON MARCH 10, 1991, I was invited to appear on NBC's *Meet the Press* along with Republican senator Phil Gramm of Texas. As the chairmen of our respective parties' Senate campaign committees, Phil and I had been invited to discuss the upcoming election cycle. Most of the questions related to the Gulf War, which was now only two months old, but about midway through the interview, Andrea Mitchell took the discussion in a different direction. She probed about some rumored backlash from my vote against party lines to give President George H. W. Bush authorization for the use of military force in the Persian Gulf to drive Saddam Hussein's troops out of neighboring Kuwait.

"Let me ask you this, to clear something up," she began. "We have heard a report that you are being removed from the Senate Budget Committee as punishment for your vote, which would be unprecedented in the middle of a congressional [term]."[1]

There I was, a freshman senator only a third of the way through my first term, and I'd gotten into a public spat with my own leadership. I hesitated before answering. Mitchell's question put me in a difficult position. It was true that I had been dropped from the Budget Committee, and it was true that I had broken with party leadership to vote in favor of President Bush's use of force. But my vote on the use of force wasn't the reason for my committee ouster. Unfortunately, the real reason was a different vote over which I was also at odds with my party leadership. I didn't want to open a new can of worms on live television, especially since it was generally understood in the Senate that members shouldn't air their internal disputes in public.

THE WHOLE STORY had begun on August 2, 1990, when Iraqi president Saddam Hussein invaded neighboring Kuwait. Shortly after the invasion, on a clear, chilly Sunday afternoon, President Bush invited five people to the White House: Republican senator Warren Rudman; former CIA director Richard Helms; National Security Advisor Brent Scowcroft; former special envoy for the Middle East and future ambassador to Russia Bob

Strauss; and me. It was a diverse, bipartisan group, and one well-suited to discuss the topic. We were all veterans except for Strauss, who had served at the FBI during World War II. Each person had a different, valuable perspective on the situation in the Middle East and how the United States ought to respond.

Sitting in a small circle on the two couches and upholstered chairs of the Yellow Room on the second floor of the White House, we undertook a serious and lengthy discussion during which each of us offered President Bush our views and recommendations on the appropriate response to Hussein's invasion.

My own views in most national security and foreign policy discussions tended to be more hawkish than those of most Democrats, but I thought that there were some necessary preconditions for military action against Iraq. First, we shouldn't do it alone. I believed it was critically important that whatever action the United States took militarily, we needed to form a strong international alliance in dealing with this issue. Second, American troops shouldn't be the first to cross the line of departure. One of our Middle East allies, a member of the Gulf Cooperation Council (GCC), ought to be the first troops to move into enemy-held territory to lessen any mistaken impression of a U.S. invasion of the Middle East. We did not want the United States to be viewed as colonizers or intruders. Third, it was essential to me that there was a clear mission, limited to expelling the Iraqi invaders from Kuwait, not an open-ended campaign in the Middle East.

But with those preconditions met, I felt that the United States was right to intervene in this invasion of Kuwait. First, I didn't believe that we could allow Kuwait to fall into the hands of a rogue dictator, especially one like Saddam, whose cold-blooded reputation had been established with his use of chemical weapons against his own countrymen during the Iran-Iraq War in the 1980s. Second, we needed to restore balance in a potentially explosive and influential region of the world. Third, and perhaps most important, we had to assert the rule of international law in a period when the United States, as the last remaining superpower, was the only country with both a moral rationale and the necessary force to do it. Saddam had wantonly stormed into a peaceful country. If the United States failed to respond, then other ambitious, aggressive warlords around the world might be emboldened to do the same thing.

President Bush took in our advice but offered no final decisions. He was wrestling with the questions of conflict in the post–Vietnam War era and had many factors to consider when weighing a military response. In addition to the necessary military considerations, the president had to decide if he would ask Congress for approval. The War Powers Resolution of 1973, passed in the wake of the Vietnam War, established specific restrictions on the president's ability to send American forces into battle, with several exceptions. In 1990, the act was still relatively untested.

I had some reservations about restrictions on the commander in chief's ability to command and direct the military, but by late 1990, I cautioned the administration against going forward with military action without congressional approval. By that time, the sentiment in the Congress was shifting in favor of military action, and it looked like a resolution authorizing the use of force might pass. The result would be the same—Bush would commit U.S. military in the Persian Gulf—but with Congress's approval, the mission was in a much stronger political position. Passing force authorization would not be easy, however, since the legislation would have to gain the support of enough Democrats, who then held a majority in both Houses.

The debate in Congress was fierce. Saddam's invasion of Kuwait was widely condemned, but our country hadn't, at that point, been involved in a major conflict since Vietnam, and there was a real fear that putting American troops on the ground in the Middle East would draw the United States into another military and diplomatic quagmire with thousands of American casualties. The question gripped the attention of Washington politicos and dominated the Sunday-morning talk shows, editorial pages, and political news cycle throughout the winter of 1990–91.

I felt very strongly from the start that the United States would be compelled to take military action, which put me on the opposite side of the debate from many of my fellow Democrats.

But questions remained about our new role in the post–Cold War environment, among them whether the United States had the will to take the risks, and whether our military forces were sufficiently prepared to launch an offensive. To help answer the latter question, I accepted the invitation of Majority Leader George Mitchell to join him and six other Democratic senators on a fact-finding mission to the Middle East.

On December 13, 1990, we left from Andrews Air Force Base for a whirlwind tour of the Middle East. The trip was businesslike—no cultural entertainment or sightseeing. We only had a few days to meet with leaders in multiple countries to get a better current understanding of the region and the level of preparedness for war. We had candid discussions with

King Fahd of Saudi Arabia, Sheik Jaber Al-Ahmad Al Sabah of Kuwait, and Prime Minister Yitzhak Shamir of Israel, as well as their key military and intelligence leaders. My interest was to get their views on the situation and the appropriate response and to discover what they were willing to do to support it.

A highlight of the trip was a thorough briefing by U.S. general Norman Schwarzkopf and his key advisors, during which I was able to ask very specific questions about the readiness of our armed forces. I came away convinced that we were trained, equipped, and ready for the task at hand.

By the end of the trip, Majority Leader Mitchell was opposed to granting the president force authorization. He was not against military action altogether, but he wanted to give the economic sanctions, imposed by the United Nations shortly after the invasion of Kuwait, more time to take effect. It was a close decision for the other Democratic senators on the trip as well, but in the end, they followed the lead of their majority leader. I had great respect for Senator Mitchell—who, not everyone realized, was himself an Arab American politician—as a voice of moderation and reason. But the trip had answered many of my most pressing questions and strengthened my belief that we should grant the administration congressional authorization to use force. That put me squarely on the opposite side of most of my Democratic colleagues in the Senate.

A short time later, I was invited, as chair of the DSCC, to a meeting of the Democratic leadership in the Senate to discuss the situation in the Gulf. It was instantly apparent that I was the only person in the room in favor of granting force authorization.

I hadn't been reluctant to voice my opinion publicly and had agreed to numerous media interviews on the situation in Kuwait in which I argued for the necessity of military intervention with international support. Almost immediately, my office was deluged with an outpouring from constituents who opposed my position. Initially, the letters and phone calls ran nine to one against committing American troops or engaging in offensive action, and many of those who called my office were understandably emotional. At several points, I took a number of the phone calls personally, in order to relieve some of the staff and interns from the intensity of the calls and to get a better idea of the depth of my constituents' feelings. I fully understood their anxiety, particularly about the safety of sons and daughters who could be sent to fight, and I took their views into consideration. But I believed that I was making the right decision. If my decision proved to be so unpopular in Virginia that I lost my next election, I was fully prepared to accept those consequences.

By the start of 1991, pressure from concerned Virginians was unrelenting. Then, on January 8, President Bush formally requested congressional support for military force as a response to Saddam's invasion. At that point, the debate accelerated and took on a new level of intensity. On January 9, the Senate brought the force authorization resolution to the floor. Debate lasted for three days, after which the closing vote was set for Saturday afternoon, January 12, 1991, just a few days ahead of the January 15 deadline that the United Nations issued to Saddam to withdraw his forces from Kuwait.

In the final days leading up to the force authorization vote, it was too close to tell which way it would go. As with all important and controversial votes, there was plenty of arm-twisting, phone-calling, and debate going on behind the scenes, and it was apparent that many legislators were still wrestling with their consciences.

One influential senator who still appeared to be undecided in the final days of debate was Al Gore. Al and I were both invited to the majority leader's office a few days before the vote to discuss the Gulf situation. Throughout that meeting, he listened to the arguments of both sides, but he remained so evenhanded that I couldn't be sure which side he'd ultimately come down on.

In the remaining hours of debate on Saturday, January 12, Gore rose to speak on the Senate floor. Typically, most senators aren't present in the chamber during floor speeches, and when Al rose to speak at around 9:30 a.m., I was still at home, preparing to drive to the office. I happened to catch Al speaking on C-SPAN and hung around the television for a few minutes to listen. I still didn't know which way he planned to vote, but I listened for almost ten minutes as he methodically summed up the arguments against force authorization. Disappointed at apparently having failed to persuade him, I got in my car and headed for my office in the Russell Building. When I arrived, my legislative director, Kerry Walsh Skelly, greeted me with "Congratulations! You got Al."

Dumbfounded, I replied: "We got Al? But I watched most of his speech."

"Right at the end," Kerry said, "he came around and said he was going to vote for authorization."

Of course, Al had listened to others and not just to me, but I was very pleased to have had a hand in his decision.

Later that day, the Senate voted, 52–47, to support the president's request for force authorization, including ten Democrats in the "aye" column.

Five days after the vote, on the night of January 17, I was working late in my Senate office with the television tuned to CNN when the first U.S. bombs fell on Baghdad. My staff was tense and eerily quiet as we watched, for the first time, a military action unfold in live coverage. The scene in my office, where no one within sight of a television could tear themselves away, was being replayed in homes and businesses all across America.

The bombing campaign went on for six weeks, and it wasn't until February 25, the second day of the ground war, that it became clear that we weren't going to have massive casualties, that this wasn't going to be Vietnam all over again, and that the international community would ultimately view the intervention as necessary. Only at that point did the phone calls to my office, and public opinion in general, begin to turn more positive toward intervention, though even then they were still split down the middle. In the end, the war was such a success that those of us who had made the then politically unpopular decision to support it received a boost in public opinion ratings, and most people quickly forgot how much anxiety it originally generated. If the war had turned out differently—if we had lost or suffered massive casualties—a vote for force authorization could have been politically fatal.

A FEW WEEKS after the vote on force authorization, I had an entirely different clash with the Democratic leadership in the Senate. This time, the issue was a budget bill proposed in the Budget Committee, of which I was a member. I believed that the proposed budget was fiscally irresponsible. Presenting a skewed budget is not uncommon, because, under the byzantine process of government expenditures, the budget in the Senate has little actual effect on the expenditures of the federal government. But I refused to vote for a budget, even a symbolic one, that so poorly reflected an issue that I felt strongly about: fiscal discipline.

My opposition hadn't come out of nowhere. The previous year, I had expressed the same reservations about voting for the 1990 budget bill to both the Budget Committee chairman, Senator Jim Sasser, and to Majority Leader Mitchell. At the time, I had reluctantly agreed to vote for that budget bill, but I'd made it clear that the next year's bill needed to do substantially more to reduce the deficit or I couldn't support it. When the bill was put before the committee in 1991 with no more deficit reduction than the year before, I balked. And in February 1991, I told Jim Sasser that I couldn't vote for it.

Sasser was in a tough position. His job was to get a budget through the committee, which is not always a walk in the park. The only tool he had at hand was to placate various members with support for the particular concerns of their states. This is far from nefarious—senators are necessarily looking for ways to support their state, and Jim, an experienced and talented politician, was very effective at addressing those individual requests. This give-and-take was a time-honored tradition in the Senate, and everyone knew that was how the game was played. But at a time when we had an outrageously high national debt and our spending was threatening to derail our country's fiscal future, I just couldn't, in good conscience, be a party to passing legislation that didn't deal honestly with fiscal implications and would condone the fiscal situation.

In 1991, Democrats were the majority party in the Senate, and we held thirteen seats on the Budget Committee to the Republicans' ten. Jim could have lost my vote and still reported the bill out with the votes of the other twelve Democratic senators, but the senior member of the committee, Democrat Fritz Hollings of South Carolina, also opposed the bill. As the senior member, Fritz was not going to be easily moved, which made me, as the least senior committee member, a much more likely target for persuasion. Jim asked to meet with me in my office.

"I made my position known last year," I told Jim, "and everyone knows where I stand on this. We've got to force the system to be fiscally responsible, and I don't know any other way to do it."

I said the same thing to George Mitchell when he also tried to convince me to change my mind, and he didn't press further.

In the end, the budget wasn't cut, but my seat on the committee was. Jim's official reason for dumping me was that with twenty-three members, the committee was too large, so he cut two committee positions, one Democrat and one Republican. But it was no secret that the Republican, Warren Rudman, had already planned to switch from the Budget Committee to the Intelligence Committee anyway.

I think Jim assumed that I would simply accept getting axed. In hindsight, that would have been the smoother option. But I was stubborn and indignant, and I asked to appeal the decision before the Democratic Steering Committee—the group of senators that proposes committee assignments to the Democratic Caucus. Up until that time, I'd never had any direct contact with the Steering Committee, which is effectively controlled by the majority leader. I didn't realize that, as a practical matter, the Steering Committee supports the committee chairman in any disagreements over assignments, to avoid the risk of having the whole system break down. I appealed, but the committee, not surprisingly, voted to uphold Jim's request to downsize the Budget Committee.

One senator who sat on the Steering Committee came up to me after the meeting and said bluntly, "You got screwed."

All this had happened behind the scenes, and I didn't have any intention of making it public. So, I believed the whole thing was, more or less, over.

Then, on March 10, 1991, I went on *Meet the Press*, ostensibly to talk about the Gulf War. When Andrea Mitchell asked me whether my being removed from the Budget Committee was punishment for my vote to give the president authorization for the use of military force, I was caught off guard—on live television.

My answer started out vague, but I was drawn out in the follow-up. "If I were to suggest any particular role," I said, referring to the loss of my seat on the Budget Committee, "I would suggest that it had to do with my un-willingness to report [out] a meaningless budget resolution. I've been fairly intractable on that position as well. But again, like my fellow Democrats, I vote my conscience."[2]

This was inflammatory enough, but once we were off-air, the influential *Washington Post* columnist David Broder, who was also on the *Meet the Press* panel, asked me some follow-up questions about my remarks. Soon enough, the story was in play, and I was very publicly at odds with the Democratic leadership.

Through a spokesman, Jim Sasser disputed my account of the budget flap, again citing his desire to make the committee smaller and "less un-wieldy." Both Sasser and I continued to hold our ground publicly, which only served to further highlight the rift.

Though I remained friendly with George Mitchell and was sad to see him leave the Senate in 1995, my unwillingness to toe the party line did not endear me to some Capitol Hill Democrats. Democratic Hill staffers in par-ticular, whose job I was making much harder with my vote granting force authorization, were less than pleased with what they saw as my continuing contrarianism.

But I never minded taking votes that stood against popular or political pressure. Voting against the stream on an important issue was actually one of the few times in the Senate when I felt as though my vote truly mattered. And if I were going to be disliked, I was content for it to be over issues that I was passionate about.

23

A National Soap Opera

BY APRIL 1991, Operation Desert Storm had concluded, and I planned, along with two other members of the Senate Armed Services Committee, Senators Carl Levin of Michigan and Jim Exon of Nebraska, to travel to the Persian Gulf on a fact-finding trip to survey the aftermath of the Gulf War. However, just as our plane's wheels left the runway, my press secretary got word that a new NBC tabloid-style show, *Exposé*, planned to air a segment about me that Sunday evening, only three days away.

The segment was based on unsupported rumors that had first surfaced in Virginia Beach during my time as governor. In the mid-1980s, Virginia Beach was a seaside resort city of more than a quarter million people with a sizeable population of young, wealthy, entrepreneurial types who worked hard and played hard. Once I became governor, there were a few weekends each summer when my family and I would stay at the official governor's beach cottage at Camp Pendleton in Virginia Beach. When Lynda and the girls were out of town during the girls' school vacations, I would sometimes go down without them to speak at an event or attend an official function. If I was already scheduled to be in the area, I would occasionally accept invitations to dinners or parties with supporters while I was there. There were times when I accepted invitations to parties that I would have been better off declining, and I made a mistake in doing so when Lynda couldn't join me. Part of the attraction was that this crowd felt distinctly outside of my "official duties," but it was a mistake to think that I could ever really be "off the clock," and I should have known better.

Friends and advisors eventually warned me that they had heard that rumors were circulating about my social life at the beach, but I dismissed the rumors as nothing more than a partisan whisper campaign. The rumors were sometimes so outlandish that they were hard to take seriously. The one incident that had enough specificity to directly refute was a rumor that I had attended a dinner in a Virginia Beach restaurant without Lynda in the company of a very attractive young woman. That incident was actually true, but the very attractive young woman happened to be our middle daughter, Catherine.

However, over a year after I was out of the governor's office, on May 2, 1987, there was a new twist. Lynda and I were sitting down to dinner with friends on the patio of a restaurant in Georgetown. Suddenly, two television reporters appeared with their cameras running, interrupting dinner and asking questions about a story slated for the next day's *Richmond Times-Dispatch*.

The next day, the article did, in fact, run on the front page under the headline, "Robb Denies Being at Parties at Which Cocaine Was Used," alleging that "federal prosecutors investigating cocaine trafficking in South Hampton Roads have been told by several witnesses that former Gov. Charles S. Robb—while in office—attended parties in Virginia Beach at which the illegal drug was used."[1]

Although the *Times-Dispatch* article made no indication that I was the target of any investigation, readers would only remember that my name had been linked in the media to illegal drugs, creating understandable doubt about what had been going on behind the scenes while I was in office.

The *Richmond Times-Dispatch* story spurred many other news outlets to write their own versions, which relied heavily on the anonymous "federal official close to the inquiry."

I was besieged for comment by virtually every TV, radio, and print news organization in the state. I told every one of them the same thing: I had never been in any situation where I knew that illegal drugs were present or were being used, period.

If I'd had a reputation as more of a partier, then rumors about my attendance at parties in Virginia Beach during my governorship wouldn't have caused much of a stir. But the stark contrast with my straitlaced image made the story more interesting, and my categorical denials were met with skepticism. The truth was far less interesting: if someone had or was using drugs at one of these beach house parties, the last person they'd want to do it in front of would be the sitting governor with a state police security detail.

When the *Washington Post* published a version of the story, it provoked the ire of their own ombudsman, Joseph Laitin, who wrote in an internal memo:

To do to a public figure what was done to Charles Robb on Page One of the Metro section last Monday (May 4), represents poor journalism, poor judgment, poor taste and while probably not "actionable," as lawyers are wont to say, there's something wrong with the training of editors and reporters here, or with the backup system for screening out distasteful and unwarranted material that can destroy people's reputations.

If you're going to accuse a former governor of an important state . . . of association with the use of drugs, then, by god, assign a couple of investigative reporters and get the goods on him, if it's there. Don't, by innuendo and indirection, lay it on him, in a casual, almost afterthought way, by including it in a feature update of drug users, and then attribute it to another newspaper which credits it to "an unidentified federal official." . . .

The damage is already done; only a public apology can repair it.[2]

Stories trickled out over the next two years, but I thought that the issue had withered away, until December 7, 1990, when I sat down for an interview in my Senate office with the *Washington Post*'s Don Baker and Thomas Heath. Baker, who had covered Virginia politics for many years, was a tireless, persistent, and effective reporter, and I assumed that the interview would be about the ongoing debate over American involvement in the Persian Gulf. I was caught completely off guard, however, when Baker began grilling me about a former Miss Virginia USA named Tai Collins.

Collins had appeared in an August 1988 *Virginian-Pilot* article regarding illegal drugs as only a headshot photo and brief caption stating that Collins "became friendly with Robb during her reign as Miss Virginia/ USA in 1983."[3] Some Republican operatives thought they smelled blood, however, and apparently began courting Collins assiduously. Collins then began claiming that we had had a long-standing affair and had taken trips together while I was governor.

I repeated to Baker what I had told reporters in the summer of 1988: I never had an affair of any kind with Collins or anyone else. I acknowledged having met privately with her only once during a political trip to New York when she showed up at my hotel suite and I allowed her to enter. We had a glass of wine, but when she began to give me a back rub, it quickly became apparent that she had other intentions, and I quickly ended the visit. I immediately regretted ever allowing her to enter my suite and putting myself in circumstances not appropriate for a married man.

As Don Baker continued to question me about Collins, he was so openly skeptical of my answers that I finally asked him point blank why he was treating my answers with such contempt. He looked me in the eye and said acidly, "All politicians lie."

I leaned forward and replied calmly, "*All* politicians do *not* lie."

I was particularly irritated that Baker would so categorically tar all politicians as liars. I had known a great many elected officials, on both sides of the aisle, who dealt honestly with reporters, constituents, and colleagues.

Needless to say, the interview with Baker and Heath ended a short time later, and my staff and I waited uncomfortably for a story to be published. But three months went by, and no story appeared. At the same time, Operation Desert Storm commenced in the Persian Gulf. Then, in February 1991, the same rumor was brought up again, this time by a soon-to-be-launched NBC tabloid-style show, hosted by Tom Brokaw, called *Exposé*.

NBC had apparently been contacted by a private eye named Billy Franklin, who had been peddling what he described as "Robb dirt" to reporters since the 1988 campaign. We eventually learned that Franklin had been hired by a Republican donor who had solicited money from other Republicans around the state to finance his investigation.[4] The money hadn't covered his expenses, however, and he was trying to recoup his costs by writing a book. Approaching NBC with the story could generate free publicity.

Franklin had fed NBC a film noir for the modern age, a fantasy about a powerful politician, cocaine, femme fatales, and hired goons used to cover it all up. Of course, when *Exposé* asked for proof, Franklin had none. The show's producers were apparently skeptical of Franklin, his gumshoe persona, and his sensational story, but they also recognized that breaking a scandalous story about a high-profile politician would be a surefire way to launch their fledgling show. By February 1991, NBC was seeking to interview me for the new show.

I agreed to NBC's request for an interview naively believing that I could put the rumors to rest once and for all. The rumors felt like a direct challenge to my integrity. I believed that I had developed a reputation up to that point, and through the conduct of my administration, as a straight shooter and as someone who tells the truth. I thought that if I denied these charges, the media would at the very least do the due diligence to fact-check them. Collins was claiming that we had had a long-running affair, including taking several trips together—something that could have been easily verified if it was true, but this kind of simple fact-checking never appeared in any of the reporting that I saw. This level of investigation just wasn't being reported, which made me even more determined to set the record straight.

After the interview for *Exposé*, we waited anxiously for a segment to air. There were several stops and starts before NBC told my office in the last week of April that the segment *might* air the following Sunday, April 28— the same weekend that I was scheduled to be traveling in the Persian Gulf. I was concerned about being out of the country when the story aired, but I had already asked my fellow senators to delay the trip the previous weekend for the same reason, and by late Wednesday evening we still didn't have confirmation from NBC. So, I agreed to go ahead and leave for the trip as planned after the last vote on Thursday evening. It wasn't until after our plane took off that my press secretary got word that the segment was definitely included in that Sunday's upcoming show.

Worse yet, the next morning's *Washington Post* would carry a front-page story by Don Baker describing the highlights (or lowlights) of *Exposé*'s report and reviving the content of our contentious interview, which had apparently been sitting on the shelf.

The timing could not have been worse. I was totally out of communication for most of the weekend as we traveled around what remained of a war zone. In an era before cell phones, David McCloud was only able to reach me on a landline when we landed at the U.S. air base at Incirlik, Turkey, but the call quality was bad, and it was extremely difficult for me to get a clear picture of the situation back home and how my staff was handling it. Thousands of miles away, I was unable to help with the fallout.

All I could do was to focus on the reason that I was on this trip: to survey the devastation wrought by the Gulf War. What we saw was a sobering scene of life and death. First, we helicoptered into the Kurdish area of northern Iraq. The terrain looked like an empty moonscape, as desperate refugees had picked the trees clean for shelter and firewood, leaving not a single branch for miles. Thousands of Kurds of all ages who had survived the initial Iraqi assaults were now dying from the conditions of war and deprivation: famine, unclean drinking water, and rampant disease. Children and the elderly were the first to succumb. The international community had flown in the most immediately available emergency food supplies—"Meals Ready to Eat" (MREs) made to feed U.S. ground forces in combat. But some of the MREs contained pork, so the Muslim refugees refused to eat any of them and were instead starving.

The stench of death and human waste was overwhelming. Large trenches had been dug to serve as mass graves, and survivors were lined up in a grotesque queue, carrying the bodies of their loved ones, wrapped in cloth, waiting to hand them over for burial.

I am not easily shaken or upset, but to this day I cannot forget the horror of what Saddam Hussein and his forces had inflicted on the Kurds in Iraq. The drama before me was so vivid, and so immediate, that it momentarily eclipsed all else. My own troubles back home were trivial by comparison. They seemed distant and almost unreal, as though they were happening in a parallel universe.

The rest of our trip was a blur of scene upon scene of devastation. In Kuwait and southern Iraq, we drove across the fields where oil wells, set ablaze by the fleeing Iraqis, were still burning fiercely, with black clouds stretching across the horizon. We used giant plastic heat shields to get as close to the fires as possible, to feel the immense heat and experience the size of these massive fires. We flew by helicopter along the so-called "Highway of Death," with the burned-out hulks of hundreds of destroyed Iraqi vehicles of war littering the road, some still smoking, for as far as the eye could see. Finally, we visited the spot where General Schwarzkopf had formally accepted the surrender of Saddam's army and saw the huge refugee camp that had developed right next to it.

Throughout it all, a part of my mind was still concerned about what was happening back home. The worst part was not knowing. I still had no idea how much the *Exposé* story had escalated, how Lynda and the girls were dealing with the media onslaught, or how my staff was coping. I don't think I've ever felt so completely helpless in my life.

We left the Gulf on Sunday as planned and arrived back at Andrews Air Force Base at 3:30 a.m. on Monday, April 29. Unbeknownst to me at the time, David McCloud had risen in the middle of the night to meet me at Andrews in order to give me a lift home and tell me about the events of the last three days. In what seemed like an appropriately frustrating end to the weekend, my plane had landed earlier than expected, so, not knowing that David was en route, I rode home alone in a government staff car, and David reached the air base only to find that I'd already left.

What David had wanted to fill me in on was a weekend in which a single bad story had turned into a media circus. The *Post* article on Friday had set off two full days of stories, capped by the actual airing of *Exposé* on Sunday.

When I arrived at home a little before dawn, I knew my first order of business was to talk with Lynda. It had been a terribly trying three days for her, and she was understandably upset. I reassured her that I hadn't had any kind of an affair or romantic relationship with anyone else in all the years that we'd been married, and that reassurance eased some of the tension. We talked until the sun rose and it was time for me to get ready for work.

In some ways, it was a completely normal Monday, filled with the various activities of a U.S. senator. But my life had changed dramatically. As I went about my mundane duties, a posse of cameras followed, clicking incessantly, trying to get their own shot of me as the reluctant star of a cheap soap opera.

There was also blowback against NBC for the *Exposé* episode. In his *Los Angeles Times* column, Howard Rosenberg wrote that the show "freely used guilt-by-association tactics" to create drama out of hollow accusations. Later, even Alicia Mundy, a young reporter who had already written several critical pieces about me, took NBC News to task for its handling of the story. Her piece in the *Washington Journalism Review* began, "In a piece about young women, coke parties and a recorded threat, NBC shot Chuck Robb in the halo and itself in the foot."[5] According to Mundy, NBC's respected Washington bureau chief, Tim Russert, had even lobbied the president of NBC News to drop the piece, doubting that the seven-year-old story was newsworthy.

As a longtime believer in the cardinal rule of public life—"never do or say anything that you don't want to end up on the front page of the *Washington Post*"—I certainly should have known better than to ever open the door to my hotel room under those circumstances. I had to acknowledge, sadly, that my mistake had broken that cardinal rule.

The mistake was mine alone, but it ultimately hurt my family, especially Lynda. As the daughter of one of the most forceful and controversial presidents of the twentieth century, Lynda had weathered public storms before, and she knew, almost instinctively, what to expect. But the fact that she'd been through it all before didn't make it any easier. I would like to be able to say that I helped Lynda deal with the situation, but the truth is that I think she provided more support for me.

During the turbulent months of 1991, my family closed ranks in a way I'll never forget. Our eldest daughter, Lucinda, even penned a very strongly worded op-ed piece in my defense that she shared with her mother before formally submitting it to the newspaper. Lynda wisely convinced her that publishing it would only keep the story alive even longer, so she did not submit it for publication. Nevertheless, Lucinda's willingness to publicly stand by me so unequivocally meant more to me than she could ever know.

Lynda stuck by me resolutely in this difficult period of our marriage, and her loyalty never wavered. This was the biggest mistake of my life, yet my family had paid much of the price.

Up to this point in my life, I had always taken pride in being self-reliant. I always felt I could handle almost anything—until I learned that I couldn't. For the first time, I began to truly appreciate the support of my friends, colleagues, and, most especially, family. I was grateful to learn, during the most difficult time of my life, that I am a truly lucky man.

24

The Tale of the Tape

A FEW WEEKS after the *Exposé* interview aired, and just as the commotion it caused was beginning to die down, the story was kept alive by an investigation launched by the Virginia State Police into claims made against me on the program.

From the start, the source and purpose of the investigation was unclear. The probe hadn't been initiated by a grand jury or by Virginia's attorney general, Mary Sue Terry. Under Virginia law, the only other way an investigation of a sitting elected official could be initiated was if it was ordered by the governor—Doug Wilder. When questioned by reporters, Wilder consistently said that he had no involvement in initiating the investigation.

The state police investigation itself ended with a whimper after only four days, but the mystery surrounding who authorized it grew over the next three weeks. Finally, in the first week of June, the media got wind that Governor Wilder had, in fact, authorized the investigation, and the *Virginian-Pilot* was planning to run the story on Saturday, June 8, 1991.

On the day before the *Virginian-Pilot* story was going to run, I got an urgent call from my press secretary, Steve Johnson, who told me that the *Washington Post* was planning to run a story the next day, but not about Governor Wilder's involvement in the state police investigation. Instead, the story was detailing claims by Doug that his phone conversations had been bugged, that tapes of those conversations had been passed to me, and that my staff played the tapes for the press and prominent Democrats.

The claim was completely out of the blue, and I didn't even know what tapes were being referenced. I later learned that the story was actually about a single tape, and one that I hadn't seen, heard, or even read the content of in a transcript. All I knew then was what I had been told years earlier on two phone calls from David McCloud. In the first call—in October 1988, in the final two weeks of my campaign for the Senate—David mentioned that he had been told about a tape of a phone conversation between then lieutenant governor Doug Wilder and a campaign supporter, on which Doug appeared to gloat about the political problems I was having at the time.

I was certainly curious, but I told David that my immediate reaction was that neither he nor I should have anything to do with the tape. David seemed to agree. After we hung up, I didn't think any more about it.

The second call with David was in early February 1989, one month after I'd been sworn into the Senate. David (now my chief of staff) told me that he now had the tape of Doug Wilder's conversation in his possession. Noticing my hesitation before responding, he told me not to worry, that he'd checked with lawyers, who determined it was legal to retain the tape as long as he didn't make it public. I still wasn't comfortable—regardless of what was on the tape, there could be serious fallout if he, or anyone else associated with me, ever made it public. David answered that he just wanted to hang on to it personally as evidence of inconsistencies between Doug's public and private statements about me.

In the harsh glare of hindsight, it's clear that I would have been far better off had I simply asked David to destroy the tape when I learned that he had it in his possession.

The tape again faded from my mind, until Steve Johnson's anxious phone call in June 1991, almost two years later. I immediately sat down with David and asked him to tell me the full story behind how the tape came into being.

David told me that he had learned that on October 9, 1988, Wilder was talking on a car phone with Hampton Roads real estate developer Daniel Hoffler. The call would have simply disappeared into the ether if it weren't for a Virginia Beach man named Bobby Dunnington, who had an unusual hobby: he enjoyed listening in on other people's cell phone conversations. Using completely legal electronic equipment available at any local Radio Shack, including a radio scanner and a standard tape recorder, he would randomly search the airwaves for cellular conversations, listen in, and sometimes make recordings of them. Cell phone frequencies were not then encrypted and could be listened to with something as simple as a baby monitor.

Dunnington happened, by chance, to tune in to part of Doug Wilder's conversation with Hoffler, and he taped it. He then passed the tape to his twin brother, Ricky, who passed it along to a mutual acquaintance, Bruce Thompson.

Rumors about my Virginia Beach social life were just becoming public around that time, and speculation abounded about who was feeding information to the press and keeping the rumors alive. Considering the widely reported differences between Doug and me following the 1985 elections, some wondered whether Doug or his staff might be stoking the rumor mill. Bruce Thompson believed Doug's comments on the tape supported this view and decided to give the tape to David McCloud. Since then, David told me, the only other people in the office who knew of the tape were Steve Johnson and Bobby Watson. All three staffers denied giving the tape to the media.

On June 8, 1991, the *Washington Post* put out a story about the tape, and the next day they published excerpts taken from a transcript given to the paper "by a source." Then, on Monday, June 10, a *Virginian-Pilot* story claimed that the *Post*'s source was someone in my office. Now I was incensed. The idea that someone in my office had passed such a tape along was bad enough, but, if true, it meant that that person was also not being fully candid with me about their actions.

Soon, the situation got much worse as it turned into a legal matter. On Tuesday, June 11, Attorney General Terry announced that she would ask the FBI and state police to look into allegations of wiretapping. Unfortunately, once it turned into a criminal investigation, I knew that I had to put David McCloud, Bobby Watson, and Steve Johnson on administrative leave. I didn't want to take this step, as all three had worked very hard and been loyal to me, but it was becoming clear that I didn't really have a choice.

It's difficult to fully convey the frantic pace of events during those days and the chaos it generated in my office. Before the tape story even broke, we were already stretched—we were still responding to continuing *Exposé* fallout, the Virginia State Police investigation had just withered, the threat of new rumors was keeping us constantly on edge, and throughout it all we were trying to attend to Senate business. In military terms, I felt that all we could do was set up a defensive perimeter and hope to survive yet another barrage of mortar and artillery fire.

The most absurd part of this whole fiasco was that the actual content of this now notorious tape was entirely unexceptional. When I did eventually read the transcript just before stories hit the papers in June, I couldn't understand why it had been described to me as so damaging to Doug. The worst thing that Doug had said on it was that I was "finished" politically, and the rest was insider political gossip.

The fact that something so banal could have caused so much excitement was a sad reminder of just how out of hand Doug and I had let the "feud" get with our respective staffs. There was no doubt that there were differences between Doug and me, both in policy and style, that would have been cause for some head-butting over the years. But the situation was exacerbated by the very real animus that had developed between members of our two loyal staffs. He and I both bore ultimate responsibility for not reining in the situation sooner, and it was clear that it was time for the two of us to put a stop to the political gamesmanship. We planned a meeting on June 18 at my Senate hideaway office, where we had the best chance of talking privately, and I told him everything I knew: the origins of the tape, the unsanctioned actions of my staff, and exactly what I'd known about the tape and when I knew it. We then left together for a nearby Democratic fundraiser and publicly put the talk of a "feud" to rest.

Then, on June 26, 1991, my fifty-second birthday, came the next blow: it was announced that a grand jury to investigate the wiretapping allegations was being convened in Norfolk by Robert Wiechering—the same assistant U.S. attorney who had led the Virginia Beach illegal drugs investigation in the 1980s, and who had, during the course of that investigation, interrogated grand jury witnesses about my private life.

I knew that, before I was caught off guard again, I needed to know the specific facts of what had happened in my office. So, I talked to Stuart Ross, a friend and the head of a local law firm who had not had any involvement with my Senate office. Stu and one of his law partners, Rick Simpson, agreed to conduct an internal investigation. They also became my liaisons with the prosecutor, the FBI, and state investigators, providing them with all requested documents and information, including the files and hard drives from my office.

To my relief, Stu and Rick found no evidence that my staff had anything to do with recording the conversations and that no one had knowingly violated any laws. Unfortunately, they also advised me that enough unanswered questions remained to make it untenable to have David, Steve, or Bobby return to the staff, regardless of what might result from any outside investigation of the office. Reluctantly, I agreed. On July 19, I publicly announced—but privately regretted—that I had accepted the resignations of these three staff members.

The resignations were even more unfortunate because, despite the apocalyptic tone of the "wiretapping scandal" stories, it appeared that the only law the three could possibly have violated was a rather technical communications law (18 U.S.C., Sec. 2511[1]) that made it illegal to record or publish a cellular phone conversation, though it was not illegal to possess it. The statute is so obscure that, as of the writing of this book, I know of no other prosecutions that have ever taken place under it. No one on my staff had recorded the tape, but they learned later that, in the eyes of the law, simply playing a tape privately for another person fell under the legal definition of "publishing" it. Without my knowledge, David had played the tape for Steve, who had played it for Bobby. Most disappointing was the revelation that Steve and Bobby had indeed played the tape for a *Washington Post* reporter, even though they claimed that they had done so on background and not for publication. So all three were technically in violation of the law.

I didn't agree with Steve and Bobby's decision to share the tape with a reporter, and if they had made me aware of their intentions, I would never have approved doing so. But what they did was really nothing more than typical political hijinks that are not in any way out of the ordinary. Nevertheless, David, Bobby, and Steve, along with many other members of my staff, were called to testify before the grand jury.

When used appropriately, a grand jury can be a helpful tool for federal law enforcement. The purpose of a grand jury is to review a prosecutor's case to determine whether there is enough evidence to pursue a trial. Most Americans don't realize, however, that the rules and rights of a grand jury appearance are completely different than those of a regular jury trial. The prosecutor alone has the power to decide what evidence and witnesses to present to, or exclude from, the grand jury. They can subpoena someone to testify without probable cause, and that person is not allowed to have their lawyer in the room during the proceedings (though they can ask to step out to confer with their counsel before answering a question). Witnesses do not have access to transcripts of any previous testimony in the case, but if a prosecutor can find any discrepancy in a witness's testimony with their own previous testimony—sometimes given months before—or the testimony of other witnesses, the witness can be prosecuted for perjury. The jury itself is anonymous, and the subject of the investigation has no ability to challenge a juror. With no presiding judge, the prosecutor controls the grand jury process almost completely, choosing cases, calling witnesses, and determining immunity.

As then U.S. attorney general (and later Supreme Court justice) Robert H. Jackson said:

> The prosecutor has more control over life, liberty, and reputation than any other person in America. His discretion is tremendous. He can

have citizens investigated. . . . Or the prosecutor may choose a more subtle course and simply have a citizen's friends interviewed. The prosecutor can order arrests, present cases to the grand jury in secret session, and on the basis of his one-sided presentation of the facts, can cause the citizen to be indicted and held for trial. . . . While the prosecutor at his best is one of the beneficent forces in our society, when he acts from malice or other base motives, he is one of the worst.[1]

The result is that it is extraordinarily easy for most prosecutors to get indictments. It is often said that a prosecutor could get a grand jury to "indict a ham sandwich."

Despite this seemingly unlimited power of the prosecutor, I felt confident when my turn came, on August 8, 1991, to appear before the grand jury at the Norfolk Federal Courthouse. In truth, I was probably overconfident. I saw no point in having a lawyer accompany me to Norfolk, or even formally represent me in the investigation. I had been warned repeatedly by friends who were familiar with the grand jury process that my attitude was naive, if not dangerous. But I was absolutely determined, and my hardheaded streak propelled me through the day.

The testimony itself was far less glamorous than a television courtroom scene. The questioning was in a medium-sized room, painted government-issue beige. I sat, ramrod straight, in a chair against a wall facing the two dozen or so members of the grand jury.

Wiechering stood as he posed the questions, which were nearly identical to those I had already answered for the FBI. Wiechering was poised and professional. I was confident and direct. Most of the time, I could see where he was trying to lead me, and I simply responded with the truth. It was exhausting, but in a way it was also exhilarating.

When I left the courthouse, through a scene of political theater, reporters, and klieg lights, I was happy with how I'd responded during the testimony. I had stood up to the charges against me, and I hoped that my forthright answers had put the matter of any involvement on my part to rest.

But the prosecutor extended the grand jury into the fall and winter, and a series of leaks from the prosecutor's office continued to generate news. Because grand juries are sealed, reporters are dependent on leaks in order to have anything to report. That means that the prosecutor's office can exercise complete power over the ongoing narrative by releasing only the details (proven or not) that fit their script, and reporters can quote "a government official close to the investigation" with impunity. It was easy to see how grand juries could be used to try a case in the court of public opinion.

In January 1992, Wiechering moved first on the staff member who had only worked for me for ten months, Steve Johnson. In classic prosecutorial operating procedure, Wiechering set up the investigation exactly as one would to take down a drug cartel—he pursued the most vulnerable target first and made his way up the political food chain, in the hope of bringing down a sitting senator. His next target was Bobby Watson and then David McCloud. In order to avoid a costly and damaging trial, each agreed to a plea deal in which they pled guilty to one "infraction" (even less serious than a misdemeanor), were fined heavily, and were given a one-year term of probation. Most important for Wiechering were the statements he drafted and pressured my former staff members to sign, in order to avoid a public trial, in which they admitted to "conspiring" to intentionally disclose and use the secretly taped cellular phone conversation. The word "conspiring" was important because it was how Wiechering hoped to catch his "big fish." While there was nothing that Wiechering could charge me with—not even the technical infraction of making the tape public—he was clearly hoping to use the testimony of my staff members to prove the existence of a "conspiracy" to commit an otherwise unprovable offense.

The lives of the three staffers involved in the investigation were, of course, forever altered. All three had to deal with massive legal fees and fines while trying to start new careers under the shadows of high-profile guilty pleas. In addition, the investigation and news coverage exacted a psychological and emotional toll. Even though it was obvious that I was the prosecutor's ultimate prey, I was in a stronger position than my former aides. My financial situation would allow me to pursue a protracted legal fight if necessary, something the other three were not in a position to fall back on.

David McCloud's life was completely upended, and he was nearly crushed by the financial burden of his legal bills. When the grand jury investigation began, David had worked with me for nearly a decade, and he and I were friends on a personal as well as a professional level. During the investigation, we thought it was best if we didn't communicate, and the loss of one of my closest advisors during that time was like tying a hand behind my back. Once the cloud of the federal prosecution was behind us, I was able to pick up the phone again and call David, but it wouldn't be the same as having him as my right-hand man. David couldn't return as my chief of staff after everything that had happened. My office needed to start fresh as we embarked on a tough campaign for reelection. David went on to open his own public affairs shop, and we have stayed in touch over the last two and a half decades.

David received a great deal of unfair criticism for his part in the Wilder tape episode, but he never would have felt the need to try to protect me if I had simply refrained from socializing when Lynda was traveling out of the state. Without the initial rumors from Virginia Beach, for which I alone bore responsibility, all of our futures might have been very different.

It wasn't until the grand jury investigation was well underway, after the paper trail began to emerge, that I fully understood how concerned David, and other members of my staff, had been about the potential political danger posed by Doug Wilder and his staff members. By then, I was able to see how much time and energy David and other members of my staff had spent trying to figure out ways to protect me. There was never any question in my mind that during these difficult times, David was doing everything he could on my behalf. I will always be grateful for his loyalty and personal support.

The members of my staff who had never had anything to do with the tape also paid a price. During the course of the investigation, nearly all of them were called to testify before the grand jury and had to make perp walks into the courthouse in front of the media. The general public doesn't have time to absorb and process the details of a complex story like this one, and with no quick way to sort out fact from fiction, everyone associated with the principal essentially gets marked as somehow "tainted." My staff members were a hardworking and dedicated crew who stuck together through some very tough times. In a situation where they could have broken ranks or jumped ship to save their own skins, I was immensely proud that my office had none of the infighting and turnover that is common around embattled politicians.

At some point during this seemingly never-ending dripping out of scandal speculation, I finally decided to stop trying to tell my side of the story in response to reporters' repeated questions and started responding only that I stood by my earlier statements. I was forced to recognize that my repeated denials were only fueling the fire by giving the story "legs" and that my dogged belief that the truth would come out in the end might not happen in this case.

My approval ratings, which until this point had held up much better than might be expected over the course of a solid year of negative stories, finally went into free fall. In June 1992, one public poll showed that just 30 percent of respondents thought I was doing a favorable job, compared to 69 percent two years earlier.

For over a year, Virginians had been opening their morning papers and seeing my picture next to the words "conspiracy" and "wiretapping." Whether I was indicted or not, the damage had been done. Virtually nothing had been reported about my regular Senate activities, which I had attended to without interruption. Soon, commentators and pundits were writing my political obituary, with headlines such as "Robb's Star Falling Like a Meteor."

When you are a public figure under siege, there's a tendency to want to limit your eye contact with the rest of the world. It was particularly uncomfortable to walk through the narrow subterranean hallways connecting the various congressional buildings, where I would constantly run into Senate colleagues and staff members. After each bad story, I would have to hold my head high and exchange greetings and pleasantries, all the while wondering who had read which news articles or seen which broadcasts, and whether they believed any of it.

Because I was a public figure, it's arguable that I was fair game for anything. That's not true for families, however, and my family didn't deserve what they had to go through. Lynda took the same approach as her mother had when her father faced public criticism, and during this period she would change the channel or put away a newspaper when confronted with upsetting stories. I, on the other hand, became almost obsessed with the inaccuracies being reported, and I stubbornly followed the coverage, no matter how frustrated it made me. I'm sure I would have been better off adopting Lynda's strategy, but I found myself unable to ignore the erroneous reporting.

The stress finally began to get to me. For the first time in my life, I had trouble sleeping. Even now, looking back nearly three decades later, I'm amazed at the sheer volume of painful, chaotic events that engulfed me, my family, and my staff in such a short period of time.

Among all the things that had caused me grief over the so-called "scandal" period, I found it particularly galling that Wiechering had pressured my former aides to imply in their sworn "statements" (which Wiechering had drafted) that I wasn't telling the truth. That I was accused of not being truthful bothered me more than any other accusation or rumor that had been hurled at me during this period. It went right to the core of my sense of integrity and, in my darkest hours, began to erode my sense of self.

I wouldn't have acknowledged it publicly—or perhaps even privately—at the time, but the events of the early 1990s definitely took something out of me. Where I once felt like I could trust my instincts, and that anything was possible, I found myself veering toward self-doubt. Where I had once believed that the truth would always prevail, I couldn't seem to break through the incessant drumbeat of baseless accusations. Though I continued to work hard to fulfill my responsibilities during my remaining years in the Senate, I never completely recovered the kind of drive, energy, or momentum that had marked my earlier political career.

WITH THE FALL of 1992 came the distraction of the presidential election season and the election of Bill Clinton. Things seemed to be looking up. Then, on December 10, 1992, Wiechering acknowledged that he was, in fact, planning to seek an indictment against me. That was when I made a decision that virtually everyone argued would be a huge mistake: I requested to appear before the grand jury for a second time. Even my lawyer, Chuck Ruff, advised against it.

Hiring Ruff had been a big concession for me. After months of protesting that I didn't need representation because I hadn't done anything wrong, I was finally convinced by friends and family to hire a lawyer anyway, if only to have someone who could respond to requests from the prosecutor.

Ruff reminded me that I was inviting significant additional risk by testifying again. I would be entirely at the prosecutor's mercy, answering his questions under oath, and if anything I said conflicted with my previous testimony, or that of my former staff members—none of which I'd be allowed to review—then I could be charged with perjury and have to go to trial.

But I had made my decision, and I wasn't going to back down. I knew that this was the only way to defend myself in front of the grand jurors, and the only way that they would hear my side. I thought that if they saw me rebutting Wiechering's claims, point by point, mano a mano, that I could finally put these allegations to rest.

The date of my second grand jury appearance was set for December 17, 1992, but even this proved an irritant: I had long planned to take Lynda on a surprise seven-day Caribbean cruise over that week, as a present for our twenty-fifth wedding anniversary. Unable to change the booking or get a refund, I was able to substitute our middle daughter, Catherine, in my place. I was disappointed, but Catherine sent me daily missives aimed to cheer me up and allow me to vicariously enjoy the vacation.

"Dear Daddy," went one, "today you went scuba diving. You skinned your arm on a coral rock formation. You had a great day. . . . love, Cathykins." Catherine's messages really lifted my spirits back in wintry Washington.

Finally, sixteen months after my first grand jury appearance, I again walked past the television satellite trucks, reporters, and photographers waiting for me on the Norfolk Federal Courthouse steps. It was a cold, dreary, rainy day, and I doubt if the grand jurors who'd been summoned to the courthouse were thrilled to be called in just a week before Christmas. They had been meeting monthly with the prosecutor for more than a year, watching and listening as Wiechering tried to make a federal case out of a mostly gossipy cell phone conversation intercepted by a guy in a garage.

Despite feeling the effect of the long months of stress and sleep deprivation, I was energized to be there—to have the chance to face down the questions that had been dogging me. Once more, I sat in the lone chair facing the grand jurors as Wiechering asked me to raise my right hand.

"Do you swear to tell the truth, the whole truth, and nothing but the truth, so help you God?" Wiechering said.

"I do."

For more than five hours, Wiechering lobbed question after question, trying to find a contradiction with either my previous testimony or that of my former aides. The tenor was confrontational but not emotional, and there were no outbursts on either side. We were both professionals, doing verbal combat on a very well-ordered stage. I don't tend to lose my cool easily, and this was no exception. As many Marines and combat veterans will attest, once you are trained to stay calm under live fire, you are less easily rattled by a verbal skirmish. The stakes were sky high, but a casual observer might never have known that this was anything but a very long, antagonistic interview.

By late afternoon the whole thing was over. Wiechering dismissed the grand jury, which would reconvene early in the new year and, presumably, grant the prosecutor's request to indict me. In public, I talked about the unfettered power of the prosecutor and acknowledged that the system lent itself to granting virtually every indictment sought. Privately, I held out hope.

A few days later, we were informed that the grand jury's decision was likely to come on January 12, 1993, just eight days before Bill Clinton was to be inaugurated as president of the United States. I was in my Senate office that day, working on routine business and trying to stay focused. You could feel an electric undercurrent of anticipation and anxiety running through the office, and a few reporters were camped out in the hallway. One of my staff members even threw a towel over her head and her computer screen to block out everything else.

We were waiting anxiously for a phone call from the prosecutor's office or some sort of formal announcement, when suddenly Senator John Kerry's press secretary rushed into our office and blurted out, "I just saw on the wire—they're not going to indict him!" Immediately, the office erupted, with people cheering and shouting the news to anyone within earshot.

Soon our phones began ringing nonstop with requests from the press for my reaction. I asked my press secretary to reserve time in the Senate Radio and Television Gallery so I could face the media all at once. For the first time in years, I was actually looking forward to conducting a press conference.

At 5:00 p.m., I stood in front of a crowd of reporters packed shoulder to shoulder:

I said all along I knew *how* this would end, I just didn't know *when*. Well, it finally ended today. Ultimately, the system worked, and the grand jury fulfilled its historical role to serve not only as a sword, but also as a shield to protect citizens from unjust prosecution. I would like to thank the citizens who served on the jury and who made the system work.

I happen to believe, as many of you know, very strongly, that no man is above the law and public officials ought to be held every bit as accountable as any other citizen. That said, it never entered my mind that this matter could get this far or that the system could be so abused.

I want to thank the people of Virginia, my family, my colleagues on both sides of the aisle, an extraordinary number of friends, and my staff and counsel, for standing by me. They understood that an assault on my integrity went straight to my core and they never wavered. It is now time to turn our attention to the serious challenges that are facing Virginia and the nation, and I look forward to getting on with the job I was elected to do.[2]

I then took questions from reporters, and, after about ten minutes, I was stopped by a very welcome interruption. Amid the euphoria, my staff had been able to track down Lynda, who had come straight to the Capitol Building. As I stood behind the podium, she came running into the press room, her arms held wide, and we embraced happily as the cameras flashed and the video rolled. It was an emotional moment of relief—a stark, joyous contrast to the unrelenting anxiety that had been building up in both of us for what seemed like an eternity.

PART IV

AGAINST THE TIDE

IN THE SPRING of 1918, the Imperial German Army was advancing swiftly on the western front. Germany had signed a treaty with the Russians that March, removing the Russians from the war and freeing up Germans to fight elsewhere. The German army swung into action with a major offensive in France and Belgium, hoping to crush the Allies before troops from the United States, which had only recently entered the war, could be fully deployed. By May, the Germans were within fifty miles of Paris.

Then, on June 1, the Germans encountered the U.S. Marine Corps at Belleau Wood. The Battle of Belleau Wood raged for nearly a month, and, alongside British and French troops, more than ten thousand Marines were killed, wounded, or missing in action. But the Marines, fighting through poison gas, sometimes hand-to-hand with bayonets and fists, held their ground against a far larger German force. Legend has it that this is the battle where German soldiers gave the Marines the nickname "devil dogs." It was while receiving reports of the Battle of Belleau Wood that Army General John L. Pershing is credited with the quote, "The deadliest weapon in the world is a United States Marine and his rifle." It is the words of Marine Captain Lloyd S. Williams, however, that so perfectly captured the tenacity that is part of the Marines ethos. As Williams was moving his troops forward early in the battle, French officers urged him to retreat. The day seemed lost. Williams famously shot back, "Retreat? Hell, we just got here!"

This story may be apocryphal, but it does illustrate the mindset of a Marine, an instinct for drive and persistence that I've carried with me since Quantico. Tenacity can be a great asset when you are facing stiff odds. Then again, Captain Williams didn't survive the battle.

The U.S. Senate is different from a battlefield in many ways. For one thing, it doesn't always have clear sides. There were many times when my vote had little relation to the final legislation, and when it could be hard to see what was "right." But there were also moments of clarity, when I believed that there was, unmistakably, a right side on an issue. Those were the times when a single vote could make all the difference in people's lives — whether I was on the winning side or not — because I believed that my vote among the unpopular minority sent an important message. It was on these votes that I found the most certainty in the Senate.

There is sometimes a tendency in politics to judge success based on wins and losses. In my experience, it was the times when I could speak out against legislation that I believed was fundamentally wrong—but I knew was politically popular—that I thought my voice in the Senate was most effective. Standing up for what I believed to be right was the most gratifying part of my Senate career, even if it cost me my seat.

25

Guns, Gays, and Old Glory

ON THE NIGHT of Saturday, January 16, 1993, four days before the presidential inauguration, and just four days after the grand jury's refusal to indict me, I waited in the evening chill to greet President-elect Clinton and his family when they flew into Charlottesville, Virginia. William Jefferson Clinton had chosen Monticello, the historic home of Thomas Jefferson, to launch the final leg of his preinaugural victory tour.

I had met Bill Clinton fifteen years earlier, shortly after I took office as governor of Virginia in 1982. I was walking through the rows of cubicles at the headquarters of the Democratic National Committee in Washington, D.C. Suddenly, a man popped out from behind one of the dividing walls to introduce himself. It was Bill Clinton, then only thirty-five years old, and in the midst of a two-year gap between terms as Arkansas governor. Bill had lost reelection the last time around and was making fundraising calls for his next run, with his large frame folded into one of the empty cubicles. I enjoyed our conversation, and I was immediately impressed by this relatively young politician who was, despite his recent gubernatorial loss, clearly a rising star. I could immediately see that he was an extremely effective communicator with a first-class mind and an appealing kind of charm.

After this initial meeting, Bill and I quickly developed a friendship, even though we came from different backgrounds and had different styles. Bill was a garrulous extrovert who never met a stranger, whereas I was more reserved. Where I was athletic, rigid, and disciplined, Bill was a relaxed southern politician with a penchant for junk food. Yet we shared many political values, such as a commitment to increased opportunity for all Americans, fiscal responsibility, robust national security, and leaner government.

Even when I didn't agree with him, I respected Bill's ability to synthesize his position and discuss it on the merits. Despite my personal commitment to serving in combat in Vietnam, I was enormously impressed with Bill's infamous 1969 letter to the director of the Reserve Officers Training Corps (ROTC) program at the University of Arkansas, expressing his opposition to fighting in the war. I found it remarkable that, at twenty-three years old, Bill could articulate his position so eloquently and effectively.

Bill won reelection in November 1982, and we kept in close touch while we were both southern Democratic governors, talking countless times over the phone and even traveling together on a trade mission to Taiwan with our wives. It was Lynda, with her innate and uncanny political sense, who first noticed the talent of Bill's wife, Hillary, and suggested to me that she was "one to watch."

When we launched the Democratic Leadership Council (DLC) in 1985, I had to work extra hard to recruit Bill, who was concerned about losing his strong support from the Democratic Party establishment, which viewed the DLC with suspicion in our first few years. But his ideas were so closely aligned with ours that I kept at him, and when he did join, Bill was an active and persuasive member. In 1990, Bill became chair of the DLC during the lead-up to his run for president. I assisted his campaign as often as possible and was delighted when he was elected in November 1992 because I thought he'd make a great president. Besides my father-in-law, of all the presidents I've gotten to know, Bill Clinton is the one with whom I had the closest personal relationship.

At Monticello on that Saturday night before Bill's inauguration, the mood in the crowd was festive and emotional as the Clintons' plane landed and the president-elect emerged, beaming and exultant in the glare of klieg lights. He descended the plane stairway, and as I stepped forward to greet him, he threw his arms open to embrace me. It wasn't the first time I'd been on the receiving end of one of Clinton's signature bear hugs, but this one lasted longer than most, and we clung to each other as though we were both returning from a war. And in a sense, we were. We were both emerging from a time of intense media scrutiny, a battleground where one can lose one's dignity, personal privacy, and even, for a time, one's sense of self.

Very few observers probably thought twice about that moment, reading it as nothing more than a spirited greeting between two political backslappers. But for me it was one of the all-too-rare unguarded moments in a politician's life, when there is, at least for an instant, a true human connection.

Four days later, on a bright, crisp January morning, Lynda and I watched from the platform as "the man from Hope" took the oath of office.

"Today, we pledge an end to the era of deadlock and drift," President Clinton said in his inaugural speech. "A new season of American renewal has begun."[1]

I shared in the excitement and optimism that permeated the festivities. President Clinton wasn't the only breath of fresh air in Washington in January 1993. Just a few weeks before, the Congress had sworn in its newest batch of representatives. As the chairman of the Democratic Senatorial Campaign Committee (DSCC), I'd been quietly campaigning and raising money for Senate candidates for the last two years. From the start, the 1992 Senate elections were going to be tough for Democrats. We had twenty-one seats to defend, six more than the Republicans, and in several states the incumbent Democrat had retired. Public opinion was still very favorable toward the successful 1991 Gulf War, which most Democrats had voted against.

We had a hardworking, professional team at the DSCC, including Executive Director Steve Ricchetti, Deputy Director Bob Hickmott, Political Director Don Foley, and Treasurer Tom Lehner. Throughout the tumultuous years of 1991–92, I kept my nose to the grindstone at the DSCC, with good result. We raised a then record amount of money for candidate support while reducing DSCC overhead and operating expenses so that our resources went even further. We also retired all of the previous debt the DSCC was carrying and left the organization with a respectable surplus at the end of my term as chairman.

On election night in 1992, we managed to stand our ground, and Senate Democrats retained our fourteen-seat majority. But the true success of that election was the number of women elected to the Senate. Women had served in the Senate since 1922, but largely as appointees, and never more than two had served at any given time. The Democrats had an unmatched slate of female candidates that year, including Dianne Feinstein and Barbara Boxer of California, Carol Moseley Braun of Illinois, Patty Murray of Washington, and incumbent Senate candidate Barbara Mikulski of Maryland. I made it a priority of the DSCC to funnel as much of our fundraising efforts to these glass-ceiling-shattering candidates as we could and called on Democrats to emphasize the historic nature of the "Year of the Woman." In the end, 1992 saw the election of all five female Democratic candidates.

Soon there were new faces in my Senate office as well—I was joined by a new chief of staff. After David McCloud's resignation in 1991, I had asked Roland McElroy, Senator Sam Nunn's former chief of staff, to come out of retirement to serve as my interim chief of staff, and he kept the office running effectively during a very turbulent time. Once the grand jury investigation finally ended in January 1993, I needed to find someone to fill the role on a permanent basis. Tom Lehner, who had acquitted himself well as the treasurer and budget guru of the DSCC in the last cycle, told me that he would like to be considered for the position. Tom had the skills that fit what our office needed at the time—he was personable and dependable, and combined good political instincts with common sense. When I brought Tom on board, I needed to refocus my energy and my staff in time to face a tough reelection campaign in 1994, only eighteen months away. Tom's partner in this mission would end up being Ridge Schuyler, who came on board at the same time as my new legislative director. Tom and Ridge made a formidable team, and they immediately worked to inject a sense of confidence and purpose back into my tight-knit office. They would end up staying with me for the rest of my tenure in the Senate.

We also had a little continuity in the press office, as Peggy Wilhide, who had taken over the difficult job of press secretary after Steve Johnson's departure in 1991, decided to stay on through the 1994 election.

With my office back on track and the chaos of the grand jury investigation behind us, I was looking forward to working with the new Clinton administration on a whole host of issues. Clinton's first year in office was full of promise, but it wouldn't be easy—many of the issues that the new president wanted to tackle were politically unpopular.

One of the first issues that he took on was his promise to lift the ban on gays and lesbians in the military. Up to that point, the mere fact of having a different sexual orientation (not any action or misconduct) was enough to get a service member court-martialed or, at the very least, separated from the military without an honorable discharge, a procedure that severely hampered their benefits and rights as a veteran. Throughout the 1970s and 1980s, the ban had been increasingly controversial, and a growing number of activists and politicians fought for its removal through legislation, media, and the courts.

Many assumed that, because I was a combat veteran, I would naturally oppose gays and lesbians serving in the military. To the contrary, I had long felt that it was morally wrong to discriminate against gays and lesbians serving openly in the military. The issue first came to my attention during my 1971 law school summer internship with the Marine Corps Judge Advocate General's Corps (JAG), on temporary active duty. During that summer, my job was to handle the Officer Qualification Records (OQRs) of officers who were the subject of any sort of disciplinary proceedings, reviewing the records to make sure that everything was in order and up to date. Among the files were the records of two Marine officers who—despite having served admirably, and even heroically in combat—were facing expulsion from the Corps because they were accused of being gay. They hadn't done anything that would have endangered the lives or well-being of their fellow Marines. In fact, their official records were otherwise unblemished. They were not being charged with any illegal conduct, nor had they been caught engaging in any action that would prove their guilt. They had simply been *accused* of having a nonheterosexual orientation and, based on that accusation alone, were now facing a dishonorable discharge.

I had felt instinctively, during that summer in the JAG office, that the military's exclusionary policy wasn't fair, and that sense of unfairness stuck with me. More than twenty years later, I was a U.S. senator and had a chance to do something about it. The issue had reached Congress in February 1992, nine months before Clinton's election, when the then chairman of the Joint Chiefs of Staff, General Colin Powell, stated his opposition to gays and lesbians serving openly during a House hearing on the defense budget. He was certainly in line with public opinion when he made this declaration, but I disagreed. So, in an attempt to encourage a change in thinking from inside the military, I sent a letter to General Powell, urging him to reconsider.

"The military, in my judgment, should not bar individuals from service based on who they are," I said in the letter. "Rather, it should be concerned with what they do. Like racial or ethnic origin or gender, sexual preference has no bearing on how great a contribution an individual can make to the United States."[2]

In response to the claim that gays and lesbians would have an adverse effect on unit cohesion and discipline, I wrote: "Not so long ago it was argued that the presence of minority personnel in what had previously been all-white units would degrade that confidence, and would lead to disorder. But the exemplary service of minority warriors in the Second World War and Korea, along with a national commitment to equality among the races, led to integration of the services."[3]

I went on to note that similar arguments had been made against allowing women to serve but that gender integration had nonetheless been successfully implemented as well, as demonstrated during the recent 1991 Gulf War.

The letter to General Powell was not intended to be public, but a copy of it was leaked to the press. The reaction was immediate: my office was flooded with letters and phone calls, almost all of them harshly critical. Many were shocked to hear this "radical" view coming from someone from a military background. But it was precisely because I had worn the uniform myself that I felt confident that the military could function perfectly well with people of different sexual orientations serving side by side.

On the campaign trail in 1992, Clinton had pledged to support integrating gays and lesbians into the military, and he was determined to take it on early in his administration. On his very first day as commander in chief in January 1993, Clinton issued an interim order to halt discrimination against gays and lesbians serving in the military as a temporary measure. To make the change permanent, Clinton directed the secretary of defense to draft an executive order to that effect after consultations with senior military leaders about the best way to implement the order.

Clinton, however, had underestimated the degree and impact of the opposition to this hot-button topic, which was swift, vocal, and overwhelming. Soon, the administration was on its heels, forced to accede to a longer period of "study" of the issue before Clinton would sign a final executive order—a period that would be fraught with opposition.

Part of the reason for the fierce opposition was that Clinton was, particularly in these first days of his administration, a little out of his comfort zone when it came to the military. His avoidance of the draft had been a major issue in the campaign, and the comparison with his predecessor, President George H. W. Bush, who was a naval aviator in World War II, didn't help matters. President Clinton needed to strengthen his own relationship with the military, but he didn't always hit the right notes. Soon after the inauguration, Clinton invited me to accompany him on his first-ever visit to an aircraft carrier—the USS *Theodore Roosevelt*—and his first visit as commander in chief to forces under his command. Unfortunately, he didn't make a stellar first impression. His dress that day was a little too casual, his lingo belied some unfamiliarity with the inner workings of military life, and he didn't yet project a commander-in-chief aura. The headlines the next day read: "Warship Gives Clinton a Not-So-Hail to the Chief," and "Unaccustomed Role for Clinton at Sea."[4]

None of this made the administration's position any easier, and through the summer debate raged as the issue of gays and lesbians in the military was kicked back and forth by the White House, the Department of Defense, and the Congress. The Senate Armed Services Committee—of which I was, by then, a member—held hearings, the first one at the naval base in Norfolk, Virginia, an area that was known for its strong pro-military and conservative sentiments, where opposition to gays and lesbians in the military was at its peak. Of the nine senators who visited Norfolk that day, touring submarines and talking to sailors, I was the only one who publicly opposed discriminating against gays and lesbians serving openly in uniform. But, as I told the *Washington Post,* "I just didn't feel right about ducking this occasion."[5]

Unfortunately, the president felt that he had no choice but to compromise. In July, he issued the executive order that allowed gays and lesbians to serve in the military but continued the prohibition on "homosexual conduct." In December, the administration issued Department of Defense Directive 1304.26 that translated that order into military law. Dubbed "Don't Ask, Don't Tell," it was a contradictory policy that restricted the military's efforts to discover or reveal the sexual orientation of service members or applicants while still prohibiting openly gay, lesbian, or bisexual people from military service and forcing them to live a lie in order to serve their country.

"Don't Ask, Don't Tell" was a real disappointment for those of us who believed, in the words of former conservative Republican senator Barry Goldwater, "You don't need to *be* straight to fight and die for your country, you just need to *shoot* straight."

Not surprisingly, my position was considered a political liability. Larry J. Sabato, a political scientist at the University of Virginia, told the *Washington Post:* "This issue is a big loser for Chuck Robb politically. . . . Virginians overwhelmingly oppose lifting the ban [on gays serving in the military], by numbers much higher than in the country as a whole."[6]

Instead of backing away from my stance on the issue as I approached my 1994 reelection campaign, I was determined to stand foursquare behind it. "Robb Hitches Campaign to Gay Rights" blared the headline of a *Washington Post* story in which I "condemned the 'fundamental unfairness' of anti-gay discrimination and called efforts to end it 'the last frontier of the true civil rights struggle.'" I also said at the time that "we're going to get it right in the very near future"—a prediction that I was very pleased to see come true when "Don't Ask, Don't Tell" was repealed in 2010.[7]

My support for gays and lesbians in the military was one of a growing list of issues that would virtually ensure a tough campaign in 1994.

Another hot-button topic on that list was flag burning, an issue that taps into deeply rooted feelings of patriotism, and one for which there is no real middle ground. Just as my background as a military officer had led most people to assume that I would oppose gays and lesbians serving in the military, it made them expect that I would support efforts to ban the burning of the U.S. flag. And I did—initially.

One day in 1989, Senator Strom Thurmond marched up the aisle of the

Senate chamber and thrust a piece of paper at me as I presided over the Senate from the dais.

"You're a patriot," he barked. "You fought for your country. You ought to be on this!" I looked down at the paper—it was a joint resolution proposing a constitutional amendment to ban flag burning. The resolution was in reaction to a Supreme Court decision that had just been announced upholding the rights of individuals to express their dissent by burning the American flag. I am not often sentimental, but I feel a deep sense of patriotism whenever I see the American flag being flown. I understood why, year after year, close to 90 percent of the American public supported a ban on flag burning. I was irritated and indignant that any random provocateur could willfully and legally desecrate the flag I'd fought for.

I signed on without hesitation.

I didn't think much more about the issue until I finally got around to reading the Supreme Court's official decision, written by Justice Antonin Scalia, a short time later. The more I read, the more I realized that the court was right—the act of flag burning, as abhorrent as it was, couldn't be outlawed without seriously infringing on one of our most sacred constitutional amendments: freedom of speech. But the ethereal concept of the First Amendment has a hard time competing with the visceral pull of patriotism and the flag.

The flag-burning amendment didn't pass in 1989. When it was raised again in 1990, I knew that I'd have to oppose it and that my opposition this time around would anger and alienate many Virginians. I also knew that I would appear to be waffling on an important topic. But changing my stance was the right decision, and I wanted people to understand why. So, I decided to speak on the Senate floor:

> What I am about to say is not easy for me. It is not easy to admit that you have changed a strongly held position. . . . But this is one instance where debate in the greatest deliberative body in the free world actually helped change at least one senator's mind. . . . I have been a member of the armed forces (active and reserve) for a third of a century, [and] I have never knowingly failed to stand and render appropriate honors to our flag during my adult lifetime. . . . I have also handed our folded flag to too many widows of servicemen and police officers killed in the line of duty. But despite all these experiences I am no longer persuaded that a constitutional amendment will best protect our flag.

I am persuaded instead that a preservation of the Bill of Rights is the best example that we can provide to the fledgling democracies around the world, as they face dissent and try to rise above the lessons handed down by their autocratic forebears.

My heart requires that I defend the flag. My mind tells me that our flag will be better protected, and the freedoms and values it represents will be better honored, by resisting this amendment.

I believe that in doing so, I am faithfully upholding my solemn oath to support and defend the Constitution of the United States.[8]

The proposed flag-burning amendment didn't get very far that year, but, because it's an issue that provides guaranteed political capital for those who profess their support, it continued to reappear nearly every year. The bill generally fell well short of the required two-thirds majority for a constitutional amendment to pass the Senate. With the bill's defeat assured, several colleagues urged me to protect myself politically—and regain crucial veterans' and military support I had lost on this issue earlier—by voting in favor of the resolution. But my vote was never in question.

As expected, my vocal opposition to a ban on flag burning generated a surge of anger back home in the Old Dominion. But that was nothing compared to the wrath that I incurred on the issue of gun control.

Aside from a few liberal pockets in Northern Virginia, the Commonwealth, with its large rural population and deeply rooted libertarian tradition, was a reliably anti-gun-control state. And supporters of less restrictive gun laws were backed by one of the most influential lobbying organizations in American history: the National Rifle Association (NRA).

Starting in the 1970s, the NRA had invested in a growing number of conservative legal scholars who backed the once novel notion that the Constitution confers on an individual the right to possess *any* kind of firearm, no matter how much danger the weapon poses to the general public, with no restriction whatsoever. The NRA's well-funded lobbying operation had moved that interpretation of the Second Amendment from the edge of American thought squarely into the mainstream, making it hard, if not impossible, for any politician to oppose the "gun lobby."

I had long been familiar with firearms in my personal and professional life. I remember the excitement of owning my first BB gun as a boy, and of my father teaching me, a few years later, how to use a .22-caliber rifle. In the Marine Corps, I had always qualified as either an expert or sharpshooter on the pistol and rifle ranges and had fired every individual and crew-served weapon available to the military during the 1950s and 1960s. I had also used weapons in combat and had them used against me. All in all, I was no stranger to guns, and I consistently supported their responsible ownership and use.

But there were some important points on which the NRA and I disagreed, the clearest being their stance on assault weapons. I knew from firsthand experience what assault weapons were designed for: killing large numbers of enemy soldiers in a combat environment. They simply had no rational purpose in a civilian society—individuals didn't need assault rifles to go deer hunting or to protect themselves at home. The NRA's argument that denying citizens the right to own assault weapons somehow violated the Second Amendment right to bear arms was a willful misreading of what our forefathers intended. The founders simply did not envision the need for everyday citizens to maintain weapons capable of mass killing.

I had incurred the NRA's wrath by voting for what I considered sensible restraints on gun ownership, such as the Brady Bill, named for James Brady, President Reagan's press secretary who was shot and partially paralyzed during an assassination attempt on Reagan in 1981. The law required background checks for handgun purchases, limited ownership of assault weapons to the military, the police, and collectors, and closed a gun-show loophole that allowed vendors at gun shows to sell weapons without the same limitations imposed on all other licensed firearm dealers. When the bill came up for a vote in 1993, I supported it without reservation.

I never sought to repeal the Second Amendment, nor did I seek to prohibit the ownership of firearms for hunting, recreational use, or personal protection. But each of my votes on these issues and arguments for rational restraint only added to the perception that I was culturally out of sync with many Virginians.

I could now add gun control to the growing list of hits that the opposition could easily throw at me in my 1994 reelection campaign. Patriotism, "traditional values," safety—these were core issues to both my constituents and myself, even if we sometimes held different positions. I was happy to explain my positions to skeptical constituents, but I knew that, for many reasons, a win in 1994 would be far from a sure thing.

26

An Imperfect Candidate

ONE BREEZY AUGUST afternoon in 1994, while Lynda and I were visiting with Lynda's mother during her annual late-summer holiday in Martha's Vineyard, the three of us accepted an invitation to join Jacqueline Kennedy Onassis for lunch at her home nearby.

Of all the presidential family members I've been privileged to get to know, no one intrigued me more than Jackie. She had an almost other-worldliness to her, accentuated by her high, airy voice that was nearly a whisper.

We sat on the terrace, chatting and looking out over the water, and the conversation eventually turned to my upcoming reelection campaign. The former First Lady was more knowledgeable about the issues then facing Virginia than I had expected. At one point, Jackie turned to me and, in her most emphatic tone, said, "Chuck, you just *can't* let Oliver North take your Senate seat!"

I RARELY LOOKED forward to campaigns, but as I approached the '94 campaign, I was looking forward to two things: standing up for the issues that I cared about and proving—to myself and to all Virginians—that my personal integrity remained intact. I admit that I had a bit of a chip on my shoulder—rumors had been freely conjured up and wielded throughout the state to try to tarnish my reputation. I had failed to successfully tamp them down, an almost impossible task when there were no concrete allegations to refute. If I couldn't prove them wrong, I could at least prove that they hadn't done the damage that they'd intended. I was ready to win this election, no matter who I was up against. I was ready to prove that the rumors of my political death were greatly exaggerated.

However, after what I'd been through, I was in a much weaker political position than I had been in any of my other campaigns. Not only would I have to prove that I wasn't damaged goods, I'd have to campaign with several political albatrosses around my neck. My votes on issues such as gun control, gays and lesbians in the military, and flag burning were, I believed, the right decisions, and I would stand by them. They were not, however, politically popular, and they certainly wouldn't make campaigning in Virginia any easier.

No one was better at seizing a political opportunity than Doug Wilder, and it was widely speculated that he would challenge me in the primary. In his final State of the Commonwealth address as governor in January 1994, Doug had built up the prospect that he would declare his candidacy, only to shock the audience with the announcement that "I will not seek the nomination for my party for the United States Senate in 1994, nor will I be a candidate for that office."[1] The stunned murmurs in the audience were echoed throughout the state. With Doug out of the race, most of the attention quickly focused on the main matchup: Robb v. North.

Oliver North was a larger-than-life, passionate, and polarizing figure who had captured national and international attention with his appearance before the Iran-Contra congressional hearings in the mid-1980s. America was riveted by the scandal, in which Reagan administration officials illegally sold arms to Iran in exchange for the release of U.S. hostages in Lebanon, using the proceeds to fund rebel Contras in Nicaragua, something Congress had specifically banned earlier in the decade. As he sat before the congressional committee in his Marine Corps uniform, North refused to back down over his role in the scheme and projected an aura of principled defiance that tapped into the antigovernment fervor of the time. Over the course of the hearings, North transformed himself from a rogue operator into a national Republican hero.

Facing criminal proceedings for his role in the affair, North was indicted on sixteen felony counts and convicted of three felonies, including accepting an illegal personal gift of a home security system worth $13,800 that had been bought with money from the illegal sale of arms to Iran. But his convictions in the affair were reversed on a technicality in 1991. After that, North was a highly sought-after stump speaker for Republican candidates across the country and a hot political property.

By 1993, North's name identification was as high as President Clinton's, and he had already developed a sophisticated direct-mail fundraising operation that had raised $20 million over the previous five years for political groups and to help pay his Iran-Contra legal defense expenses.[2] North would be hard to beat.

The potential drama of the race was so palpable that in 1993 a documentary crew started following around the North team. The producers had asked my campaign for access as well, and we responded that they were welcome to film public events, but we politely declined to allow them into our campaign's internal meetings. It was clear from the outset that they thought of North as the dramatic, flashy lead character of their story. The movie they produced, eventually called *A Perfect Candidate*, presents Ollie and me as caricatured versions of ourselves. Ollie is portrayed as a young, crusading rock star, making appearances before thousands of screaming, adoring supporters, whereas I'm shown as old, uninteresting, and out of touch. The producers knew that Ollie could play the young hero who would draw people to the theater. My role in that narrative was as a foil, against which they expected Ollie's campaign to ultimately triumph.

I wasn't bothered by the oversimplification—developing a simple narrative is at the heart of a campaign's ability to reach people in their busy lives. What bothered me about *A Perfect Candidate* was the film's cynical overall message about American politics: *a plague on both candidates.*

At one particularly sad point in the film, *Washington Post* reporter Don Baker, who had built his career on political reporting, is asked to identify a politician he admires, and he cannot come up with a single name. All too often, journalists and voters had looked for heroes among politicians but found fallible human beings.

I found the idea that all politicians were cut from the same crooked cloth very troubling, and yet, by the mid-1990s, it was already deeply ingrained in our culture and our media. Heavily featured in the film was North's campaign strategist, Mark Goodin, a protégé of Lee Atwater's, who most personified the "at any cost" style of campaigning that became more prominent in the 1980s. Goodin said in the film: "Getting people elected . . . has a lot to do with dividing. . . . It's like busting a big rock. You try to chip off your piece and then break the rest of it into so many smithereens that they don't matter."[3]

I found this perspective not only misanthropic, oversimplified, and over-dramatic but also plainly untrue about politics as I knew it. I believed that, more often than not, elected officials on both sides of the aisle, and the staff who supported them, had a true passion for public service. That passion can take some too far, and there are those individuals for whom winning is the only goal, but that was the exception rather than the rule.

On January 28, 1994, North officially announced his campaign, followed by appearances on a series of national television talk shows. There was a catch, however. His fame may have netted him an unusual amount of exposure for a first-time candidate, but the lingering controversy surrounding Iran-Contra meant that he didn't get as much deferential treatment from the shows' interviewers. These were his first appearances since his conviction had been overturned, and without the drama of standing up to Congress, he didn't fare nearly as well. Public opinion polls following this first round of appearances showed that North dropped as much as ten points in hypothetical matchups with me and other potential competitors.

North was also a polarizing figure within the Republican Party. Although there was a faction that was fervently committed to North, there also was a vocal faction who would refuse to support him, even when he was the nominee of their party. The latter—including almost all of the former Reaganites and Virginia's senior U.S. senator, John Warner—lined up behind his primary opponent. Though North went on to win the nomination, the battle was a particularly bloody one for the Republicans.

My own campaign kicked off with a bang.

"Defiantly declaring that he's 'never run from a fight,'" the *Washington Post* said, "Sen. Charles S. Robb today began what even he admits will be his toughest political battle ever as he formally opened his bid for reelection."[4]

"I know the campaign ahead won't be easy," I told the cheering group of supporters gathered for my kickoff event. But, I said, "This is a fight we have to win."[5]

I wasn't wrong on either account, and I was glad to have a good staff behind me. Susan Platt, my campaign manager, was one of the very few women in the country managing a Senate race, and, as far as we knew, the first woman to manage a statewide race in Virginia.

As always, my family proved to be my rock in difficult times. Lynda, still the best politician in the family, was joined by all three of our daughters on the campaign trail: Lucinda volunteered to make campaign speeches across Virginia; Catherine insisted—over my objections—on deferring her enrollment at the University of Texas Law School so she could travel around the state organizing young adults in support of my campaign; and Jennifer, who was still in high school, participated in local political events whenever her studies and sports schedule permitted. Even my brother Wick and his family, who lived in Fauquier County, Virginia, and Lynda's mother and sister, Luci, who both lived in Texas, came out to lend their support.

Almost immediately, we experienced the sometimes startling fervor of the North supporters. In April, I attended the annual Shad Planking, a Virginia political event held in rural Sussex County. As soon as I arrived,

I found myself surrounded by shouting North supporters waving Wild West–style "Wanted" posters, with my face as the supposed criminal. The large crowd began chanting and closing in on me and my small staff. For a moment, it felt like the situation could become hostile, so I went with my instincts: I pulled a blue felt-tipped pen out of my pocket and autographed the nearest poster. Instantly, the tension broke, and the antagonistic crowd transformed into a line of people eager to get their posters signed.

In June, I won the primary with a resounding 58 percent against three challengers, but with poor turnout—an indication that enthusiasm for my candidacy was hardly at an all-time high.

Doug Wilder took perfect advantage of the unexciting Democratic primary to make his own news by delivering two cardboard boxes full of signatures—some of which were reportedly collected outside the Republican convention—to the Virginia Department of Elections that got him on the ballot as an Independent. By not running in the Democratic primary, Doug avoided Virginia's "sore loser" law, which precluded candidates who lost a primary from then running as an Independent.

Wilder wasn't the only one. Marshall Coleman also decided to jump into the fray as an Independent on the eve of the primary. Coleman, who had served as Virginia's attorney general when I was lieutenant governor, was still an appealing candidate, despite running unsuccessfully for governor against me in 1981 and against Doug in 1989.

For those covering the election, this race was a dream come true: four well-known candidates would duke it out in a free-for-all. Our first round was a loosely formatted ninety-minute extended debate before a national television audience on *Larry King Live*. As both the incumbent and an unapologetic ally of President Clinton (who had had a somewhat bruising first two years of his presidency), I was a natural target for criticisms from the three other candidates. But I held my own, and most pundits opined that I'd had the best showing that night. In one revealing moment, we were all asked who we would vote for if we were not in the race. North and Coleman both ducked the question, and Wilder declared with a smile that he would still vote for himself. I was surprised to find that my honest answer—I would vote for Doug—was noted in the media as a high point for the debate.

The next major joint appearance was a July 9 American Legion convention in Richmond, where we were all scheduled to make speeches during the proceedings. I knew that I'd face fierce opposition from the crowd of veterans because of my support for gays serving openly in the military and my opposition to a flag-burning amendment to the Constitution. Feeling like Daniel in the lion's den, I stepped up to the podium and launched straight into the most contentious issues rather than waiting for my opponents to exploit them.

"I'd like to be able to throw you some red meat," I said. "But if I did, I wouldn't be true to my beliefs."[6]

The response was about the best I could have hoped for: polite, muted applause. I considered it a partial victory when a grizzled old veteran came up to me as I was leaving and said: "Senator, you've got guts. I'm not voting for you, but you've got guts."

When Oliver North addressed the same crowd later that day, he gave them exactly what they wanted to hear. With his misty-eyed sincerity and unstintingly conservative positions, he roused the assembled to their feet. A *Washington Post* headline read, "Veterans Groups Give North a Hero's Welcome."[7]

At the campaign's second debate on July 16, held at the Virginia Bar Association's annual meeting, I wasn't at the top of my game, and the rigid format allowed each candidate the opportunity to critique my record uninterrupted and unchallenged. I was absolutely hammered in the debate, and it marked the low point of my campaign. The single benefit was that this allowed me to reach my nadir well before Labor Day, when most voters actually begin to pay attention to campaigns.

By the end of the summer of 1994, I was down but not yet out. At the third and final debate of the race the day after Labor Day at Hampden-Sydney College, Doug Wilder and Marshall Coleman, who were trailing far behind in the polls, adopted a "nothing-to-lose" strategy of going after both Ollie and me hammer and tongs. I was doing well until I got a question on fiscal discipline.

I've never believed in sugarcoating fiscal discipline, and I was seriously frustrated by my opponents' promises of a plethora of new social programs and significant tax cuts while also pledging to reduce the national debt. I had taken a strong and very public stand in favor of President Clinton's Deficit Reduction Plan of 1993. Debt reduction was the issue that I had talked to Clinton about constantly during his campaign, bringing it up at every meeting and during every phone call. I must have sounded like a broken record. After a rapid increase of the national debt—the accumulation of each year's overspending, or deficit—during the tax cutting and military spending of the Reagan years, I was anxious that Clinton's first budget address the problem. If it didn't, then he would own the problem himself, and his chances of stemming the tide of red ink would be lost for the remainder of his presidency. When Clinton unveiled the Deficit Reduction Plan of 1993 (formally called the Omnibus Budget Reconciliation Act of 1993), the plan was attacked from both sides, decried as the "largest tax increase in history," and as a program of "draconian" spending cuts that would gut many legislators' pet projects. The debate over the plan was heated, and it only barely passed, requiring Vice President Al Gore to cast a tie-breaking vote in the Senate.

I wholeheartedly supported Clinton's deficit reduction plan and wanted to take it even further. To show how serious I was, I proposed a bill in 1993 that would increase the gas tax by far more: ten cents per year for five years, for a total increase of fifty cents. Based on solid data from the Congressional Research Service, my modest proposal was grounded in the fact that U.S. gas prices were far lower than those of any other industrialized nation. Raising them over a five-year period would help us begin to wean ourselves from dependence on foreign oil and had the added benefit of freeing ourselves from one of the biggest yokes binding us to the politically volatile Middle East. As I argued in my floor speech introducing the legislation: "In the 1970s, our dependence on foreign oil cost us jobs; in the early 1990s, it cost us lives." It was a fiscally responsible solution that was supported by virtually no other politician and was wildly unpopular with voters. Understandably, my proposal had little support from my fellow legislators and did not carry the day. It did, however, provide much fodder for my future political opponents.

During the Hampden-Sydney debate, I used a line that I had employed several times before to dramatize my point in an attempt to underscore my commitment to the hard choices needed for real fiscal responsibility. Turning to Ollie, I said, "I would take food from the mouths of widows and orphans" if that's what was necessary to bring down the deficit.[8]

Hearing murmurings from the audience, I added, "I know that's not a popular line."[9]

"That's a *stupid* line," Doug shouted, and the audience howled.[10] The remark was classic Doug—pithy, funny, and incendiary all at once.

The line became infamous almost immediately, and the North staff quickly began organizing the "Widows and Orphans for North" campaign, complete with bumper stickers, which was, admittedly, quite clever.

With the debates behind me, I set off for a grueling ten-day, one-hundred-stop tour to every corner of Virginia that got me out of the Senate and into the state. I hoped to counter the impression that I had "gone Washington" and to reconnect with the many supporters whom I'd come to know over my years in politics.

During the tour, I often stayed with these supporters in their homes. These were not million-dollar mansions but the normal two- or three-bedroom homes of the local Democratic leaders—the pastors, teachers, school principals, or town doctors who were respected in their communities and whose word carried weight. I would often arrive at supporters' homes late in the evening, and we might have a chance to talk before turning in. After a good night's sleep, we'd chat over an early cup of coffee at their kitchen table.

The ability to wake up in someone else's home and share breakfast provided the time and space for real conversations about their concerns. I was able to get to know them in a more personal way rather than just shaking hands at photo-ops. The tour worked its intended magic, and instead of being wearied by the pace, I entered the fall campaign invigorated.

Meanwhile, Doug's campaign was in free fall. In many respects, the Hampden-Sydney debate was both its high-water mark and its last hurrah. I'd already been endorsed by several major national organizations, and through August and early September I received a series of endorsements from prominent leaders in the African American community, including an influential group of Black ministers, State Senator Henry Marsh (Doug's former college roommate), and the revered civil rights leader Oliver Hill.

Soon enough, Doug's campaign appeared to be coming in for a crash landing. New public opinion polls showed Doug trailing badly in the race—one even showed him trailing me with African American voters. On September 15, less than two months before Election Day, Doug officially dropped out of the race.

"I am a realist," Doug said in a statement. "I know when to hold and when to fold them."[11]

A few days after Doug's withdrawal, I requested a private meeting with him. Virginia's Democratic Party was dispirited and bruised by the fractious battles between us, and I wanted to do what I could to unify it again. Doug graciously agreed to endorse me when the time was right.

In late September, as the pressure increased, North made the first of a series of untimely mistakes. In an interview, he called me an "Eighth and Eye Marine," implying that my active duty in the Marine Corps had been largely ceremonial. I am, in most cases, slow to take offense, and I tried to avoid ostentatious public displays and performances. But this time North had simply gone too far.

To respond, I called a press conference on the street in front of the Marine Barracks in Southeast Washington, and, for the first time in my campaign, I blasted North directly and unambiguously. Throwing a three-inch-thick file folder containing my entire, unedited military record down on the table in front of me, I angrily accused Ollie of delivering a particularly low blow that was designed to go right to my credibility and my integrity. North, I told the assembled reporters, "has had real problems with the truth," and I was "not going to continue to let him get away with the deceptions that have taken place."[12]

The perception that he wasn't always fully truthful had always been North's Achilles' heel. Back in June 1993, even the conservative-leaning *Reader's Digest* ran an article titled, "Does Oliver North Tell the Truth?"

Then, in early October, at what should have been an easy event with high school students, North told the audience that he'd never lied to Congress. This was despite North famously saying, in the televised, sworn congressional testimony that we'd all watched a few years before: "I misled the Congress. . . . I did so with a purpose."[13] The lie was so blatant that most of the political world was simply stunned.

It also further exacerbated his rocky relationship with many Republican Party leaders, and the nonendorsements that had been plaguing his campaign continued full force. Virginia's Republican senator John Warner had not only backed Coleman's independent bid, but he had also persuaded several prominent national Republicans to either do the same or simply withhold their support from North. Robert "Bud" McFarlane, the national security advisor under Reagan and North's former boss at the White House, said on CBS's *60 Minutes* that North was "not someone you want in public life."[14] Woody Holton, son of former Republican governor Linwood Holton, declared that "Virginia has gone from George Washington, who could not tell a lie, to Oliver North, who could not tell the truth."

A few days after the event with the high school students, Jim Webb—a fellow Marine, former secretary of the Navy, and undersecretary of defense under Ronald Reagan—organized a press conference at the Iwo Jima Memorial with five other Vietnam veterans, including my friend and colleague Senator Bob Kerrey, and my battalion commander in Vietnam, Colonel Roger Barnard. The six veterans praised my record and criticized North for having attacked it. Webb, who was also a classmate of North's at the Naval Academy, said: "We have marveled at the exaggerations and the missteps [North] has brought to the public arena. . . . Most of us remained silent. But it has become imperative for anyone who respects the Marine Corps as an institution to say, 'Enough is enough.'"[15]

Within a week, North's campaign went into full lockdown. His staff restricted all media access to their candidate, and reporters voiced their complaints in print.

But North was not down for the count, and he had his share of effective moments as well. He ran a simple television ad featuring former Lebanon hostage David Jacobsen looking directly into the camera as he says: "I know politicians like to point their fingers at Oliver North about Iran-Contra. They weren't there. I was. If it weren't for Ollie North, I would never have seen my family again. I'm making this ad because I want you to know Oliver North is one of the finest men I've ever known."

Other former hostages publicly disputed Jacobsen's comments, but to this day, the Jacobsen spot remains, in my opinion, one of the single most persuasive political ads ever created in any political race. I felt my eyes mist up when I saw it, and if it could have that kind of effect on me, I could only imagine the effect it would have on most voters. The day after the ad aired, a Mason-Dixon poll showed North up by four points.

On October 21, Doug Wilder reentered the scene, this time as a supporter. At a local Democratic event in Northern Virginia, Doug and I stood onstage with President Clinton, and Doug pledged to fully support my campaign. Clinton noted that our truce and handshake onstage in front of him reminded him of the Palestinian and Israeli leaders Yasir Arafat and Yitzhak Rabin in the same pose thirteen months before. "Peace is breaking out all over," the president said.[16]

In the end, Doug campaigned for me up until Election Day, and we made several appearances together, effectively putting to rest any potentially distracting stories about a "feud."

Then, less than ten days before Election Day came an unexpected development. Former First Lady Nancy Reagan was asked about her husband's onetime National Security Council aide during an interview on PBS. Mrs. Reagan, whose husband had declined to support North, replied: "Ollie North—oh, I'll be happy to tell you about Ollie North. I know Ollie North has a great deal of trouble separating fact from fantasy." Mrs. Reagan paused for applause and laughter before going on. "And he lied *to* my husband and *about* my husband, kept things from him that he should not have kept from him, and that's about what I think of Ollie North."[17]

It was a huge blow for North's popularity, especially among mainstream Republicans. President Reagan himself remained silent after the incident and did not make any appearances for his former aide. Lynda and I expected President Reagan to sit this election out after seeing him at the funeral of former president Richard Nixon earlier that year. While Lynda and I were gathering before the service with other First Families, we spoke with Nancy and Ronald Reagan for several minutes. Almost immediately, I noticed something strange: every comment or question I directed to President Reagan was answered by his wife. This was highly unusual because Reagan had always been a garrulous, warm, engaging conversationalist. Neither Lynda nor I had ever seen the former president so quiet, or Nancy Reagan so forward. When we were walking away, I said to Lynda, "I think there's something wrong with him." We found out shortly after the 1994 election that President Reagan was then in the early stages of Alzheimer's disease.

In Ollie's final days on the campaign trail, the pressure mounted, and his string of gaffes continued. At one point, he referred to President Clinton as a "bonehead" and then responded to a reporter's follow-up by shooting back, "He's not *my* commander-in-chief."[18] North also suggested making Social Security voluntary, an idea his campaign immediately tried to walk back when it was roundly ridiculed.

Yet none of North's blunders diminished the enthusiasm of his huge army of true believers. Indeed, it seemed to energize them even more, and the crowds that turned out for his rallies during the last couple of weeks of the campaign set records everywhere they were held. Somewhat unexpectedly, the fervor of North's supporters worked to my advantage as well—the prospect that North could actually be elected helped me to energize and motivate voters who might otherwise have stayed away from the polls altogether.

As the clock ticked down and the race was still "spandex-tight," as one newspaper called it, my supporters were encouraging me to take North on a little more directly. I was always reluctant about going negative, but I also knew that it was important that I show voters that I really wanted to win. So, I decided to borrow a technique from Senator Howell Heflin of Alabama and wrote a humorous singsong chant that I first used at a Roanoke rally a week before Election Day, starting quietly and building up to a crescendo:

My opponent
is a document-shredding,
Constitution-trashing,
Commander-in-chief-bashing,
Ayatollah-loving,
arms-dealing,
drug-condoning,
Noriega-coddling,
Swiss-banking,
law-breaking,
letter-faking,
self-serving snake-oil salesman,
who can't tell the difference,
between the truth and a lie.
Just ask Nancy Reagan!
Just ask President Reagan!
Just ask Norman Schwarzkopf!
Just ask Colin Powell!
Just ask anyone who worked with him!

Audiences loved the mantra, and many took to chanting it along with me.

No matter how much momentum we developed, however, we knew that North's organization had the ability and resources to put together the most effective GOP "get-out-the-vote" effort that Virginia had ever seen. North's campaign also had the support of the self-described "Christian Coalition," which would be distributing its supposedly "nonpartisan" voter guides in churches across the state the Sunday before Election Day. We'd be up against a massive and well-oiled machine.

By Election Day, both campaigns had done everything they could possibly do; now it was up to the voters to decide in what had clearly become the most closely watched U.S. election of the year.

I voted early—by 7:00 a.m.—to get maximum news coverage and remind as many of my supporters as possible to vote before they headed to work. Then I went back to the campaign headquarters to do interviews and make thank-you calls to key supporters.

On a day when the Republicans were expected to do well nationwide and "Ollie's Army" appeared to be going strong, many Virginia Democrats braced themselves for a loss. North's staffers had been wagering with reporters—not about who would win, but how big North's margin of victory would be. They had even booked the cavernous Richmond convention center for what was expected to be "a huge victory party, a celebration of a political revolution."[19] My campaign had reserved the comparatively modest ballroom of a hotel in Tysons Corner, which was, according to the *Washington Post*, "supposed to be the scene of a wake." The *Post* continued:

> Instead, at the surprisingly early hour of 8:30 p.m. the Tysons party for embattled Sen. Charles S. Robb turned into a raucous explosion of relief and joy, as Democratic supporters leaped onto chairs to see early results and hugged one another in amazement. At the Richmond Centre, by contrast, the few hundred fans of Republican nominee Oliver L. North on hand looked gloomy and strangely overwhelmed in a cavernous room expected to hold thousands, while their hero huddled behind closed doors in a hotel several blocks away.[20]

Less than three hours after the polls closed, Ollie telephoned me, saying simply: "You won. Govern well."

When all the votes were counted, I had won reelection by only 55,000 votes out of more than two million cast. Turnout of registered voters proved to be the highest of any nonpresidential election in Virginia's history, and I received 46 percent of the vote, beating Ollie by only 3 percent.

According to Warren Fiske at the *Virginian-Pilot*, Marshall Coleman, who garnered 11 percent of the vote, drew votes equally from both sides and had little impact on the outcome.[21] The *Pilot*'s columnist Guy Friddell noted that throughout the campaign, "Coleman kept his poise, never lost his grace, and won many friends."[22] Despite being on the opposite side of several campaigns with Marshall, we have become friends over the years and now even attend the same church in McLean.

As in any close race, there were numerous factors that might have proved decisive. Certainly, the strong edge I enjoyed among female voters and my overwhelming support among African American voters helped push me over the top, but some fundamental doubts about Ollie North, and concerns about the kind of agenda he would support, also worked in my favor.

My campaign had raised and spent some $5.6 million. This would have been a record for a U.S. Senate campaign in Virginia, except that North's campaign had spent more than $20 million, a nationwide record for a state election at that point, with the exception of Michael Huffington's failed

Senate campaign in California that same year. There was something comforting about the fact that a seat in the Senate didn't necessarily go to the highest bidder.

For me, the victory was about more than a second term. After all that had transpired over the past four years—the rumors, investigations, and attacks on my character that chipped away at my very sense of self, I felt vindicated by the voters. It was a race that looked stacked against me: a midterm election with a president in the midst of a rocky first two years, in which I was outspent four to one and faced three serious challengers. I hadn't capitulated on any of the politically hazardous stances I'd taken during my first term because I still believed those stances were right. I decided that I was going to win on my record or not at all, and victory on those terms was sweet.

At around 10:00 p.m. on election night, I walked onstage in the Tysons ballroom packed with a euphoric crowd. In front of a bright wall of red and white balloons, surrounded by Lynda and our daughters, I leaned into the microphone. Remembering the same euphoria at the victory party for my gubernatorial win nearly fifteen years before, I used the line that expressed my feelings perfectly, yet again: "How sweet it is!" The crowd responded with jubilation.

The celebration that evening had an almost giddy air of relief to it, that this hard-fought campaign was finally over. But our celebration would be short-lived: by the next day, vote tallies showed that Republicans had trounced Democrats across the country. The "Republican Revolution," led by Newt Gingrich wielding his "Contract with America," was just beginning.

27

Taking a Stand

THE SENATE THAT I returned to after my 1994 reelection was particularly tumultuous. The 104th Congress opened in January 1995 at a time of growing politicization and disenchantment. In only two short years, the sense of optimism following Clinton's 1992 victory had completely evaporated and was replaced by increasingly poisonous partisan sniping and gridlock. Representative Newt Gingrich had led the Republican Revolution of 1994—sweeping victories by congressional Republicans in the House and Senate with a message that directly opposed President Clinton's major policy initiatives.

I may have survived the Republican tidal wave of 1994, but it had taken out enough Democrats for us to lose control of both the House and the Senate. Now the Republicans—who last had responsibility for running both houses of Congress forty years before—would be in charge, chairing the committees, setting the agenda, and controlling the debate. Life on Capitol Hill was clearly going to be different.

In addition to the losses, several of my Senate colleagues—from both sides of the aisle—announced in the early days of the new Congress that they would be retiring at the end of their terms. Democrats Sam Nunn, David Pryor, Bill Bradley, Paul Simon, and Bennett Johnston, Democratic leader George Mitchell, and Republicans Warren Rudman, Jack Danforth, Alan Simpson, Nancy Kassebaum, Bill Cohen, and Hank Brown—all would be gone from the Senate by the opening of the 105th Congress. These were all solid and very able public servants, but, more importantly, they all made a point of reaching out to find workable solutions and avoiding partisan gridlock. Many of them would end up being replaced by more ideological senators, further eroding the mainstream coalition that helped make the system work.

Throughout the mid-1990s, the level of antigovernment rhetoric escalated alarmingly. "Communist sympathizer," once the worst thing you could call a public figure, was now surpassed by the pejorative "Washington insider." The resurgence of anti-big-government sentiment added to the growing chasm of mistrust that many citizens felt toward federal institutions. And the new Republican majority, led in the House by Speaker Gingrich and guided by the philosophy of downsizing government, was in the perfect position to benefit from the public's discontent. The Republicans began aggressively pushing a return to "traditional values," an innocuous-sounding moniker for a movement rooted in intolerance. Political commentator and politician Pat Buchanan personified the movement's regressive thinking in his speech at the 1992 Republican national convention: "The agenda [Bill] Clinton and [Hillary] Clinton would impose on America—abortion on demand, a litmus test for the Supreme Court, homosexual rights, discrimination against religious schools, women in combat units—that's change, all right. But it is not the kind of change America wants. It is not the kind of change America needs. And it is not the kind of change we can tolerate in a nation that we still call God's country."[1]

Virginians already knew me well enough to realize that I wouldn't be jumping on the Republican's so-called "traditional values" bandwagon anytime soon. But, in truth, I was culturally out of step with many Virginians on several hot-button issues. I had already publicly supported gun-control measures, opposed a constitutional ban on flag burning, and supported the rights of gays and lesbians to serve openly in the military.

It was into this atmosphere that, in May 1996, legislation was introduced in the House and Senate called—misleadingly—the Defense of Marriage Act (DOMA). At its core, DOMA would allow states to refuse to recognize same-sex marriages performed in any other state.

From the beginning, it was clear that DOMA had a lot more to do with pandering to the culturally conservative agenda than somehow "defending the institution of marriage." In one *Washington Post* article, Republican backers of the bill decried that an "extremist homosexual agenda" would "threaten the nation's social structure."[2]

It was also designed as a wedge issue—the Christian Coalition, a right-wing voter-mobilization organization founded by Pat Robertson, promised that they would make DOMA "a major issue in the ['96] campaign."[3] At the time, 68 percent of Americans believed that same-sex marriage should be illegal, compared to only 27 percent who supported it.

When the bill was scheduled for debate on the Senate floor in September 1996, I decided to prepare a speech, not for the press or the campaign trail but for my fellow senators. I worked with my staff on a speech for nearly two weeks, going through many revisions with Ridge Schuyler, Susan Albert, and Kim Anderson. I wanted the speech to be rational and well-reasoned—a speech that actually would be listened to by other senators and their staff members, one with the potential to change their minds.

On September 10, 1996, the day that I was due to give the speech, my chief of staff, Tom Lehner, came into my office to talk.

"Before you go down to give this speech," Tom said, "I just feel like I have to say this: I understand that you are taking the position that you feel is right. But Virginia is still a politically and socially conservative state, and there will be serious consequences in four years if you make this speech."

From a political perspective, Tom was completely right, and he was doing his job as my chief of staff by warning me of the consequences.

"I appreciate you raising the political concerns," I said. "And I know that you have my best interests at heart. But I think that this is an important moment to take a stand."

A short time later, I rose to speak on the floor of the Senate. "Despite its name," I said, "the Defense of Marriage Act does not defend marriage against some imminent, crippling threat. Maintaining the freedom of states to define a civil union or a legal right to benefits cannot—and will not— harm the strength and power of marriage. Neither can it diminish the love between a husband and a wife, nor the devotion they feel toward their children."[4]

I went on to address the argument that this bill stopped the federal government from dictating to the states on the issue of marriage. On this point, the bill was entirely superfluous: the states have never been able to legislate for each other and arguing that this was to "protect" a federal statute was egregious and totally unnecessary.

These are important issues . . . and they deserve a full discussion, but they are not the issues that make this debate so difficult—or so important.

For beneath the high-minded discussions of constitutional principles and states' rights lurks the true issue which confounds and divides us: the issue of how we feel about intimate conduct we neither understand nor feel comfortable discussing. . . .

For the vast majority of us who don't hear that particular drummer it's difficult to fully comprehend such an attraction. But homosexuality has existed throughout human history. And even though medical research hasn't succeeded in telling us why a small but significant number of our fellow human beings have a different sexual orientation, the clear weight of serious scholarship has concluded that people do not choose to be homosexual, any more than they choose their gender or their race. Or any more than we choose to be heterosexual.

And given the prejudice too often directed toward gay people and the pressure they feel to hide the truth—their very identities—from family, friends and employers, it's hard to imagine why anyone would actually choose to bear such a heavy burden unnecessarily. . . .

I believe it is time for those of us who are not homosexual to join the fight. A basic respect for human dignity—which gives us the strength to reject racial, gender and religious intolerance—dictates that in America we also eliminate discrimination against homosexuals. I believe that ending this discrimination is the last frontier in the ultimate fight for civil and human rights. . . .

Most of us are uncomfortable discussing in public the intimacies of life. And most of us are equally uncomfortable with those who flaunt their eccentricities and their nonconformity, whether gay or straight.

But in the end, we cannot allow our discomfort to be used to justify discrimination. We are not entitled to that indulgence. We cannot afford it. But doing the right thing is not always easy and I know this is not an easy vote even for those who may agree with my argument.

It is, in a very real sense, a test of character and I hope as many colleagues as possible will take time to reflect before casting their vote. If enough of us have the courage to vote against the Defense of Marriage Act, I believe we can convince the president to do what I know in his heart of hearts he knows he should do to this discriminatory legislation. A nation as great as ours should not be enacting the Defense of Marriage Act.

Ultimately . . . I would say to our fellow Senators: you don't have to be an advocate of same-sex marriages to vote against the Defense of Marriage Act. You only have to be an opponent of discrimination. . . .

I'll conclude today with the words of a courageous American whom I seldom quote, but to whom I'm eternally indebted. President Lyndon Johnson often said, "It's not hard to do what's right, it's hard to know what's right." We know it is right to abolish discrimination. And if we reflect on what this bill is—an attempt to discriminate—rather than on what it is packaged to be—a defense of marriage—we will come down on the right side of history.[5]

When I finished my speech, Senator Barbara Boxer of California came up to me and said, "Chuck, this is political suicide for you." Coming from a liberal-leaning state, Senator Boxer knew she could vote her conscience and oppose DOMA without risking a huge political backlash. But it was clear that I'd get hammered in Virginia. And because DOMA was slated to pass overwhelmingly, regardless of my vote against it, I appeared to be tilting at windmills, sacrificing precious political capital for the sake of a losing cause. Many other political allies expressed similar sentiments, trying to persuade me to sit out the vote. And more than one Senate colleague said to me: "You're absolutely right about DOMA, and I'd like to vote against it. But I can't—I'd never get re-elected." I understood their quandary, but for me it wasn't a question.

As predicted, DOMA passed the Senate overwhelmingly, 85–14. The result was sad but not surprising. Neither was the fact that I was the only southern senator to vote against the bill. There was still a sliver of hope among those of us who opposed the bill that President Clinton might veto it. He'd made no secret during his 1992 campaign that he supported basic human rights for gays and lesbians. But Clinton had been burned politically by the blowback from the 1993 "Don't Ask, Don't Tell" controversy. Now, in the midst of a reelection campaign, he didn't want to rock the boat again, even if the polls did, by then, show him well ahead of his opponent. Discomfited by what he felt he had to do, Clinton signed the legislation in the middle of the night on September 21, 1996, with no signing ceremony and no press invited. I was disappointed that the president signed the bill at all, though I understood why he thought he had to do it. His ambivalence about the law seeped into his subsequent statement that "the enactment of this legislation should not, despite the fierce and at times divisive rhetoric surrounding it, be understood to provide an excuse for discrimination, violence or intimidation against any person on the basis of sexual orientation."[6] Over a decade later, the politics had changed, and both Bill and Hillary Clinton publicly urged the Supreme Court to strike down the bill he had signed into law.

My fellow Virginians relentlessly expressed their displeasure with my DOMA vote in 1996. "Robb is hopelessly out of touch with the typical Virginian," went one characteristic letter to the editor. The criticism was not, however, completely universal. *Washington Post* columnist Richard Cohen, who had not shied away from criticizing me in the past, opened a column with these words:

"If there is anything wrong with Washington, it is Chuck Robb," I wrote in 1994, cavalierly wasting the Virginia senator and former Marine (Bronze Star) with a single blast from my mighty word processor. I now would like to amend those remarks: If there is anything good about Washington—anything wonderful and inexplicable and, sometimes, downright confusing—it is Chuck Robb. . . .

Probably I do Robb no favor by highlighting his vote on this matter. But people are always telling me about Washington, about the sort of town it is and the sort of people who live here and how everyone's a moral coward. Sometimes, I get to believe this stuff myself and then someone like Robb comes along and—whether you agree or not—makes a stand on moral principle.[7]

I certainly preferred the bouquet to the brickbat, but in truth neither was really appropriate. Gay rights was one of those issues that I was sure would prove itself in the long run. I strongly believed that legalized discrimination against gays and lesbians would follow laws banning interracial marriage or denying women the right to vote into the dustbin of American history. It's unthinkable today that any U.S. judge would publish a ruling that read: "Almighty God created the races white, black, yellow, malay and red, and he placed them on separate continents. . . . The fact that He separated the races shows that He did not intend for the races to mix."[8] But in 1967, a judge used that argument in a Virginia trial court to rule against interracial marriage in a case that would eventually become *Loving v. Virginia.* At the time, many otherwise reasonable people agreed with it, a fact that today seems unfathomable. I believed that Americans would look back many years later at DOMA and be similarly incredulous at the blatant, shortsighted, and unfair discrimination it represented.

In 2015, when same-sex marriage became legal in all fifty states, I was gratified to see reporters whom I had long respected, such as Jeff Schapiro at the *Richmond Times-Dispatch,* describe my support for the issue almost twenty years earlier as "the long view on gay marriage."[9]

In truth, voting against DOMA was one of my most uplifting votes in the Senate. I was completely sure of where I stood on the issue, and the bill was crystal clear. I knew that my vote would have political ramifications, but what is the point of being reelected, I thought, if I didn't make a difference while I was in office?

28

Bayview

IN APRIL 1997, my office was visited by a group of African American farmers, led by John W. Boyd Jr., a Mecklenburg County farmer and president of the National Black Farmers Association. The farmers were in desperate need of the loans that farmers often depended on to purchase seed and equipment in the spring, paying the loan back after the harvest. Their complaint was that the United States Department of Agriculture (USDA) had, for many years, denied them farm loans for one reason only: the color of their skin. Black farmers had been accusing the USDA, which some of them called "the last plantation," of unfair treatment for years, and the USDA had responded by saying, "we're investigating the claims," delaying a decision on the cases until the statute of limitations on the alleged violations had run out.

It was not surprising for me to find, after twenty years as an elected official, that discrimination still existed in America. I'd seen it in Virginia when my administration fought to promote women and people of color to leadership positions in the state government. I'd seen it again just the year before when the Defense of Marriage Act (DOMA), which discriminated against gays and lesbians, passed overwhelmingly. However, it was both surprising and incredibly frustrating to find that, in 1997, systemic discrimination against African Americans within a federal government agency was still alive and well. This was the type of discrimination that defies the very idea on which our government was founded.

I told the *Richmond Times-Dispatch* at the time, "It's hard to imagine anything more disheartening than to be struck down by the very hand you thought was there to help you up."[1]

In December 1997, I was able to arrange a meeting at the White House between President Clinton, Agriculture Secretary Dan Glickman, and about a dozen Black farmers. The meeting served to spur public attention and action from the USDA, which had been dragging its feet on the issue. My staff and I worked over the next three years to get the farmers temporary relief and restitution, and to eliminate the discriminatory practices.

Then, after years of effort by many advocates, in 1999 the farmers won the largest civil rights settlement in history.

Regrettably, it is not always so easy to identify discrimination in our country or to point to a responsible party. There are times when discrimination is so ingrained in our culture that it is much more difficult to see and nearly impossible to fix.

Such was the case in Bayview, a predominantly African American village that had been populated by freed slaves after the Civil War. I visited Bayview with a few members of my staff in 1998 after learning about it from a series in the *Washington Post*. Bayview is on the Eastern Shore peninsula—a slice of rural Virginia cut off from the rest of the state by the Chesapeake Bay— and to reach it by car we had to drive across the Bay Bridge and through part of Maryland. When we arrived, we found that the paving stopped short of the village, so we parked the car and walked the rest of the way on a dirt road covered in clam shells.

What I saw was a community from a different century. They had no modern conveniences, no stores, no public facilities, and few public utilities. According to the *Washington Post*, "Only six of the 52 houses have indoor toilets and running water; only three are up to building code."[2] The houses had changed little since the Great Depression.

Escorted by local organizers, I stepped into a small shack to visit with the residents. The shack had only two rooms, neither with anything that would distinguish it as a kitchen or bathroom, just thin walls and a roof that leaked. A rudimentary outhouse was the only bathroom, and water came from a pump that was sometimes contaminated from the waste.

"There is no question," I told reporters, "that the people who live in this area are living under conditions that are simply unacceptable."[3]

But for all its deprivations, I was struck by the quiet dignity of this little village, where the residents of Bayview had lived, largely on their own, for decades. Far from helpless, they had inspiring organizers, including two indomitable self-taught community leaders named Cozzie Lockwood and Alice Coles.

My staff and I immediately began to investigate ways to get the giant machinery of the federal government to help the community. The greatest challenge was that our effort was politically unpopular—aid to Bayview would cost money but provided few political gains for proponents. It was similar, in that way, to the issue of the discrimination against Black farmers by the USDA and to too many other issues that never see the light of day. Our advocacy was not met with opposition but with apathy.

Thankfully, my staff was both skilled and persistent, and we did have some allies—including Thurgood Marshall Jr. in the Clinton administration— who helped us get some balls rolling. After nearly a year of advocacy, in May 1999, I joined the Bayview community in the tiny Holmes Presbyterian Church to deliver federal aid totaling $4 million. That wasn't nearly enough to achieve everything that the Bayview residents needed—it would take funding from many sources at the state, local, and federal level over the next several years to bring Bayview up to livable standards. But the community celebrated each victory and was rightfully proud of each step forward.

The struggle for Bayview is the struggle for the American idea of equal opportunity. Reality diverged from that ideal, and we worked, to the best of our ability, to make it right. What little my staff and I were able to achieve during my time in office was just a start. There was—and still is—so much more work to be done—in Bayview and in the countless other communities where injustice and inequality are ingrained in the very way of life.

Sometimes it was difficult, as an elected official, to see the impact of our work. This was one of those rare moments when a problem struck very close to home and my staff and I were able to help out, even if it was just to give the community a little boost. Alice Coles said it best on that day in the Holmes Presbyterian Church when she came up to the podium to speak, surrounded by poster boards covered with housing plans for the future 140-unit village: "The sun has risen on Bayview."[4]

29

A Passion Play

ON THE MORNING of May 27, 1997, I was sitting in the gallery of the United States Supreme Court, waiting to hear oral arguments. The court was considering the constitutionality of the recently enacted line-item veto law, and I had been invited, along with several other senators who had played a leading role in the passage of the legislation, to hear the arguments. Before arguments began, as was the custom, a decision on a previously argued case was read by Justice John Paul Stevens. In a unanimous decision, the court had ruled that the president wasn't immune from civil suits filed against him for acts done before taking office and unrelated to the office. The decision meant that the sexual harassment case filed by Paula Jones against Bill Clinton could proceed while he was the sitting president. A murmur instantly spread throughout the courtroom, and reporters scurried out the door to phone their editors.

BILL CLINTON'S PRESIDENCY had seen a conservative backlash that sparked not only political opposition but brutal character attacks as well. Bill and Hillary both seemed to excite unusually strong emotions among pundits and ordinary Americans alike. Despite his resounding reelection victory over Kansas senator Bob Dole in 1996, Bill remained a polarizing figure into his second term. The cacophony of negative commentary, which had dogged him since the beginning of his first presidential campaign, seemed only to grow louder as time went on. But it all seemed to be background noise, until the start of 1998.

On January 20, 1998, I was standing in the Grand Entrance Hall of the White House, at a reception following a ceremony in which my old Marine Corps tactics instructor at Quantico, retired major general James L. Day, received the Congressional Medal of Honor for his service in the Korean War.

"Chuck!" I heard President Clinton call out. "Come on over here a second. I want you to meet someone."

I no longer remember who the president wanted me to meet that day, but I do remember that, as we stood talking, I could tell that his mind was elsewhere. I had never seen him so distracted and disengaged from our conversation, which was highly unusual for the legendary communicator.

The next day, I realized why President Clinton hadn't been himself when I saw the story splashed across the front page of that morning's *Washington Post*: "Clinton Accused of Urging Aide to Lie."[1] The story opened with the startling revelation that independent counsel Kenneth Starr was investigating whether the president had had an affair with a young White House intern named Monica Lewinsky, and whether he'd then asked her to cover it up.

Over the next few months, I watched in disbelief as Starr carried on an investigation that strayed from legitimate inquiry into a political inquest. Starr had been authorized by Congress in 1994 to investigate the failed Whitewater land deal, which he did for three years with little result. Then, in January 1998, Starr's office received a tip about an affair with Lewinsky, uncovered in the course of the unrelated sexual harassment case brought by former Arkansas state employee Paula Jones.

Starr pursued the charges of infidelity with a zeal that some interpreted as a sort of vendetta, while others saw it as a justified response to President Clinton's actions. The battle was taken to a new level on September 11, 1998, when the House of Representatives publicly released the independent counsel's findings, dubbed "the Starr Report," which was packed with uncomfortably graphic details about the president's relationship with Monica Lewinsky. The following month, the House Judiciary Committee voted to launch a congressional impeachment hearing against President Clinton.

There were points throughout the hearings when I thought that the president would have no real choice but to resign. Government business was practically paralyzed, and the office of the president was being severely weakened.

On December 19, 1998, the Republican-led House voted to impeach President Clinton on two out of four articles—then only the second impeachment of a president in our country's history. The process of impeachment is complex with good reason: it *should* be difficult to remove a sitting president without true cause. The founders designed the process with extraordinary checks and balances: the House of Representatives acts essentially as a grand jury, deciding whether or not to indict, and then the Senate serves as the trial court, with the chief justice of the Supreme Court presiding. Unlike a jury trial, however, the prosecution needs only a two-thirds majority of the Senate to achieve a guilty verdict. If the Senate found President Clinton guilty, he would be immediately removed from office. I was prepared, reluctantly, to take on that responsibility, but it was a far cry from what I'd come to the Senate to do. And sitting in judgment of my friend of then almost twenty years would be difficult to say the least.

I had taken part in the earlier Senate impeachment trials of U.S. District Court judges Alcee Hastings and Walter Nixon in 1989—unusual events in and of themselves—but this was a far more complicated and delicate situation. Like most of my Senate colleagues, I had, while the House deliberated, been studying books on constitutional history as well as impeachment, including sitting Supreme Court chief justice William Rehnquist's 1992 book *Grand Inquests: The Historic Impeachments of Justice Samuel Chase and President Andrew Johnson*. I felt a sense of responsibility to our forebearers and was pleased that most senators seemed to approach our role with similar gravitas.

The trial began on January 7, 1999, and Chief Justice Rehnquist presided, wearing his judicial robe and displaying an unexpected sense of humor that helped break the tension. On February 9, after we had heard from witnesses and both the defense and prosecution had made their cases, the trial went into final deliberations. These were going to be held in closed session, so, for four days, the Senate chamber was sealed and television cameras were banned during the proceedings. With the bright lights of C-SPAN uncharacteristically absent, the proceedings seemed cast in a soberly dim light. A guard was posted at each door, and all one hundred senators were required to be present for the arguments, creating a scene in the chamber unlike any I'd ever experienced. Every senator seemed to take their role very seriously, considering the evidence as objectively as possible, and many of us avoided the news media altogether while the trial was taking place—highly unusual for a group not known to be camera-shy.

The trial had been exhaustive, the evidence presented substantial, and the legal talent impressive. If the charges against the president were true, I felt compelled to vote "guilty," and I couldn't help but assume that many fellow senators felt the same way. I hadn't discussed my own position with any of my colleagues, and when I rose to speak on the Senate floor on February 11, I'm not sure that they had any idea which way I planned to vote.

I wanted my speech to explain, as precisely as possible, the rationale upon which my votes were based. But, having closely studied constitutional history in the preparation of my remarks, I was also very conscious that I was speaking not only to the present but also to the future. If, at some time in the future, America found itself going through another presidential impeachment process, I wanted my words to be as useful to future generations as my predecessors' words, 150 years earlier, had been for me.

I was conscious that, as I said in my speech to the Senate, "removing a president is not the same as punishing a citizen in a court of law," and a president was still subject to the rule of law. I continued:

Some [have] argued that since the president's oath requires him to faithfully execute the laws, any violation of those laws should thereby warrant his removal from office. While that argument may be appealing, it simply was not the standard adopted by the framers. Their standard was narrowly confined to treason, bribery, or other high crimes or misdemeanors. And it is against this standard that we are called upon to judge the conduct of this president.[2]

On the first article of impeachment—accusing the president of perjuring himself before the grand jury—I was simply not convinced of his guilt beyond a reasonable doubt. After all the arguments and evidence were presented, I didn't see clear evidence that he had made statements to the grand jury that were false. I *was* convinced that he had made false statements in his deposition for the Paula Jones case, but the House hadn't voted to impeach him for that.

"So, while I am convinced that the president lied to us," I continued, "I am not convinced beyond a reasonable doubt that he lied to the grand jury, which is the sole basis for the first of the two impeachment articles. . . . On article I, therefore, I will vote not guilty."[3]

I then took issue with the unfairly written second article of impeachment, designed to garner the constitutionally required two-thirds concurrence of the Senate by lumping multiple allegations together:

Drafted in the disjunctive and containing seven subparts, each alleging a separate act of obstruction of justice, the bundling of these allegations would allow removal of the president if only 10 senators . . . voted to convict based solely on subpart 1 and a different group of 10 senators voted to convict based solely on subpart 2, and so on. . . .

Such a pleading is not allowed under the Federal Rules of Criminal Procedure and would be thrown out by every federal court in the land. . . . We simply cannot remove a president from office with an article of impeachment that so clearly violates constitutional standards that we are required to follow.

On article II, therefore, I will vote not guilty.[4]

Of the fifty senators who voted "not guilty" on the second article, I was, to my surprise, the only one to make this particular argument. After my speech, a number of my fellow senators, several of them respected constitutional lawyers, even complimented me on my reasoning.

On February 12, 1999, the Senate voted not to convict President Clinton on either charge. Votes on both counts fell far short of the required two-thirds for conviction. Joining the forty-five Democratic senators who voted not guilty on both counts, ten Republicans voted not guilty on the first count and five on the second. The constitutional challenge to Clinton's presidency was finally over.

Outside the Senate chambers, the outcry was shrill and moralistic. In the end, I believe President Clinton may have been saved politically because of the House's overzealousness. The Republicans' scorched-earth strategy ultimately backfired: Bill Clinton was beaten up so thoroughly in the media by his opponents that he actually became a more sympathetic figure.

JUST OVER A month after the vote on impeachment in the Senate, I was seated in the cavernous ballroom of the Washington Hilton, attending the annual Radio & TV Correspondents' Dinner along with thousands of other guests. My table was close enough to the stage for me to study President Clinton's expression. He sipped water constantly, his face immobile, as ABC's Jackie Judd stepped up to the stage to receive the association's award. Judd was being honored for her coverage of the president's indiscretions.

When Judd came to the podium to accept her award, President Clinton rose, shook her hand, and politely said, "Congratulations, Jackie."[5]

"This is so very, truly unexpected—truly—which makes it all the sweeter," Jackie said. "And I appreciate the president's graciousness this evening."[6]

The sheer oddity of the moment was lost on no one, least of all Fox News Channel's Jim Mills, whose dubious honor it was to introduce the president directly after Jackie Judd's acceptance speech.

"This is not awkward," Mills deadpanned to the assembled guests, who sat murmuring, aware they were witnessing a surreal moment in American politics.[7]

Mills echoed the sentiments of many in the room when he said to the president and First Lady, "After the kind of year we've all had, we would certainly understand it—all of us in this room—why you would not want to be here in the same room with us tonight."[8] That Clinton went to the dinner and shook Judd's hand seemed to be sending a message about the value that he placed on good journalism in our country—even when that reporting didn't sing his praises. And it showed how a president could handle a tumultuous period with grace. I wasn't surprised that Bill received three separate standing ovations that night.

As a senator, it was difficult and unpleasant for me to participate in the impeachment trial of the president of the United States. This was, however, one of those rare moments in the Senate when it felt as though we were a part of history. It was a tumultuous time, but one in which we were keenly aware of the effect of our decisions on future presidencies. It was also one of the most gut-wrenching experiences I had in the Senate, not because Bill was a fellow Democrat, but because I had to sit in judgment of a friend.

30

Against the Wind

A CARTOON IN the *Richmond Times-Dispatch* in January 1999 portrayed me as a football player at a coin toss in the middle of the field. I'm depicted standing across from a player who is wearing a jersey marked "Allen" and is twice the size of anyone else on the field. The referee is turning to me and saying, "Before I flip the coin, are you *sure* you want to go through with this?"[1]

The truth was that, a year earlier, when former Virginia governor George Allen announced his intention to run against me for the U.S. Senate, I was already planning to retire. I'd now spent nearly two decades as a statewide elected official, including two terms in the Senate—and the thought of six additional years had simply lost its appeal.

My 1994 race against Oliver North had been completely different. Motivated in large part by the fact that I'd spent so much of my first term defending myself from rumors, I still had something to prove by being reelected. When I won back my seat in 1994—in the middle of the Republican Revolution—it felt like a vindication.

But by 1998, I didn't feel the same way about running for reelection. Since coming to the Senate, my life had been dictated by a legislative schedule over which I had almost no control. I had grown increasingly disenchanted with the gamesmanship of legislating. I was particularly frustrated by common practices used by both sides, like adding unrelated and politically incendiary amendments to a bill simply to force the other side to take hard votes. Increasingly, the Senate seemed to be becoming an environment of constant posturing and partisan gridlock. I knew that I didn't want to spend the rest of my life as a legislator.

Margaret Edds of the *Virginian-Pilot* hit the nail on the head when she wrote, "Robb has to be asking himself whether another round on the rubber chicken circuit is worth the toll."[2]

But I was equally determined not to simply abandon my seat to Allen. Allen had declared unusually early in the political cycle—December

1998—well before I had planned to announce my retirement. Dropping out after his announcement without a strong successor in place would look like I was walking away from a fight—something I wasn't willing to do. I had seen that storyline play out in my 1988 race when Paul Trible, the sitting Republican senator, dropped out, and I had sailed to victory with 71 percent of the vote.

If I could find a strong Democratic candidate to run in 2000, then I could still step away from the race in good conscience and retire on my own terms. So, in early 1999, I quietly began to make inquiries about potential successors for the Democratic nomination for my Senate seat, initially sharing my plans only with Lynda. I had to keep the search absolutely secret because if word got out that I was trying to find a credible candidate to take my place, even whispers that I wasn't fully committed would limit my political effectiveness.

Our first and strongest effort was with Don Beyer, whom we invited, along with his wife, Megan, to our home for dinner. Don would have been a great candidate—he had served for eight years, from 1990 to 1998, as lieutenant governor and had developed high name recognition and widespread respect among Virginians for his charm, wit, and intellect. We talked it over at dinner, and Megan appeared excited to take on the challenge. Lynda and I turned in that night with high hopes that he'd say yes. But the next morning, Don declined. He knew how tough an opponent George Allen would be, and he hadn't fully recovered, either emotionally or financially, from his 1997 loss to Jim Gilmore in the governor's race. I was surprised and disappointed, but I understood.

Unfortunately, other Democrats who could have run strong campaigns also declined to challenge Allen. So, I moved on to my final—admittedly unorthodox—option.

Jim Webb had strong family ties to Southwest Virginia. He had served with the Marines in Vietnam, written the highly praised novel *Fields of Fire*, and served, under Ronald Reagan, as secretary of the Navy and then deputy secretary of defense. Webb would clearly make a strong candidate in a race for the U.S. Senate in Virginia. The only problem was that, at the time, he was a Republican.

In the 1994 Senate election, Webb had surprised many political observers by supporting me over his Naval Academy classmate, and fellow Republican, Oliver North. Flying with me between campaign stops, he seemed to hint broadly that he might like to run for the Senate himself someday and that it wouldn't necessarily have to be as a Republican. So, after Don Beyer had declined to run, I set up a lunch with Webb to sound him out.

"With your credentials," I said, "you could do well as a pro-defense Democrat in Virginia."

Unfortunately, Jim's response was unambiguous. He had no interest, he said, in running against George Allen. I hadn't expected Webb to be an easy sell, but I was somewhat surprised that he wasn't even willing to consider the idea.

After Webb turned me down, I knew I had run out of options. No one who had enough experience, organization, and financing to run a competitive race was willing to take on George Allen. I couldn't blame them. Allen posed a formidable challenge.

Young, ambitious, and riding a wave of popularity following his gubernatorial term, Allen—the son of legendary Redskins football coach George Allen Sr.—was universally acknowledged to be a star on the rise in Virginia politics. Despite having been born in California and spending most of his life there, Allen had successfully adopted a "down-home" persona, complete with cowboy boots and chewing tobacco. Allen was a tax-cutting Republican with a Reaganesque ability to boil complex issues down to sound bites. Many remembered him for his challenge to Virginia Republicans during my 1994 race against Ollie North to "enjoy knocking [Democrats'] soft teeth down their whining throats."[3] Subtlety was never Allen's forte.

Allen's advantages in the 2000 race were remarkably similar to those I'd had during my first Senate race in 1988: he had finished his gubernatorial term two years earlier with strong approval ratings and high name identification, been succeeded by a clean Republican sweep of the statewide offices, and his party held majorities in the Senate and the House, in both Richmond and Washington. But he'd have one additional advantage that I had lacked in both 1988 and 2000: he was running as a Republican in Virginia in a presidential election year. In 1988, the Democratic nominee, Michael Dukakis, won less than 40 percent of the vote in Virginia. The Democratic candidate in 2000, Al Gore, was expected to do better than Dukakis had but certainly not to win Virginia. Involvement by the national party would help Allen far more than it would a Democratic candidate.

On balance, the only advantage that I could nominally claim over George Allen was incumbency, but even incumbency could sometimes be a political detriment. I'd held statewide office for a long time, and, during my

Senate term, my name had been repeatedly associated with controversy. It didn't matter anymore that the rumors about me weren't true because they had become a part of the political landscape. At some point, voters simply get tired of incumbents about whom they've heard endless negative stories and decide to make a change at the ballot box.

Allen was viewed as the odds-on favorite. But when I had run out of options for a Democratic challenger, I knew that I had only one choice. Instead of announcing my retirement on my own terms, I would run—and I'd give it my best shot. I knew that the race wouldn't be easy and that I'd be viewed as an underdog, but stepping aside and handing the seat to Allen simply wasn't an option. I certainly had no intention of ending my political career as a quitter.

When I kicked off my campaign at Northern Virginia Community College on March 26, 2000, I told a crowd of supporters, "[Allen] and some of his supporters can't understand why I won't roll over and play dead, but I remind you, and I remind him, that I know how to fight."[4]

Once the battle was joined, my competitive instincts took over, just as sharp as they had been when I had first gone to Quantico almost forty years before.

"No warrior I ever met in Quantico was intimidated by big talk, big-heeled boots and a big chew of tobacco," I said at the kickoff.[5]

I decided from the start that if I was going to get into this race and give it my all, I wanted to follow the Frank Sinatra rule of politics: I was going to do it "my way." That meant that I wouldn't speak in platitudes or catchphrases, and I would stand by my positions that were sometimes seen as "too liberal" for my state, such as a woman's right to choose, the Equal Rights Amendment, the constitutionality of flag burning, gay rights, and gun control. As I'd say later that summer, "I'm proud of my record, and I'm ready to run on that record."[6]

At the Democratic state convention that June, supporters noted how "enthused" I had become, and the press remarked on my renewed appetite for the fight. The *Roanoke Times* said that my supporters "cast themselves as an underdog army, preparing to storm the hill held by a deeply entrenched force."[7]

One editorial noted after the convention that, "at the pace set Saturday, it is going to be a long, hot and entertaining summer."[8]

The summer of 2000 would be entertaining, but for my campaign it would also be challenging. After many years working in Washington, D.C.,

I needed to hit the road to reconnect with my state and reintroduce myself to the voters as I had in 1994. By 2000, it had been nearly fifteen years since the end of my gubernatorial administration, and there were many new voters who knew very little about me. So, I set the ambitious goal of visiting all of Virginia's 135 counties and independent cities in the three months leading up to Labor Day.

This was made even more challenging by my Senate schedule. While Allen, whom the *Washington Post* called "nominally a corporate lawyer with a giant Richmond law firm," had the luxury of campaigning full-time, I was on a fifteen-minute tether to the Capitol for roll-call votes whenever the Senate was in session.[9] And, the *Post* noted, "stopping in all 95 counties and 40 independent cities would be daunting even for somebody without a day job."[10]

But our efforts started to pay off. As the summer wore on, Allen's lead began to shrink, and headlines like "Virginia's Senate Campaign Suddenly Looks Close" were invigorating.[11]

After our first debate in early August, the *Virginian-Pilot* noted that "Former Republican Gov. George F. Allen delivered some of the most biting laugh lines and got most of the laughs," but also noted that the audience gave me credit "for making the best case to voters."[12] But Allen's campaign did effectively spin one impromptu moment for their political gain. Toward the end of the debate, I lost my train of thought momentarily while rebutting a list of charges, and threw in at the end of the list, off the cuff: "I can't think of what it was, but you're equally wrong on that issue."[13] The audience laughed, and I made light of it, but Allen's campaign expertly presented the slipup in postdebate spin as evidence that I was tired and disoriented, effectively portraying me as old and out of touch.

Playing up this contrast, Allen's ads always seemed to be shot in bright lights or brilliant sunshine, with George and his family all wearing bright, bold colors and looking especially vigorous—an energy my own campaign ads lacked. The *Virginian-Pilot* even awarded one of my commercials, which had been shot with state-of-the-art equipment at considerable expense, the "Worst Editing by a Serious Contender" award, noting that an "otherwise decent campaign ad" failed in the last shot, which looked down from above on me working at my desk. "Unfortunately, due to the camera angle, Robb appears to be dead asleep."[14]

Age was a weakness that I didn't anticipate. Having been elected lieutenant governor at thirty-eight and then governor at forty-two, I had spent most of my political career concerned about being perceived as too young. However, Allen's campaign so smoothly contrasted our images, playing up Allen's own relative youth, that I did not recognize how significant of a factor this issue would be in voters' minds until it was cited in a public survey after the election was over.

On Labor Day—traditionally the first official day of the fall campaign— the race truly kicked into high gear. The *Daily Press* commented that, as I walked in the Buena Vista Labor Day parade, I was making a kind of "mad dash, racing from one side of the street to the other, in an effort to shake hands with as many voters as possible. When you're running behind, Robb seemed to acknowledge, a sprint might be in order."[15]

When it came time for the speeches at the Buena Vista Labor Day festivities, all of the candidates and elected officials sat onstage in folding chairs.

"On one side [of the stage] sat a long line of state, local and federal Republican officeholders and candidates," said the *Daily Press*. "On the other side—reserved for Democrats—sat Robb, Virginia's last surviving statewide Democratic official."[16]

I had a little over two months to show the state that I had the fortitude to withstand the Republican takeover of Virginia.

At our September 26 debate, Allen found another effective way to undercut one of my strengths. My reputation as a senator was, as the *Washington Post* put it, one of "a workhorse . . . not a showhorse."[17] I had found that working behind the scenes to gather bipartisan support for legislation was sometimes the most effective strategy to see a bill passed, and I didn't like to add my name to bills just to build up my resume. Allen played up my lack of posturing as inaction, using the line that "a Senate seat is a terrible thing to waste" in the debate.

As September turned into October, there were times when I found myself frustrated by my campaign's seemingly intractable inertia. Ideally, a campaign will generate its own energy and momentum, sweeping the candidate along. I had felt that sort of vitality and energy during the 1994 race, but this campaign was different, flatter, and, as the weeks ticked down in the last two months, I began to feel a sense of futility. That feeling was exacerbated by the fact that I was unenthusiastic about the prospect of another term in the Senate.

Sensing my mood in the weeks leading up to the election, one reporter asked whether I would run again in six years if I won reelection.

"Well, I certainly don't want to die in the Senate," I replied honestly.

But I worked hard to keep my game face on, and thanks to my tireless campaign team and family, we seemed to be closing a dwindling but tenacious gap in the polls. Lynda, who continued to be the best campaigner in the family, even carried on with her vigorous schedule despite breaking her rib in a fall.[18]

"Dead Heat Gets Hotter in Campaign's Final Days," read one *Roanoke Times* headline in late October.[19] The piece cited a public poll that had me within three percentage points of Allen.

Endorsements on both sides kept rolling in. I was honored to receive the endorsement of retired Marine generals Anthony Zinni, Carl Mundy, and Charles Wilhelm—two of whom (Zinni and Mundy) had also endorsed the Republican nominee for president. Whether or not their endorsement had much effect on the polls, the support of my fellow Marines certainly energized me.

My opponent used several endorsements—such as NARAL, the Human Rights Campaign, the Virginia Partisans Gay & Lesbian Democratic Club, and the Sierra Club—to portray me as out of step with the values of most Virginians. Well-meaning supporters sometimes suggested that I try to distance myself from these organizations, but I never considered it. Ultimately, I think that voters don't cast their ballots based on a checklist of issues— they vote for the candidate that they are comfortable with. I wouldn't gain people's trust by backing away from my friends or my positions on controversial issues.

Another boost came from one constituency that had had my back throughout the campaign—the African American community. I had received the endorsement of several African American organizations early in the campaign, while Allen had never garnered much support among African Americans, partly because of earlier flaps involving a Confederate flag displayed in his home and a "decorative" noose hanging in his office.

One of my most effective joint appearances came only ten days before Election Day at the Gold Bowl Classic—the hugely popular annual football game between Virginia Union University and Virginia State University, two historically Black colleges. I asked Doug Wilder to appear at the game with me, and when people saw the two of us together, working the crowd, they rose to their feet, cheering at the sight of the formerly "feuding" Democrats pulling together. In the end, all the talk of a so-called "feud" over the years was mainly just that: talk. I always respected Doug enormously and supported his campaigns in every way that I could. And I was immensely pleased to be able to count on his support in each of my races, including this one.

Allen also attended the game, but he was mostly ignored by the crowd. Years later, Allen told me that this was the moment in the campaign that worried him the most.

Then, less than a week before Election Day, our campaign was dealt a serious blow. Jim Webb, whom I'd approached to run in this election himself, surprised me by publicly endorsing George Allen.

Jim was at least nominally on my side at the start, but, as I learned later, his surprise shift was spurred by an event that had little to do with me: the attack on the USS *Cole* by terrorists while refueling at a port in Yemen. In Webb's mind, the need for the *Cole* to refuel in Yemen—instead of at sea, where it was far less risky—was caused by President Clinton's gutting of the military budget, for which I was implicitly responsible because I hadn't done enough to take the Clinton administration to task over issues of national security.

In a strange twist, Webb, running as a Democrat, would later challenge Allen in his next race in 2006. After Jim won the Democratic nomination, he called and, aware of the irony, asked for my support. "Well, this isn't at all awkward," he joked. I was happy to hold a fundraiser for Jim at our home with former president Bill Clinton as the guest of honor, and I was delighted when he won the seat.

In my 2000 race, Allen had been using my connection to Clinton, who had just been through the bruising impeachment scandal, throughout the campaign, constantly referring to my "Clinton Values." But I simply refused to deny my close association with the president.

"One of the things that I think political candidates make a mistake in doing," I told reporters, "is to try to run away from their friends. . . . I don't think it would be credible for me to say, 'Hey, I don't know the guy.' We've been personal friends for 20 years."[20]

It also happened that, unsurprisingly, I frequently agreed with Clinton and was happy to stand by my positions.

At nearly the same time as Webb's endorsement of Allen, my friend and volunteer finance director, Tim Ridley, gave me some more bleak news: our campaign was looking at a significant shortfall of funds, despite the tenacious fundraising by Sheila Dwyer and Fran Katz. We needed over half a million dollars to pay for the television buy we had already reserved for the final week, with no time left to raise the additional money.

Devoting significant personal money to campaigns is perfectly legal, protected by the First Amendment, and a number of successful candidates have done it. But I was never comfortable with what was sometimes interpreted as the "buying" of campaigns.

The ad buys themselves weren't necessarily crucial to the outcome of the race, but canceling would have been essentially throwing in the towel—breaking faith with all of those who had been working their tails off on my behalf. So, with reluctance but a clear conscience, I authorized the personal funds transfer.

As we neared the finish line, I felt like the campaign had spun out of my control. I was unhappy with the misleading ads that were being run against me, and I was put off by the ugly tone of some of the response ads that the Democratic Senatorial Campaign Committee was running on my behalf. I felt like a spectator in a contest where, in better times, I would have felt more in control of my game plan. I was also frustrated by the relative lack of movement in the polls, which consistently showed me within the margin of error, but one to four percentage points behind Allen.

In the frantic last few days of the campaign, I experienced a strange mixture of exhaustion, anticipation, and relief that the campaign was almost over.

"Entering the home stretch, this race is too close to call," began the *Daily News-Record* on the Saturday before Election Day. "This week, the Mason Dixon poll that had once given Allen a double-digit lead called it a dead heat. Allen led 47 to 45, within a 3 percent margin of error."[21]

Finally, Election Day was here. Lynda and I, along with our daughters, went to the polls early as a family to vote and to greet our local supporters and the media. I also stopped by some local polling places to thank the volunteers before going home to begin making phone calls to thank as many supporters as I could. At around 2:30 that afternoon, the first exit poll results came in. They showed Allen leading me by about three or four points.

As the afternoon wore on, I felt a kind of numbness. I wasn't particularly sad or angry, nor was I surprised or indignant. I simply knew Allen had won.

That evening, before heading to the events and getting in front of the cameras, Lynda and I sat down for a quiet family dinner with our daughters.

"I'm not giving up, even now," I told them, "but there's a good chance we won't make it, and I don't want you to think the world will come to an end if we don't."

Two of my daughters began to tear up, and one reprimanded me, "Daddy, you can't say that!" I reassured them that even if I lost, the sun would still rise the next morning, life would go on, and we would still have each other. After sharing some very anxious and emotional hugs, we all had a chance to pull ourselves together before heading out to the Democratic "victory party."

The truth was that I was prepared to lose this race—my first loss in twenty years in elective politics. I knew that I had given it my best shot, and I hadn't handed Allen an easy win. When all the counting was done, I lost to Allen by only four points in a state where, on the same ballot, Republican George Bush had beaten Democrat Al Gore by eight points in the presidential race.

We knew the outcome by the time we reached the victory party at a Mc-Lean hotel. I stepped on stage, surrounded by Lynda, our daughters, and a crowd of family and friends. I was so glad that my indefatigable brother Wick could come in from Fauquier County and that he brought my mother, who was then in her eighties. Even Lynda's mother had come all the way from Texas to lend her support.

As I looked out into the ballroom, I could see that it was packed with hundreds of my campaign volunteers, staffers, friends, and family members who had supported me in good times and bad. The numbness that I had felt during the day gave way to a great mix of emotions: gratitude to the people who'd worked so hard for me, sadness at having disappointed them, and relief that my political wars were now over. Though a friend had pulled together a couple of things I might want to say in my speech, I knew when I entered the hall that I didn't want to use any notes—I wanted to express my feelings and emotions as they came to me.

"First, let me say how much I appreciate all of you being here and sticking with us over a very long period of time. I was thinking this afternoon how I was going to thank everybody individually, and it occurred to me that I was going to be here all night if I thanked everyone who has meant a great deal to me, to my family, to some of the things that we've worked on together."

From offstage, a supporter shouted, "It's the least we could do!"[22]

The crowd erupted in applause, and I smiled broadly, swallowing hard to keep my emotions in check. This was the heart of my time in office, these people gathered around me. They had stood by me when I took politically unpopular stances and when I was mired in rumors. And now, when my time in office was finished, they were gracious and supportive.

We stayed at the hotel for a long time after my concession speech, shaking hands, embracing friends, and thanking everyone within earshot for their support. Finally, when there were no more hands to shake, I bade farewell to those still assembled, gathered my family, and headed for the car. My political career, and, to a great extent, my everyday life in the public eye, was finally over.

31

Free at Last

WHEN I WOKE up on the morning of Wednesday, November 8, 2000, the day after Election Day, I felt as though a burden had been lifted from my shoulders. But the mood throughout Washington that day was strange. To the country's surprise and dismay, it was not at all clear after the initial results came in whether Vice President Al Gore or Governor George W. Bush had won the presidency. The vote was so close that Gore, who had called Bush to concede earlier in the evening, had to make a second call to his opponent to take back his concession. The race came down to the contested electoral votes of a single state, Florida, which was undergoing a recount. Meanwhile, neither side could fully celebrate or plan the transition with any certainty.

Just two days after the election, Lynda, her mother, and I joined other members of former First Families at an event marking the two-hundredth anniversary of the White House. It was an impressive gathering of political luminaries for what was, to all appearances, a festive affair. But the mood in the White House was subdued by the looming question of who would be the next occupant of 1600 Pennsylvania Avenue. Neither President Bill Clinton nor former president George H. W. Bush was quite sure what to say, as each had a very personal stake in the contest—Clinton rooting for his vice president of eight years and chosen successor, and Bush for his son. I'd known, and liked, the elder Bush for many years. He was a universally pleasant, personable man and always superb company at social functions. I had never seen Bush as uncharacteristically ill at ease as he seemed that evening.

In the long reception hall on the second floor of the White House, I stood talking with former presidents Gerald Ford and Jimmy Carter. Everyone was being very gracious to me, offering words of comfort on my election loss two days prior.

"There are worse things than losing an election," President Ford said. "Look around this room—everyone here has lost an important election." He was right. Standing in the room were the families of former presidents

Johnson, Nixon, Ford, Carter, Reagan, Bush, and Clinton, all of whom, at some point in their lives, had lost an election.

Over a month later, I was performing one of the traditional duties of a senator leaving office: carving my name inside my Senate desk. I wasn't inclined to do the traditional graffiti at all—it felt a little like a self-glorified trapping of the office—but my staff convinced me that I was not exempt from a tradition that went back nearly a century. It was while I was taking a knife to the inside of my desk drawer that I got word that the Supreme Court had made the monumental decision to hand Florida, and the presidency, to George W. Bush. The next day, Gore conceded. A few hours later, Lynda and I attended Al and Tipper Gore's holiday party. The party had been planned months before, and the Gores decided to go ahead with it, despite the unusual circumstances.

The party started out somber, as the guests weren't entirely sure if they were allowed to be merry in front of their obviously disappointed hosts. But soon the mood shifted, and the party became quite lively. Later in the evening, I noticed, when chatting with Al, that his face was flushed and sweat had soaked through most of his shirt, as if he'd just finished a strenuous workout. I later saw press photos of the event that showed Al dancing up a storm, releasing all the pent-up tension of the preceding weeks and months.

WHEN YOU WIN an election, everyone you see—from friends to complete strangers—offers congratulations and best wishes. It's an old, but true, adage: everyone loves a winner. When you lose an election, however, most people have absolutely no idea what to say to you. Suddenly there's not much to talk about, and for some people no reason to talk, now that your political power is gone. One notable exception was John Warner, my Republican colleague from Virginia, who graciously stopped by my office the day after the election to offer his condolences on my loss, almost apologizing for having endorsed my opponent, at the risk of otherwise losing the chairmanship of the Senate Armed Services Committee. There were also many people who made a point of thanking me for my service. It was very gratifying to hear constituents tell me, "I really appreciated your stand" on an issue that was important to them. In some cases, though, it felt almost as if I were hearing my own eulogy.

Surprisingly, the person who took my loss hardest was Lynda. She later explained that it wasn't because she especially wanted me to stay in politics, or loved being a political spouse, but because she felt as if she had lost part of her identity. Though Lynda was not enthusiastic about being a Senate wife at first, she formed close friendships with the other Senate spouses. For years, she was active in the Senate Wives Club (which she helped to rename the "Senate Spouses Club"), serving in a leadership role and even helping them to secure a special room in the Capitol Building for Senate spouses. Lynda quickly found new endeavors, but to this day she remains active with the former and current Senate spouses and still takes great pleasure in attending their events. In an era when politics has become increasingly polarized and impersonal, Lynda has managed to carry on a tradition of good manners, grace, and lifelong friendships among elected officials, their staff members, and their families.

Before I stepped down, I closed out my Senate office and tried to make sure the members of my staff had jobs to move on to. I made calls, gave advice, and generally did everything within my power to help everyone find their next move. When it was nearly time to clear out, my staff had a surprise for me: they had purchased my official chair, the one that I'd used on the floor of the U.S. Senate. They presented the chair to me as a gift along with a framed "Ode to Courage" that contained a photo of me during my time in Vietnam and the Senate Record of several of what they considered my most courageous speeches on the floor of the Senate. Ridge Schuyler, my former legislative director, completely without my knowledge, had also nominated me for the John F. Kennedy Presidential Library Foundation's "Profile in Courage Award" in 2001, preparing and submitting a detailed application enumerating some of the politically unpopular votes and initiatives I'd taken during my Senate career. I had been extremely fortunate to have many loyal and dedicated staff members helping me throughout my career, and I was genuinely touched by their thoughtfulness as my time in the Senate came to an end.

ON JANUARY 20, 2001, George W. Bush was sworn in as the forty-third president of the United States. As a now former senator, I was invited to all the usual inaugural activities, which are generally congested affairs, overflowing with elected officials and politicos of all stripes. I decided not to attend any of them, except for one. After watching some of the inaugural festivities on television from the warmth and comfort of my home that morning, I got in my car and drove out to Andrews Air Force Base to see Bill Clinton off.

On Inauguration Day, all of Washington's attention focuses, understandably, on the incoming president. For the outgoing president, who has spent the last four or eight years being arguably the most powerful and most watched person on the planet, the sudden shift of attention can be bewildering. The transition of power is abrupt: the former president and their spouse leave the Capitol via helicopter immediately following the inaugural swearing-in ceremony and head to Andrews Air Force Base. From there, they fly to their postpresidency home. They go from national security briefings one day to listening to the news from their kitchen table the next.

The formal departure ceremony held at Andrews Air Force Base is a moving, sometimes difficult event. Though I'd been in Vietnam when Lynda's father had left office, I knew that his departure had been an emotional one for the whole family and that they had always felt especially grateful to the friends who'd come to see them off, including then congressman George H. W. Bush. Though they were in different political parties, Bush, ever the gentleman, had paid his respects to his fellow Texan, and LBJ and his family had never forgotten it.

I drove out to Andrews in a bone-chilling rain and joined the crowd of people assembled in an airplane hangar for the final departure ceremony. When he gave his farewell remarks, Clinton reminisced about his two terms in the White House. Then, much to my surprise, he said: "I don't want to start calling names around—afraid I'll never stop. But I do want to thank one person in particular for coming out here today and for meaning so much to me these last 8 years. Sen. Chuck Robb, thank you for being here. You are a wonderful man. Thank you."[1]

He raised his hand in a quick salute in my direction and the TV cameras picked me out in the crowd, sitting with my fellow well-wishers. I was very touched by his gesture. Because there was a lull in the official inaugural events between the formal swearing-in and the parade, the clip of Clinton's kind words about me was picked up by all the networks. It was ironic—if I'd been seeking the limelight on that day, when every politician in town was on parade, it would have been nearly impossible to find it.

After the speech, Clinton walked slowly toward his waiting plane, along with Hillary (then New York's newest senator) and daughter Chelsea. The now former president was indulging in one of his favorite pastimes, working the rope line, while several of his cabinet members, who had arrived unprepared for the weather, stood outside in the freezing rain at the foot of the plane's steps. I was particularly struck by Larry Summers—who, as secretary of the Treasury, had been fifth in line for the presidency just a few hours before—shivering in the raw elements with only a scarf around his neck and no topcoat, a mere mortal once again.

Shortly after the inauguration, I received a box in the mail at my home in McLean. Inside was a golf putter and a handwritten note on a presidential note card from Bill Clinton, dated January 20, his last day in office.

Chuck–

I wanted you to have this putter I used in the White House as a memory of our golf together—I hope we'll both play a little more now.

Thanks for your friendship–

Bill

Two weeks later, Clinton sent me a note when my name appeared as the answer to a clue in the *New York Times* crossword puzzle, which Clinton famously worked, in ink, every day. He had torn out the puzzle, circled where he'd filled in "Robb," and scrawled in the margin: "You made the New York Times crossword puzzle. You will always be my leader." I loved the idea of him sitting at his home in upstate New York, in an armchair, 250 miles from the buzzing Oval Office, working on a crossword puzzle, and being tickled when he saw my name.

A FEW WEEKS later, I did something that I hadn't been able to do in many years: I went to Home Depot. Then I went home and built some sturdy shelves to hold all of the files that hadn't gone with my official Senate papers to the University of Virginia Library.

Having the time for home improvements was still a bit of a novelty. When I was in the Senate, I had to be almost constantly on call while we were in session because I had no control over when a committee meeting would go on the calendar or when a vote would be called. Most long weekends or breaks were occupied with travel to foreign lands for my trio of national security–related committees, or with commitments in Virginia. More recently, any available "free" time had been taken up by the campaign. While I enjoyed being busy, I was also happy to have control over my own schedule once again.

As a newly former politician, I started my home improvements and planned to hold off making any serious professional commitments for at least a few months. I joined the other weekend warriors, eagerly tackling projects and settling into the routines of life that didn't involve going into an office every day.

I enjoyed having more flexibility to travel with my family and to visit them for dinner for no special reason. Lucinda and Jennifer both lived close enough to join us for Sunday dinner with some regularity.

Lucinda had continued her lifelong interest in education by heading up the recruitment of highly regarded professors from across the country for The Teaching Company (now called The Great Courses), which produced recorded video lectures on a wide variety of fascinating topics. She traveled frequently, sitting in on lectures and courting new talent, but she lived in Arlington, only a short drive away.

When I left the Senate, Jennifer had graduated from Duke the previous year, and she had had the foresight to complete a teaching certificate at the same time as her bachelor's degree in mathematics, so she went right into a job as a calculus teacher and head field hockey coach at Langley High School near our home in McLean.

Unfortunately, Catherine wasn't as close as either her mother or I would like to have had her. She had pleased both her father and mother by following up her undergraduate degree at the University of Virginia (where I attended law school) with law school at the University of Texas (Lynda's alma mater), but she continued to live in Texas, where she had a clerkship with a federal district judge. Her location did have the added benefit of allowing Catherine to spend more time with her grandmother, who was then in her late eighties. And Catherine quickly developed a thriving practice in Austin as an intellectual property lawyer specializing in First Amendment issues.

With our children all conducting lives of their own, it was Lynda who was most affected by my increased presence around the house in 2001. She and I were always very independent individuals, and it was during this time that she became fond of saying, "I married you for life, but not for lunch!" Yet we soon developed a standing midday date of a hot meal at our dining room table, something I referred to lovingly as "Lunches with Lynda." It turned out that some of our best conversations took place over the midday meal, when we could take a few minutes to reflect with each other about the goings-on of the day. Lunches with Lynda quickly became a highlight of my day and the thing I would miss the most if I were unexpectedly whisked back into a nine-to-five job.

There were many things that I enjoyed about having additional flexibility in my schedule, but I don't think that anyone who knew me thought that my version of retirement would be sedentary. After a few months, I began to think seriously about several of the opportunities being proposed by friends and colleagues.

While the 2000 presidential election recount was still going on, there was speculation that I might end up in a Gore administration cabinet. And indeed, the "let's talk as soon as this thing is settled" comments came from both Al Gore and his running mate, Joe Lieberman. But the most unexpected call came after George W. Bush was finally declared the winner.

Vice President–elect Dick Cheney tracked me down by phone in December 2000, just after I arrived in Austin, Texas, where my family was getting ready to celebrate the Christmas holidays with Lynda's mother. We had a pleasant fifteen-minute phone conversation, in which he reminded me about President-elect Bush's desire to have at least one Democrat in his cabinet and probed my interest in a spot related to national security, the same area that I would likely have been interested in under a Gore administration.

"I appreciate your call," I told him, but I wasn't sure that it was actually a good idea. I reminded Dick that, although my views on fiscal conservatism and most national security issues were not likely to give the Republicans indigestion, my position on social issues—"guns, gays, and Old Glory"—would create havoc in his ranks. My position on these issues were well-known, I wouldn't back away from them, and there simply wasn't a point in stirring up animosity on both sides of the aisle. Dick thanked me for my candor, and I wished him well.

With the cabinet off the table, there were a variety of other opportunities proposed to me in my post-elected life. Some offers would have been quite lucrative, but they didn't particularly interest me. Others involved more of a figurehead position, which didn't seem to promise much meaningful or rewarding work. I politely declined. There were a few, however, that appealed to my abiding interest in public policy, in areas like national security, intelligence, and fiscal responsibility, while giving me a role that was more substantial.

I took on roles with the Board of Visitors of the U.S. Naval Academy (which I eventually chaired), the MITRE Corporation (a federally funded research and development corporation), George Mason University, Harvard's Institute of Politics at the Kennedy School of Government, the Marshall-Wythe School of Law at the College of William and Mary, and the board of trustees at the Center for the Study of the Presidency, among others.[2]

It wasn't long before my dance card was full. Before I knew it, I had taken on more than I'd planned initially, and I once again had little time for my home improvement projects.

I'm sure that many of my friends and colleagues wondered what I was doing with my time now that I no longer went down to the Capitol every day. People often seem to assume that former politicians spend their days pining to be back in office. The truth was that my feelings about post-Senate life were best summed up in three words: free at last!

32

The Green Zone

IN THE FALL of 2001, I taught a seminar at nearby George Mason University that focused on many of the hot-button national security public policy issues of the day. On the morning of September 11, 2001, I was finishing my preparations to teach the seminar that evening, when I heard on the radio that there had been an explosion at the World Trade Center in New York City. I went immediately to the television, flipped it on, and sat in shock as I saw the first tower collapse in a cloud of dust and rubble. Like most Americans, I stayed glued to the television, transfixed, for most of the rest of the day. The destruction of the Twin Towers and the attack on the Pentagon, which is only about five miles from our home, was simply beyond anything I had ever imagined happening here, and it evoked the most profound sense of helplessness I'd ever felt.

What I really wanted to do was return to active duty in the United States Marine Corps. I yearned to once again be a lean, green fighting machine, and go with our troops to fight whoever was responsible for this unprecedented horror. It was a feeling powerfully reminiscent of my drive to go to Vietnam back in the 1960s. For the first time in the ten months since I'd lost my election, I even missed being in the Senate. I wanted to be in a position to do something, to get the full intelligence and national security briefings as events were unfolding, and to be a part of structuring a response.

Unexpectedly, I would get a chance to serve again in a public national security role, but that opportunity wouldn't come for another few years. In 2001, I didn't get to ship out with my fellow Marines, but my position teaching a seminar at George Mason University allowed me to see another side of these unfolding events.

All classes were canceled on the evening of September 11, but we met again the following Tuesday. As I expected, my students, a thoughtful group of mostly middle-aged professionals, engaged in a very lively, insightful discussion on everything from security ramifications to the ongoing conflicts in the Middle East.

There was one student—an African American midlevel executive in his fifties—who had stayed mostly quiet throughout the class. Just as we were about to end, he spoke up.

"I realize you all don't know this," he said, "but I'm a Muslim." For the next five minutes, as he described his own feelings about 9/11 and the repercussions he'd seen on Muslim Americans as a group, you could have heard a pin drop. The conversation up to that point had been thoughtful and by no means anti-Muslim, but it had been missing the perspective of a Muslim American. He was both extremely patriotic and proud to be a Muslim, and he was able to give a voice to a group of people—American Muslims—that many of us knew little about. His contribution gave all of us a better understanding and broader perspective on the horrible events of the previous week.

Nationwide, the struggle to understand the attacks turned into a public outcry so deafening that, in November 2002, Congress created the National Commission on Terrorist Attacks upon the United States—better known as the 9/11 Commission—to investigate what had happened. Then, in 2003, President Bush made the decision—after invading Afghanistan, where the 9/11 terrorists had trained—to invade Iraq. The president justified his decision by citing intelligence reports that Iraq had developed weapons of mass destruction and had conspired with al-Qaeda in the 9/11 attacks on the United States. Along with much of the country, I watched on television as then secretary of state Colin Powell made a detailed case to the UN Security Council in February 2003 that Saddam Hussein's government had weapons of mass destruction. George Tenet, then the director of the CIA, was seated at Powell's right elbow throughout the testimony, a clear signal to insiders that the intelligence community supported what Powell was presenting. Because I had always seen Powell as candid and well informed, I had no reason, at that point, to doubt his testimony.

Political support in Congress was easier for the president to rally in 2003 than it had been for the first President Bush in the 1991 Gulf War. A majority of Democrats had opposed the 1991 war, but after the military intervention proved to be successful with minimal American casualties, some of those who had opposed it suffered at the ballot box. In 2003, it was seen, therefore, as politically prudent to support the invasion, particularly for any Democrat with ambitions for higher office.

I wasn't in office when the debate about invading Iraq in 2003 began, but I think that many assumed that I would support the invasion. As a senator, I had advocated for intervention on several occasions, including the 1991

Gulf War, but I did not blindly support America committing troops overseas. In each case where the use of American military had been put before Congress, I had taken care to evaluate the specifics of the situation, both militarily and politically, before coming to a decision.

I did not want, as I said during the December 1995 debate over the commitment of American troops to a multinational enforcement effort in the Bosnian War, for America "to act as the world's policemen," but we should act "when it is the United States, and only the United States, that can end aggression and bloodshed." In Bosnia, I believed that "without U.S. leadership, there would be no peace."[1]

I had seen the carnage firsthand when I traveled to Sarajevo in October 1995 to gather information on the military and political situation. What I had seen was a city ravaged by a conflict that had lasted four years and had become the bloodiest European conflict since World War II. In between meetings with British general Rupert Smith, the commander of the UN Protection Force, and Alija Izetbegović, the largely titular president of the Republic of Bosnia and Herzegovina, we saw the haunting sight of the stadium that had housed the opening ceremony for the 1984 Winter Olympics. The stadium itself was torn up, an empty shell of twisted metal pitted with holes from mortars. Around the stadium, the soccer fields had been dug up, and victims of the conflict were buried there, row by row. Ten years before, the site had witnessed the glory of the world's finest athletes. But the besieged city simply had no other place to put the bodies, and now the playing fields were unrecognizable under rows and rows of mounded earth and crude wooden grave markers.

When the debate about intervention reached the Senate, I believed it was essential for us to say what we mean and mean what we say, and genocide was a clear red line that should be drawn and enforced.

"Without U.S. leadership and active participation on the ground," I said in my December 1995 speech to the Senate, "the peace will end and the carnage will continue. And we now represent the last best hope to bring the war in the Balkans to a close."[2]

Unfortunately, the relatively few casualties of the 1991 Gulf War had created an unrealistic expectation that wars could, and should, only be fought when there was little or no risk to American lives. Having served in combat, I had seen some of those risks.

"I have seen war," I said. "I have had men literally die in my arms in combat. . . . It's not easy. But the cost of freedom is high. . . . The question we face is whether the lives of American servicemen and servicewomen are worth risking to stop it? And I believe that that risk is appropriate. I believe we have a moral responsibility to act."[3]

I believed that this moral responsibility to act was present in Bosnia in 1995 and in the 1991 Gulf War. In the case of the 1991 Gulf War, I had decided that the president had secured all of the necessary components for an intervention: a strong international alliance, a Middle East ally that would be the first to cross the line of departure, and a clear, achievable military goal.

However, in 2003 I felt that there were two essential pieces missing from the proposed invasion: there was no broad international support, nor was there a clear plan for what to do once our troops got to Baghdad. I believed that these were necessary preconditions for initiating a conflict.

I was not an elected official by the time of the 2003 invasion of Iraq and therefore did not have to consider my public position too carefully until I was contacted by former congressman Steve Solarz. Steve was putting together a group of former military and political leaders to demonstrate bipartisan support for the invasion, and he asked me to participate. But without international support or a clear plan once we reached Baghdad, I respectfully declined to sign on to the Solarz group or to support the 2003 invasion of Iraq.

The invasion of Iraq went forward, but questions were quickly raised about our reasons for going in. When no complicity between al-Qaeda and Iraq on the 9/11 attack could be documented and no weapons of mass destruction were found following the invasion, the American public, by early 2004, was clamoring for answers. President Bush decided to establish a commission to investigate.

Around that time, I was at a board meeting of the MITRE Corporation in Los Angeles. At the end of three long days of meetings, I was closing my briefcase and preparing to head for the airport, when MITRE's chairman, Jim Schlesinger, pulled me aside. Jim asked if I'd mind if he recommended me to serve on a new presidential commission called the WMD Commission, formally known as the Commission on the Intelligence Capabilities of the United States Regarding Weapons of Mass Destruction. The purpose of the commission was to look into errors in the intelligence regarding WMDs that led, in part, to the 2003 invasion of Iraq.

I told Jim that I didn't yet know enough about the commission to say yes.

He countered with, "you can always decline if you're asked," leading me to believe he might have already made the recommendation.

I arrived home from California well after midnight, and in the wee hours of February 6, 2004, I received a call from Andy Card, President George W. Bush's chief of staff, asking me if I'd be willing to not only serve on the commission but also serve as cochair. I responded that I was certainly interested, but the only way I would consider taking on *that* role was to discuss it face-to-face with the president.

To my immense surprise, Card offered to have the president stop by my house on the way back from an event in Northern Virginia later that morning. I was immensely flattered—it was incredibly uncommon for a president of the United States to make a house call—but I thought it would be more appropriate if I came to the White House. So early that afternoon, less than twenty-four hours after Jim Schlesinger had first mentioned the commission to me in Los Angeles, I stepped into a black White House sedan. From the moment it pulled out of our driveway until we reached the executive entrance to the White House, right next to the Situation Room, the black sedan didn't make a single stop—anywhere. I stepped out of the car and was met by Andy, who escorted me straight to the Oval Office, without stopping for security or breaking stride, where President Bush was waiting. It was unlike any other trip to the White House I had ever made.

After a warm and frank conversation with the president, in which he assured me that the commission would have his full and unqualified support, with no interference by any government agency, I agreed to take on the assignment.

The president wanted to make the announcement right away, so, just minutes before we walked into the White House Briefing Room with the president, I met the man who would be my Republican cochair and become my partner and friend: U.S. Court of Appeals judge Larry Silberman. Larry held a well-deserved reputation as a bright, quick-witted insider with the White House and the legal hierarchy in Washington. Coincidentally, it was Larry who had written the opinion that overturned, on a technicality, the felony convictions of my 1994 Senate opponent, Oliver North. Nevertheless, Larry and I hit it off right from the start. We were in total agreement that we would remain completely independent from White House influence. If any indication to the contrary was ever discovered, we would both resign together very publicly—a politically devastating move for the incumbent in a presidential election year. After the announcement, Larry and I agreed on a time to meet the next day to get the commission up and running.

When I had a moment to reflect, I was humbled, and a bit surprised, that the president had asked me to serve in this role. Not only was I a member of the opposite party, but I had declined to support the 2003 Iraq War. This commission was specifically investigating the flawed intelligence gathering that had led the United States into that war. If I had been so inclined, a timely statement about administration abuses and a resignation from the commission could have seriously hurt his reelection campaign in 2004. My integrity had been grist for the mill when I was in public office, so the president's trust in me, when I held such a strong card, was gratifying.

With the clock ticking, the WMD Commission was up to full speed in a matter of weeks. Joining Silberman and me were six other commission members from both sides of the aisle: Rick Levin, president of Yale University; John McCain, Republican senator from Arizona; Henry S. Rowen, former chairman of the National Intelligence Council; retired admiral Bill Studeman, former deputy director of the CIA; Charles M. Vest, former president of MIT; and Patricia Wald, retired chief judge of the U.S. Court of Appeals for the District of Columbia.

All of the commission members met together occasionally, but the day-to-day work was carried out by our staff of some of the best talent that the legal and intelligence community had to offer, including Mike Leiter, then assistant U.S. attorney for the Eastern District of Virginia; Brett Gerry, who was at a prominent law firm; and Vice Admiral Scott Redd, who had most recently been the deputy administrator and chief operating officer of the Coalition Provisional Authority in Baghdad, the transitional government of Iraq.

We set up shop in a small cluster of highly secure rooms in the New Executive Office Building, half a block from the White House. Methodically but urgently, we began interviewing members of the intelligence community who had had a role in the flawed intelligence gathering that had led to the dramatically erroneous assessments before the 2003 invasion of Iraq.

We held no public hearings or news conferences. Much of the information that we were dealing with was highly classified, and a nonpublic approach helped elicit candid responses from witnesses and made it clear that the commission was an actual fact-finding body, not a publicity stunt.

In the end, we wrote our official report in both a highly classified version of about seven hundred pages with seventy-four recommendations, and an unclassified version with sixty-eight of the recommendations and identical language wherever possible.

"We conclude that the Intelligence Community was dead wrong in almost all of its pre-war judgments about Iraq's weapons of mass destruction," we wrote in the unclassified report. "This was a major intelligence failure." The problem lay in the collection and analysis of the information gathered by the intelligence community, but, we said, "after a thorough review, the Commission found no indication that the Intelligence Community distorted the evidence regarding Iraq's weapons of mass destruction. What the intelligence professionals told [the president] about Saddam Hussein's programs was what they believed. They were simply wrong."[4]

Our recommendations to move on from this failure were all geared toward not repeating the same errors. Most importantly, we recommended restructuring the nation's intelligence community, including expanding the writ of the FBI beyond domestic law enforcement and creating the new National Security Bureau within the FBI to handle counterintelligence. This was a hard sell within the agency, but after some wrangling with FBI director Robert Mueller, a fellow Marine combat veteran and UVA Law School classmate whom I'd known for years, the new bureau was up and running.

We presented our report to President Bush in March 2005, thirteen months after we began. Too many serious reports from prestigious commissions end up only gathering dust on shelves, so Larry and I were very gratified with the president's formal acceptance of 95 percent of our recommendations. In the end, President Bush dealt with the commission honestly, followed through on his promises, and didn't flinch on anything that he told us he would do. Though I understood that a number of my fellow Democrats did not hold President Bush in high esteem, when we worked together, he was always a straight shooter.

The most vocal opposition to the WMD Commission's report came not from disagreements with any of our conclusions or recommendations but from those who had always wanted the commission to assign pointed culpability on the administration. Assigning blame was not a part of our mandate as defined by the executive order establishing the commission, and few, if any, members of the WMD Commission would have signed up for such an undertaking. Our task from the beginning was to find out what happened and how it might be fixed—to lay out the facts, not embark on a political inquest. I thought it was a good indicator of our success that the intelligence organizations whose failures were most heavily cited in the report later asked me and other members of the commission to come speak to them so they could learn more about how we had come to our recommendations.

Unexpectedly, the success of the WMD Commission spurred a whole new wave of professional opportunities, at a time when I was, technically, retired. Following the release of our report, Larry Silberman recommended that President Bush appoint me to what was then called the President's Foreign Intelligence Advisory Board (PFIAB), a group of nongovernmental advisors who counsel the president on intelligence practices and operations. In addition, I was asked to serve on the FBI Director's Advisory Board and the Secretary of State's International Security Advisory Board, where I chaired the WMD Terrorism Task Force and was even named acting chairman of the full advisory board for a brief period. It was reassuring that, in the midst of a Republican administration, a Democrat was trusted to advise on national security and intelligence issues.

I didn't know it at the time, but serving on the WMD Commission was yet another unexpected opportunity that started a whole new chapter of my career.

The next page in that chapter began on a cold and rainy Saturday morning in early 2006. I was working at home when I received a phone call from Lee Hamilton, the former chairman of the House Foreign Affairs Committee and vice chairman of the 9/11 Commission with whom I had recently begun serving on the PFIAB. Lee asked if I would consider serving with him again, this time on a new bipartisan organization created by Congress which he had agreed to cochair, alongside former secretary of state Jim Baker: the Iraq Study Group (ISG). The ISG was a bipartisan commission established by Congress to study the war in Iraq (then in its third year), assess the situation, and make policy recommendations for moving forward.

I already had a full plate, but it was a fascinating opportunity squarely within my area of interest, so I agreed.

On March 15, 2006, the members of the ISG were formally announced. In addition to Lee Hamilton and me, the Democratic members were former president of the National Urban League Vernon Jordan, former Clinton chief of staff Leon Panetta, and former secretary of defense Bill Perry. On the Republican side, the lineup was Jim Baker, former Supreme Court justice Sandra Day O'Connor, and former senator Alan Simpson. Two initial members were later replaced—former New York mayor Rudy Giuliani missed our first two meetings because he was running for the Republican nomination for president, and former CIA director Bob Gates had to step down because he was appointed to be secretary of defense. They were replaced by former attorney general Ed Meese and former secretary of state Larry Eagleburger, respectively.

To get the best advice in every area, we recruited more than fifty highly regarded professionals—someone from nearly every think tank in town—to form expert working groups, and we asked a number of four-star generals and admirals to serve on a senior military advisory panel.

Throughout the course of our investigation, which took nine months to complete, we met with congressional leadership, officials from the State Department, intelligence agencies, and the military, former national security advisors, and reporters who covered Iraq. We also met with leaders from home and abroad, like Secretary-General of the United Nations Kofi Anan, former president Bill Clinton, and British prime minister Tony Blair, who we had to schedule by teleconference because time was running short. In the end, the commission consulted with more than 170 leaders and experts, both in and out of government, in the preparation of our report.

One of the most important pieces of research, however, was a trip to Iraq to observe the situation on the ground and meet the people directly involved. We left on August 30, 2006, and during our first two days in Iraq, we met with Prime Minister Nouri al-Maliki and all of the top political leadership of Iraq, as well as the most senior members of the U.S. military, intelligence, Department of State, and Department of Defense leadership. Then we broke into smaller teams for two days in order to meet with as many knowledgeable representatives as possible of the various ethnic and religious factions in Iraq, including many prominent Shia, Sunni, and Kurdish leaders. Overall, my assessment of the key personnel was mixed. The Kurdish leaders stood out as organized and effective, while al-Maliki, the U.S.-approved Shia leader, instilled less confidence. Al-Maliki lacked a leader's charisma, and I was skeptical of his ability to bring together a nation divided by violent factionalism.

All of these meetings took place within the heavily fortified Green Zone, where almost all of the Iraqi officials, and a very large percentage of U.S. military and civilian officials, lived and worked. In truth, many of the Iraqi military and civilian leadership and U.S. forces never left the Green Zone, which had such luxuries as water, electricity, and even American fast-food chains. Our meetings in the Green Zone were all helpful, but I knew that

I couldn't get a real feel for what was happening on the ground by staying within sight of a Pizza Hut. I wanted to get out to see firsthand the conditions faced by the combat forces and Iraqis generally.

Before we left American soil, I had made a request to visit areas outside the Green Zone. Once in Iraq, I repeated my request. I specifically asked to travel to Anbar Province and Fallujah, the areas where some of the fiercest fighting of the war was taking place. I sensed some uneasiness from the State Department and military leaders about my safety, but arrangements were made for me to board a Blackhawk helicopter just after dawn on our third day in Iraq and fly to a Marine forward operating base (FOB), where I received a comprehensive briefing from the commanding general and his senior staff officers.

As we traveled in an armored convoy to tour the area outside the FOB, I also had the chance to talk to the two Marines with me in the Humvee about their last operations, relations with civilians, and how things were going on the ground. I learned from these Marines that—at least from their perspective—morale was as high as you could expect under the circumstances and that they felt like there was a workable plan in place. This ground-level perspective was as useful as the high-level briefings and an important addition to them.

When I got back to the FOB, I learned that an armored convoy was going to be traveling to Ramadi later that morning, and I requested to join it.

This request was more than the leadership was prepared to grant and was denied. As soon as I returned to the Green Zone from the FOB, I asked, pointedly, who had denied my request. A young foreign service officer confessed that he believed it was too dangerous, and if I died on this additional leg of the trip (even though I said I'd sign a waiver accepting full responsibility), it would set back diplomatic efforts taking place in this area. With that explanation, I held my temper and made a very pointed request to go out again the next morning (the day we would leave to fly back to the United States), to visit another area where heavy fighting had been taking place. The request made its way up the chain and eventually the order came back from General George Casey, commander of the Multinational Force Iraq, to "take him wherever he wants to go."

The next thing I knew, the Army had issued a classified operations order to take me out the following morning. We left at dawn for a ground combat patrol into Dora, the scene of some of the heaviest fighting anywhere close to the Green Zone.

I think it startled the convoy commander when I asked to halt the convoy in front of a group of young Iraqi men so that I could ask some questions. Speaking through an interpreter, I was able to ask the men some basic questions about who they were and how they lived. According to the two most talkative, they were a mix of Sunni and Shia. When I asked them how they were able to live together, they said that they were the members of an extended family. Although they were all of military age, the men told me that they were students, though it was hard to comprehend how they went to school amid the violence. The conversation, which couldn't have lasted more than ten minutes, helped me to form a far more accurate picture of what life was like for average citizens trying to live through the devastation of this war.

As we left Iraq, I was more convinced than ever that we needed a new strategy if we were going to reduce U.S. presence in the country. In order to give the fledgling Iraqi government a chance at success, we needed to stabilize the security situation on the ground, particularly in Baghdad. I strongly believed that, before we began to draw down our forces, we should temporarily increase our troop commitment for a short period—a temporary surge of American military force.

I never advocated for a surge of U.S. forces at this point in the conflict as the way to "win" or continue the war—instead, I saw it as a way to hand over a relatively stable situation in the Iraqi capital city. I felt strongly that we had a moral obligation to give this Iraqi government—which we had created—at least a chance to succeed. The United States had started this conflict in 2003 as a preventive (and arguably preemptive) war. At that time, I had declined to support the decision to initiate the war, but I believed that, three years later, we had far too much skin in the game to just walk away. We couldn't, in good conscience, suddenly pull out our troops and leave the Iraqis at the mercy of sectarian violence. And if we were going to maintain our credibility on the international stage, we could not fly our troops out with the capital city crumbling in our wake.

At the same time, I didn't believe that we could leave U.S. troops in Iraq indefinitely. I wasn't confident in the prospects for a politically stable Iraq—we couldn't just expect them to instantaneously function as a full-fledged democracy—but I felt that if there was ever going to be peace in Iraq, it ultimately needed to be achieved by Iraqis.

The other members of the commission were less enthusiastic. By the time we were all on the flight back home to Andrews Air Force Base, I was the lone vocal advocate of a temporary surge. We continued to talk about what should be included in the final report, but when we reviewed the first draft of the report's outline, there was no mention of a pre-drawdown surge.

I was fairly convinced that we would lock in the basic elements of our recommendations at the ISG's next plenary meeting, but, as luck would have it, I had a long-standing conflict and couldn't attend. So, I drafted a brief memo to my fellow commission members that read, in part:

> Without being overly dramatic, I believe the Battle for Baghdad is the make or break element of whatever impact we're going to have on Iraq and the entire region for at least a decade—and probably much longer. In my judgment we cannot afford to fail and we cannot maintain the status quo. . . .
>
> My sense is that we need, right away, a significant short term surge in U.S. forces on the ground, augmented where possible by coalition partners. . . . I believe we will just end up playing whack-a-mole if we take too many currently committed forces from areas where they now have some degree of control. Our military is as capable as any fighting force anywhere, but time is of the essence and if we don't successfully complete Operation Forward Together [to quell the insurgency in Baghdad] by spring we lose. Too many of our troops are needlessly at risk of being picked off by snipers or blown up by IEDs. It's time to let our military do what they're trained to do on offense—without being overly constrained by a zero casualties or collateral damage approach. . . .
>
> If the ISG report is going to have any real impact it's going to have to be bold and consequential. I believe that recommendations currently deemed a bridge too far will be viewed differently after our November elections. I'm very much aware of the difficulties inherent in this brief rant and I look forward to participating in all discussions after next week.[5]

I also opened up some back-channel communications with General Peter Pace, then chairman of the Joint Chiefs of Staff, to get some feedback from the service chiefs. Pete seemed open to it initially, but after a few weeks his responses seemed much more noncommittal, from which I inferred that he was getting a lot of pushback from some of the individual service chiefs.

When it came time for the final report, we didn't hold a vote on what was included but instead went through rounds of negotiations and edits until we had unanimous sign-on from all ten ISG members. We all realized that any dissents or separate statements would detract from its effectiveness. The concept of the surge was obviously important for me, so, at one of our last meetings, Jim Baker, Lee Hamilton, Bill Perry, and Ed Meese came up with language they thought everyone might agree to: "We could, however, support a short-term redeployment or surge of American combat forces to stabilize Baghdad, or to speed up the training and equipping mission, if the U.S. commander in Iraq determines that such steps would be effective."[6]

It was a compromise, but one that I felt worked. We had a deal.

On November 29, 2006, we assembled in the Willard Hotel in Washington at 6:00 a.m. for the formal rollout of our report, including a briefing for the president, another for the Congress, and a public press rollout.

At our briefing for the president, he thanked the members of the ISG for taking on the assignment, but he was noncommittal. He then invited everyone to offer any remarks on the report, starting to his right, where I was sitting. I focused, not surprisingly, on my advocacy of a temporary surge. And as I shook hands with the president at the conclusion of our briefing, I mentioned to him, "You ought to take a close look at the surge provision." I thought I detected some enthusiasm, not then evident for the entire report, when he replied that he planned to do just that.

During the press rollout we did countless interviews, but I got the most feedback from the fact that I had, during the press conference, pulled out the chair for Justice O'Connor when we all sat down on the main dais. Apparently, a number of TV stations doing live coverage focused on that small natural gesture as we all walked in. Maybe because the tension over what to do in Iraq at that time was so great, a little common courtesy made a lasting impression with viewers.

It is hard to gauge the impact of the Iraq Study Group report. The goal of the commission wasn't to motivate political action or rouse public sentiment, which was why we didn't hold public hearings or court media attention. We were there to find solutions to the complex and serious problems with our involvement in Iraq.

The seventy-nine recommendations that we outlined in the report were both short- and long-term, involving changes both to internal U.S. agencies and external diplomatic efforts. The recommendations were meant to be quietly implemented without fanfare. And several of them were.

The most publicly quoted aspect of the report was not one of the formal recommendations, but the pre-drawdown short-term surge in troop levels. From my perspective, the surge achieved the limited purpose of giving the Iraqi government some amount of stability in the capital and breathing space before American troops were withdrawn. It also demonstrated to the international community that we weren't planning to "cut and run" from our obligations in Iraq. It was never designed as a way to "win" the war or meant to continue a permanent engagement there. Sadly, I didn't see a way to "win" the war outright without a massive, long-term escalation of forces—a strategy that I did not see as viable and for which our country was not ready. It was clear to me that a traditional victory, complete with a formal surrender, was not in the cards.

In general, I was supportive of American military intervention when it was necessary to stop acts of atrocity, such as genocide, because I believed in America's moral responsibility to act when it was possible to make a difference. But I also believed that intervention needed to meet certain criteria before we engaged in any military action, and my skepticism that the 2003 Iraq War would meet those criteria ended up being justified. I hoped that any work that I could do on either the WMD Commission or the ISG would at least help to mitigate some of the damage that the conflict had caused, both at home and abroad.

In the end, my work on these commissions proved to be an unexpected and rewarding final chapter of my work in public life.

PART V

EPILOGUE

As THE LOW-COUNTRY sky shifted from pitch-black to dark blue, hinting at the approaching dawn, I stood listening to the advancing drum line of boots pounding the asphalt in unison, followed by a full-throated, singsong cadence: One-Two-Three-Four!

It was the spring of 1998, and I was visiting the Marine Corps boot camp at Parris Island, South Carolina, where a giant sign above the entrance proclaims, "We Make Marines." I was there to witness the conclusion of the last challenge of the recruits' training: the grueling "Crucible."

As I stood silently watching the recruits, I experienced once again the odd mix of nostalgia and adrenaline that washes over me when I reenter the military realm. The scene embodied a great deal of what I still found so compelling about the Marine Corps—despite any differences of race, gender, or socioeconomic background, these young men and women could come together to find common purpose and common ground. Whether they knew it or not, these young Marine recruits were developing a value system and a rare camaraderie that would remain with most of them for the rest of their lives and help them become more disciplined and productive citizens. Their kinship and commitment to public service, even in today's "me-first" culture, made these young recruits a part of a special and elite few.

The sun wasn't due to rise for another half hour, and the early-morning mist made it difficult to tell how far down the road the ground-pounders were. Finally, I began to make out the approaching silhouettes. Two groups of Marine recruits, divided according to gender, sounded distinctly male or female until they drew closer and their voices gradually blended into one.

33

Over the Horizon

In 2019, for my eightieth birthday, a group of my friends—Martha Marks, Ben Dendy, Susan Albert (now Susan Carr), and Debbie Keefe—threw me a party that I'll never forget. In every corner of Martha's beautiful Alexandria home and spilling out onto porches and lawns were many of the stalwarts with whom I had worked through the last forty years of my life as a public official.

There was Steve Ricchetti, whom I had hired as a young executive director of the Democratic Senatorial Campaign Committee (DSCC) back in 1990, his phone buzzing every few minutes with new presidential poll numbers on his current boss, former vice president Joe Biden. Chuck Dolan, whom I had hired to run the Democratic Governors Association, was nearby, catching up with Stewart Gamage.

Sheila Dwyer, who had played so many roles in my Senate office and always seemed to know everyone, was in the middle of a small group of my former Senate staff members. Nearby was Laurie Naismith, who served as one-third of my very first political staff in the lieutenant governor's office and went on to be my secretary of the Commonwealth, chatting with Congressman Don Beyer. In the opposite corner was Ridge Schuyler, who ran my policy shop in the Senate with skill and a strong moral compass, deep in conversation with his usual partner-in-crime in that office, my former chief of staff Tom Lehner.

Gesturing with his ornate cane was former senator John Warner, who, despite our difference in parties, was always a good friend and colleague. John was telling a story to former ambassador Lloyd Hand and his wife, Ann, a couple whose charm and intelligence had made them fixtures in Washington. I met Lloyd and Ann when the former was chief of protocol for Lynda's father, and they have been among our dearest friends for more than fifty years. Both Lloyd and John had recently marked their ninetieth birthdays, but they still came to celebrate my reaching a mere eighty.

There were also people who were notable in their absence. Three of my close friends and colleagues were very ill by the time of the party, and by the time of this writing, all three have passed away. Governor Jerry Baliles was a good friend and a worthy successor in the governor's mansion. Alan Diamonstein and Bill Thomas had, along with Al Smith, whom we lost back in 2008, formed the core of my "Kitchen Cabinet." All three were crucial supporters in every race I ran and were very much a part of the extended family.

These and so many others were the people who made my time in public office what it was. Martha's living room was packed with small groups of people animatedly telling stories of exploits from offices, campaigns, CODELS, and legislatures. There were tales of our shockingly small lieutenant governor's office in the Bell Tower in Capitol Square, tales of the prison breaks during our gubernatorial administration, and tales of harrowing flights over the jungles of Africa. The cacophony of storytelling was so loud that anyone trying to talk to me had to practically shout.

What struck me in the midst of this merriment was that this group wasn't there just for me. They certainly didn't come to benefit somehow from my political power—at my age and in my health, I was clearly never going to run for office again. This joyous crowd had come—some a great distance—to see each other. This is the side of politics that we don't always see, in part because it doesn't always happen this way. The staff of politicians don't always end up as godparents to each other's children, but this amazing group of individuals did. They represent the heart and soul of my career, and, more than forty years after my first run for office, they were still together, still laughing and remembering.

All night, we shared our remembrances of the past and our fears for the future. These people had devoted their time and their energy to public service, and in several conversations I had that night, one of them would look me in the eye and ask, "What are we going to do?" The topic wasn't always the same, but the worry was. It was a concern for the future of our country and our democracy, and for what we are leaving behind for our children and grandchildren.

There are a few topics that I keep going back to—long after I've left office—and still read articles about in my home office, sometimes late into the night. One that I believe to be the most damaging to our future is the national debt. With the national debt increasing at the unsustainable rate of over a trillion dollars a year, I continue to believe that we simply can't ignore the long-term implications of putting our country further and further into debt. We shouldn't get any credit for really solving a problem by funding government programs if we're just going to leave the bill for our children and grandchildren.

However, I've also learned more in recent years about the lives and circumstances of the people most in need of those government programs. Policymakers frequently focus on numbers, and it is easy to see programs and their impacts as figures on a tally sheet. What I've seen more of in the last few years is the human element—the lives of those affected by poverty, discrimination, displacement, natural disasters, and other hardships both in America and around the world. Seeing the human element has led me to the conclusion that we have to do more to find new and different ways to address the issues that we face.

We are also living through a health crisis unlike any we've seen in the last hundred years. As I write this, the coronavirus pandemic has shut down schools and businesses and has confined the majority of Americans—including myself—to their own homes. Unemployment reached 14.7 percent in the spring of 2020—the highest it has been since the Great Depression. This crisis is a moment of true emergency, when it is necessary for the government to borrow, but we have to acknowledge that that money, though warranted, is not free. That money will ultimately have to come from all of us, as taxpayers, and will be a burden on future generations. We must take on that burden today by beginning to pay it down now and creating a plan for repayment, just as a homeowner pays down a mortgage.

What we're left with is what I believe to be the fundamental dilemma of our era: how to address the critical needs of those suffering and in special need in our society, without bankrupting future generations. I believe that we have a duty to help, particularly during this crisis, but that we also need to commit to a plan to pay for that help. That would mean either cutting back on existing programs or raising the government's revenue, which would undoubtedly require us to move back toward a more progressive system of taxation. We will have to expect those who have more to contribute more, through reforms such as increasing the income tax rate at the top tax brackets, and through a reexamination of the tax rates on long-term capital gains. This won't be politically popular, but it would return a sense of fiscal responsibility to our progressive ideals and pay for the critical programs to help those in need.

Much of my further contemplation in my retirement years has been driven by this same mix of reevaluation of the facts and a hard look at the impact on real lives. We are now, as a society, taking a hard look at how we treat others, in particular women and people of color.

As I write this, protests are happening across the country and around the world to highlight the unequal and unjust treatment of people of color by the police. The fight against this injustice is a movement that I wholeheartedly support, even though I don't think that learning to actively protest in my ninth decade is in the cards. I always thought that President Lyndon Johnson captured the spirit of our continuing struggle with systemic racism when he addressed a 1965 commencement ceremony at Howard University:

> Freedom is not enough. You do not wipe away the scars of centuries by saying: Now you are free to go where you want, and do as you desire, and choose the leaders you please.
>
> You do not take a person who, for years, has been hobbled by chains and liberate him, bring him up to the starting line of a race and then say, "you are free to compete with all the others," and still justly believe that you have been completely fair.
>
> Thus it is not enough just to open the gates of opportunity. All our citizens must have the ability to walk through those gates.
>
> This is the next and the more profound stage of the battle for civil rights. We seek not just freedom but opportunity. We seek not just legal equity but human ability, not just equality as a right and a theory but equality as a fact and equality as a result.[1]

I now have a greater understanding of the fact that my own path was eased by what I can more easily identify as a system imbued with white male privilege. This certainly wasn't something that I knowingly exploited, but I can now see just how much I've benefited from simply being white, straight, and male. Factors beyond my control have resulted in doors being opened that others had to fight to break down—like there was a "get out of jail free" card in my pocket that I didn't, at the time, know was there. I had the system at my back instead of having it throw obstacles in my path.

Our society has also been struggling recently with the experiences of women, and the additional challenges they face in both their professional and personal lives. I have been particularly moved by the personal stories told by those who have faced these challenges. I was drawn into this topic more deeply by stories like that of Dr. Christine Blasey Ford and her accusations of sexual assault during the confirmation hearing of now Supreme Court justice Brett Kavanaugh. Like many others, as I watched Dr. Ford's testimony on television and read about her story, I found myself thinking of the last time that a Supreme Court nominee was accused of inappropriate behavior by a woman—the 1991 confirmation hearings of Supreme Court justice Clarence Thomas.

Confirming judges to the Supreme Court is one of the tasks of the U.S. Senate, and one that I took very seriously as a senator. As the highest authority of one of the three coequal branches of the federal government, the Supreme Court's impact on American life is often much more significant than some might realize. As a senator, I believed that presidential appointments should be judged almost exclusively on their qualifications for the office, not their ideologies, party affiliation, or honestly held political or religious beliefs. When I voted to confirm Justice Thomas, I knew that we had clear differences in our ideology, but I believed then that if we were going to hold presidents accountable, they should have reasonably wide discretion in making executive decisions, especially in matters relating to military action, international affairs, and judicial choices. That's why elections matter. I believed that the Senate had a duty to closely scrutinize the qualifications and fitness of each person a president put forward, but that those inquiries should focus on whether the nominee had the necessary intellect, experience, temperament, and judgment to sit on the bench.

Judgment became a real question for me when accusations of sexual harassment by Thomas's former colleague, Anita Hill, were raised. That's why I publicly called for a delay in the confirmation proceedings so that Hill could be heard by the Judiciary Committee and made it clear that my vote rested on hearing Hill out. If, on hearing all the evidence, I concluded that Clarence Thomas was in fact guilty of deliberate sexual harassment, then I would not have voted to confirm him to the Supreme Court.

I never doubted that Anita Hill was a credible and serious witness. What I didn't fully appreciate in 1991 was the full extent of the harm that could be done by nonphysical sexual harassment, and I came to the conclusion then that Thomas was not fully aware of the effect that his comments were having on Hill.

I am no longer in a position to vote on Supreme Court nominees, but, with increased introspection and a good deal of reading, my views on the appropriate criteria for approving them have changed. Watching the increasingly partisan nature of these lifetime appointments over the last twenty-five years, I have come to the conclusion that, due to the frequent 5–4 divisions of the court, the ideology of prospective judges need not be entirely ignored in the decision to confirm a nominee.

Spurred in part by the nomination process of Justice Kavanaugh, my understanding of sexual harassment and assault has also broadened. As far as I was concerned, sexual assault had always been a disqualifier for any nominee, and I thought that Dr. Ford gave genuine and convincing televised testimony before the Senate Judiciary Committee during Kavanaugh's confirmation hearing. Whereas I once made a distinction between purely verbal harassment and physical assault, I have come to realize just how damaging verbal harassment can be, particularly in a workplace setting. More than twenty-five years later, I have a deeper understanding of the effect that Thomas's actions could have had on Hill.

Dr. Ford's testimony came in the midst of a larger movement of increased awareness of sexual harassment and assault. As we have begun to address these topics more openly, I have read many stories of the brave women who chose to share their own experiences. Hearing these accounts has helped many of us who have never been the target of such behavior become much more aware of its impact on the victim, even years after the incident occurred.

Moving forward, I think that we need to do more to raise awareness among both genders of how this behavior can affect women. Much of the current movement is seeking to do just that, and to recognize the courage of the women who have stepped forward to tell their stories. Anyone who is willing to put themselves through public excoriation in order to bring forward allegations of sexual abuse, harassment, or intimidation by those in power deserves to be heard. It has to be our job, ultimately, to listen.

While more work needs to be done, I think that progress is being made and more women are being heard. There is another issue, however, that I believe to be threatening our democracy itself, and it is getting worse. One of the greatest challenges facing our country is the ideological divide. The politics of division, which was used so effectively in the 1994 Republican Revolution, and then fostered over the last quarter century, has become widespread and pervasive. Sadly, during the presidency of Donald Trump, misinformation has been used to solidify a narrow political base and divide the rest of the country.

Much of what is missing in the kind of ugly tribalism that I see taking over our political system today is the respect that is formed by listening to the other side. Senator John McCain, my longtime friend from across the aisle, put it so effectively in 2017 when he told Naval Academy graduates:

I believe in Americans. We're capable of better. I've seen it. We're hopeful, compassionate people. And we still have leaders who will uphold the values that made America great, and a beacon to the oppressed.

But I don't take that for granted. We have to fight. We have to fight against propaganda and crackpot conspiracy theories. We have to fight isolationism, protectionism, and nativism. We have to defeat those who would worsen our divisions. We have to remind our sons and daughters that we became the most powerful nation on earth by tearing down walls, not building them.[2]

John didn't live long enough to see this fight through, and I fear that neither will I. So, all I can do is to promote the solution that I see today and hope that it applies as thoroughly to the future. I see the country at a crossroads. Special interests, using millions in political contributions, are creating and influencing systems—health care and the environment, for example—to work more for them than for all American citizens. These systems are broken, and it is hurting Americans of all backgrounds and political affiliations. And yet, the tribalism that is worsening with each twenty-four-hour news cycle is pushing us so far apart that we are frequently unable to work together long enough to come up with sensible solutions.

I've seen special interests pull people apart before. In the 1980s, the Democratic Party was at a similar crossroads. Overtaken by special interests and bogged down by identity politics, we needed, as a party, to return to our common core values to reconnect with the American people. Back then, we formed the Democratic Leadership Council (DLC) in order for the Democratic Party to reclaim our bedrock issues, such as economic growth, a strong national defense, fiscal responsibility, and a commitment to national service, while also reinventing social programs for those in need and providing greater opportunity for the working men and women of our country.

Today we, as Americans, also need to work harder to come together to reclaim our own shared core values. This doesn't have to mean that we agree on everything, but how we disagree matters. Instead of arguments that simply disparage the other side, an argument over the best way to reach our goals—one with opposing but not demonizing views—will result in a better system. I've always felt that encouraging debate and allowing that debate to change and improve policies is what makes our democracy different from an authoritarian regime.

The tribalism that is pulling our democracy apart doesn't have to prevail. For our democracy to hold together, its citizens must share a commitment to the common good. In order to fix our problems, we are going to need a renewed commitment to citizenship that overcomes tribal allegiances.

What I am advocating for is patriotism, which should not be confused with nationalism. I do not believe that all Americans have to look a certain way or have a certain background. What binds us is not a shared ethnicity but a shared commitment to America's fundamental ideals. I think that patriotism has gotten a particularly bad reputation in the last twenty years, as it has been co-opted by segments of the political spectrum that have confused patriotism with nationalism. One can be fully patriotic—devoted to our nation and fellow citizens—without seeking to expel one type of person from our shores. One can also be a patriotic progressive, devoted to our country and our democracy, and at the same time committed to policies that care for those in need. I consider myself a patriotic progressive who believes deeply that citizenship is both a gift and a responsibility.

"Citizenship is the glue that binds us together as a country," I said in a 1986 speech as chairman of the DLC. "It is both the means that enable us as a nation to meet the challenges we face, and the end that entitles each of us to share the blessings which our common efforts secure."[3]

Just as our government itself derives its power from the people, it depends on our participation to survive. A democracy only holds together when our freedoms are balanced with rules that are derived from a shared moral understanding. In order for democracy to respond to our needs, I believe it is important that we participate in it and devote something of ourselves to the benefit of our broader community.

I don't think it's necessary for everyone to run for public office, but I do believe that every American should afford their country some amount of public service. In the same speech in 1986, given at the National Press Club in Washington, I called for universal national service as "a responsibility of citizenship." I went on to say:

We need to stop selling the American people short. They know that our nation's progress has been built on hard work and shared sacrifice. And they know that America is one nation, not just a place where millions of individuals act out their private destinies.

They understand that citizenship means much more than that— citizenship means there are times when we have to subordinate private pursuits to national purpose; it means paying our way today, and not mortgaging our children's future. It means compassion for our less fortunate fellow-citizens. And it means making personal sacrifices to promote common goals—like excellence in public education, safe neighborhoods, a healthy environment, and a strong national defense. . . .

I believe that the American people will respond to a new summons to civic duty and responsibility—if only we have the courage to sound it.[4]

I've always felt that, having had the good fortune to have been born in the United States—with all of its rights and privileges—we ought to accept an obligation to make sure that our children and their children have the same opportunities we've had. I've tried to emulate that belief in my service in the military and elected office, and when I entered the Senate, I proposed legislation, along with Senator Sam Nunn and several others, to create a program of universal national service. The negotiations over the legislation were long and hard, and we were proud to emerge, after compromises on both sides, with a national community service program called AmeriCorps. The program was a good first step that gave young people a nonmilitary way to serve their country in sectors such as education, public safety, and environmental conservation. But, with only twenty thousand participants per year initially (that number has since been significantly increased), it was far from universal. I see our next step as the creation of a national service program that reaches every young American citizen. The universality of service is important because when service is a shared experience, it can bring together Americans from all walks of life, helping to break down barriers between social, ethnic, racial, socioeconomic, and religious groups. I believe it can create Amitai Etzioni's apt metaphor of America not as a melting pot, where all of our differences should be melted together and indistinguishable, but as a mosaic, where the differences in color and shape combine to make a larger, stronger, more beautiful whole.

Today, universal national service may not yet have the political support that it will need, but I believe it is just as, if not more, necessary if we are to break through the tribalism and restore a commitment to the common good. Because without a commitment to our national community, our differences could well pull us apart.

Most organizations that are fighting to make a difference in our society are not looking for a man in his eighties to lead a revolution. I continue to support all of those who are tirelessly advocating for those who have less, for those who have been discriminated against, and for a society in which everyone can enjoy the God-given rights and freedoms due all human beings, in America and around the world. My hope is that by highlighting some of these issues here, by using whatever platform I have, I might encourage others to continue the fight.

Perhaps if we were at a more tranquil period in American history, I would not feel the need to add these thoughts to the end of my story. But each era has had fundamental threats to democracy, and I want us to make sure we meet ours. How our nation responds to its crises will determine what kind of democracy our country, and our children and grandchildren, are left with long after I'm gone.

Our country faced a critical choice last year, and I was immensely pleased and relieved when my longtime friend Joe Biden was elected president. Watching the campaign and its aftermath unfold, I was struck by the different choices being presented. That choice became more apparent when, on January 6, 2021, rioters stormed the U.S. Capitol, spurred on by unsupported claims of election fraud, to prevent the certification of the electoral college vote through violence. The insurrection exposed a long-standing fissure in American politics which, if left unchecked, would undermine confidence in our democracy, both at home and abroad. Fortunately, the insurrection was subdued, the certification was completed, and the inauguration proceeded without further incident.

I believe that, with the inauguration of Joe Biden, America chose the path of empathy, integrity, and sound leadership. Joe understands that leading the country is about bringing people together, not just chipping off your piece of the electorate and working to destroy the rest. Watching the inaugural ceremonies, I saw reason for hope in the eloquence of the next generation and the beginnings of the restoration of bipartisanship. I felt the promise of the American dream when Kamala Harris became the first female, first Black, and first South Asian vice president. I'm again confident that our nation's best years are still ahead of us. We have the ability to live up to those values that so many have fought and died for—to be the land of the free and the home of the brave. America can once again deserve respect, both at home and abroad, and be a beacon of freedom and hope around the world.

34

Always a Marine

A FEW YEARS ago, Lynda and I celebrated our fiftieth anniversary by hosting a dinner for friends and family at our home. I stood up during the dinner to thank everyone for coming and, as I said to Lynda, "to brag about you for just a second." To which she responded that I should "keep it short."

"I just want to let you know that not only is she very special to me," I said, "but she has a couple of distinctions that you wouldn't normally know about unless you've kept track of presidents' daughters' weddings. Only eight daughters of presidents have been married in the White House, and Lynda is both the only such bride in the last one hundred years, and the first to get to celebrate her golden wedding anniversary. I'm lucky enough to rate a footnote in that accomplishment."

To commemorate the occasion, I gave Lynda a ring that now nestles between her engagement and wedding rings. It is called an eternity ring, because that's how long I want our relationship to last.

At our anniversary dinner, Lynda got up to speak next. "I told Chuck that I was going to go for the gold. And then, after that, I wanted to renegotiate our contract." Everyone laughed.

"I haven't been visited by your lawyers yet!" I quipped from my seat.

"I was waiting for this party," Lynda replied in a perfect deadpan. "There are several good lawyers here."

Lynda, who inherited her father's talent for public speaking, went on to introduce many of the friends, family, and members of our wedding party—a few donning their original bridesmaids dresses. Then she summed up the evening perfectly:

The thing that makes us the luckiest is that we have so many friends. They say that the thing that makes you live the longest is being surrounded by people that you love and call as friends. We're lucky to have here . . . so many of you who, even if we're not related by blood, we're related by love. And that is a great gift. My mother used to say that the most important thing that you can give someone is memories. And that is what y'all have done.

KNOWING THAT, AS my friend Bill Clinton used to say, "I've got more sunsets behind me than ahead of me"—I am now older than the last four presidents and the last eight commandants of the Marine Corps—I'm in a position to reflect upon my life and what, if anything, I've learned. Not surprisingly, the lessons that have stuck with me the longest were the ones that I learned first: be polite, be respectful, and be honest. They are simple rules, taught to me by my parents and reinforced in the Marine Corps, that I have tried to live up to throughout my life. And I credit these lessons with any success I have had. I can't claim to be gifted with an overabundance of a single talent—I would never be mistaken for a rocket scientist, I was never drafted into professional sports, and I can't carry a tune in a paper bag. But I have tried to bring the values of kindness, respect, and honesty, along with a strong work ethic, to everything I do. I haven't always succeeded, but what successes I've had, and the relationships I've made along the way, are the result of sticking to those lessons I learned when I was young. I also benefited enormously from the very special woman I was lucky enough to marry and the three bright, talented, and thoughtful daughters we were fortunate enough to bring into the world.

A few years ago, I noticed that the unsolicited advertisements I used to get for life insurance had turned into advertisements for assisted living facilities and were now straying into ads for burial plots. I was being told cheerily that, at Cedar Hill Cemetery, I was "already pre-approved!" I know how to take a hint. When the time comes, if I'm lucky enough to meet St. Peter, I'm ready.

When I do go, I know that I will likely be remembered more as a governor or senator of Virginia. Those were certainly defining roles in my life, but I see myself first and foremost as a Marine. When I look in the mirror, the reflection is that of a man early in his ninth decade, but I still picture myself as a lean, green fighting machine. Though I still tell myself that I'll get back in fighting shape next season, my retirement years have constantly reminded me of the "Serenity Prayer," which I have always admired:

God, grant me the serenity to accept the things that I cannot change, the courage to change the things I can, and the wisdom to know the difference.

In the last few years, I've only been back to the Capitol to pay my respects after the passing of leaders whom I admired, such as President George H. W. Bush, Justice Ruth Bader Ginsburg, Representative John Lewis, Senator John McCain, and First Lady Nancy Reagan. These services have naturally left me thinking more about my own. When we attended the funeral of my friend John McCain in 2018, I was moved yet again by one of the first songs that echoed through the nave of the National Cathedral: the Navy hymn, "Eternal Father, Strong to Save." I'd also like that hymn performed at my own funeral, along with the verse asking for divine guidance for the Marine Corps:

> Eternal Father, grant, we pray,
> To all Marines, both night and day,
> The courage, honor, strength and skill
> Their land to serve, Thy law fulfill;
> Be Thou the Shield forevermore
> From ev'ry peril to the Corps.

I know that those best chapters of my life—meeting Lynda, serving in public office for over twenty years, having three almost-perfect daughters—none of them would likely have happened if I hadn't first joined the Marines.

Al Grasso, then president and CEO of the MITRE Corporation, summed it all up particularly well at a small ceremony to celebrate my stepping down as chairman, my retirement from the board, and the dedication in my name of a new auditorium at MITRE's headquarters. At the ceremony, Al pointed out the plaque affixed to the wall just outside the hall that listed all of the various positions and offices I'd held. Each was an important and significant part of my life. Next to each position was a date signifying when it began and when it ended. But, as Al noted: "If you read the very last line of the plaque, it has no date to it. It just says, 'U.S. Marine.' Once a Marine, always a Marine."[1]

Writing this book has forced me to put my life in black letters on a white screen, and to edit it down to a length that could be published as something short of a doorstop. I've had to examine for myself what I hoped to achieve out of life, and I believe that it is best summarized as: I wanted to do the best that I could do. I strove to develop a reputation for truth, honesty, and fairness. I tried to lead with respect and integrity. I hoped to be judged on my deeds. And I was determined to run a three-mile course, in full combat gear, in under eighteen minutes.

ACKNOWLEDGMENTS

THERE ARE SOME who sit down to write about their life and see the words flow onto paper almost effortlessly. I am not one of those people. I am not, as friends and family can attest, even the best storyteller in my household—that accolade is held by my wife.

But I did, when I first began to consider this venture, have an idea of what I wanted to accomplish. I had read the masterfully narrative memoirs of Kay Graham (*Personal History*) and Ben Bradlee (*A Good Life*), and knew that I wanted to accomplish something in that vein. Unfortunately, my own style is much closer to Jack Webb's character in the old television show *Dragnet*: "Just the facts, Ma'am." So, I knew that it would be essential to have some very able partners to get this done, and I have been assisted over the years in the writing of this book by many friends, volunteers, and professional storytellers.

There were three phases in the development of this book, a project that has spanned several decades. In the first phase, I brought on one of the writers who had assisted Ben Bradlee with his memoir, Barbara Fineman Todd. Barbara took my handwritten notes on yellow legal pads, carefully talked through them with me, and helped me piece together a very rough account of my life to that point.

I next worked with another very talented writer named Lisa Dickey, who helped me organize a full draft and draw out more details where they were lacking. Then several years passed in which my work on the manuscript made slow but steady progress. There were several very able writers, researchers, and assistants who helped me during this period, including Phillip Cantelon of History Associates Incorporated, and fellow Marine Chip Jones.

I met my final literary partner, Alice McKeon, by chance, and we immediately struck up a particularly good working relationship. It was a fortuitous meeting—Alice, a graduate of William & Mary who had worked professionally in politics at the state and national level, and whose grandfather had served in the Marine Corps during Vietnam, couldn't have had a better background and understanding of the events during my years in the Marine Corps and in public service thereafter. Alice is very smart and has a

335

creative mind that helped me pull the complex project together. A talented writer, Alice has helped me to further focus my story and draw out the themes. She has been a positively ruthless editor, managing to help me to cut enough to keep the book from becoming a doorstop, while still finding creative ways to sneak in stories that were important to me. She is also a top-flight detective—asking questions that I had never considered and fact-checking so diligently that I am sure she knows more about my life at this point than I do. Most importantly, Alice kept me focused on telling my story—with the bark off—with all of the truth and clarity that we could muster. Over the course of the last five years that we have worked together, Alice and I were able to transform the hard facts of my life into a narrative.

Of course, there are so many more people who have contributed to this project over the years with their time, materials, memories, editorial skills, and wisdom that it is impossible for me to have a comprehensive list here. But I would be remiss if I did not mention: Bob Brown; Susan Albert Carr; John Casteen; Peter Cleveland; Ben Dendy; Connie Desaulniers; Brian Detter; Betty Sue Flowers; Stewart Gamage; Cathie Lechares; Tom Lehner; David McCloud; Don McKeon; Harry Middleton; David Nelson; Terry Paul; Steve Ricchetti; Ridge Schuyler; David Solimini; Tim Sullivan; Julia Sutherland; Tony Townes; and Stephen Wells; as well as Mark Lawrence, Claudia Anderson, and Chris Banks at the LBJ Presidential Library.

I would like to give a special thanks to my longtime friend Bill Clinton for his generous and very gracious foreword, and to his staff, led by Tina Flournoy, for their help and support through the process.

In addition, I'd like to thank the staff at the University of Virginia Press, who have been endlessly supportive and helpful with our many questions throughout the publication process: Eric Brandt, Helen Chandler, Charlie Bailey, Ellen Satrom, Susan Murray, Emily Grandstaff, Jason Coleman, and Emma Donovan.

I would like to thank my siblings, Wick, David, and Trenny, for their support, as well as a healthy supply of old family stories and photos.

There have been countless campaign workers, volunteers, and staff members who have provided invaluable assistance to me over the years and who are simply too numerous to mention in the book. Know that Lynda and I are forever grateful for everything that you have done for both of us.

It is important to note that, regardless of the help that I have received, I take full responsibility for the content of this book. I have captured situations and conversations, often recorded contemporaneously, to the best of my memory and verified as much as possible with secondary sources. However, it is still an account of my life through my own eyes, and there are bound to be, after eighty-one years, some things that I remember differently—and other things that I don't remember at all.

I couldn't have done any of this without the memory, support, and storytelling of the love of my life, and my wife of more than fifty-two years, Lynda. I also want to thank our daughters, Lucinda, Catherine, and Jennifer, and their husbands, Lars and Josh, for supporting this endeavor from its inception. Being a "Boppa" has always brought joy to my life, and I hope that one day our grandchildren—Madeline, Austin, Lawrence, Charlie, and Joshie—will read this book and be able to learn a little more about their grandfather and the people, places, priorities, and events that shaped his life and the family and friends he cared so much about.

NOTES

Preface

1. Tom Sherwood, "Robb Wrestles with Memories," *Washington Post,* November 12, 1985.
2. Leslie Pockell and Adrienne Avila, *The 100 Greatest Leadership Principles of All Time* (New York: Grand Central Publishing, 2007).
3. Theodore Roosevelt, "The Man in the Arena," Paris, France, April 23, 1910, Humanities Texas, https://www.humanitiestexas.org/sites/default/files /TRManintheArena_0.pdf.

1. The Path to Quantico

1. Betty Beale, "Robb's Background Local," *Sunday Star* (Washington, DC), September 24, 1967.
2. Beale, "Robb's Background Local."
3. John Carmody, "Robb More Than a Poster Soldier," *Washington Post,* October 8, 1967.
4. "For the Robbs, Wedding Is Also a Homecoming," *New York Times,* December 1, 1967.
5. "For the Robbs, Wedding Is Also a Homecoming."
6. Earl Swift, "A Serviceman to the Core," *Virginian-Pilot,* October 1, 2000.
7. Swift, "A Serviceman to the Core."
8. "President Visits Nort'n," *The Scanner,* USS *Northampton* CC-1 Command Ship, April 1962.

2. The President's Daughter

1. Edwin Lahey, "Lynda on a Date," *Washington Post,* January 21, 1966.
2. Dorothy McCardle, "The LBJ Daughters Make Their Own Marks," *Washington Post,* December 8, 1963.
3. "Lynda Johnson Tells the Story behind Her Engagement," *McCall's,* November 1967.
4. Claudia Alta Johnson, *A White House Diary* (New York: Holt, Rinehart and Winston, 1970), 558.
5. C. A. Johnson, *A White House Diary,* 552–53.

6. C. A. Johnson, *A White House Diary,* 553.

7. Maxine Cheshire, "Vietnam on Waiting List for Capt. Robb?," *Washington Post,* October 15, 1967.

3. A White House Wedding

1. *Once in a Lifetime,* video file, 1967 film by the White House Naval Photographic Center, LBJ Presidential Library and Texas Archive of the Moving Image, https://texasarchive.org/2010_00110.

2. Judith Martin, "Geoffrey Beene's Aim: Royal Romanticism," *Washington Post,* December 10, 1967.

3. "Diploma Caps 25-Year Effort," *Madison Wisconsin State Journal,* May 16, 1988.

4. *Once in a Lifetime,* video file, 1967 film by the White House Naval Photographic Center, LBJ Presidential Library and Texas Archive of the Moving Image, https://texasarchive.org/2010_00110.

5. C. A. Johnson, *A White House Diary,* 598.

4. The Weight of War

1. "Telephone Conversation between President Johnson and the President's Special Assistant for National Security Affairs (Bundy) Washington, May 27, 1964, 11:24 a.m.," Document 53, in *Foreign Relations of the United States, 1964–68,* vol. 27: *Mainland Southeast Asia: Regional Affairs* (Washington, DC: U.S. Department of State); Original Source: Recording of a telephone conversation between the President and McGeorge Bundy, Tape 64.28 PNO 111, Recordings and Transcripts, Johnson Library, https://www.mtholyoke.edu/acad/intrel/vietnam/lbjbundy.htm.

2. "Telephone Conversation between President Johnson and the President's Special Assistant for National Security Affairs (Bundy) Washington, May 27, 1964, 11:24 a.m.," Document 53, in *Foreign Relations of the United States, 1964–68,* vol. 27: *Mainland Southeast Asia: Regional Affairs* (Washington, DC: U.S. Department of State); Original Source: Recording of a telephone conversation between the President and McGeorge Bundy, Tape 64.28 PNO 111, Recordings and Transcripts, Johnson Library, https://www.mtholyoke.edu/acad/intrel/vietnam/lbjbundy.htm.

3. Michael Beschloss, *Taking Charge: The Johnson White House Tapes, 1963–1964* (New York: Simon and Schuster, 1997), 248.

4. Beschloss, *Taking Charge,* 269.

5. Beschloss, *Taking Charge,* 269.

6. "Lyndon Baines Johnson Quotes," Lyndon Baines Johnson Museum of San Marcos, https://lbjmuseum.com/lyndon-baines-johnson-quotes/.

7. Claudia Alta Johnson, *A White House Diary* (New York: Holt, Rinehart and Winston, 1970), 589.

8. Lyndon B. Johnson, *The Vantage Point* (New York: Holt, Reinhart and Winston, 1972), 430.

9. Thomas Percy, *Reliques of Ancient English Poetry, Consisting of Old Heroic Ballads, Songs and Other Pieces, of Our Earlier Poets* (London: Templeman, 1839), 264.

10. L. B. Johnson, *The Vantage Point,* 431.

11. Tom Wicker, "Johnson Says He Won't Run," *New York Times,* April 1, 1968.

12. C. A. Johnson, *A White House Diary,* 644.

5. Boots on the Ground

1. Don Reeder, "Robb 'Just a Marine' to Men, Cong," *Salem (OR) Statesman,* August 1, 1968.

2. Charles S. Robb to Lynda J. Robb, May 31, 1968.

3. Charles S. Robb to Lynda J. Robb, May 31, 1968.

4. Charles S. Robb to Lynda J. Robb, May 5, 1968.

5. Earl Swift, "A Serviceman to the Core," *Virginian-Pilot,* October 1, 2000.

6. Charles S. Robb to Lynda J. Robb, April 8, 1968.

7. Charles S. Robb to Lynda J. Robb, May 5, 1968.

8. Charles S. Robb to Lynda J. Robb, May 30, 1968.

9. Charles S. Robb to Lynda J. Robb, August 5, 1968.

10. Charles S. Robb to Lynda J. Robb, August 5, 1968.

6. Bulletproof

1. Charles S. Robb to Lynda J. Robb, May 13, 1968.

2. Charles S. Robb to Lynda J. Robb, May 22, 1968.

3. Lynda J. Robb to Charles S. Robb, May 30, 1968.

4. Charles S. Robb to Lynda J. Robb, audio recording, 1968.

5. Lyndon B. Johnson to Charles S. Robb, October 24, 1968.

6. Lyndon B. Johnson to Charles S. Robb, October 24, 1968.

7. Lynda J. Robb to Charles S. Robb, July 30, 1968.

8. President's Daily Diary, July 31, 1968, LBJ Library.

9. Lyndon B. Johnson to Charles S. Robb, May 3, 1968.

10. Lyndon B. Johnson to Charles S. Robb, September 3, 1968.

11. Charles S. Robb to Lynda J. Robb, audio recording, 1968.

12. Charles S. Robb to Lynda J. Robb, February 23, 1969.

7. Returning Home

1. "Robb Meets Daughter at Last," *Milwaukee (WI) Journal,* April 26, 1969.
2. Lynda J. Robb to Charles S. Robb, April 5, 1968.
3. Lynda J. Robb to Charles S. Robb, April 6, 1968.
4. Lynda J. Robb to Charles S. Robb, June 5, 1968.
5. Lynda J. Robb to Charles S. Robb, June 6, 1968.
6. Charles S. Robb to Lynda J. Robb, June 6, 1968.
7. Lynda J. Robb to Charles S. Robb, June 8, 1968.
8. John H. Chafee to Melvin Laird, "Memorandum for the Secretary of Defense: Allegations of Indiscriminate Killings Involving Major Robb's Unit in Vietnam," December 15, 1969.
9. "'Heavy-Duty Litigator' Has Colorful Past," *Concord Monitor,* September 23, 2012.
10. Jim Rutenberg, "The Man behind the Whispers about Obama," *New York Times,* October 12, 2008.
11. Charles S. Robb, "Remarks by Major Charles S. Robb, II U.S. Marine Corps," Kiwanis Club, Buckhead, Atlanta, Georgia, October 13, 1969.
12. Robb, "Remarks by Major Charles S. Robb, II U.S. Marine Corps," Kiwanis Club, Buckhead, Atlanta, Georgia, October 13, 1969.
13. "Johnson's Son-in-Law Discusses Pacification in Vietnam," *La Salle Magazine,* La Salle University, Spring 1970.
14. Beth Gillin, "Robb's Charm, Not Message, Wins Applause," *Philadelphia Inquirer,* February 18, 1970.
15. Robb, "Remarks by Major Charles S. Robb, II U.S. Marine Corps," Kiwanis Club, Buckhead, Atlanta, Georgia, October 13, 1969.
16. Robb, "Remarks by Major Charles S. Robb, II U.S. Marine Corps," Kiwanis Club, Buckhead, Atlanta, Georgia, October 13, 1969.
17. Paul M. Bourke, "The Man Who Knew Too Much," *New York Times,* March 12, 2018.

8. A Growing Family

1. Carol Morello, "A Quiet Fighter in His Toughest Battle," *Washington Post,* October 10, 2000.

9. Larger than Life

1. Hal Rothman, *LBJ's Texas White House* (Texas: Texas A&M University Press, 2001), 252.
2. Juan Castillo, "40 Years after Woodlawn Bus Tragedy, Survivors Recall Horror,

Then Outpouring of Compassion," *Austin American-Statesman,* December 26, 2012.

3. Haynes Johnson and Jules Witcover, "LBJ Buried in Beloved Texas Hills," *Washington Post,* January 26, 1973.

4. Michael O'Donnell, "How LBJ Saved the Civil Rights Act," *Atlantic,* April 2014.

5. "Annual Message to the Congress on the States of the Union. January 8, 1964," in *Public Papers of the Presidents of the United States: Lyndon B. Johnson* (Washington, DC: U.S. Government Printing Office, 1965).

PART II. THE NEW DOMINION

1. Robert Wickliffe Woolley, "Politics Is Hell," autobiography, final draft, prepared circa 1946, Box 44, Robert Wickliffe Woolley Papers, 1842–1956, Library of Congress, Washington, DC, https://hdl.loc.gov/loc.mss/eadmss.ms011186.

10. STEPPING INTO THE FRAY

1. Donald P. Baker and Glenn Frankel, "Chuck Robb: Va. Candidate Still Emerging from the Shadow of LBJ," *Washington Post,* September 13, 1981.

2. John McCain and Mark Salter, *The Restless Wave* (New York: Simon and Schuster, 2018), 321.

3. Clare Crawford, "Lynda Robb Couldn't Help Being Born to a Politician, But She's Uneasy Married to One," *People* magazine, August 1, 1977.

4. Crawford, "Lynda Robb Couldn't Help Being Born to a Politician, But She's Uneasy Married to One."

5. Hubert H. Humphrey, "Remarks by Senator Hubert H. Humphrey," University of Virginia Law School, Charlottesville, February 15, 1973.

6. Ward Sinclair et al., "The City He Loved Says Farewell to Hubert Humphrey," *Washington Post,* January 16, 1978.

11. A FUTURE WORTHY OF HER PAST

1. Donald P. Baker, "Robb Takes Offensive in First Va. Debate," *Washington Post,* May 5, 1981.

2. Baker, "Robb Takes Offensive in First Va. Debate."

3. Carla Hall, "Lynda Robb, the Feminist Surprise," *Washington Post,* May 12, 1979.

12. NO HIGHER HONOR

1. Celestine Bohlen and Denis Collins, "Top Hats, Ear Muffs and a Bit of History," *Washington Post,* January 17, 1982.

2. Patricia E. Bauer, "Robb Assumes Post, Gets Mansion Keys," *Washington Post,* January 17, 1982.
3. Donald P. Baker, "Robb Pledges Greater Role for Minorities and Women," *Washington Post,* November 8, 1981.
4. Glenn Frankel and Donald P. Baker, "Robb Sworn in as 64th Governor," *Washington Post,* January 17, 1982.
5. Patricia Sullivan and Michael D. Shear, "Hunter B. Andrews Dies," *Washington Post,* January 15, 2004.
6. Jeff E. Schapiro, "Schapiro: The Pols Who Lent Personality to Va. Campaigns," *Richmond Times-Dispatch,* November 4, 2014.
7. Celestine Bohlen, "Virginia's Bill Killer," *Washington Post,* February 22, 1983.

13. The Democracy of Opportunity

1. Glenn Frankel and Donald P. Baker, "Robb Sworn in as 64th Governor," *Washington Post,* January 17, 1982.
2. Charles S. Robb, "Remarks by Charles S. Robb," National Press Club, Washington, DC, April 3, 1986.
3. "Robb's Address: A Plea for Austerity," *Washington Post,* January 19, 1983.
4. "Robb's Address: A Plea for Austerity."
5. Tom Sherwood and Sandra Sugawara, "Robb Proposes Broad Changes on Many Issues," *Washington Post,* January 12, 1984.

14. The Aristocracy of Merit

1. Michael Isikoff, "Race Relations Distinguish Robb's First Year," *Washington Post,* January 9, 1983.
2. Isikoff, "Race Relations Distinguish Robb's First Year."

15. The Long, Hot Summer

1. Arthur Brisbane, "Area Swoons in 'Almost' Record Heat," *Washington Post,* June 9, 1984.
2. Lee Hockstader and Molly Moore, "Manhunt: Search Widens for 4 Slayers Who Fled Va. Death Row," *Washington Post,* June 3, 1984; "Four Escapees from Va. Death Row Continue to Elude Police in 4th Day," *Washington Post,* June 5, 1984.
3. "Robb's Focus: Taxes, Education, ERA, and Crime," *Washington Post,* January 12, 1982.
4. "Two Who Fled Prison in Richmond Recaptured," *Washington Post,* June 30, 1984.

5. Molly Moore and Tom Sherwood, "5 Guards Fired after Probe of Death-Row Breakout," *Washington Post*, July 6, 1984.

6. John Ward Anderson and Martin Weil, "Va. Prisoners at Mecklenburg Hold 7 Hostages," *Washington Post*, August 5, 1984.

7. Tom Sherwood and Molly Moore, "Robb Takes 'Full Responsibility' for Prison Problems—Robb Addresses Assembly," *Washington Post*, January 10, 1985.

8. Sherwood and Moore, "Robb Takes 'Full Responsibility' for Prison Problems—Robb Addresses Assembly."

16. CLEAN SWEEP

1. Mark Shields, "The Robb Revolution," *Washington Post*, November 5, 1985.

2. Molly Moore and Donald P. Baker, "Charges Fly in Va. Races," *Washington Post*, November 11, 1985.

3. Tom Sherwood and Donald P. Baker, "Long Costly Campaign Ends in Va.," *Washington Post*, November 5, 1985.

4. Philip Smith and Donald P. Baker, "New View of Va. Emerges: Baliles Ticket Shoved Stereotypes Aside," *Washington Post*, November 6, 1985.

5. Donald P. Baker and Molly Moore, "Robb Closes with Call for Spending," *Washington Post*, January 9, 1986.

6. Baker and Moore, "Robb Closes with Call for Spending."

7. Tom Sherwood, "Robb: New Image for State," *Washington Post*, January 1, 1986.

8. Sherwood, "Robb: New Image for State."

9. Sherwood, "Robb: New Image for State."

17. SACRED COWS

1. Charles S. Robb, "Democratic National Convention Day 3," video file, 03:26, C-SPAN, https://www.c-span.org/video/?124439–1/democratic-national-convention-day-3.

2. Phil Gailey, "For a Mondale Friend, One Question Lingers," *New York Times*, November 16, 1984.

3. Phil Gailey, "Dissidents Defy Top Democrats; Council Formed," *New York Times*, March 1, 1985.

4. Paul Taylor, "Democrats' New Centrists Preen for '88," *Washington Post*, November 10, 1985.

5. Taylor, "Democrats' New Centrists Preen for '88."

6. Charles S. Robb, "Remarks by Charles S. Robb," National Press Club, Washington, DC, April 3, 1986.

7. Al From, *The New Democrats and the Return to Power* (New York: Palgrave Macmillan, 2013), 72.

8. From, *The New Democrats and the Return to Power,* 72–73.

9. From, *The New Democrats and the Return to Power,* 73–74.

10. From, *The New Democrats and the Return to Power,* 73–74.

11. "Hard Truths about Race," *New York Times,* April 26, 1986.

12. David Sigal, dir., *Crashing the Party* (Warren River County, NJ: Passion River Films, 2016).

13. Sigal, dir., *Crashing the Party.*

18. Pandora's Box

1. Tyler Whitley, "Democrats Can't Win with Politics of Race, Wilder Aide Contends," *Richmond Times-Dispatch,* November 24, 1986.

2. Michael Hardy, "Appeals to Race Said to Fail," *Richmond Times-Dispatch,* November 24, 1986.

3. Donald P. Baker, "Wilder Skips Trip with Robb," *Washington Post,* November 21, 1985.

4. Baker, "Wilder Skips Trip with Robb."

5. Baker, "Wilder Skips Trip with Robb."

6. Baker, "Wilder Skips Trip with Robb."

7. Judy Griswold to Charles Robb, "Governor's Office Campaign Activity/Wilder & Joint Campaign," memorandum, undated.

8. Donald P. Baker, "Wilder Going His Own Way," *Washington Post,* October 2, 1986.

9. Donald P. Baker, "Wilder Picks His Fights," *Washington Post,* December 3, 1986.

10. Baker, "Wilder Going His Own Way."

11. Baker, "Wilder Going His Own Way."

12. Charles Robb to L. Douglas Wilder, November 30, 1985.

13. Charles Robb to L. Douglas Wilder, August 20, 1986.

14. Donald P. Baker, "Robb Says Wilder Has Alienated Him," *Washington Post,* December 4, 1986.

15. Baker, "Wilder Picks His Fights."

16. R. H. Melton, "Robb, Wilder Meet to Seek End of Feud," *Washington Post,* December 18, 1986.

17. Melton, "Robb, Wilder Meet to Seek End of Feud."

19. A New Challenge

1. Peter Hardin, "For Robb, Globe-Trotting Provides Quiet Schooling," *Richmond Times-Dispatch,* April 21, 1987.

2. Hardin, "For Robb, Globe-Trotting Provides Quiet Schooling."
3. Donald Baker, "Robb Launches Va. Senate Campaign with Warning against Complacency," *Washington Post,* April 8, 1988.
4. R. H. Melton and Donald P. Baker, "Va. GOP Puts Black on Ticket—Dawkins to Oppose Robb in Senate Race," *Washington Post,* June 12, 1988.
5. Mary Jordan, "Dawkins-Robb Rebukes Increasingly Personal," *Washington Post,* October 5, 1988.

20. THE MOST EXCLUSIVE CLUB

1. Robert Caro, *Master of the Senate: The Years of Lyndon Johnson* (New York: Vintage, 2003), 109.
2. Wendy Benjaminson, "Lady Bird Johnson, Fingering a Locket She Received When . . . ," UPI, January 3, 1989.
3. Kent Jenkins Jr., "Robb Takes Senate Seat with Style," *Washington Post,* January 4, 1989.
4. It took the time and effort of many people to make our Senate office run smoothly, including, but certainly not limited to, the following: Will Allcott, Amy Anderson, Adam Anthony, Francine Archer, Rebecca Barrett, Jessica Battaglia, Jennifer Bennett, Shelley Brown, Alfred Campos, Catherine Carpenter, Benjamin Clausen, Herb Cupo, Suzie Dabkowsi, Samantha Dallaire, James Dennis, Dominique Duncan, Gwyn Dutton, Rebecca Filomena, J. J. Gertler, Martha Gibbons, Mia Gomes, Jeremy Grant, Robert Gray, Tricia Grondin, Tela Hansom, Ralph Hawkins, Mike Henry, Ty Hicks, Carla Howard, Charlotta Jacobson, Rob Jones, Scott Jones, Rick Kahlenberg, Katy Kale, Debbie Lawson, Torian Lee, Dave Link, Wyatt Little, Augustus Mays, James Migliaccio, Karen Miller, Wendy Morigi, Elizabeth Musick, Erica Nash-Thomas, Dee Outlaw, Bill Owens, Erica Paulson, Amy Sander, Lula Sawyer, Dan Sheehan, Abigail Spanberger, Bobbie Spear, Shelly Spears, Pat Spurlock, Karen Stanley, Rae Steinly, Bill Sutey, Nicole Venable, Lawrence Webb, Rich Williams, and Jay Winik.

21. DISTANT LANDS, FARAWAY LIVES

1. Charles S. Robb, "Cambodia between Horror and Hope," *Washington Post,* June 5, 1990.
2. Charles S. Robb, "Trip Report of Senator Charles S. Robb, Chairman, East Asian and Pacific Affairs Subcommittee, August 13–22, 1993," United States Senate, Committee on Foreign Relations, 103rd U.S. Congress.
3. Thomas W. Lippman, "A Murder Investigation with 1 Million Victims," *Washington Post,* July 8, 1995.

4. Charles S. Robb, "Trip Report of Senator Charles S. Robb, Chairman, East Asian and Pacific Affairs Subcommittee, August 13–22, 1993," United States Senate, Committee on Foreign Relations, 103rd U.S. Congress.
5. "Robb Barred from Seeing Dissident," *Washington Post,* August 20, 1993.
6. Charles S. Robb, "Trip Report of Senator Charles S. Robb, Chairman, East Asian and Pacific Affairs Subcommittee, August 13–22, 1993," United States Senate, Committee on Foreign Relations, 103rd U.S. Congress.

22. ISSUES OF WAR AND PEACE

1. *Meet the Press,* NBC, March 10, 1991.
2. *Meet the Press,* NBC, March 10, 1991.

23. A NATIONAL SOAP OPERA

1. Michal Hardy, Jeff E. Schapiro, "Robb Denies Being at Parties at Which Cocaine Was Used," *Richmond Times-Dispatch,* May 3, 1987.
2. Joseph Laitin to Ben Bradlee and staff; Meg Greenfield and staff, May 7, 1987.
3. Rose Ellen O'Connor, "Robb Enjoyed Glitzy VA Beach Social Scene," *Virginian-Pilot* and *Ledger-Star,* August 28, 1988.
4. Donald P. Baker, "Robb Probe Had Support of GOP, Instigator Says," *Washington Post,* May 17, 1991.
5. Howard Rosenberg, "NBC Nightly News: How Mighty Have Fallen," *Los Angeles Times,* May 1, 1991; Alicia Mundy, "Victim of Exposé—Chuck Robb? Or NBC?," *American Journalism Review,* July/August 1991.

24. THE TALE OF THE TAPE

1. Robert H. Jackson, "The Federal Prosecutor," *Journal of Criminal Law and Criminology* 31, no. 1 (1940): 3–6, doi:10.2307/1137244, https://www.jstor.org/stable/1137244?seq=1#page_scan_tab_contents.
2. Charles Robb, "Indictments Dropped on Eavesdropping Charges," C-SPAN, January 12, 1993, news conference in Senate Radio and Television Gallery, http://www.c-span.org/video/?36960–1/indictments-dropped-eavesdropping-charges.

25. GUNS, GAYS, AND OLD GLORY

1. William J. Clinton. "Inaugural Address," Speech, Washington, D.C., January 20, 1993, American Presidency Project, https://www.presidency.ucsb.edu/documents/inaugural-address-51.

2. Charles S. Robb to Colin Powell, March 4, 1992.
3. Charles S. Robb to Colin Powell, March 4, 1992.
4. Barton Gellman, "Warship Gives Clinton a Not-So-Hail to the Chief," *Washington Post,* March 13, 1993; Richard L. Berke, "Unaccustomed Role for Clinton at Sea," *New York Times,* March 13, 1993.
5. Kent Jenkins Jr., "Into Troubled Waters," *Washington Post,* May 11, 1993.
6. Kent Jenkins Jr., "Opposing Gay Ban Could Hurt Robb," *Washington Post,* May 10, 1993.
7. Kent Jenkins Jr., "Robb Hitches Campaign to Gay Rights," *Washington Post,* May 10, 1994.
8. Charles S. Robb, "Statement of Senator Charles S. Robb, Consideration of S.J.Res. 332" (Senate floor statement, Washington, DC, June 26, 1990).

26. AN IMPERFECT CANDIDATE

1. L. Douglas Wilder, "Virginia State of the Commonwealth Address," video file, 41:18, C-SPAN, January 12, 1994, https://www.c-span.org/video/?53739-1/virginia-state-commonwealth-address.
2. Kent Jenkins Jr., "Fundraising Prowess Makes North a Force," *Washington Post,* March 22, 1993.
3. R. J. Cutler and David Van Taylor, *A Perfect Candidate* (1996); "A Perfect Candidate: Mark Goodin's Thinking Changes," video file, 1:10, YouTube, posted by Bill Pascoe, March 6, 2010, https://www.youtube.com/watch?v=KweT34C5i-k.
4. Kent Jenkins Jr., "Robb Takes up 'a Fight,'" *Washington Post,* March 14, 1994.
5. Jenkins, "Robb Takes up 'a Fight.'"
6. Peter Baker, "Veterans Groups Give North a Hero's Welcome," *Washington Post,* July 10, 1994.
7. Baker, "Veterans Groups Give North a Hero's Welcome."
8. Kent Jenkins Jr. and Donald Baker, "Robb's Opponents Hammer away at His Personal Life," *Washington Post,* September 7, 1994.
9. Jenkins and Baker, "Robb's Opponents Hammer away at His Personal Life."
10. Jenkins and Baker, "Robb's Opponents Hammer away at His Personal Life."
11. "Wilder Quits in Virginia," *Chicago Tribune,* September 15, 1994.
12. Kent Jenkins Jr., "Robb Flays North over Remark on War Record," *Washington Post,* September 29, 1994.
13. Kent Jenkins Jr. and Donald Baker, "Didn't Lie to Congress, North Tells Students," *Washington Post,* October 5, 1994.
14. Donald Baker, "North Tries to Discredit Censure by Ex-Colleague," *Washington Post,* September 10, 1994.
15. Kent Jenkins Jr., "Six Veterans Bash North, Push Robb for Senate," *Washington Post,* October 8, 1994.

16. Tyler Whitley and Peter Hardin, "Wilder Endorses Robb 'Peace Is Breaking out All Over,' Clinton Jokes as Old Foes Unite," *Richmond Times-Dispatch,* October 22, 1994.
17. "The 1994 Campaign: Virginia; Mrs. Reagan Denounces Oliver North on Iran Affair," *New York Times,* October 29, 1994.
18. Donald Baker, "North Backs away from Comments on Capabilities in Gulf," *Washington Post,* October 11, 1994.
19. R. H. Melton, "For Robb, an Explosion of Relief, for North, Unexpected Defeat," *Washington Post,* November 9, 1994.
20. Melton, "For Robb, an Explosion of Relief, for North, Unexpected Defeat."
21. Warren Fiske, "Character Issue Hurt North, Exit Polls Show," *Virginian-Pilot,* November 9, 1994.
22. Guy Friddell, "Frayed Robb, Flawed North—Both Have Been Redeemed," *Virginian-Pilot,* November 9, 1994.

27. Taking a Stand

1. Nicole Hemmer, "Speaking of Family," *U.S. News and World Report,* June 16, 2015.
2. John E. Yang, "House Bill to Stop Gay Marriages Has Stormy Start," *Washington Post,* June 13, 1996.
3. Yang, "House Bill to Stop Gay Marriages Has Stormy Start."
4. Charles S. Robb, "Senate Session: The Senate Debated the Defense of Marriage Act," video file, 2:50:50, C-SPAN, September 10, 1996, https://www.c-span.org/video/?74897-1/senate-session.
5. Charles S. Robb, "Senate Session: The Senate Debated the Defense of Marriage Act," video file, 2:50:50, C-SPAN, September 10, 1996, https://www.c-span.org/video/?74897-1/senate-session.
6. William J. Clinton, "Statement on Same-Gender Marriage," September 20, 1996, in *Public Papers of the Presidents of the United States: William J. Clinton* (Washington, DC: U.S. Government Printing Office, 1996).
7. Richard Cohen, "Voting One's Conscience," *Washington Post,* September 17, 1996.
8. Loving v. Virginia, 388 U.S. 1 (1967).
9. Jeff E. Schapiro, "Schapiro: A Virginian Who, Almost Alone, Took the Long View on Gay Marriage," *Richmond Times-Dispatch,* April 28, 2015.

28. Bayview

1. Greg Edwards, "Glickman Sees Progress; Farmers Red," *Richmond Times-Dispatch,* August 20, 1997.

2. Sylvia Moreno, "A Blessing for Bayview," *Washington Post,* December 25, 1998.
3. Ted Shockley, "Robb Visits Bayview, Promises Help," *Eastern Shore News,* July 8, 1998.
4. Donna Bozza Rich, "Robb Brings Aid Totaling $4M to Bayview, New Roads, Exmore," *Eastern Shore News,* May 26, 1999.

29. A Passion Play

1. Susan Schmidt, Peter Baker, and Toni Locy, "Clinton Accused of Urging Aide to Lie," *Washington Post,* January 21, 1998.
2. Charles S. Robb, "Statement of Charles S. Robb on the Trial of William Jefferson Clinton, President of the United States," U.S. Senate, Washington, D.C., February 11, 1999.
3. Charles S. Robb, "Statement of Charles S. Robb on the Trial of William Jefferson Clinton, President of the United States," U.S. Senate, Washington, D.C., February 11, 1999.
4. Charles S. Robb, "Statement of Charles S. Robb on the Trial of William Jefferson Clinton, President of the United States," U.S. Senate, Washington, D.C., February 11, 1999.
5. William J. Clinton, "1999 Radio and Television Correspondents' Association Dinner," video file, 12:48, C-SPAN, March 18, 1999, https://www.c-span.org/video/?121876-1/1999-radio-television-correspondents-dinner.
6. Jackie Judd, "1999 Radio and Television Correspondents' Association Dinner," video file, 13:00, C-SPAN, March 18, 1999, https://www.c-span.org/video/?121876-1/1999-radio-television-correspondents-dinner.
7. Jim Mills, "1999 Radio and Television Correspondents' Association Dinner," video file, 14:57, C-SPAN, March 18, 1999, https://www.c-span.org/video/?121876-1/1999-radio-television-correspondents-dinner.
8. Jim Mills, "1999 Radio and Television Correspondents' Association Dinner," video file, 15:24, C-SPAN, March 18, 1999, https://www.c-span.org/video/?121876-1/1999-radio-television-correspondents-dinner.

30. Against the Wind

1. Gary Brookins, "Before I Flip the Coin . . . ," *Richmond Times-Dispatch,* January 1999.
2. Margaret Edds, "Robb Faces No Cakewalk in 2000," *Virginian-Pilot,* December 13, 1998.
3. Lisa Rein, "Women's Vote Could Tip Close Contest," *Washington Post,* October 23, 2006.

4. Dusty Smith, "Robb Digs in as Senate Race Starts," *McLean Times*, March 29, 2000.

5. Smith, "Robb Digs in as Senate Race Starts."

6. Todd Jackson, "Senate Candidates Allen, Robb Exchange Barbs at The Homestead: Debate Looks at Records," *Roanoke Times*, August 6, 2000.

7. Childs Walker, "Democrats Pin Hopes on Robb Victory," *Roanoke Times*, June 4, 2000.

8. Guy Friddell, "U.S. Senate Race Promises Long, Hot Summer Full of Big Talk," *Virginian-Pilot*, June 5, 2000.

9. R. H. Melton, "Robb Hits the Road to Keep His Day Job in U.S. Senate," *Washington Post*, June 15, 2000.

10. Melton, "Robb Hits the Road to Keep His Day Job in U.S. Senate."

11. Francis Clines, "Virginia's Senate Campaign Suddenly Looks Close," *New York Times*, June 19, 2000.

12. Holly A. Heyser, "Robb, Allen Tangle in First Senate Debate," *Virginian-Pilot*, August 6, 2000.

13. David Lerman, "Allen Attacks Robb," *Daily Press*, August 6, 2000.

14. Dave Addis, "Candidates' Cheap Attacks Put Smear on Election," *Virginian-Pilot*, November 3, 2000.

15. David Lerman and Terry Scanlon, "Senate Campaigns Kick Off with Labor Day Festivities," *Daily Press*, September 5, 2000.

16. Lerman and Scanlon, "Senate Campaigns Kick Off with Labor Day Festivities."

17. Craig Timberg, "Fading into Senate Background," *Washington Post*, October 28, 2000.

18. Laetitia Clayton, "Lynda Robb Campaigns in Area Despite Broken Rib," *Northern Virginia Daily*, October 16, 2000.

19. Childs Walker, "Dead Heat Gets Hotter in Campaign's Final Days," *Roanoke Times*, October 22, 2000.

20. Bob Lewis, "Robb Won't Run from Clinton Linkage," *Fairfax Journal* (Associated Press), August 11, 2000.

21. Andrew Scot Bolsinger, "Robb, Allen Race Too Close to Call," *Daily News-Record*, November 4, 2000.

22. Charles S. Robb, "Robb Concession Speech," video file, C-SPAN, 00:20, November 7, 2000, http://www.c-span.org/video/?160365-1/robb-concession -speech.

31. Free at Last

1. William J. Clinton, "Former President Clinton Farewell Rally," video file, 14:50, C-SPAN, January 20, 2001, https://www.c-span.org/video/?162048-1/former -president-clinton-farewell-rally.

2. I would be remiss if I didn't mention all of the worthy organizations that I have worked with in the years since I left the Senate: Board of Visitors at the United States Naval Academy (chair); Landowners' Economic Alliance for the Dulles Extension of Rail (cochair); the President's Intelligence Advisory Board; the Secretary of State's International Security Advisory Board (chairman, WMD-Terrorism Task Force); the FBI Director's Advisory Board; the Iraq Study Group; the Critical Incident Analysis Group; the Afghanistan Study Group; Institute of Politics at Harvard University (Fellow); Marshall Wythe School of Law at William & Mary (Fellow); the Council on Foreign Relations Independent Task Force on Pakistan and Afghanistan; the Space Foundation; the Thomas Jefferson Program in Public Policy; the Bipartisan Policy Center; the National Committee on U.S.-China Relations; the Aspen Institute/Rockefeller Commission to Reform the Presidential Appointments Process (co-chairman); the Center for Infrastructure Protection Advisory Board; the Center for the Study of the Presidency and Congress Advisory Board; the Robertson Foundation Advisory Board; the Batten School of Leadership and Public Policy Advisory Board at UVA; the Homeland Security Policy Institute Advisory Board at George Washington University; the Iranian Nuclear Development Task Force at the Bipartisan Policy Center (co-chairman); the Concord Coalition; the Pew/Peterson Foundation's Committee for a Responsible Federal Budget; the Research Strategies Network; the National Museum for Americans in Wartime; Strategic Partnerships LLP; GMU's Critical Infrastructure Protection Program; and the Center for Strategic and International Studies.

32. The Green Zone

1. Charles S. Robb, "Senate Session," video file, 7:08:20, C-SPAN, December 13, 1995, https://www.c-span.org/congress/?chamber=senate&date=1995-12-13.
2. Charles S. Robb, "Senate Session," video file, 7:09:45, C-SPAN, December 13, 1995, https://www.c-span.org/congress/?chamber=senate&date=1995-12-13.
3. Charles S. Robb, "Senate Session," video file, 7:11:10, C-SPAN, December 13, 1995, https://www.c-span.org/congress/?chamber=senate&date=1995-12-13.
4. Commission on the Intelligence Capabilities of the United States Regarding Weapons of Mass Destruction, *Report to the President* (Washington, DC: U.S. Government Printing Office, 2005), https://www.govinfo.gov/app/details/GPO-WMD/.
5. Charles S. Robb to members of the Iraq Study Group, "Notes from Chuck Robb," 2006.
6. The Iraq Study Group, James A. Baker, and Lee H. Hamilton, *The Iraq Study Group Report: The Way Forward—A New Approach* (New York: Vintage, 2006), 73.

33. Over the Horizon

1. Lyndon B. Johnson, "To Fulfill These Rights," Commencement Address Delivered at Howard University, June 4, 1965, *Public Papers of the Presidents of the United States: Lyndon B. Johnson II* (Washington, DC: U.S. Government Printing Office, 1966), 301, 635–40, https://www.humanitiestexas.org/sites/default/files/LBJToFulfillTheseRights_0.pdf.
2. Eli Meixler, "'It's Time to Wake Up.' Read John McCain's Speech to Naval Academy Graduates," *Time*, October 31, 2017.
3. Charles S. Robb, "Speech at the National Press Club," Washington, D.C., April 3, 1986.
4. Charles S. Robb, "Speech at the National Press Club," Washington, D.C., April 3, 1986.

34. Always a Marine

1. Al Grasso, "Welcome to the Charles S. Robb Auditorium," 2017.